UP

Merry Christmas & Happy New Year in 2019

CLOSE

Sharon Patrick

AND PERSONAL

FRIENDSHIP WITH GOD

SHARON PATRICK

Endorsements

Sharon's many intimate moments with Jesus are inspiringly documented in her yearly devotional. You will be touched with how God can become so real in your daily walk and the many ways that He speaks to those who seek Him. *Up Close and Personal: Friendship with God* will excite you into desiring a fresh walk with the Lord, knowing that He wants to communicate with you daily. Sharon's devotional will minister to your heart and show you how God wants to lead, guide, and comfort you through life by His Holy Spirit.

Penny Funkhouser
Pastor of Heartbeat Ministries International

For decades now, I have watched Sharon grow from a seeker of the Lord to one who is truly sold out to His will and purpose. Her hunger for Jesus is a day-by-day experience of earnest expectation to know Him. I've found her book, *Up Close and Personal: Friendship with God,* not only genuinely engaging, but beneficial to a deeper understanding of who the Holy Spirit is and what He does in our daily lives. Sharon's insights are revelatory and easily applicable from the rich backdrop of her life experiences. You'll find yourself laughing and shedding a tear simultaneously as she shares her revelations from the Lord. Through *Up Close and Personal: Friendship with God,* you'll be personally impacted by Sharon's deep understanding of trust and relationship with the Lord. I believe that every truth seeker will be touched by the heart of this wonderful woman of God.

Dan Funkhouser
Pastor of Heartbeat Ministries International

Up Close and Personal: Friendship with God

Copyright 2017 © Sharon Patrick

ISBN # 978-0-692-95966-4

Unless otherwise noted, all Scripture citations are taken from the *New King James Version* of the Bible (NKJV). New King James Version®. Copyright © 1982 by Thomas Nelson. Used by permission. All rights reserved.

Scriptures marked AMP are taken from the *Amplified Bible* (AMP). Copyright © 2015 by The Lockman Foundation, La Habra, CA 90631. All rights reserved.

Scriptures marked CEB are taken from the Common English Bible. All rights reserved. No part of these materials may be reproduced or transmitted in any form or by any means, electronic or mechanical, including photocopying and recording, or by any information storage or retrieval system, except as may be expressly permitted by the 1976 Copyright Act, the 1998 Digital Millennium Copyright Act, or in writing from the publisher.

Scriptures marked ESV are taken from The Holy Bible, English Standard Version. ESV® Permanent Text Edition® (2016). Copyright © 2001 by Crossway Bibles, a publishing ministry of Good News Publishers.

Scriptures marked GNT are taken from the Good News Translation® (Today's English Version, Second Edition). Copyright © 1992 American Bible Society. All rights reserved.

Scriptures marked HCSB are taken from the Holman Christian Standard Bible. Copyright © 1999, 2000, 2002, 2003, 2009 by Holman Bible Publishers, Nashville, TN. All rights reserved.

Scriptures marked KJV are taken from the *KING JAMES VERSION*, public domain.

Scriptures marked NASB are taken from the New American Standard Bible, Copyright © 1960, 1962, 1963, 1968, 1971, 1972, 1973, 1975, 1977, 1995 by The Lockman Foundation.

Scriptures marked NET are taken from the New English Translation. NET Bible® copyright ©1996-2006 by Biblical Studies Press, L.L.C. http://netbible.com. All rights reserved.

Scriptures marked NIV are taken from the *New International Version* (THE HOLY BIBLE, NEW INTERNATIONAL VERSION®, NIV® Copyright © 1973, 1978, 1984, 2011 by Biblica, Inc.® Used by permission. All rights reserved worldwide.)

Scripture quotations marked (NLT) are taken from the Holy Bible, New Living Translation, copyright © 1996, 2004, 2007 by Tyndale House Foundation. Used by permission of Tyndale House Publishers, Inc., Carol Stream, Illinois 60188. All rights reserved.

Scriptures marked TLB are taken from the Living Bible (TLB). The Living Bible copyright © 1971 by Tyndale House Foundation. Used by permission of Tyndale House Publishers Inc., Carol Stream, Illinois 60188. All rights reserved.

Author contact information: Sharon777Patrick@gmail.com

Editor: Renée Gray-Wilburn

Cover design: Esperto Creative, LLC
P.O. Box 1561, Sisters, OR 97759
Phone: 503-816-6584
Owner: Torrey Sharp, Designer: Tim Green

Author photo: Lois Jacobson
Lois' Inspirational Photography
Phone: 719-351-7938
e-mail: loiscj7771@msn.com

Cover sculpture by Mark Patrick: markpatrickstudio.com

Interior design: Satoshi Yamamoto

Publisher: Sharon Rose Publishing, Colorado Springs, CO, 80919

Printed in the United States of America.

Acknowledgments

To my God and Savior, Jesus Christ, and the Holy Spirit: my constant companion, healer and friend.

To my loving and supportive husband, Mark.

To my priceless daughter, Sasha, and her incredible family, Nate and Emery.

To Sandy for your faithful prayers and your unwavering friendship, godly insight, and your and Stan's astounding generosity.

To my praying friends Carol, Jan, and Nancy—thank you!

To God's chosen champion editor, Renée Gray-Wilburn, who made it all come together on paper.

And finally, to my sweet son, Levi, who went home to be with Jesus in 2010. It's because of your godly testament in life and death that God put this book in my heart.

Foreword

I have known Sharon Patrick and her husband, Mark, for more than a decade. For most of those years I have known them from afar because that is how I preferred it. They suffered a grief so raw and devastating in the death of their son, Levi, that I turned away to preserve my own comfort zone. But over the past seven years, my wife and I were brought together with them by unexpected events, and I finally dared to hear their emerging story. I was touched and changed, and began to open my eyes to the loss they had suffered and the deep friendship with God that undergirded it. *Up Close and Personal: Friendship with God* is Sharon's daily devotional, and it offers you the benefit of sharing her triumph over unspeakable tragedy and absorbing it for your own edification.

As a daily devotional, this book will sneak up on you, and overwhelm you with its depth and intimate revelations. Get ready. It will take time, but as you read *Up Close and Personal: Friendship with God*, you will be swept up in Sharon's journey with God. On certain days, you might feel small by comparison, as I did, because your own path does not compare, but that's okay. I assure you, she is a special friend whom God has sent to open your heart and mind to realms of glory beyond your imagining. As you continue reading, you'll come to understand that your journey is just as beautiful, just as meaningful, just as full of promise and purpose as hers. (Perhaps you haven't opened your spiritual eyes full wide yet. Keep going.)

Having finished the devotional, I can say with confidence that Sharon has been called by the Holy Spirit to share this journal. It is a mosaic of moments and insights that will add up to a picture so wonderful, that in the end your mind will think better thoughts, your heart will dream better dreams, and your soul will tap into an endless fountain of joy that has always been yours. Let her story sweep over you, as it did me, day by day. Let it challenge you, convict you, provoke you, encourage you, enlarge you. This is what fellowship is supposed to be like among members of God's family. No two of us are the same. I pray that you are ready to receive *Up Close and Personal: Friendship with God* as a good gift from your sister Sharon Patrick, and from your heavenly Father.

Finally, as you read, I pray that you will truly know that you, too, have a story, and it is much better than you think.

Stephen Bransford
Award-winning novelist, screenwriter, and author of the biographical story, The Last Photograph *(Thomas Nelson, 1995, www.stephenbransford.com).*

Introduction

Have you ever felt as though circumstances or sudden unimaginable news has blocked your airway, taking your breath away? Or worse, causing your heart to stop?

I have, as inconceivable anguish nearly caused my heart to stop on March 27, 2010, when my beloved son, Levi, met with sudden death at the age of nineteen. Traveling in a Jeep as a passenger, Levi went to be with Jesus when a faulty tire exploded, causing the vehicle to roll.

Levi was in many ways a typical teenager. But in other ways, he was exceptional. He was typical in regards to school and work duties; however, he was exceptional in relationship with God and others and in sharing his faith in Jesus. The evidence of this came when over 2000 people attended his memorial service, and over 200 hundred committed their lives to Christ. His godly legacy continues, not only through the testimonies of others, but through this book. For such a young man, he experienced a life well lived.

Nine months after Levi's passing into glory, God spoke to me from Revelation 1:11, *"What you see, write in a book."* I believe what you are about to read is the result of God's request.

Two years into my grief process, the numbness of the reality of Levi's death began to subside. While quietly sitting in my prayer chair, I heard the Holy Spirit whisper, *"Sharon, I am the breath of the Almighty. A part of you died when Levi died, but I'm going to breathe life back into you again."* In that instant, a vision came to me of a person who appeared dead lying on the ground as an emergency medical technician performed mouth-to-mouth resuscitation. Oddly, it was the rising and falling of the person's chest that caught my attention.

The Holy Spirit showed me that He was the one administering the resuscitation, and the person on the ground could easily be you or me. Jesus said, *"It is the Spirit who gives life...the words that I speak to you are spirit, and they are life"* (John 6:63).

Through the counsel, hope, and comfort of His Spirit, and through His Word, our chest also rises and falls—spiritually speaking—with the breath of His life. Throughout Psalm 119, David cried out repeatedly: "Revive me O Lord; revive me according to Your loving kindness, and according to Your word, revive me" (see Psalm 119:25, 88). As long as we are on the earth, we'll cry out like David, "Revive us, Lord!"

Conceived by the Holy Spirit, the experiences recorded here don't only reveal Christ in my grief process but also years of powerful revelation and testimonies from walking with Jesus moment to moment, day by day, and year by year.

This walk also includes my husband, Mark; my daughter, Sasha; my son-in-law, Nate, and other family members and friends.

Although this book reflects my personal journey, I understand that you're traveling your own road and are in need of the comfort, encouragement, and guidance of God, Jesus, and the Holy Spirit as well.

Had it not been for the breath of the Almighty, I'm certain that I would've died of grief. But God, in the depths of my sorrow only held me closer. And by breathing His life and vision into my broken heart, He took me deeper, plunging me into the depths of His everlasting love.

The Spirit breathing life back into me came about through the process of this book. My path at times, although rocky with anger, confusion, and questions, was also paved with joy at the continued revelation of our living hope, Jesus Christ.

As you read of God's unfailing love and faithfulness, it's my hope that you encounter the very heart of God for yourself as He meets you on each page, manifesting healing to your spirit, soul, and body.

I can assure you, *whatever* you're going through, no matter how difficult, you have God, Jesus, and the Holy Spirit as your infallible first responders. They'll breathe life back into you, and you will surely live.

Clues

Look, I am coming soon!

Revelation 22:7 (NLT)

After Levi's death, my husband and I were looking for clues when we journeyed into our son's bedroom. We longed for any sign that might indicate his foreknowledge of departure: a journal, a note, anything that would help make sense of the unspeakable grief we were experiencing.

Levi's bedroom was uniquely his own: sport trophies lined the shelves, medals hung from his desk, posters decorated the walls, and like many teenagers' bedrooms, clothes were scattered on the floor. Looking around, I could not help but wonder, *Jesus, were You speaking to Levi about his homecoming, and if so, did he comprehend it?*

On the earth, Levi was a special young man, but in some respects, he was a typical teenager. He dreamed of one day being an NFL draft pick, therefore, our college scouting included football. He liked guns and girls, and he was only five weeks shy of high school graduation.

Unfortunately, his bedroom revealed no secrets, but a thought came to me. With revered anticipation, my husband and I picked up Levi's Bible and slowly turned the pages. Some clues began to emerge.

We were at a loss for words, seeing the stars Levi had drawn in pencil all around Revelation 22:7, 12–13, and 16: *"[7]Look, I am coming soon! Blessed are those who obey the words of prophecy written in this book… [12]Look, I am coming soon, bringing my reward with me to repay all people according to their deeds. [13]I am the Alpha and the Omega, the First and the Last, the Beginning and the End… [16]I, Jesus, have sent my angel to give you this message"* (NLT).

I believe Jesus was speaking directly to Levi, His son and our son, to prepare him for his heavenly home. Today is a New Year and a new day. Have you considered spiritual preparation for your eternal destiny? If not, I encourage you to turn your heart to Jesus, and receive Him as your Savior. He's your Beginning and your End. He can make you ready at a moment's notice.

New Year's Promise

You crown the year with Your goodness,
and Your paths drip with abundance.

Psalm 65:11

Most of my life, with anticipation, I looked expectantly to the New Year and to the new beginning it brings. But not this year; this was my first New Year without Levi since his heavenly departure ten months earlier. I had no interest in starting the year without him. I don't know how things are beginning for you in this new year, but I would like for you to take comfort in the encouraging words God shared with me:

"This new year, I will do a new thing and lead you in a new plan by a new way. New thoughts will solidify your new foundation. Instead of the rubble of grief, you will have new and living stones. Look to Me, My love. There will be paths that you have not walked in which You need Me to navigate the way. Let Me be your guide, your GPS (God's Positioning System), your compass. I am the Way, the truth, and the life. I am the Light of your life. I alone can guide you through the dark and unknown rugged paths, as well as the smooth ones. You must stay close to Me even when enjoying the easier road, because at any given moment there could come a rough spot. You don't want to be caught off-guard, thinking that because the path is smooth you can let go of My hand. Your hand in Mine at all times is the ONLY way you will make it through. All of my paths are mercy and truth."

Are you ready to put some of last year's circumstances or events behind you? Are you trusting God for new and greater things in the year ahead? Let's take hold of the promise in Psalm 65:11 that reads: *"You crown the year with Your goodness, and Your paths drip with abundance."* I'm taking God at His Word today and throughout the year. Will you join me?

Going through the Motions

*These people draw near to Me with their mouth,
and honor me with their lips, but their heart is far from Me.*

Matthew 15:8

In my youth, attending church was not something I wanted to do, but up until the age of eighteen it was expected. With lip service, I sang the songs. I knelt and said the prayers. But my heart was far from God.

At age twelve when I was inducted into Holy Communion, I had more interest in the new white dress, gifts, and attention I received than communion's significance. Although Catechism classes never transformed my heart, graduation still occurred when the priest said, "Receive the Holy Ghost." I thought, *Who is the Holy Ghost?*

Sadly, "going through the motions" is a global issue. Many attend church, confess their sins to an authority figure, do good deeds, and take communion, only giving way to a false sense of eternal security. Some, through requisites, have met God. Many have not.

Through these institutional rituals, and with no personal participation, I was told I was eternally secure and right with God, although I had never encountered God, Jesus, or the Holy Spirit for myself. Steeped in sin, God was the last person on my mind.

The Good News had not yet penetrated my heart. There is one God and one mediator between God and men—Christ Jesus (see 1 Timothy 2:5). God set Old Testament priests in place *only* until our High Priest, Jesus, came into the world. He alone is man's mediator, God, and Savior, who forgave sin and granted right standing.

At twenty-eight years old, thankfully, Jesus made Himself known to me in the back woods of Colorado where I became born again and received His Holy Spirit. I am no longer going through the motions. My heart is completely His.

It is possible to go through ritualistic ceremonies and miss the truth of salvation: *"I am the way, the truth, and the life. No one comes to the Father except through Me [Jesus]"* (John 14:6, brackets added).

Are you just going through the motions? If so, God is waiting for you! If you're willing, He will turn your heart from all formulas holding no meaning into a real and personal relationship with Him.

Everlasting Father

*I will be a Father to you, and you shall be My sons
and daughters, says the LORD Almighty.*

2 Corinthians 6:18

F ather's Day is a day to show appreciation for not only our earthly fathers but our heavenly Father as well. Today's opening scripture comforts my heart.

In the Bible we read more about sons than about daughters. However, in many instances, where *son* is mentioned, it also includes women, referring to mankind. Nevertheless, whenever the Bible specifically mentions women, my heart stands at attention.

Because of the effect this passage had on me, I had an overwhelming sense that God was preparing me for my dad's death. In His loving kindness, He further anchored me in truth: My dad's death would not leave me fatherless. Six months later, on Christmas Day, my dad departed to greet His heavenly Father.

There are many reasons for the loss of a parent. For those of you who feel as though you have been deserted due to such a loss, please take comfort in the words of David: *"When my father and my mother forsake me, then the LORD will take care of me"* (Psalm 27:10).

God, speaking through the prophet Isaiah, said, *"Even if a mother should forget her child, I will never forget you"* (Isaiah 49:15, GNT).

Unfortunately, parental abandonment is a part of fallen humanity. However, Isaiah also prophesied: *"For unto us a Child is born…and His name will be called … Everlasting Father"* (Isaiah 9:6).

Jesus told His disciples before His ascension, *"I will not leave you orphans; I will come to you"* (John 14:18). In His physical absence, Jesus sent His Spirit to accompany and comfort us. Therefore, we are never without the aid of our Everlasting Father. And the good news is that whether you are a believer or a nonbeliever, He always lends a helping hand.

Are you *feeling* fatherless today? Take God's words to heart, and know that when you turn to Jesus Christ, you are never Fatherless.

The Safe

For there is nothing covered that will not be revealed,
and hidden that will not be known.

Matthew 10:26

While walking and praying, a vision came to my spirit of a lone, moderate-sized, locked safe. With plastic explosives in hand, Jesus approached the safe and attached the putty-like substance to its hinges, blowing the door off. Kneeling down on one knee, He looked inside the safe, finding papers with secrets written on them and records of wounds that had been hidden away for some time, along with pain, shame, and guilt.

This is how it may be for some of us. Although noted for securing valuables, a safe can also serve as a hiding place. As humans living in a fallen world, I believe there are times we go to the safe deposit box of our heart where we leave confidential items, close the door, spin the dial, and then walk away.

For our omnipotent Father, Son, and Holy Spirit, nothing is too difficult for them—even safe cracking. The Godhead knows the code to your heart, and having made Him the Lord of your life, permission to turn the dial is a given. But they'll also do whatever it takes to save your life, even if that includes blasting their way in.

Some people go to the grave having never opened their safe deposit box. The same goes for the strongbox of our soul, where hurts can remain unseen and untouched. As believers, it's best to grant Jesus entry and allow Him to deem what's valuable and what's not, because there is *"nothing covered that will not be revealed, or hidden that will not will not be made known"* (Matthew 10:26). If you have locked shame and guilt in the vault of your heart, Jesus bore that and more on the cross. His promise in Isaiah 61:7 is that instead of shame, we would receive double honor.

"Before [God] *formed you in the womb* [He] *knew you"* (Jeremiah 1:5, brackets added). So truly, whatever you're hiding is not a secret to Him. He knows you inside and out. Allow Jesus access to the safe deposit box of your heart so you can be healed of old wounds and pain once and for all.

Three in One

For there are three that bear witness in heaven:
the Father, the Word, and the Holy Spirit; and these three are one.

1 John 5:7

Even with the Holy Spirit's insight, it's impossible to comprehend the fullness of this truth: The Godhead is One.

Today's writing is complied largely of what God says about Himself. Besides, who can describe God better than God Himself? Of His many characteristics, I enjoy His confidence. He knows who is King of the hill and has no qualms declaring it. God is sure of Himself and has no identity issues. He says, *"For I am God, and there is no other; I am God, and there is none like Me"* (Isaiah 46:9).

No gods claiming to be God, other than the Lord God Almighty, can say they created the universe, nor can they say they've given life to mankind. Nor is there any other god who died for the sins of mankind. He communicates clearly: He is *"God the LORD, Who created the heavens and stretched them out, Who spread forth the earth and that which comes from it, Who gives breath to the people on it, and spirit to those who walk on it"* (Isaiah 42:5).

Referring to the three being one, the scriptures say about Jesus, *"'They shall call His name Immanuel,' which is translated, 'God with us'"* (Matthew 1:23). Revelation 19:13 records the name of Jesus as *"the Word of God."* Similarly, John 1:1 tells us, *"In the beginning was the Word, and the Word was with God, and the Word was God. The Word became flesh [who is Jesus] and dwelt among us"* (John 1:14, brackets added). Jesus is God.

The Spirit of God was on the scene of creation hovering over the face of the waters when the earth was without form and void, and darkness was on the face of the deep (see Genesis 1:2). *"The Spirit of God has made me, and the breath of the Almighty gives me life"* (Job 33:4). The Holy Spirit is God.

For now, the divine mystery of the Godhead remains. However, my prayer is that through these passages, clarity and trust have blossomed in your heart. Truly, *"The LORD our God, the LORD is one"* (Deuteronomy 6:4).

Conception Protection

Stand therefore, having girded your waist with truth…

Ephesians 6:14

Therefore gird up the loins of your mind…

1 Peter 1:13

While reading our opening scriptures, the Lord gave me a vision of a woman in a heavy metal chastity belt, with a padlock securely fastening the front of the belt. The Holy Spirit spoke to me about the vision: *"As physical loins are girded with a chastity belt and cannot conceive and give birth, so the loins of your mind, when girded with the belt of truth, cannot conceive and give birth to the lies of the devil."*

Gird is not a term widely used outside of the Bible or Christian circles. The definition means "to gird up, to gird around or about,"[1] restraining on every side. It "is used metaphorically of the loins of the mind."[2] With physical loins restrained, impregnation is impossible. In addition, any spiritual conception of lies in the mind is out of the question when our thoughts are belted with God's truth.

Isaiah 11:5 says about Jesus, *"Righteousness shall be the belt of His loins, and faithfulness the belt of His waist."* Jesus, too, restrained Himself on every side, from anything contrary to His Father's will.

In the human body, there are two areas in which conception or procreative power lies, and both are in the loins: The physical loins, which produce children, and the loins of our mind or imagination, which produce whatever our heart or mind believes and thinks on.

First Peter 1:13 encourages us *"to gird up the loins of your mind."* By doing so, we are watchful for the incoming lies of the enemy and any attempts at conception.

Do you have conception protection against the lies of the enemy? *"Because the carnal mind is enmity against God…"* (Romans 8:7), and because we are not to *"… be conformed to this world, but be transformed by the renewing of your mind"* (Romans 12:2), spending time in God's presence, praying, and meditating on His Word will provide us with the necessary divine conception protection.

Holy Spirit Gardening 101

The LORD God planted a garden.

Genesis 2:8

When my husband decided we should landscape our property, I grumbled and complained about the timing because we had all summer to landscape. It was now fall. Bible college was to begin in one week, and my mind was busy preparing for another year of teaching classes there.

As I worked on my knees in the dirt pulling weeds in the hot sun, my thoughts wandered. I should be in my office praying, reading the Bible, and studying to ready myself for teaching the students.

In preparing the soil for landscaping, there was a large variety of weeds that needed to be removed. I encountered unwanted plants with roots two to three feet long, some backbreaking to pull, others impossible to remove without the use of a shovel. Even with gloves, some were prickly to the touch. As I pulled these pesky plants, they seemed to multiply. As far as I was concerned, I was done with this weed job! Becoming impatient, I was tempted to pull only the ones that were easy to uproot and lay landscape fabric over the remainder.

As I worked, I heard God speak to my heart, *"Isn't that so true of the weeds in the soil of your heart? It is easier to pull the weeds that uproot easily, and to lay the fabric over the ones that seem difficult. But nothing is too difficult for Me; not even the weeds in your heart."*

Jesus said in Matthew 15:13, *"Every plant which My heavenly Father has not planted will be uprooted."* Ecclesiastes 3:1–2 states, *"[1]To everything there is a season… [2]a time to plant, and a time to pluck what is planted."*

As Master Gardener, God has big plans for the garden of your heart. He knows when the time is right to pull any weeds that have taken root. Allow Jesus to freely till the soil of your heart. You will be amazed at how your garden grows! Consider today's message a lesson in Holy Spirit gardening.

Hell, Fire, and Brimstone?

Hell from beneath is excited about you,
to meet you at your coming; it stirs up the dead for you.

Isaiah 14:9

Even among professing believers, hell is a controversial topic. But I believe that just as heaven is for real, so is hell.

It is often said that a loving God would not allow people to dwell in a place of eternal punishment. It's true; God does not condemn people to hell. Jesus Himself says, "*16For God so loved the world that He gave His only begotten Son, that whoever believes in Him should not perish but have everlasting life. 17For God did not send His Son into the world to condemn the world, but that the world through Him might be saved. 18He who believes in Him is not condemned; but he who does not believe is condemned already, because he has not believed in the name of the only begotten Son of God*" (John 3:16–18).

Condemnation is present, however, not because of God, but because there are those who choose not to believe. Their own unbelief condemns them, not God.

Instead of hell, fire, and brimstone, I'd like to present the Good News of the gospel of Christ. Adam and Eve's choice separated us from God. However, Jesus, through His death on the cross and His resurrection, reconciled us back to God. "*We have peace with God through our Lord Jesus Christ*" (Romans 5:1). God "*is longsuffering toward us, not willing that any should perish but that all should come to repentance*" (2 Peter 3:9).

The most important eternal choice you will make in your earthly life is to believe or not to believe in the name of the only begotten Son of God, Jesus Christ. Like Paul in 2 Corinthians 5:20, as an ambassador for Christ, and as though God were pleading through me, I implore you on Christ's behalf, be reconciled to God.

God and heaven's inhabitants are excited to meet you at your coming!

Eternal BFF
(Best Friends Forever)

*Ointment and perfume delight the heart, and the sweetness
of a man's friend gives delight by hearty counsel.*

Proverbs 27:9

The sweetness of my best friend, Sandy, consists of innumerable characteristics, but one that stands out is the hearty counsel, in which the Lord gifted her. With a Master's degree in social work, Sandy is one who helps people solve and cope with problems in their everyday lives. I have often ribbed Sandy that God gave her that degree for me, as it has benefited me greatly.

In 1993, sailing on separate seas in life, Sandy and I were two vessels God chose to dry-dock for repairs at the same church. He christened our friendship in a class titled "Search for Significance." Anchored in our identity in Christ, our search became a deeper reality.

One of my favorite memories of Sandy is bringing her as a guest to the Bible college I attended. The Holy Spirit came upon her in such a way that she began to stagger like a drunken sailor and speak in tongues. The disciples too, when filled with the Holy Spirit, spoke in tongues and appeared drunk, as Peter told onlookers, *"15these are not drunk, as you suppose…. 16But this is what was spoken by the prophet Joel:'17… I will pour out of My Spirit on all flesh'"* (Acts 2:15–17). Endued with power from on high, both the disciples and Sandy were out of character as the joy of the Holy Spirit filled their hearts (see Acts 2:1–4).

Our divine course continues. And like Paul, *"We are hard-pressed on every side, yet not crushed; we are perplexed, but not in despair; persecuted, but not forsaken; struck down, but not destroyed"* (2 Corinthians 4:8–9). We've raised, graduated, and married some of our children and sadly, buried my son. With our foundation on the Rock of Jesus Christ, along with prayer and Bible study, God continues to grow and preserve our friendship.

My prayer is that God has or will bring you an earthly, eternal best friend. What a friend we have in Jesus, but what a friend God gives us in others!

JANUARY 11

Armed and Dangerous

Behold, I give you the authority to trample on serpents and scorpions, and over all the power of the enemy, and nothing shall by any means hurt you.

Luke 10:19

Walking through the aisles of a home improvement store, my husband blurted out, "Sharon, look! That man has a gun strapped to his hip!" My first thought was, *No one will mess with him.* Then I heard the Lord say, *"How many of My people know they are armed and dangerous against the devil?"*

Hidden in our spiritual man resides an armory filled with the power and authority of Jesus Christ. Although locked and loaded, the church is not fully aware of her menacing capabilities against the attacks of the enemy. Therefore, some are ineffective in wielding their God-given weapons.

American citizens hold the right to openly carry firearms. In the spirit realm, the legal right to "open carry" God's weapons also exist. We wouldn't allow a mortal enemy to threaten or gain entrance into our homes. Nor should we tolerate the devil's threats of entry into our lives, as Jesus *"disarmed principalities and powers"* (Colossians 2:15).

The scenario in the home improvement store led me to take a gun safety class. I left knowing how to wield my weapon. A correlation also came to me regarding the well-educated women who taught this class and how God, too, has placed gifted teachers within the body of Christ who are effective in training others to handle spiritual weapons. The Holy Spirit is our ultimate Teacher, but as believers, we are not independent but interdependent—learning from one another.

As weapon-toting believers, it's wise to humbly secure all the training God has for us and utilize our spiritual arsenal efficiently and effectively in our battle against the schemes of the enemy. Jesus has made you armed and dangerous, embrace His grace, and He'll teach you how to use your weapons.

Heavenly Rodeo

…bringing every thought into captivity to the obedience of Christ.

2 Corinthians 10:5

I once lived on a horse ranch, which meant plenty of activity. Our neighbor Alan, a professional cowboy, participated in local rodeos. My family and I had the pleasure of attending some of his events. As I watched him wrestle steers and rope calves, the Spirit gave me a revelation of these competitions, showing how they relate to us taking our thoughts captive.

Steer wrestling, also known as bulldogging, begins when the cowboy motions the gatekeeper to release the steer from its corral. Once loosed, horse and rider chase the steer at full gallop. The rider then drops from his horse onto the animal, grabbing the animal by the horns. Since it's a timed event, he wrestles the steer to the ground as quickly as possible.

Another timed event is calf roping, where a calf runs out of the gate as a rider on horseback attempts to throw a lasso around its neck. The cowboy then dismounts his horse, runs to the calf, and strives to restrain it by tying three of its legs together. When completed, the cowboy throws his hands up to let the judge see that he has brought the calf into submission.

The revelation came twofold. Like the bulldogger, the moment a thought in our mind elevates itself against the knowledge of God, we are to jump on it and wrestle it to the ground, bringing it into the submission of Christ. In addition, when our thoughts have been brought into the obedience of Christ, like the calf roper, we should throw up our hands and thank God for the victory!

In regards to your thought life, you've probably been in this rodeo arena before. But, instead of sitting in the stands enjoying the rodeo, maybe it's time to get into the arena of your thoughts and take them captive like a cowboy ropes and wrestles steers.

The Divine Diet

The fruit of the Spirit is self-control.
Galatians 5:22

For many years I have taught on and lived a lifestyle of fasting. Often, people would say to me, "All that fasting keeps you slim, doesn't it?" I'd reply, "No, it's the Spirit's fruit of self-control dwelling within my spirit that keeps me at a balanced weight."

Each New Year, I try to steer clear of the onslaught of "fad diet" information, as fitness regimes and product sales inundate our culture. The American diet changes continually. One year low-fat foods are healthy, and the following year they're bad, and round and round it goes.

It's evident, living in a fallen world, that our physical body can be affected, and medical conditions or medications can cause people's weight to get out of balance. However, God is greater than this fallen world, and He has a Divine Diet to keep your body, the temple of His Holy Spirit, functioning like a well-oiled machine.

Instead of chasing the vacillating ways of the world or even going to food for comfort, we can turn to the Holy Spirit and Scripture for God's balanced diet plan. Notably, there are varying body types, but each one can be healthy within its proper frame. Please don't attempt to attain the world's idea of male and female perfection; it's a bold-face lie! With God, all things are possible, including you coming to a place of contentment of how wonderfully God created you!

Blessed in my youth, I viewed my parents as naturalists. With the exception of homemade sweets, we ate foods considered to be "raw and clean." There are simple steps we can take to shed pounds or to live healthier just by getting back to basics with the foods from the earth that God provided.

To begin the Divine Diet, consult the Great Physician for help. Since the majority of the battle of the bulge is in the temptation to overdo, or do it unhealthily, one diet advantage of living in tandem with the Spirit is the fruit of self-control (see Galatians 5:23). My advice is to go with God and not the fad!

No Horns, No Red Cape

...nor give place to the devil.

Ephesians 4:27

The devil is *not* an imaginary being. Look around your world. Or, better yet, read your Bible. The serpent of old lurked in the Garden. Without success, he tempted Jesus in the wilderness, entered into Judas Iscariot, prompted Ananias to lie to the Holy Spirit, and repeatedly hindered the apostle Paul.

You may wonder why I'm writing about Satan. It's because God wants us to understand the importance of knowing our enemy. Many describe the devil as a rival or adversary—one who opposes us as a competitor or combatant. Although he's a defeated foe since Jesus disarmed principalities and powers at the cross (see Colossians 2:15), he still seeks to take us out.

Commanders of our armed forces are not ignorant of the tactics of the enemy, nor are they oblivious to their position. We, too, are to have a keen sense concerning the devil's whereabouts and his inroads into our lives, as we look to our Commander in Chief, the Lord Jesus Christ.

The deceiver has no new tricks. He presents old conspiracies with bold new ideas, but under it all, we will find his same old schemes of lies and accusations.

Satan is the ruler of darkness. Synonyms for *darkness* are *shadiness* and *obscurity*. When we are unaware of his strategies, blindness, deception, and entrapment will be our lot. Ephesians 6:12 reminds us that we do not wrestle against people, but against every spiritual host of wickedness in the heavenly places.

I like what God says: *"Who will contend with me? Let us stand together. Who is My adversary?"* (Isaiah 50:8). Jesus living in us is our only power over Satan. By God's grace, or ability, we can stay diligent, keep watch, submit to God, resist the devil, and he will flee!

Love at the Cross

God demonstrates His own love toward us,
in that while we were still sinners, Christ died for us.

Romans 5:8

One day while praying, fasting, and walking in a remote area, a woman driving a car approached me and asked, "Do you need a ride?" I sensed she was new in the area, as it was not odd for locals to be out walking. I responded, "No, thank you, I'm enjoying walking." She blurted out, "Will you be my friend?" I understood God was at work. I said, "Yes, I will."

The following day, odd temple gods surrounded us in her living room, and tarot cards served as wallpaper. During casual conversation, she suddenly screamed out, "I have bullets in the garage; I will kill myself!" I responded, "Because God loves you, He sent me here to help you."

She had no kind words about God, nor would she allow prayer. I asked her, "*If there is one thing that you might ask God for, what would it be?*" She answered, "For my husband to come and live with me." Tired of their location, she moved to Colorado without him. I told her I would pray to God on her behalf.

I kept my promise. The following day she called with excitement, saying, "My husband is relocating!" I responded, "See how much God loves you?" As I spoke these words, God spoke to me, and His words pierced my heart: "*My love isn't based on answered prayer; it's based on the cross of Jesus Christ. What if her husband decided not to move to Colorado? Your response to her reveals that answered prayer is the foundation of My love, and not the cross.*"

We often, inaccurately, equate His love with answered prayer. Although God delights to answer prayer according to His will, there are many factors involved in receiving answers. Our prayers *appeared* unanswered when we prayed for Levi's safety and he died. We prayed to raise him back to this earthly life, but he went to heaven. Does this mean God does not love us? Certainly not! You too must set your eyes on the cross of Christ where God demonstrates His love for you, and not on answered prayer.

Will You Still Love Me?

Simon, son of Jonah, do you love Me?

John 21:16

After the birth of my two children, the Lord posed an unusual question to me yearly. For eleven years, I always responded no. Then I attended a convention where I met Julie Ann Allen, who authored the book, *You Only Think God Is Silent.*[1]

Riveted is the only word that came to mind as Julie shared her story. Her husband, working as a hydro-geologist, was in a large pit one day extracting soil samples. Before inspecting the trench, the track hoe operator filled the hole, burying her husband alive.

At that time, Julie's fondness toward God puzzled me. How does becoming a widow on your thirty-eighth birthday and left alone to raise two young children warrant praise? How was God protecting your family? Where were His mighty angels?

I left the convention speechless. God then asked me His unusual, annual question: *"Would you still love Me if anything happened to the children?"* Until this time, I didn't think to ask what He meant by this. Now, I scrutinized my thoughts: *What could happen to my children? We pray for them and fully trust the Lord with them. God gives His angels charge over them, promising protection and health.* After meeting the widow, my response to God was, "Yes, Lord, I'll still love You if anything ever happens to the children."

Eight years later, after leaving the morgue and lying on a hotel bed in confusion and anguish, I sensed God's presence. My heart wept, as I said, "Don't talk to me. You just broke my heart." God responded, *"You said you'd still love Me if anything ever happened to the children."* My heart questioned, "And You're holding me to that now?" For a millisecond, there was silence between us.

God speaks life, and His words never return void, accomplishing what He pleases (see Isaiah 55:11). Although God didn't break my heart, it was broken. His loving reminder came so the devil's destructive hooks couldn't penetrate it. That night He scooped me up in His mighty arms, which are able to save. He'll do the same for you regardless of your circumstances. Simply fall into His already open, loving arms.

His Communion Table

For as often as you eat this bread and drink this cup,
you proclaim the Lord's death till He comes.

1 Corinthians 11:26

Although my friend Carol and I haven't seen each other face to face for many years, we continue our friendship over the phone. The majority of our conversations include Jesus and all He's doing in our lives. A recent call was no exception.

The Spirit spoke to Carol about taking vitamins and supplements, but ultimately, God wants her to trust in Jesus and the healing He has provided. He reminded her that by receiving His holy communion and putting her faith in Him, it's His body that heals and His blood that forgives. These are the sources of her divine health. Yet, because her natural body is the temple of the Holy Spirit, she still bears the responsibility for taking care of herself by eating well and exercising. As useful as natural remedies are, she's not to rely on them but rather on God's finished work.

When Carol shared her revelation, the Holy Spirit rocked my world with revelation for me personally! Brokenhearted, I needed healing! What better way to obtain healing than by receiving the Lord's Supper?

Since our phone conversation and the Spirit's unique revelation to me, communion has been a daily part of my life. A portion of 1 Corinthians 11:26 reads, *"as often as you eat this bread and drink this cup...."* Revelation came! I can take communion, as often as I like and as many times a day as I want, in order to remember my Lord's death and all that He provided through it, until He returns.

This book contains my personalized revelations from the Holy Spirit. I pray that you'll also receive your own gift from God, as He gives you a personal revelation of the Lord's Supper. If you don't take communion on a regular basis, I encourage you to seek the Lord about how it can help manifest healing for you. You're always welcome at His communion table.

Natural and Spiritual Combat

Endure hardship as a good soldier of Jesus Christ.

2 Timothy 2:3

S hortly before my son's passing, I received an invitation to speak at his Bible study. My first thought was, *Lord, what would You have me share with an all-male group?* The Lord's response was, *"What do you think of when I say the word combat?"* My heart responded, *I think of soldiers and weapons.* At that moment, the Lord opened my eyes to multiple comparisons of natural and spiritual combat, which I will share throughout this book.

Combat is a conflict in which two forces fight and oppose one another. Both camps possess numerous similarities, and each has specific marching orders. In warfare, each faces an enemy, which camouflages itself, seeking to destroy. Although conquered, Satan still poses a threat in his efforts to level us. Because your adversary the devil walks around like a roaring lion seeking whom he may devour, life-saving instructions for being sober and vigilant are necessary for both warriors (see 1 Peter 5:8). The word *sober* indicates being free of intoxicating drink, while *vigilant* denotes being awake and alert.

As spiritual soldiers, we are not to be drunk with wine, but to be filled with the Spirit (see Ephesians 5:18). Natural soldiers, if inebriated on the battlefield, may possess a greater sense of fearlessness, but they are less likely to be attentive and more likely to be injured or killed. On the other hand, the ones who are watchful and exhibit self-control have better odds of staying alive. In spiritual warfare, we too will be safer when we are watchful and not staggering in the works of the flesh but filled with the Spirit (see Galatians 5:19–23).

One motto of the United States Armed Forces is: "Never Leave a Man Behind." God never leaves a man or woman behind, no matter our condition on the battlefield. By His grace, continue to live free from the intoxication of the world, stay alert and in close communication with your heavenly Commander, and your victory against the enemy is sure.

Life and Death

The day you die is better than the day you are born.
Better to spend your time at funerals than at parties.
After all, everyone dies—so the living should take this to heart.
Sorrow is better than laughter, for sadness has a refining influence on us.
A wise person thinks a lot about death,
while a fool thinks only about having a good time.

Ecclesiastes 7:1–4 (NLT)

If we belong to Christ, truly the day we die is better than the day we are born. This passage granted me significant meaning after my mother and son departed for heaven. Then, on Christmas Day, in 2014, my dad also died, receiving the indescribable gift of meeting Jesus face to face.

Viewing my dad's lifeless body, I was reminded that each life comes to a mortal end. This caused me to reflect on how I was presently living. I asked myself, "Am I walking out Christ's example to the fullest?" Most often, we don't know when our soul will be required of us. Therefore, I want to live with a heart of wisdom, for my days on earth are but a breath (see Job 7:16).

I find the statement *"sadness has a refining influence on us"* to be as true today as it was thousands of years ago. The sadness of my son's death had an astounding, eternal refining influence on me.

Death is not a coveted topic; after all, even the mere mention of the word can be viewed as a negative confession. This thinking contradicts Ecclesiastes 7:4, "A *wise person thinks a lot about death, while a fool thinks only about having a good time."* The wise think about death and realize that it is, in fact, a part of life until Jesus returns.

In Job 14:5 we read, *"You have decided the length of our lives. You know how many months we will live, and we are not given a minute longer"* (NLT). If you have not yet received Christ as your Savior, then today salvation has come to your house. Scripture reveals that a funeral can be the very occasion that provokes a time of serious reflection, not only of your present life, but your eternal destiny. Are you living today with an eternal perspective?

It's All in the Timing

To everything there is a season, a time for every purpose under heaven.

Ecclesiastes 3:1

In 2009, God spoke to me saying, *"2009 is My time to bring forth certain promises I have for you."*

With His statement, I began to think about times and seasons of life, beginning with conception, gestation, and birth. There's a time to plant and harvest. The sun and moon also hold a time to shine. God ordained a year to consist of 365 days. He placed a certain number of days in each month. A day holds 24 hours, and a minute contains 60 seconds.

In Acts 2, there was an appointed time for New Testament believers that wasn't available to Old Testament saints: the *fullness* of Pentecost—the time when Jesus sent the Holy Spirit to indwell believers.

Times or *seasons* in the Greek language mean "a fixed or special occasion, an individual opportunity," or something in "due season."[1] God ordained the plans and purposes for Jesus on the earth. It was only a certain time that came for the Wise Men to see the star in the East. When the fullness of the time had come, God sent forth His Son, born of a woman (see Galatians 4:4). Fulfilling Scripture, John the Baptist came at a certain time to baptize Jesus. God also ordained Jesus' time to die, rise, and ascend. Jesus' return to the earth is not even in His own hands. That, too, is in God's timing.

Jesus said to His disciples, *"It is not for you to know times or seasons which the Father has put in His own authority"* (Acts 1:7). God has times and seasons for our lives that are in His authority alone.

With Jesus as our example, why would we doubt that our times are not also in God's hands? He alone knows the due season for the special occasions in each of our lives: *"God who holds your breath in His hand and owns all your ways…"* (Daniel 5:23).

I encourage you to believe, be patient, and look expectantly to God for the things He has for you in His time. It seems God is never early, and never late, but always right on time.

True Love

The Lord *does not see as man sees; for man looks at the outward appearance, but the* Lord *looks at the heart.*

1 Samuel 16:7

One day in the '80s, I noticed a man covered in tattoos selling hot dogs under the shade of an umbrella. Curious about his business, I approached him to ask questions. He politely answered me, but he also began telling me about Jesus. Miffed, I thought, *I did not ask you about Jesus.* However, for this man, business and Jesus weren't separate topics.

He spoke fondly of Jesus, as if they were good friends. I listened respectfully without response as he told me how much Jesus meant to him. At a time when tattoos weren't popular, I thought, *How can this be? He is fully tattooed. How does he know God loves him?* I had no ink on my skin and no knowledge of Christ's love for me. I heard Jesus died on a cross, rose from the grave, and was in heaven, but how did that concern me? I lived on earth. What good was Jesus to me, unseen?

The man continued, "Jesus loves you!" It was all I could do to hold back a torrent of tears. There seemed to be a force—a love—emanating from him that brushed up against my broken heart, causing my protective shell to crack. The man knew nothing of the weight of my sin crushing me. I politely said good-bye, never to see him again. His words not only pierced my heart, but they became *tattooed* on my heart.

The stranger was not ashamed of the gospel of Christ, for it is the power of God to salvation for everyone who believes (see Romans 1:16). One week later, at a drug party in the woods, I became born again by the Holy Spirit from above. That was in 1986.

As you share God's love with others, you won't always see what God is doing behind the scenes. In obedience to the Holy Spirit, you tell of His love, which He demonstrated on the cross through Jesus, and He takes care of the rest, permanently tattooing lives and hearts. I encourage you to not be ashamed to speak of this "True Love."

Power Twins

So He said to them, "This kind can come out by nothing but prayer and fasting."

Mark 9:29

Today my title stems from a chapter in a book called, *The Walk of the Spirit— The Walk of Power,* by Dave Roberson. Apparently, Dave too was introduced to a life of prayer and fasting in his Christian walk. I agree wholeheartedly with his term, *power twins,* which he refers to as prayer and fasting. [1]

I have twin sisters, Mary and Margaret. To me, they are power twins. On my behalf, the dynamic duo prayed for me with fasting, which opened my heart to receive Christ, sparing me from eternal damnation.

When I was newly saved, I asked God, "Why are my twin sisters paving the way spiritually?" He said, *"two put ten thousand to flight"* (Deuteronomy 32:30). True to His Word, this is exactly what my power twin sisters have done, and continue to do, wielding Christ's authority over the demonic forces in our family through prayer and fasting.

Some translations of the Bible omit the word *fasting* in our opening scripture. Previously in this book, I have mentioned the lifestyle of prayer and fasting God graced me with, along with its benefits. This writing is another example of a godly "Hoorah!" of me living a life with the power twins.

I consider fasting a booster to prayer. Together they boost the manifestation of our spiritual blessings in the heavenly places into the natural realm. God once told me, *"Fasting is like Miracle Grow."* Miracle Grow is a fertilizer that boosts the soil, causing vegetation to grow "miraculously."

Matthew 6 gives us directives for giving, praying, and fasting. Many people continue to give and pray but consider fasting a work of the flesh. But, in truth, giving and praying can also become works. My hope is that you haven't quit giving and praying, or made them religious rituals. But, neither do you want to forget the power twins of prayer and fasting. Together these spiritual disciplines create a powerful lifestyle!

Jesus, the Word

But you stand here awhile, that I may announce to you the word of God.

1 Samuel 9:27

Most vocations come with an instruction book, whether that's education through a handbook or a set of tools for the trade. No matter the calling, the proper implements make the process less daunting and more enjoyable.

The best life instruction book is the Holy Bible. In Daniel 10:21 we read, *"But I will tell you what is noted in the Scripture of Truth."* The Scripture of Truth is our lifeline and our plumb line.

My greatest treasure is Jesus, who is the Word:

¹In the beginning was the Word, and the Word was with God, and the Word was God… ¹⁴The Word became flesh and dwelt among us. (John 1:1, 14)

He was clothed with a robe dipped in blood, and His name is called The Word of God. (Revelation 19:13)

The word of our God stands forever. (Isaiah 40:8)

Wielded like a hammer, His Word demolishes the lies we believe. As a fire, it incinerates all ungodly thinking. Countless times we've cried out for direction or instruction, and His Word becomes *"…a lamp to* [my] *feet, and a light to* [my] *path"* (Psalm 119:105, brackets added). Since *"every word of God is pure,"* it too contains a healing balm, yielding medicinal effects for any wound (Proverbs 30:5).

My twin sisters consider the Word of God so essential that when I became born again, they sent me a Bible via Federal Express. They told me, "Just as you eat food for your physical body, you must daily eat this book and allow God to nourish, grow, and sustain your spirit man." I took their advice, and because of their example, I also now love Jesus, the Word.

"As for God, His way is perfect; The word of the LORD is proven" (Psalm 18:30). Today's technology provides ample ways to obtain the Word of God. Jesus said, *"It is written, 'Man shall not live by bread alone, but by every word of God'"* (Luke 4:4). Jesus' life-giving words, whispered by His Holy Spirit, will sustain us—spirit, soul, and body. Is God's Word part of your daily diet? If not, begin eating from it today.

A Beautiful Gift

*They were all filled with the Holy Spirit and began to speak
with other tongues, as the Spirit gave them utterance.*

Acts 2:4

Shortly after my salvation experience, my sister Margaret, who is incredibly smart and most often sensible, came to visit me. However, during this stay I began to question her sanity, as she began to tell me about the gift of tongues mentioned in 1 Corinthians 12. Tongues are unusual because they are not natural but spiritual.

At the time of my sister's visit, I refused the invitation to receive the gift Jesus had for me, thinking it was just too strange. The apostle Paul writes, *"The natural man does not receive the things of the Spirit of God, for they are foolishness to him; nor can he know them, because they are spiritually discerned"* (1 Corinthians 2:14). At this time, I was spiritually undiscerning, and the gift of tongues seemed foolish to me.

But, really, tongues are not all that strange. First Thessalonians 5:23 tells us that we are triune beings, possessing a spirit, a soul, and a body. Our soul speaks a language, which can be English or any other language. So why should we think it's strange for our spirit man to also have a language?

Two weeks later at a backyard barbeque, two women asked me, "Have you received everything your Father has for you?" I thought to myself, *I'm twenty-eight years old. What does my dad have that he hasn't already given me?* In their enthusiasm, they forgot to tell me they were referring to my heavenly Father. I told them that I wanted everything God had for me! They laid hands on me and instructed me to ask Jesus to baptize me with the Holy Spirit and fire. Immediately, an unknown language rolled off my tongue like a sweet melody. It was exactly as Jesus said: *"... these signs will follow those who believe:...they will speak with new tongues..."* (Mark 16:17).

God's ways are unnatural to our physical senses. God is not natural; He is a Spirit. It takes faith to receive salvation, and it takes faith to speak in tongues. Don't hesitate any longer. This amazing gift is waiting for you!

The Voice of God

My sheep hear My voice, and I know them, and they follow Me.

John 10:27

My dad had always been a man of few words. When I became a child of God, God spoke to me, saying, *"Because your dad didn't talk much, I will always talk with you."* God has kept His promise. I can't imagine a relationship with Him void of two-way conversation.

People often ask me, "How do you hear God? How do you know it's Him speaking? What does He sound like?" Jesus desires for all of His children to hear His voice.

Jesus said, *"My sheep hear My voice"* (John 10:27). Are you His sheep? If you're His and of His flock, my intention is for you to grow in recognizing His voice in your life. If you're not His sheep, you only need to humbly ask the Shepherd, and He'll open the gate for you to enter and become a part of His flock.

God speaks to us in various ways: by His Spirit through the scriptures, in dreams or visions, or through our circumstances. He also speaks through people, impressions, and the still, small voice of His Spirit.

My personal testimony of hearing God's voice began shortly after my salvation experience. While preparing to go to church, an impression came to my heart: *"Mark will be in church."* My heart responded, *No, Lord! He can't come there. That is our place.* I didn't want to share God or my church with my former boyfriend. When I arrived at the church, I knew I had heard God because Mark was present.

As my relationship with God progressed, I began writing down words I heard, scriptures that came alive, or pictures that came to mind. By journaling, I could refer back to these expressions, checking for accuracy, clarity, and confirmation. It's impossible to record thirty years of hearing God's voice on this page, but as you continue to read this book, I pray that God will enrich your recognition of His voice in your own life.

A Universal Dart

Those the Father has given Me will come to Me, and I will never reject them.

John 6:37 (NLT)

While traveling in Russia, an opportunity arose for me to pray for a woman. As I prayed, in my spirit I saw a man who I understood to be the devil. He approached this woman, and at point-blank range, shot her in the chest. When he fired the gun, it was not a bullet but an arrow that came out. Attached to it was a white flag with the word *Rejection* written in black letters. Penetrating her heart, it protruded about four inches out of her back. As I continued to pray, the Lord revealed the enemy's intent for the embedded projectile—he wanted her heart immobilized for life.

Rejection is terribly hurtful. Unfortunately, everyone—including Jesus—has experienced it. Even worse, sometimes we live with it for a lifetime. Its definition makes my blood curdle because it contains traits of Satan himself. *Rejection* implies refusing, turning down, or spurning. To drive my point home, when we spurn someone, we look down on, turn our back on, or abandon that person.

The Holy Spirit revealed the woman's heart trouble. Many people, including me, had seeds take root at a very young age due to believing that God is One who spurns or turns His back on mankind. However, God is the exact opposite. The outstretched arms of Jesus on the cross are proof of that. They bid us all to come.

In Psalm 27:10, David wrote, *"When my father and my mother forsake me, then the LORD will take care of me."* Sadly, betrayal comes. In a perfect world, there would be no struggle with dysfunction in relationships; however, in this less-than-perfect world, we can turn to God Almighty. He'll never turn you away or reject you. *"God is love"* (1 John 4:8).

If rejection is a dart that has pierced your heart, take a moment to pray and talk it over with God. Let Him know what you're feeling and thinking. God doesn't want your heart to be rejection's target, but rather a target for His great love.

Dreams that Rattle

Train up a child in the way he should go,
and when he is old he will not depart from it.

Proverbs 22:6

Eternal change came to me on December 7, 1991, when I had a dream in which my two-year-old son, Levi, died in a drowning accident. Although it was a horrible dream, I was relieved when I prayed to resuscitate him and he began to breathe again. Upon waking, dread and anguish lanced my heart. Thankfully, peace also surrounded me, knowing it was only a dream. In my heart I also believed the Spirit of Christ within me was not only able but willing to raise Levi *if* something were ever to happen.

I held my son more dearly and became acutely aware that he was at my mercy to train him up in God and for God. Urgency stirred my heart. By God's grace, as his mother, it was my responsibility to present Jesus to Levi. I did this through example and opportunities. For a time, we had devotions before school. I also encouraged quiet time with God through prayer and Bible reading. Another way I influenced him was with committed relationships among our church family.

Twelve years later when Levi was fourteen, I dreamed a second time that he passed away. Five years later the dream became a reality. Unlike my former dreams, in real life, the prayers of our family and friends didn't bring Levi back.

As parents, we cry out to God for a balance of love and boundaries in raising children. I felt our boundaries were rather strict, but I also believe they were mixed with God's kindness. Thankfully, our children grew to know and love Christ and to respect us as parents.

If you're a parent, you'll stand before God and give an account as to how you took care of the gifts He entrusted to you. Children are a gift and reward from the Lord (see Psalm 127:3). I encourage you to take every opportunity He provides to help them know Christ. If you don't do it, who will? Train up your children in the way they should go. Their eternal destiny depends on it.

His Harvest

Therefore pray the Lord of the harvest to send out laborers into His harvest.

Matthew 9:37

I received an invitation from the Lord in the form of an impression to attend a New Age seminar. Prayerfully considering the event, the Lord revealed our opening scripture, personalizing it by emphasizing "His harvest" instead of "the harvest."

For His kingdom purposes, Jesus led me to this New Age seminar where He wanted to harvest souls. His mission's objective was the speaker and her assistant.

Despite her passion, the speaker's words were meaningless babble. It was a "how to" in overcoming addictions and routine cycles of negative behavior. People may experience temporary freedom with secular ideas, but when they encounter Christ, His truth sets them permanently free.

There is a biblical process involved in breaking sinful behavior. The process is known as "pulling down strongholds." Strongholds are ideas that are contrary to God's thoughts (see 2 Corinthians 10:4). As we replace the lies we believe with the truth of God's Word, the transformation of our mind begins, and these ungodly beliefs and patterns fall away (see Romans 12:2).

I felt pity and compassion for the speaker and was burdened for the crowd because I didn't have the platform to speak God's transforming truth on their behalf. Nevertheless, I understood that God was at the helm of this harvest.

God had me share my testimony (found in the July 5–14 devotionals) with these two ladies. God alone knows what He accomplished in this New Age vineyard, as the women have not crossed my path since.

As the Spirit leads, we venture into His vineyards and allow the Lord of the Harvest to reap wherever and whomever He desires, as He gave His life as a ransom for many (see Mark 10:45). Sitting in that meeting was irritating, but for the sake of souls it was worth it. Jesus said to His disciples, *"the harvest truly is plentiful, but the laborers are few"* (Matthew 9:37).

Will you allow yourself to be a willing laborer in the vineyards of His choice?

Promises, Promises

There has not failed one word of all His good promise, which He promised.

1 Kings 8:56

We often hear the phrase, *promises, promises,* spoken in a sarcastic or negative manner. This refers to one who makes a promise but is known for not keeping it. Considering this expression and God's promises, I thought of how we can turn this cynical phrase into a life-giving one.

I'll never forget the day many years ago when I was in a Sunday morning church service, and a woman boasted about God keeping His promises. I was beside myself as she told of her recent widowhood that left her with five children. I thought, *If God were a promise keeper, you would not be a widow!* I admit, I had a lot of growing to do in grace and knowledge!

Today, I also now possess a testimony, that after the death of my son, God has kept His promises. I would like to encourage you: Never once has He failed to keep His Word that He vowed to do for me. He said He came to heal the brokenhearted, and He did. He promised He wouldn't leave us comfortless—not only when we mourn, but at all times. He guaranteed that when we call on Him, He would answer. God has kept every promise to me, and I know He does the same for you, as *"the Lord is not slack concerning His promise"* (2 Peter 3:9).

Abraham, a man of faith, *"did not waver at the promise of God through unbelief"* (Romans 4:20). We do well to do the same. Unlike Abraham, we have the limitless faith of the Son of God available to us at all times in our spirit man.

Have you felt at one time or another that God has let you down and not kept His promises? I have. I assure you, as you sit with Him and talk it over, He'll unveil to you His unseen ways—maybe not all of them, but the ones you need to know about.

Promises, promises. The Promise Keeper keeps them all!

Renewed Wedding Bells

Behold, I will do a new thing, now it shall spring forth; shall you not know it?
Isaiah 43:19

When leaving a cabin where I spent time in prayer and fasting, the Lord spoke suddenly, saying, *"Mark is going to ask you to marry him again. I'll give you the ring of your dreams and the honeymoon you never had."*

When I arrived home, my husband, Mark, approached me and asked, "Would you marry me again?" My heart burst with joy at the confirmation! God was truly doing a new thing! I didn't share my story with my husband, but a couple of nights later he asked, "What do you think of us getting married again?" At this time, I let the cat out of the bag.

Two years passed, and the topic of renewing our vows rarely came up. The word from Isaiah in our opening passage is *"now."* For me, this event was two years past due. I continued to pray, sensing that God wanted me to follow Him as He led my husband.

After twenty years of marriage, the renewal of our vows came about in an intimate setting in our home with close friends. Now that we had children, it was our desire for them to travel with us on our honeymoon to Israel. The trip was amazing. The Bible came more alive and reinforced our family belief that Jesus Christ is Lord.

In hindsight, God did this "new thing" in our marriage so we could withstand the indescribable heartache that lay ahead two years later when Levi died. I don't have solid evidence of divorce statistics after the death of a child, but I know that grief is crushing and puts a tremendous strain on a marriage.

God is good. And in traveling to Israel, He was doing a "new thing" for Levi too, which not only solidified his commitment to Christ, but in some way it prepared him for his entrance into eternity.

Are you believing God to do a "new thing" in your life, your marriage, or your family? God is a Man of His Word, and if He said it, you can expect it!

Speech Class

You have given him his heart's desire,
and have not withheld the request of his lips.

Psalm 21:2

While raising my children, I had a desire to take a speech class at a local college for the sole purpose of preaching the gospel. Now as an empty nester, it seemed the perfect time.

Our first speech was one of introduction. I asked my class partner to acquaint the audience with my belief in Christ. He asked, "Are you really religious?" My enthusiastic reply was, "I'm a radical believer in Jesus Christ!" He responded, "I don't believe in religion; I believe in 100 percent science."

Although God brought us together, I sensed conflict ahead, as we were polar opposites. The Lord said to me, *"Sharon, let your partner pick all of the topics."* God was telling me He was at the helm, and I could trust Him no matter how contrary the subject matter.

For our final speech, we blindly picked a topic from an envelope. Knowing the professor and I weren't on the same page spiritually, I prayed before choosing. Relieved, I thanked God for my topic of trustworthiness, and left the classroom.

My partner ran down the hall after me, calling my name. He voiced a desperate plea, saying, "The professor said I could trade topics with you if you're willing." Curious because of his noticeable distress, I asked, "What's your topic?" He replied, "Forgiveness. I don't know a thing about forgiveness! I think that's your department." I was elated. God was faithful to my desire to preach His gospel in a speech class.

My final twenty-minute speech was on the forgiveness of Jesus Christ. I could sense the Holy Spirit's power and presence overwhelm me, and I was reminded of the words of the apostle Paul: *"I am not ashamed of the gospel of Christ, for it is the power of God to salvation for everyone who believes"* (Romans 1:16).

Do desires burn in your heart? God hasn't forgotten them. Ask the Lord if it's time for your long-awaited dreams to come to pass. He gave me the longing of my heart, which was to preach the gospel. Anything you ask according to His will, He will also do for you.

What's in a Name?

*You will conceive in your womb and bring forth a Son,
and shall call His name Jesus.*

Luke 1:31

One day during my first year of marriage, I was sitting on a hillside having a devotional time with God. I read 1 Corinthians 14:13: *"Therefore, let him who speaks in a tongue pray that he may interpret."* Childlike faith sprang up in my heart, as I was less than a year old in the Lord. Since I pray in tongues, I took God at His Word, asking Him to make this word alive in my life. I began to pray in tongues, and then I began to pray in English, or with understanding. As I did so, I heard words that were unfamiliar to me because God said, *"You are praying for your children."* My black-and-white response was, *"Lord, I don't have any children!"* He continued, *"You will have children. You'll have a son, and you'll name him Levi."*

God not only got my attention, but He made it known to me that He does what He says He'll do. He told us in Scripture to ask to interpret a spiritual tongue. I did, and He answered. Naturally, I thought my first child would be a boy. When my daughter came first instead, I figured I didn't hear God accurately. However, Levi followed soon after.

If God can send a message to Mary through the angel Gabriel about her conception, birth, and name of her Son, He can speak to you and me through His Holy Spirit about the conception, birth, and names of our children.

Coming face to face with God on March 27, 2010, Levi came to the fulfillment of his name and its meaning—"united in harmony and joined to God."

If you're a parent beginning your family, if you ask God, I believe He'll tell you the names He's chosen for your children. If you've already named your children, you can be in prayer that your grandchildren will have the names that God ordained for them from before the foundation of the world. Names are important to the Lord, so seek Him as to what He would like for your children or grandchildren to be called.

The Mute Button

I will restrain my mouth with a muzzle.

Psalm 39:1

My friend Jan and I both have had sons depart for heaven. One day as we spoke on the phone and her own words registered in her ears, she said, "Listen to me complain." Grieving together, I responded, "Jan, I'm guilty too." I said, "We should hit the mute button, as I'm sure God would want to hit it as well." Although brokenhearted, we still had things in which to be thankful.

An ungrateful heart catches each one of us from time to time. *Complain* means to "express dissatisfaction or annoyance about a state of affairs or an event."[1] Jan and I were dissatisfied with our difficult circumstances, as any parent would be.

As I read 1 Corinthians 10:10–11, I was reminded that when we murmur, we open a door in our lives for the devil and his destruction. Written for our example, this passage discourages us from engaging in this type of speech. Some Old Testament characters complained, and the destroyer destroyed them. When we complain, God will not destroy us, but we will experience repercussions from our choice of words. Grumbling also dishonors our heavenly Father as our caretaker. What parents like to hear their children gripe?

The writer of Philippians admonishes us to *"do all things without complaining and disputing"* (2:14). I have not yet reached perfection in the counsel of the apostle Paul, *"12but I press on, that I may lay hold of that for which Christ Jesus has also laid hold of me.... 14I press toward the goal for the prize of the upward call of God in Christ Jesus"* (Philippians 3:12, 14).

Please join Jan and me today, as we give thanks with a grateful heart! We're all able to hit the mute button, putting a muzzle over our mouths and our complaints.

Willingly Abused

I lay down My life…. No one takes it from Me,
but I lay it down of Myself. I have power to lay it down.

John 10:17–18

Remembering the Lord's death in communion, a picture of the physical abuse Jesus endured came to mind. Jesus said He'd suffer many things from the elders, chief priests, and scribes, and He'd be killed and then raised back to life on the third day (see Matthew 16:21).

It all happened as Jesus prophesied. At His arrest, *"⁶⁷…they spat in His face and beat Him; and others struck Him with the palms of their hands, ⁶⁸saying, 'Prophesy to us, Christ! Who is the one who struck You?'"* (Matthew 26:67–68). Then, they pressed a crown of twisted thorns on His head, placed a reed in His right hand and mocked Him (see Matthew 27:29). Stripping Him, they divided His garments and cast lots (see Luke 23:34). Crucifying Him, they pounded nails into His hands (see John 20:25) and pierced His side (John 19:34).

Once, while reading Isaiah 50:6 regarding Jesus, I sensed the presence of Jesus, as He said to me, *"I gave My back to those who struck Me and My cheeks to those who plucked out My beard. I didn't hide My face from shame and spitting."* How can we understand His willingness to lay down His life for us? *"He was oppressed and He was afflicted, yet He opened not His mouth; He was led as a lamb to the slaughter, and as a sheep before its shearers [He was] silent"* (Isaiah 53:7, brackets added). Although innocent, Jesus willingly took the sin and penalty that was due mankind and never spoke up in self-defense.

Jesus, God's sufficient blood sacrifice—spirit, soul, and body—provided redemption once and for all. The joy set before Jesus was you and me. He endured the cross, despising the shame, nakedness, insults, and torture (see Hebrews 12:2).

First John 5:11–12 reads, *"¹¹this is the testimony: that God has given us eternal life, and this life is in His Son. ¹²He who has the Son has life; he who does not have the Son of God does not have life."* I pray you won't reject Jesus, who willingly gave His life for you. For in Him, my dear friend, is eternal life.

Prayer, Your Oxygen Mask

Praying always with all prayer and supplication in the Spirit.

Ephesians 6:18

One day, in my mind, I saw myself seated in an airplane putting on an oxygen mask. This image brought about a correlating thought: Prayer is like putting on an oxygen mask. Since oxygen is essential to sustain life, prayer then, is the oxygen or life-support system that sustains ourselves and others.

Before take-off, flight attendants convey emergency instructions, which include directions for passengers to put on their own oxygen mask first then that of another passenger who needs assistance. There is validity for this logic: In a life-threatening situation, without oxygen for ourselves, we'd be unable to assist others. In my spirit, I saw myself following these directives with prayer. Only after I put on my oxygen mask of prayer will I be able to aid others.

With the word *spirit* defined as "breath," it's the Spirit of God whose breath sustains us.[1] Psalm 104:29 reads, *"You take away their breath, they die and return to their dust."* Without His life-giving breath, our physical body and spirit is dead. Without His oxygen or life-giving breath in our prayers, our lives and ministry to others will also lack life. However, replenished and revived with oxygen—as we are with oxygen masks on—we can minister to God, ourselves, and give aid to others.

I appreciate many things about Jesus, but one is His prayer life. As the Son of Man, by turning to His Father in prayer, He put on His oxygen mask. Jesus said, *"For their sakes I sanctify* [set apart] *Myself, that they also may be sanctified by the truth"* (John 17:19, brackets added). Jesus, for our sake, set Himself apart to God; He then turned and infused us with that same life-giving oxygen of the Holy Spirit!

Are you laden with oxygen through prayer? With Jesus as your example, you can rise early in the morning, long before daylight, depart to a solitary place, and pray (see Mark 1:35). Or, perhaps mid-morning, afternoon, or evening work better for you. Those too are perfect times to talk with God. Whenever you pray, you'll fill yourself with His rich life-giving oxygen so you can then administer it to others.

A More Opportune Time

*Now when the devil had ended every temptation,
he departed from Him until an opportune time.*

Luke 4:13

The devil diligently threw every temptation at Jesus that he could muster. With no success, the Bible says he departed from Him until *"an opportune time."* *Opportune* depicts a moment well chosen or particularly favorable or appropriate. I've never given the devil credit for being smart, but this scripture proves me wrong.

Not only is the devil hard working, although he's defeated, he's a crafty mastermind, watching and waiting for the best time to strike again.

Have you ever experienced relief knowing that the enemy has departed from you and the pressure has eased? I have! Despite this, his absence is short lived. Jesus said, *"Watch and pray, lest you enter into temptation. The spirit indeed is willing, but the flesh is weak"* (Matthew 26:41). Since the devil plotted to come to Jesus at an opportune time, it's wise for us to not ignore our foe. Through prayer we watch for the devil's return with temptation in our own lives. It's a tool that keeps the devil's attempts of attack at bay or even thwarts them all together.

Jesus told His disciples before His arrest at the Mount of Olives, *"Pray that you may not enter into temptation"* (Luke 22:40). After Jesus Himself rose from prayer, He found the disciples sleeping from sorrow. He asked them, *"Why do you sleep? Rise and pray, lest you enter into temptation"* (Luke 22:46). Has Jesus ever found you asleep spiritually?

Colossians 4:2 tells us to *"devote [ourselves] to prayer with an alert mind and a thankful heart"* (NLT, brackets added). I encourage you today to maintain an alert mind in prayer, for with it you can lay aside the sin or temptation that may beset you (see Hebrews 12:1). And hold onto a thankful heart, which enables good things, including grace, to abound in your situation. Staying alert, watchful, and thankful will help expose the "opportune time" that the devil may have planned for you.

Gone Fishin'

Come, follow Me and I will show you how to fish for people.

Matthew 4:19 (NLT)

In order to find the best fishing holes, you must have an expert guide or someone native to the area. For a crackpot—expert—fisherman, I recommend Jesus. He has innumerable fish stories; each one unique but true!

Like an expert guide, Jesus gets into your boat (see Luke 5:3) to help you find the best fishing holes for souls. No matter the fight, He's skilled in getting the fish on His hook and into His net. Some spots will yield a large catch; others, only one. Although some fishermen prefer the larger catch, in the kingdom of God, if you hook only one it's still considered a great day of fishing and a good spot because *"there is joy in the presence of the angels of God over one sinner who repents"* (Luke 15:10)!

Although I live in the majestic Colorado Rockies, I'm not a fan of fishing in quiet ponds or meandering streams. I have limited patience there. Deep-sea fishing is what piques my interest. If I'm going to fish, I prefer living large. I desire all the excitement that goes with each catch, and my hope is to fill the boat to capacity with a variety of fish. Clearly, I'm a fisherman who prefers to fish for the multitudes.

However, it's not about me. I'll trust my Guide and His expertise. Moreover, when He tells me to launch out and let down my net for a catch, whether it's in the deep or the in the shallows, I won't lean on my own understanding. I'll follow His expert instructions.

In John 21:3, Simon Peter said to the men, *"'I am going fishing.' They said to him, 'We are going with you also.'"*

Are you ready to go fishing for souls? Allow Jesus to be your Guide, and He'll take you right to your catch!

Live Poet Society

*For God so loved the world that He gave His only begotten Son,
that whoever believes in Him should not perish but have everlasting life.*

John 3:16

I do not consider myself to be a poet, nor have I expressed interest in poetry. In grade school, complaints were my only response to poetic assignments! However, since becoming a Christ follower and carrying the limitless ability of the Spirit within my spirit, it's amazing what comes forth: poetry from God! He's not only a poet but a poet who speaks life!

For You
I love *you!*
For *you* I died,
For *you* I was raised.
For *you* I will ever praise,
For with *you* I will ever be.
For it is *you* I long to see.
I loved *you* on My knee;
I loved *you* on My tree.
My love for *you* will always be.

God goes to considerable lengths to encourage us to comprehend His great love for us, including the gospel poetically spoken.

God demonstrates His own love toward us, in that while we were still sinners, Christ died for us (see Romans 5:8). *"The LORD has appeared of old to me, saying: Yes, I have loved you with an everlasting love; therefore with lovingkindness I have drawn you"* (Jeremiah 31:3). Everlasting love…who can fathom that? I can't! However, I believe it because God said it. And *"God is not a man, that He should lie… Has He said, and will He not do? Or has He spoken, and will He not make it good?"* (Numbers 23:19). God loves you!

Jesus loved us and washed us from our sins in His own blood (see Revelation 1:5). *"He will quiet you with His love"* (Zephaniah 3:17). *"He loved us first"* (1 John 4:19). God … is rich in mercy, because of His great love with which He loved us (see Ephesians 2:4). These passages are just a few examples of His great love for us. Take time today to respond to God's love for you. Perhaps you could even write a poem back to Him, expressing your appreciation.

Devil's Dart Board

Above all, taking the shield of faith with which you will be able to quench all the fiery darts of the wicked one.

Ephesians 6:16

Most of us are acquainted with the game of darts, which includes a circular board with a bull's eye at the center. Do you ever feel Satan has made you his target and your heart his bull's eye when he throws his fiery darts at you?

Once when I worked as a manager for a Christian ministry, I was approached by a non-management employee, who asked, "Are you speaking at the meeting?" As a department head, the meeting was a big event that I had expected to take part in.

I responded, "No, I'm not."

She then replied, "I am! I've been asked to present the offering message."

The devil used her words in an attempt to snare me. I felt overlooked since I was a manager and she wasn't. In that moment, I heard the Lord whisper, *"Sharon, put up your shield."* Immediately in the spirit, I saw my shield of faith go up. Satan's fiery darts of rejection hit that shield and fell, smoldering at my feet.

Professional dart players often use a wrist-snap movement to throw, allowing for more acceleration and accuracy. God showed me how the devil throws darts: He is precise, and his aim is intentional. However, the devil wasn't the expert he thought he was when he launched his flaming darts of lies and accusations at me. They never hit their target, which was my heart.

Taking up our shield of faith is similar to the workings of Israel's Iron Dome. This system design allows interception and destruction of incoming short-range rockets and artillery shells. Likewise, as believers, we have a defense system in the form of the shield of faith, which enables us to resist the enemy's incoming fiery darts.

Take up your shield of faith every day. And, *"Above all else, guard your heart, for everything you do flows from it"* (Proverbs 4:23, NIV). As you do, every fiery dart of the enemy will be extinguished.

This Is Only a Test

But He knows the way that I take;
when He has tested me, I shall come forth as gold.
My foot has held fast to His steps; I have kept His way and not turned aside.
I have not departed from the commandment of His lips; I have treasured the
words of His mouth more than my necessary food. But He is unique, and who
can make Him change? And whatever His soul desires, that He does.
For He performs what is appointed for me, and many such things are with Him.

Job 23:10–14

One morning the Lord woke me at 1:58, saying, *"The title of your next message will be 'The Three B's: Born Again, Baptized in Water, and Baptized in the Holy Spirit.'"*

At God's direction and with diligent prayer, I held a meeting titled "The Three B's" at a local hotel. I felt like I did all the Lord had asked of me. However, the meeting didn't go as I envisioned. I left disheartened.

The following morning in prayer, I asked, "Lord, what went wrong? I thought I did all You asked of me." God then led me to our opening scriptures. I sensed Him saying, *"This was a test for you to step out in faith and obedience to My directions. You have come forth as gold. Your foot held fast to My steps, and you didn't turn aside from all that I commanded you. You treasured the words of My mouth more than your necessary food through fasting. However, I am unique, and whatever My soul desires, that I do. I performed what was appointed for you."*

Have you ever stepped out in faith and obedience and found things didn't go as you had hoped or expected? Perhaps it's only a test. Your part is to obey God to the best of your knowledge, and the results are up to Him. The clay shouldn't tell the potter what to do! *"Does not the potter have power over the clay?"* (Romans 9:21). *"As the clay is in the potter's hand, so are you in My hand"* (Jeremiah 18:6). God is unique, and who can change Him? Whatever His soul desires, that He does, performing what is appointed for you.

As a man or woman in right standing with God through Jesus, praying and obeying is the best you can do. But, as you do, your steps will be ordered by Him.

Combat Authority

Let every soul be subject to the governing authorities.
For there is no authority except from God,
and the authorities that exist are appointed by God.
Therefore whoever resists the authority resists the ordinance of God,
and those who resist will bring judgment on themselves.

Romans 13:1–2

Authority is a combat essential. It's mandatory for all armies, including God's troops. Joshua succeeded Moses in leading the Israelites. Nearing Jericho, Joshua saw a man who identified Himself as the Commander of the Lord's army. *"Joshua fell on his face to the earth and worshiped, and said to Him, 'What does my Lord say to His servant?'"* (Joshua 5:14).

Like Joshua, you and I are servants or servicemen under the authority of our Supreme Commander, our highest-ranking officer, the Lord Jesus Christ. *"He is the head of the body, the church"* (Colossians 1:18) *"and the head of all principality and power"* (Colossians 2:10).

The Hebrew word for leader comes from the root word *commander*, which means "(chief) ruler" or "occupying the front."[1] Jesus holds the front lines of the body of Christ. His role as Commanding Officer is to appoint, authorize, or set things in order, which He established in the government, church, work, and family.

Although imperfect, God established human authority for our good. In 1 Peter 2:18, servants are instructed to be submissive to their masters with all fear; not only to the good and gentle, but also to the harsh. Recruits have a responsibly to pray for those in authority, and by this obedience, we're promised His protection and peace (see 1 Timothy 2:1–2). *"When He [Jesus] was reviled, [He] did not revile in return; when He suffered, He did not threaten, but committed Himself to Him who judges righteously"* (1 Peter 2:23, brackets added). While submitting to frail human leadership, Jesus was ultimately submitting to God. We are to follow the example of Jesus.

God also delegated to every enlisted person, including you, His spiritual authority, which is power over the enemy (see Luke 10:19). Remember, it's by your delegated authority in Jesus Christ that Satan submits to you. Don't be afraid to use your authority today against the plans of the enemy.

Appropriate Affections

All whose knees have not bowed to Baal,
and every mouth that has not kissed him.

1 Kings 19:18

The god Baal has an in-depth history in the Holy Bible. Baal became the proper name for the most significant god in the Canaanite pantheon. Baal's main function was thought to be making land, animals, and people fertile.[1]

We often hear 1 Kings 19:18 referring only to those people who *"bowed their knee to Baal."* To my knowledge, I hadn't heard about people *kissing* Baal until the Holy Spirit revealed this to me in a time of prayer and fasting. Not only did they bow their knee, but they also kissed the idol! The word *kiss*, as a verb, means "to touch with the lips as a sign of love…reverence, or greeting."[2]

The Lord showed me that I was kissing Baal when I agreed with the lies of Satan. Does that ring your bell as it rang mine? At one time or another, everyone has made agreements with the lies of the devil. So it follows that, on occasion, we have all kissed Baal!

I began fraternizing with Baal by believing the lies of the feminist movement in the '60s and '70s: the lie that God favored men over women. In numerous cultures, people continue to kiss statues of religious deity. As believers in Christ, we don't kiss statues, but when we embrace ideas contrary to God, or place our attention and affection on people or things other than God, we are, in effect, kissing Baal.

In my early years with Christ, as I prayed and read my Bible, God began to show me the truth: He not only loves women, but He has no favorites. Little by little, I began to stop cuddling up to Baal and the lies.

God warns, *"You shall have no other gods before Me"* (Exodus 20:3). Let's keep affection and worship within their proper boundaries, resisting all kisses of the enemy and allow God to *"kiss [us] with the kisses of His mouth"* (Song of Solomon 1:2, brackets added). As Psalm 119:103 tells us, His words are sweeter than honey to our mouth.

Paralleled Times

Certain Epicurean and Stoic philosophers encountered him [Paul].
And some said, "What does this babbler want to say?"
Others said, "He seems to be a proclaimer of foreign gods,"
because he preached to them Jesus and the resurrection.

Acts 17:18 (brackets added)

It appears that ancient times parallel our modern day. As disciples of Christ, and sadly, in a nation professing Christianity, because we preach Jesus crucified, the resurrection, and the ascension, like Paul we are babblers proclaiming a foreign god in the eyes of the world.

Recently, I've been thinking much about the unrest of our world as well as the condition of America. It's a known fact that society rapidly declines as it rejects God and His Word. Today there are bills, amendments, and resolutions that are in total opposition to God's will for mankind, freely passed as law.

There is nothing new under the sun. In the book of Judges 17:6, we read that *"everyone did what was right in his own eyes."* For our nation's Supreme Court, my prayer is for a realization that there is One Supreme Judge to whom they and all mankind *"will have to give account"* (1 Peter 4:5). Even in the days of Isaiah, the prophet wrote *"...woe to those who call evil good, and good evil"* (Isaiah 5:20).

As believers, *"we know that we are of God, and the whole world lies under the sway of the wicked one"* (1 John 5:19). In 1 John 2:15, we're told that we're not to love the world or the things in the world and that if anyone loves the world, then the love of the Father is not in that person. The world and its gods represent the antitheist of God.

In heartfelt prayer, with the signs of the times, I asked the Lord, "How are we to make a difference as Christ followers, when today's society is in opposition to Your will at every turn?"

As if receiving orders from a five-star general, God disclosed my personal ministry marching orders and how He wants me to approach the conflict we're up against today. As you read the rest of this story in the following devotional, I encourage you to begin to ask the Lord for your own marching orders.

A Life-Changing Answer

Avoid foolish and ignorant disputes, knowing that they generate strife.
And a servant of the Lord must not quarrel but be gentle to all,
able to teach, patient, in humility correcting those who are in opposition, if
God perhaps will grant them repentance, so that they may know the truth,
and that they may come to their senses and escape the snare of the devil,
having been taken captive by him to do his will.

2 Timothy 2:23–26

As I touched on in yesterday's devotional, pondering the conditions around the globe, I wondered what exactly we, as believers facing opposition to God's holy standards, are to do. After all, there seems to be no regard for His principles of righteousness and holiness in our "anything goes" society. I wondered what our response should look like as Christ followers.

It wasn't long before I met a woman who unashamedly voiced her opinions and beliefs about the institution of family, which were contrary to God's. She said to me, "That was blunt, wasn't it?" Stunned, I immediately turned inward to ask, "Lord, how should I respond?" The impression came to tell her about my family, when God said, "Say to her, 'Speaking of blunt...'"

I had no idea how God was going to finish His statement, but trusting Him, I said to the woman, "Speaking of blunt, since the death of my son, I'm more straightforward in telling people about their eternal destiny. One day you'll have to stand before God and give an account to Him of how you lived your life. Jesus paved the way, paying the price for your sin. Jesus came to turn you from darkness to light, and from the power of Satan, to God. To receive His gift, believe and call on His name, and you will be saved."

At this point, she appeared ready to find the nearest exit. However, I knew the Holy Spirit penetrated her heart. After this encounter, I again prayed to God, pleading, "How are we to speak Your truth with an attitude of love in the face of views so false and diametrically opposed to Yours?" He answered me by illuminating our opening passage. Read it again, then ask God for yourself, "Lord, how am I to carry out my ministering marching orders?" He'll be faithful to show you, and your answer may make an eternal impact in the life of someone else.

God's Valentine

I have not concealed Your lovingkindness.

Psalm 40:10

Two days after meeting the woman I discussed in yesterday's devotional, I found myself praying fervently for her when God suddenly spoke a poem to me on her behalf. With pen in hand, I could scarcely keep up with His pace of revelation.

As His love and passion for her overwhelmed my heart, I saw a large, shiny, red gift bag. In the bag were a card, the newly penned poem, a living plant, and a heart-shaped box of chocolates. With Valentine's Day only two days away, God's purposes were plain to me.

Knowing next to nothing about this woman, or if she'd even receive me, as a messenger of the Lord, I obediently did as He instructed. I knew from experience that even if I encountered resistance, it wouldn't have been an indication that the plan was not from God. He reassured me long ago that when I yield to Him and simply do as He asks, no matter what the outcome, the results are His responsibility. Thankfully, things went flawlessly that day as I presented her with her Valentine's Day gift from Jesus:

Poetry of God

Jesus

The God who is Savior and Friend
The Son of God who apprehends and defends
The God made flesh who took our sins away,
The lover of our soul who steals our heart away!
The Christ, the Risen Lord, who opens heaven's doors
He will come again, in time
He asks today, "Will you be My Valentine?"

Although of secular origin, God chose to touch this woman with His love through the idea of Valentine's Day. Do you know that you, too, are God's beloved? He loves you as much as He loves Jesus! He loves you as much as He loves this woman. He also wants to present you with a gift bag filled with His love. Today, will you be His Valentine? He loves like no other!

Fruit to Eternal Life

They should repent, turn to God, and do works befitting repentance.

Acts 26:20

In regards to sin, *repent* indicates that someone is thinking differently or reconsidering by turning away from thoughts and actions that are contrary to God. By repenting, we turn our back on old thought patterns and habits and turn toward God.

In his address to King Agrippa, Paul recounted his instruction from Jesus: *"18To open their eyes, in order to turn them from darkness to light, and from the power of Satan to God, that they may receive forgiveness of sins...."* And that *"20...they should repent, turn to God, and do works befitting repentance"* (Acts 26:18, 20).

For the last two days, I've written about a certain woman. Today I'll share the conclusion of that story, which models repentance. Two years passed when I again ran into this lady, who previously and unashamedly voiced her opinions about the government's kind of marriage and family. At our meeting, she recalled that Valentine's Day when we met in detail. Profusely hugging and thanking me, she said, "When I met you I was in a bad place." That place was a homosexual relationship. One month after our first meeting, she turned away from that relationship and began attending church with a boyfriend, where she gained a new realization of God's love for her.

This woman didn't meet me, but she met Jesus in me. Jesus strengthened her with His grace to take to heart the things God revealed to her through me. She demonstrated what Paul suggested: *"...that they should repent, turn to God, and do works befitting repentance."* She began to think differently about living contrary to God's will for her life. In doing so, she "repented" and turned from that sinful relationship to God.

God's forgiveness and grace are available to you in this moment to help you repent or turn from anything contrary to His will for your life. His Holy Spirit is present to work in you or with you to *"do [or accomplish] works befitting repentance"* (brackets added).

Concealed Carry

But we have this treasure in earthen vessels.

2 Corinthians 4:7

One day I did something I don't normally do. Running late, I carried my purse into my exercise class. During the workout, I repeatedly glanced at my handbag because I was carrying a concealed weapon.

As I thought about the people in the class and the gun in my purse, the Lord shared an analogy with me between my concealed firearm and the Holy Spirit hidden in my heart, as well as the hearts of other believers.

Those in the exercise class were not aware of my 38 Special. Nor were they aware that, if the need arose, I was prepared to defend them or myself in any life-threatening situation. It felt as though I was engaged in spiritual covert operations with the Holy Spirit.

Although I live in this world, thank God, I am not of this world! As believers, we are hidden in Christ, in God. I enjoy the thought of hiding. Not as someone posing, but rather knowing that in this wild and crazy world, there's a secret place within our spirit, where we dwell hidden with God. In this world, darkness surrounds us. However, as we go about God's business, Isaiah 45:3 is there for us: *"I will give you the treasures of darkness and hidden riches of secret places that you may know that I, the Lord, who call you by your name, am the God of Israel."*

People may not be aware of the unseen cooperation between me and the Holy Spirit or that I have a concealed weapon. Rest assured, He works through us as Christ followers to defend others against the schemes of the enemy. Whatever the need, the concealed treasure within emerges in a calculated manner with love, deliverance, healing, or encouraging words, firing a decisive round.

If you do not yet have your spiritual conceal carry permit, go to Jesus, receive the salvation He provided for you, and He will issue one to you.

Covenant Rainbow

*I set My rainbow in the cloud, and it shall be for the sign of the covenant
between Me and the earth. It shall be, when I bring a cloud over the earth,
that the rainbow shall be seen in the cloud; and I will remember My covenant
which is between Me and you and every living creature of all flesh;
the waters shall never again become a flood to destroy all flesh.*

Genesis 9:13–15

As a new believer, I began reading the Bible from its beginning. Nine chapters into the book of Genesis, I stumbled upon the pot of gold at the end of a rainbow. Astonishment filled my heart, as I read our opening passage for the first time.

Since childhood, science had imposed the rainbow's meaning in my heart and mind, but in reality, it's much more than a display of prisms reflecting light in droplets of water. It's the sign of a loving God, keeping His covenant promise with Noah. He set His rainbow in the clouds as a covenant that He would never again flood the earth and its inhabitants.

No matter where you live on the earth—from the North or South Pole to the deepest jungle—not one single human can escape the rainbow in which God chooses to adorn the skies. Scientists research its elements; it permeates movies, literature, music, and logos. Living at approximately 600 B.C., the age-old prophet Ezekiel also referenced the rainbow in the sky on a rainy day (see Ezekiel 1:28).

The Bible records a rainbow around the throne of God that has the appearance of an emerald (see Revelation 4:3). The rainbow is more than science or a slogan; it's God's idea!

Don't be misled today with the world's meaning or historic folklore concerning the rainbow. God's original intent for the rainbow still stands, which is a guarantee that He won't be asking you to build a boat to escape flood waters! Every time you see the rainbow, be reminded that our God is a covenant keeper. If He will keep this promise, He will keep His other promises as well. What promise do you need Him to keep in your life today? He is faithful!

Inheritance Spending

In Him also we have obtained an inheritance.

Ephesians 1:11

One of my husband's co-workers received what I thought to be a substantial inheritance. This man's gift came from his uncle in the form of $300,000. My husband's blue eyes turned green with envy with each new story the man shared as to what he purchased, which was anything and everything he desired.

Considering this man's spending, I couldn't help but think of the body of Christ and our inheritance in Jesus. Although the man's gift was limited, we have unlimited wealth in Christ. I'm not speaking merely of monetary blessings, but of the endowment of peace, hope, joy, companionship, and above all, the promise of the eternal inheritance—a relationship with God, here and now and beyond; the relationship that Jesus provided for us through His death (see Hebrews 9:15).

How many of us appropriate our spiritual inheritance as freely as this man spent his earthly one? On occasion, it appeared the man lacked wisdom, which should accompany an inheritance (see Ecclesiastes 7:11). Proverbs 20:21 cautions, *"an inheritance gained hastily at the beginning, will not be blessed at the end."*

As born-again believers, we've all obviously taken hold of His inheritance of salvation, which is only the beginning of the abundance of His will and testament. There is so much more! Portions of our inheritance are available to us on earth, but other incorruptible portions, which won't fade away, are reserved for us in heaven (see 1 Peter 1:4)

Although He is God, Jesus, as the Son of Man, is obviously a good man, and *"a good man leaves an inheritance to his children's children"* (Proverbs 13:22). As His kids, we bear rights to an inheritance, which never ends, and the blessing is for our children's children as well.

Agree with Psalm 16:6 today by declaring, *"The lines have fallen to me in pleasant places; yes, I have a good inheritance."*

People Pleasing

For do I now persuade men, or God? Or do I seek to please men?
For if I still pleased men, I would not be a bondservant of Christ.

Galatians 1:10

P aul believed he was a chief among sinners (see 1 Timothy 1:15). I believe he was chief among the "politically incorrect" who attempt to please God and not people.

While taking a college English course, my professor instructed us to write an essay on a sexually immoral topic. As believers, we are in the world, but we are not of the world. Although I was *in* the English class, as a Christian, I was not *of* the class. I'm also not of the class that pleases people, but rather God. It didn't matter to me if I received an F or was out $500 for the cost of the class because of my decision.

Voicing my disgust in an email to the professor, I quoted the apostle Peter from Acts 5:29: "[I] *ought to obey God rather than men*" (brackets added). I had received responses to previous correspondence with him, but I received none on this matter. I then approached him in class, revisiting my original email. Because I spoke God's Word, which is living and powerful and sharper than any two-edged sword, I could tell that it pierced through my professor's thoughts and motives of his heart. He ultimately backpedaled, allowing me to write an essay of my choice. I completed the class with an A+.

Paul said, *"The world has been crucified to me, and I to the world"* (Galatians 6:14). *"For all that is in the world, the lust of the flesh, the lust of the eyes, and the pride of life, is not of the Father but is of the world"* (1 John 2:16). He also said in Galatians 4:16, *"Have I therefore become your enemy because I tell you the truth?"* This world has no hold on me. If you meet me in person, you'll find that I'm much like my brother Paul, a bondservant of Christ, who doesn't please men.

Are you in the class of the world, pleasing men, or in Christ, pleasing God? Don't be content to please man. God has a much better way for us when we step out in faith and choose to please Him alone.

Text Me

*Call to Me, and I will answer you, and show you
great and mighty things, which you do not know.*

Jeremiah 33:3

When I noticed an emoji smiley face on my cell phone from a friend's text, I thought, *I bet God would like a text from us!*

In today's forms of communication, how many of us think to figuratively text God? Do we leave Him a smiley face, conveying our elated emotion or thanks? Do we text just to say hello, or that we're thinking of Him, or to ask what's on His heart? Since texting is something done between friends, I believe God, as our dearest Friend, would enjoy equal consideration.

As handy as texting can be, it has also enabled a great disconnect in the vital role of face-to-face conversation. God's favorite form of communication with us is still as He had with Moses—*"face to face as a man speaks to his friend"* (Exodus 33:11). King David called on the Lord morning, noon, and night, and we can do the same. God will hear our voice (see Psalm 55:17). God longs to receive a text from you, or expressing it another way, He loves to connect with you. In Colorado, texting while driving is illegal, but talking with God is not!

"Out of heaven He let[s] *you hear His voice, that He might instruct you"* (Deuteronomy 4:36, brackets added). Every line of reception on God's end, which would allow us to hear His voice, is open. And, like a popular cell phone slogan, He says, "Can you hear Me now?"

When we call on God, His answer is never like that of our robotic-voiced smart phones, who respond, "I'm sorry. I cannot process anymore requests right now. Please try again later." You'll never hear God say, "You're breaking up." With Him, you won't experience busy, lost, or failed calls. If you do experience a delay when calling God, know that He is righteous, and He ponders how to answer (see Proverbs 15:28).

I know God doesn't object to me giving out His phone number, which is Jeremiah 33:3. Don't hesitate to call or text. He's waiting to hear from you. And please, spread the word!

The Devout

Cornelius…a devout man and one who feared God with all his household,
who gave alms generously to the people, and prayed to God always.

Acts 10:1–2

The Lord spoke to me about a modern-day Cornelius, saying, *"There are many people today like Cornelius. They're devout in their attitude toward Me, they fear Me, and they generously give alms through monetary gifts, food, and clothing. They pray always, and like Cornelius, I'm coming to their home to give them something more."*

In prayer, Cornelius encountered an angel, who said, *"Your prayers and your alms have come up as a memorial before God"* (Acts 10:4). Cornelius's devotion didn't go unnoticed. God was about to do something wonderful for him and his family.

Despite his sincerity, God determined that Cornelius and his family needed something more than devotion; they needed the Author of Salvation, Jesus Christ. In this divine encounter, Peter preached to Cornelius, his family, and his relatives that whoever believes in Jesus will receive forgiveness of sins. While Peter was still speaking, the Holy Spirit fell on all those who heard the word, and the gift of the Holy Spirit was poured out on them. They spoke with tongues, magnified God, and were immediately water baptized (see Acts 10:43–48).

Are you like Cornelius? Are you devout in your attitude toward God? Your affection for God isn't in vain. God has more for you! Your adoration is your stepping stone to Jesus, who said, *"…everyone who has heard and learned from the Father comes to Me"* (John 6:45). Somewhere Cornelius heard and learned about God and came to Jesus. As a young girl, I too heard and learned from the Father, and years later, fulfillment of that promise came to me.

Cornelius received Peter's words, not as words from man but from God, and said, *"We are all present before God, to hear all the things commanded you by God"* (Acts 10:33).

Has God sent a type of Peter to your house? My prayer is that you, like Cornelius, would take God at His Word. Believe in Jesus. Allow the Holy Spirit to fall on you, and begin to speak with tongues, magnify God, and be baptized in water.

Rogue Wave

Suddenly a terrible storm came up, with waves higher than the boat.
Matthew 8:24 (TLB)

A rogue wave is large, unexpected, dangerous, and very unpredictable; and often comes from directions other than the prevailing wind and waves. I once watched a documentary called *Abandoned*, a story about *Rose Noelle*, a forty-foot trimaran yacht that encountered a rogue wave while sailing in the southern Pacific Ocean.[1]

The sixty-foot monster wave blindsided this crew, turning them upside down. Half submerged under water, the captain attempted to calm his inexperienced crew, explaining to them that the yacht wouldn't sink because of its design, which consisted of three side-by-side hulls. Despite his efforts, the crew strongly distrusted their captain's ability. But he maintained a steadfast faith that they would all make it out alive. Although anticipating a quick rescue with the ship's distress beacon, they ended up drifting on the sea for 119 days.

Like a rogue wave coming out of nowhere, the devil hits us with circumstances to toss us about or turn us upside down, making us believe we'll sink and not survive. And, like the crew of *Rose Noelle*, we are sometimes leery of trusting the ability of our skilled, seafaring Captain, Jesus.

After four months at sea, although elated with land in view, the crew of *Rose Noelle* found themselves in even more danger. As the yacht approached the rocky shore-line and the crashing surf, their vessel began to break apart in shark-infested waters. At times, just before our rescue, the devil will bring about even fiercer circumstances in an attempt to destroy us. However, we must continue to trust our Captain until we are safely on shore.

In the end, each crewmember of *Rose Noelle* was safely rescued. Has the devil brought a rogue wave into your life? Circumstances may tempt you to distrust your Savior, but He is trustworthy in every way. Look at the cross. Through it, He has rescued every distressed, seafaring soul, including yours.

Safe Borders

And when they went from nation to nation, and from one kingdom to another people; he suffered no man to do them wrong.

1 Chronicles 16:20–21 (KJV)

Six months after Levi crossed over to be with Jesus, my husband took a job in Canada. While visiting him during the fall months, the country was exploding with color. The invigorating autumn air beckoned me to get outside and walk. However, as a woman in another country and with my husband working long hours and unable to join me, caution needed to stroll with wisdom. I realized there was the possibility that I might encounter dangerous people or even wild animals.

As I prayed about my situation, God spoke to me from our opening passage, reassuring me that, although I had traveled to another nation, He wouldn't let anything or anyone harm me—grizzly bears or otherwise. As God demonstrated His nearness through this passage, my heart exploded with His peace and joy like the fall colors around me.

Our Father God is loving and fiercely protective, and is mindful of us at all times. Psalm 139:3, 5 is a touching descriptive of just how mindful He is. *"³You comprehend my path and my lying down, and are acquainted with all my ways…. ⁵You have hedged me behind and before, and laid Your hand upon me."* Today you can reflect on this psalm of David and his words describing God's tender care for you, no matter what your location.

I know that God cares for you as much as He cares for Jesus and me. Whatever path you're contemplating, or even if you've taken the wrong path or have gone ahead of Him, He watches over you to guide and protect. He let me know on that beautiful fall day that His mighty arms of protection held me wherever I went—even in another country! With His assurance, I confidently went for a walk.

Golden Birthdays

There is hope for a tree, if it is cut down, that it will sprout again.
...Yet, at the scent of water it will bud and bring forth branches like a plant.

Job 14:7, 9

Wonder filled my heart as I read Job's words. Since water is essential for the survival of all life—plant, animal, or human—I envisioned a human heart that had been cut down, dead, and dry. Like a tree, our heart will bud again and bring forth branches at the *very scent* of the living water of the Holy Spirit.

As I write, I'm overlooking one of the largest bodies of water on the planet: the Pacific Ocean. With the distinct smell of seawater rising to my nostrils, my heart cries out for the scent of God's life-giving water in my grief process.

Today is significant and special for me, as it would be Levi's golden birthday. Today, on February 24, he would be turning 24. In heaven where all birthdays are golden, he is soon to celebrate his fifth. Although he is forever young and content with Jesus, I have long wondered, *Lord, will my heart bud again?* Since his passing, I have experienced certain areas of my life, like a felled tree, that are in need of heaven's dew.

Because Levi is now experiencing every spiritual blessing in the heavenly places, I'm asking the Lord for a birthday gift in his stead in the form of the scent of water so my heart may bud again.

Maybe you're encountering similar thoughts in the circumstances of your life. As there is hope for a tree if it's cut down, there's hope for you and me. Together, we can stand on God's promise that at the *very hint of the scent* of His living water, these areas of our lives will bloom again.

Allow God to visit you today, so He can greatly enrich you and cause His river of life to overflow the banks of your heart. Then, people can't say, *"there is no help for them in God"* (Psalm 3:2).

His Nail-Pierced Hands

…casting all your care upon Him, for He cares for you.

1 Peter 5:7

My heart swelled with anger that my beloved Levi was gone—dead. Sitting on my sofa, I saw Jesus standing directly in front of me in a vision. He wore a white robe belted with a red sash. His expression was kind and compassionate. With His palms cupped upward, as though waiting to receive something from me, He whispered, *"Sharon, place the anger in My hands."* Spiritually obedient, I visualized myself putting the anger in His hands. As soon as I did this, my anger disappeared.

Justified or unjustified, anger is something with which every human struggles—from infants to the elderly. I believed that the anger I was experiencing in the death of my son was warranted. After all, we are praying Christian parents. We entrusted Levi to God from the womb and beyond. However, because the anger was hurting me, Jesus wanted to take it from me. The priceless pearl of this encounter was the manifest love and presence of Jesus Christ Himself, which only fueled my ability to hand the rage over to Him.

Since we live in this world, earthly circumstances have the potential to affect our heart. It may not be anger at the death of a child, but whatever it is, Jesus cares for you more than you know. He wants nothing separating you and Him. The power of His love and presence in that moment, in that vision, anchored my broken and angry heart in quiet calm. My prayer is that you see Jesus as He truly is: your best friend and the One who is always there for you and never fails you.

Is there something He's asking you to place in His hands? Pierced for you and for me, His hands can hold anything you put in them. I can assure you that His promise is true: You can cast *"all your care on Him for He cares for you"* (1 Peter 5:7).

Victory Banner

*But God forbid that I should boast except in the cross
of our Lord Jesus Christ.*

Galatians 6:14

As I took communion this morning, I heard Jesus say, *"Because of My body and because of My blood, you can boast of My victory!"*

I immediately remembered the anthem sung by the Israelites at the Red Sea: *"¹I will sing to the LORD, for he has triumphed gloriously; he has hurled both horse and rider into the sea. ² The LORD is my strength and my song; he has given me victory"* (Exodus 15:1–2, NLT).

Some days the battles are demanding, and the truth of victory appears to be camouflaged, as it did for the Israelites with their backs to the sea. However, God caused them to prevail. He's also caused us to be victorious! We can *boast* and thank God, *"who gives us the victory through our Lord Jesus"* (1 Corinthians 15:57).

What is your ovation in Christ? Is it the healing He provided? Perhaps it's eternal life, knowing Him (see John 17:3). We can all flaunt the countless spoils we've gained in Christ's conquest at the cross.

I personally boast in Christ's cross and His victory over death. This truth has become more alive to me since my son's physical death. Because of the body and blood of Jesus, I can say, "Oh, death, where is your sting? Oh, Hades, where is your victory?" Death cannot hold my son because it couldn't hold Jesus; because Jesus is alive and well, so my son is alive and well. I can say with assurance, *"Death is swallowed up in victory"* (1 Corinthians 15:54).

Take time today to wave your victory banner in the face of the enemy, and open your mouth in song to the Lord. *"For He has done marvelous things; His right hand and His holy arm have gained Him the victory"* (Psalm 98:1). *"In God we boast all day long, and praise Your name forever"* (Psalm 44:8).

Lil' Preacher Man

Out of the mouth of babes…

Psalm 8:2

When Levi was only five, God began his ministry. However, I didn't become aware of this until fourteen years later at his death.

My husband invited a foreign couple into our home of whom we knew little about. After a pleasant evening meal and conversation, I excused myself to prepare the guest room. As I made up their bed, to my surprise, the man appeared in the doorway, apologizing profusely, saying, "I can take the couch, and my girlfriend can take this room." I didn't realize that they weren't married.

My husband explained to me later that while I was making preparations for our guests, our son was having a Spirit-led conversation with them. Apparently, Levi informed them that they could not sleep together if they weren't married! Because of their country's heavily imposed marriage tax, they had lived together for almost fifteen years. The truth of God, spoken from our beloved son, changed their lives.

About one year later, with their next visit to America, my husband and I were attendants at their wedding. To this day, they remain married. As our son now sits with Jesus, angels, and others of the heavenly family, I believe He sees the fruit of his reward, which was his obedience to speak the truth without compromise. God bless and keep you Lil' Preacher Man! I look forward to the day that I'll see you again.

For those of you who are living together unmarried, it's still God's plan today for a man and a woman to marry instead of living a compromised lifestyle.

The following is a conversation between the young prophet Jeremiah and God: "*⁶…Lord GOD! Behold, I cannot speak, for I am a youth.' ⁷But the LORD said to me: 'Do not say, "I am a youth," for you shall go to all to whom I send you, and whatever I command you, you shall speak'*" (Jeremiah 1:6–7).

No matter your age or circumstances, always choose to speak as the Lord commands you, in unwavering obedience, as you may very well change lives in the process.

Things Above

If then you were raised with Christ, seek those things which are above,
where Christ is, sitting at the right hand of God.
Set your mind on things above, not on things on the earth.

Colossians 3:1–2

Have you heard it said: Christians are so heavenly minded we're no earthly good? God once told me that those who are heavenly minded are every bit of earthly good!

With our mind set on things above where Christ sits and not on things of the earth, how is it that we're not a benefit to God and His plans? By rising to pray a great while before daylight, Jesus set His mind on things above, and look at all the earthly good He accomplished! Jesus looked up to heaven, blessed and broke the loaves, and the disciples fed the multitudes (see Mark 6:41). *"Abraham lifted his eyes and looked, and there behind him was a ram caught in a thicket"* (Genesis 22:13). As Jesus ascended into heaven, the disciples looked steadfastly toward heaven, and after His departure they were every bit of earthly good.

Encouragement comes from 2 Corinthians 4:18—*"while we do not look at the things which are seen, but at the things which are not seen. For the things, which are seen are temporary, but the things which are not seen are eternal."* If you look at the things that are seen, consider yourself hoodwinked, because this world is under the sway of the wicked one, and ever-increasing darkness surrounds us. However, as heavenly minded inhabitants living on earth, we possess spiritual eyes to behold the things that are above so we can be every bit of earthly good for God.

Those who live according to the flesh set their minds on the things of the flesh, but those who live according to the Spirit, the things of the Spirit (see Romans 8:5). Seek the things that you have in Christ, for yourselves and for others. Look up to Him who is sitting at the right hand of God, interceding for you and pouring out every spiritual blessing from His heavenly throne.

Puzzled

For this reason a man shall leave his father and mother and be joined to his wife.

Mark 10:7

It was September 28, 1998. As the pastor read announcements, I read Mark 10:7. Instantly, Jesus spoke to me: *"Levi will leave you and Mark at a young age. Cling to him and embrace him, for your days with him will be short."* At the time, Levi was only two. Where was he going? Perceiving God spoke, but not understanding, in light of the passage I assumed Levi would marry at a young age, maybe even before his older sister.

Seventeen years passed when the topic of marriage came up among my two children and me. I shared the secret of what God had spoken. Without God's clear interpretation, we were left to our own ideas as to the meaning of God's peculiar message. Our discussion took place one month before Levi's death.

Two days after Levi died, the Lord quickened our opening passage, saying, *"Levi married the Lamb."* The marriage the Lord had in mind and the one I had in mind were millions of miles apart.

Mary and Joseph also heard puzzling statements from Jesus. At twelve, Jesus went missing. Diligently searching, they found Him sitting in the synagogue. Mary asked, *"'48Son, why have You done this to us? Look, Your father and I have sought You anxiously.' Jesus responded, 49'Why did you seek Me? Did you not know that I must be about My Father's business?' 50They did not understand the statement which He spoke to them"* (Luke 2:48–50).

What wasn't to understand? The angel had spoken directly to them in regards to the birth and conception of Jesus, along with God's plan for Him concerning mankind. Were Mary and Joseph dull of heart?

I don't believe the hour had come for God to open their understanding. Likewise, when God spoke to me in 1998, it wasn't His appointed time to reveal that Levi "leaving" us meant he would depart for heaven and marry the Lamb. This is the marriage all are invited to, and will take part in, when they believe on the name of Jesus.

If God is speaking peculiar things to you, do as Mary did, and ponder them in your heart (see Luke 2:19). At the proper time, their meaning will be revealed.

My Dwelling Place

Surely I will not go into the chamber of my house, or go up to the comfort of my bed; I will not give sleep to my eyes or slumber to my eyelids, until I find a place for the LORD, a dwelling place for the Mighty One of Jacob.

Psalm 132:3–5

Although David was looking for a resting place for the Ark of the Covenant, these scriptures came alive in my heart in relation to the intimacy David pursued and experienced with God.

Having put our faith in Christ, in our spirit we have a resting place in God and He in us. Despite this truth, my earthly desire continues, as did David's, that I don't go to the comfort of my bed or give sleep to my eyes until I have found a place for the Lord within my day.

Unlike David, New Testament believers are free at any time to fellowship with God through His indwelling Spirit. But I still like David's idea of finding a place for God before retiring at the close of our day. Personally, if I didn't engage in this practice daily, I'd feel as if I've ignored Jesus, not giving Him the focused attention He rightfully deserves.

Before committing to live in a home, knowing there's a private place for prayer is a priority for me. Even when building our home, we designed a special room for the purpose of prayer. Imitating Jesus, time alone with God is important to me. I need the Lord of my life at the beginning of my day, to lead and guide me until the end of the day.

Beginning in the Garden, God's desire has always been to spend time with us. Where is your dwelling place with God? You may not have the availability of a private room, but you may have a favorite chair or a spot in the woods. Wherever you're comfortable, sit with your Savior. I can assure you, talking with Jesus at any given place and time—even if it's in the shower—is always the best choice. Don't wait another moment. He's looking for and anticipating your coming.

Humpty Dumpty

The Spirit of the LORD is upon Me… He has sent Me to heal the brokenhearted.
Luke 4:18

awoke straight out of sleep, weeping and praying in tongues. It was 3:00 a.m., January 24, 1993. An hour had passed when the prayer and sobbing subsided. Then I heard the Lord quote an English nursery rhyme to me: *"Humpty Dumpty sat on the wall, Humpty Dumpty had a great fall; all the king's horses and all the king's men couldn't put Humpty together again."*

Immediately, in a vision, I saw a stunning crystal vase. Suddenly, it was a heap of slivered fragments as the vase shattered. I sensed this was a picture of my heart. Then I heard Jesus say, *"Although all the king's horses and all the king's men couldn't put Humpty together again, I am the King who can put you back together again."*

I thought, *Who doesn't experience heartache?* Nevertheless, without interpretation, expectancy filled my heart with His promise. The apostle Paul wrote, *"²¹to die is gain…²³having a desire to depart and be with Christ…is far better"* (Philippians 1:21, 23). Do you *really* believe that to die is gain or to be with Christ is far better? I do! While meditating on this passage, I found myself looking back to the events of 1993. In that 3:00 morning hour, I was at the foot of Levi's bed weeping and praying in anguish. He was two at the time.

Twenty years later, the Holy Spirit revealed the meaning of the event. The weeping, anguish, and fervent prayer were what I'd experience seventeen years later in Levi's death. Truly, for Levi to die was gain, and for him to be with Christ is far better. These small but profound truths sustained me in my grief process.

I don't understand why God waited all these years to share this mystery with me, but I relate to King Nebuchadnezzar's words to Daniel: *"Truly your God is the God of gods, the Lord of kings, and a revealer of secrets"* (Daniel 2:47).

With God, there's an appointed time for everything, including the manifestation of His healing revelation. God's never late, and He's faithful to His promise: *"I have come to heal the brokenhearted."*

Just as Jesus healed my brokenness, the King can also put you back together again.

Envision Resurrection

Jesus said to her, "I am the resurrection and the life."

John 11:25

While surfing the internet, my spirit leaped within me when I came across a conference advertised in Albany, Oregon, with featured speaker, Mahesh Chavda. I asked the Lord if He wanted me to attend this event, but I didn't hear a response.

Getting away to pray and fast at my usual retreat, I selected a cottage that I hadn't stayed in for quite some time. Going through the cabin's media content, surprisingly, it contained only videos and CDs of Mr. Chavda! What are the chances of that? Chuckling, I said, "Lord, I'm going to Oregon!"

The meeting was ablaze with the fire of the Holy Spirit and His gifts: gifts of faith, tongues, interpretation of tongues, and healings (see 1 Corinthians 12).

During this time, Jesus appeared to me in a vision dressed in a white robe with a red sash. Dark shoulder-length hair and glowing olive skin enhanced His dark beard. Facing me with His palms open and standing next to a cave with its stone rolled away from the entrance, He revealed His unmistakable nail prints (see Luke 24:40). Looking directly into my eyes, He said, *"I am the resurrection and the life."* Then, the vision disappeared. In my heart, I said, *"Lord, I believe You are the resurrection and the life. Do You want me to study this topic?"* I sensed no response.

Five years later the vision's meaning came about in the fiery furnace of faith, with my son's exit into eternity. As Jesus directed me once again to John 11, I read *"25I am the resurrection and the life…. 26Do you believe this?"* (vv. 25–26). Jesus empha-sized: *"Do you believe this?"* The choice was before me. My heart responded with the help of His grace: "Yes, Lord I believe."

If you're in a crisis of faith, challenged in believing that Jesus is your resurrection and life in your current circumstances, my prayer is that God will bring you to the full persuasion of this truth as He has me. In your life, Jesus is who He says He is: the resurrection and the life.

Combat Unity

Behold, how good and how pleasant it is for brethren to dwell together in unity!

Psalm 133:1

An important trait among soldiers is unity. Without it, chaos reigns and objectives are difficult, if not impossible to achieve. As a military directive, we can read Philippians 2:1–4, which instruct us to be like-minded and friendly. In addition, we are not to do things with selfish ambition, but in humility, honoring others to a greater degree than we do ourselves. As we look to our own interests, we should also pay close attention to the needs of others.

The book of James tells us: *"where envy and self-seeking exist, confusion and every evil thing are there"* (3:16). We could say the weapons of the devil are strife, division, and confusion, with which he can quickly dismantle a perfectly integrated unit. As warriors for Christ, our weapons are love, kindness, and humility, which work to build morale and unity among the troops.

Our Commander in Chief, Jesus, desires for His army to move in unison. As the body of Christ, *"God has set the members, each one of them, in the body just as He pleased"* (1 Corinthians 12:18). We're all responsible to do our part, and as we do, things will function more smoothly as God designed.

While fighting the good fight of faith, it's our military duty to embrace grace and keep the unity of the Spirit in the bond of peace. In this foxhole of life, there will be offenses and disagreements, but *"if it is possible, as much as depends on you, live peaceably with all men"* (Romans 12:18). This means, not only with our brothers and sisters in Christ, but with all mankind.

In what ways can you promote unity within your ranks? How about relationships within your family, church, or work? These are strategic areas in which the devil would like to divide and conquer. Despite this, as you put on love, which is the bond of perfection (see Colossians 3:14), you will defeat the enemy's schemes.

Fit for Purpose

…useful for the Master, prepared for every good work.

2 Timothy 2:21

As a babe in Christ, I realized the devil could hear my prayers, so I prayed silently, "Lord if I could help You with anything, I think it would be the broken-hearted." At the time, with my past life experiences, I felt equipped.

The following night attending church, I approached the guest speaker after he gave an invitation to receive prayer. He prayed over me in tongues, then walked away with no interpretation in English. I considered that to be a useless prayer. For those not familiar with tongues, it's one of the Holy Spirit's gifts recorded in Scripture (see 1 Corinthians 12 through 14). This spiritual tongue, or language, spoken by believers in Christ, is not of this world and is a language that can be interpreted.

Moments after the man walked away from me, his wife approached me. She also prayed in tongues, but then spoke in English, saying, "The Lord has called you and anointed you to heal the brokenhearted." I was stunned, as God directly answered my silent prayer. It was clear that this woman heard from the Lord. This was my first encounter with God speaking to me through this gift of tongues and interpretation of tongues (see 1 Corinthians 12:10).

At that time, in my naivety, I thought I had experienced enough heartache to minister to the brokenhearted. Little did I know that the ultimate heartbreak would follow twenty-four years later with the death of my son. Now that God has molded me through that experience, I feel the Jesus the Master has prepared me in greater ways to aid and comfort those with broken hearts.

How might God want to use your struggles and pain for His service? Psalm 139:16 says, *"Your eyes saw my substance, being yet unformed. And in Your book they all were written, the days fashioned for me, when as yet there were none of them."* If you allow Him, God has the well-laid plan to turn any tragedy into triumph.

Bow in Humility

And bowing His head, He gave up His spirit.

John 19:30

One day, in a conversation with a woman, she told me she couldn't forgive a co-worker. The following day while taking communion, God said, *"Because of My body and because of My blood you can bow…in humility."* He was referring to this woman. Because she was a Christian, she did have the ability to bow in humility and forgive the co-worker. To *bow* means "to bend the head or upper part of the body as a sign of respect."[1]

Jesus, being God, expressed humility toward His heavenly Father and mankind, as He willingly bowed His head and gave up His spirit. *"He humbled Himself and became obedient to the point of death, even the death of the cross"* (Philippians 2:8). Because of Christ's example, through His Spirit we're now able to bow in humility toward God and one another, forgiving others as Christ forgave us.

Psalm 149:4 reads, *"He adorns the humble with salvation"* (HCSB). By bowing our knee to Jesus and His sacrifice on the cross, we receive His forgiveness through salvation. A centurion who stood opposite Jesus on the cross humbly bowed his heart in worship, saying, *"Truly this Man was the Son of God!"* (Mark 15:39).

God has given *"[9][Jesus] the name which is above every name, [10]that at the name of Jesus every knee should bow, of those in heaven, and of those on earth, and of those under the earth, [11]and that every tongue should confess that Jesus Christ is Lord, to the glory of God the Father"* (Philippians 2:9–11, brackets added). This passage is all inclusive: every knee should bow.

Consider if you've truly bowed in worship and humility toward God. Or, perhaps you need to bow in humility toward someone who needs forgiveness. Today is the day the Lord has made for you to take a knee and bow before the cross.

Our Supply Closet

Now in the morning, having risen a long while before daylight,
He went out and departed to a solitary place; and there He prayed.

Mark 1:35

Does the picture of Jesus rising early to commune with His Father beckon you as it does me? As born-again children of God, with the indwelling Holy Spirit, we have the sacred privilege of communing with the Godhead at any time. However, if Jesus thinks it's significant to rise early, find a solitary place, and pray, then it's important to me too. We can be encouraged by His words in Matthew 6:6, *"But thou, when thou prayest, enter into thy closet, and when thou hast shut thy door, pray to thy Father which is in secret; and thy Father which seeth in secret shall reward thee openly"* (KJV). The Greek definition for *closet* is "secret chamber, storehouse."[1]

One day while in the breakroom of my workplace, I observed the custodian standing inside the supply closet loading a cart with toilet paper, paper towels, soap, and other janitorial supplies. At that point, I had a revelation about that closet and the "secret place." With supplies kept in the closet, it was a necessary for the custodian to go to the storehouse daily and obtain the provisions for the duties of the day.

In John 9:4 we read the words of Jesus, *"I must work the works of Him who sent Me while it is day; the night is coming when no one can work."* Jesus also went daily into His Father's storehouse through prayer and fellowship. He too filled His cart, so to speak, with the supplies needed for each day. As He went about His Father's business, God rewarded Him openly with signs, wonders, and miracles. His promise is the same for us when we pray in secret: He will reward us openly.

Take time each day to go to your secret supply closet to pray and fellowship with God. There, He will give you all of Himself and everything you need to go about your Father's business.

Generous versus Stingy

There is one who scatters, yet increases more; and there is one who withholds more than is right, but it leads to poverty.

Proverbs 11:24

As a new believer and wife, I watched my husband receive various blessings. Although his blessing was my blessing, I believed the lie that God favored him over me because it looked as though he was given more. At this time, the Lord spoke to me from our opening scripture, saying, *"There is one who scatters, which is your husband, and he is increasing. There is one who withholds more than is right, that is you, and it leads to poverty."* Pierced! The two-edged sword, the Word of God, had my attention. God also told me, *"The generous soul will be made rich."*

I came from a family of fourteen. With my old mindset, if I gave away what I had, there would never be enough! Eighteen and tightfisted, I left home. My husband, obviously, left home generous and openhanded.

When I had young children I didn't work outside the home. Believing that money was the only thing to give, I assumed I had nothing to offer. Then I was reminded that *"he who waters will also be watered"* (Proverbs 11:25). God began to show me how I could bless others apart from money. One way was by being hospitable. Romans 12:13 tells us to distribute *"to the needs of the saints, given to hospitality."* *Hospitality* means "the friendly reception of guests or strangers." At one time, I had seventy-five guests in my home! God's message was loud and clear: He gave me gifts to give to others.

"But whoever has this world's goods, and sees his brother in need, and shuts up his heart from him, how does the love of God abide in him?" (1 John 3:17). By thinking I had nothing to offer, I was actually withholding from others in need. Thankfully, I no longer believe this way.

God has also given you gifts to help others, be it money, time, kindness, or prayers. Whatever your gifts, they are valuable. Distribute them, and you'll find that it's more blessed to give than receive!

Master's Degree

She had a sister called Mary, who also sat at Jesus' feet and heard His word. But Martha was distracted with much serving, and she approached Him and said, "Lord, do You not care that my sister has left me to serve alone? Therefore tell her to help me." And Jesus answered and said to her, "Martha, Martha, you are worried and troubled about many things. But one thing is needed, and Mary has chosen that good part, which will not be taken away from her."

Luke 10:39–42

Most of us can associate ourselves with one or the other of these famous sisters. Personally, I am Mary's clone. I appreciate Jesus' uncluttered, yet powerful response to Martha's plea for help: "Martha, Martha, you are worried and troubled about many things." I can only assume Martha believed that Jesus would see the situation her way.

I've often regretted not furthering my college education to receive a degree on paper. Although licensed and ordained from a Bible college, I considered attending a Christian university. Yet, I sensed God tell me that I could never glean there what I've gleaned from Him at His feet. In addition, like Mary, Jesus assured me that by His grace, I too have chosen the one thing that is needed, and that good part is something *no one* can take from me. Instead of head knowledge, I've received the degree of a lifetime, and that's a priceless, living relationship with Jesus.

I'm not discrediting a college education, but college isn't for everyone. Many of the uber-rich have never stepped foot into higher education. There are people with degrees in theology who've never met or sat at the feet of Jesus. In addition, with little or no education, Jesus qualified fishermen, tax collectors, and prostitutes. His disciples in Acts 17:6 turned the world upside down. The Lord encouraged me one day, saying, *"Sharon, you have a Master's degree, and you received it at My feet."*

Throughout your day, make every effort to not become distracted, worried, and troubled about the things around you like busy beaver Martha. Instead, choose that "one thing" like Mary did, which is to sit at the feet of Jesus. Learn from Him and receive the degree of a lifetime. If you're uncertain about your educational direction, stop here at the feet of Jesus, and commit your plans to Him. Know that whatever course of training He leads you to will be the very best education you can get.

Spiritual Morse Code

A strength to the needy in his distress, a refuge from the storm.

Isaiah 25:4

S.O.S. is the international Morse code distress signal. In popular usage, *S.O.S.* became associated with such phrases as, "Save Our Ship" or "Save Our Souls. But, in actuality, *S.O.S.* doesn't stand for anything, and it's not an abbreviation. It was chosen because it's easily transmitted into Morse code.[1]

During our lifetime, I'm sure you and I have put out many distress signals. The following are a few of my own acronyms for the famed code:

S.O.S.—Saints Overcoming Satan

They overcame him by the blood of the Lamb and by the word of their testimony, and they did not love their lives to the death.
Revelation 12:11

S.O.S.—Same Old Stuff

You have skirted this mountain long enough...
Deuteronomy 2:3

S.O.S.—Sharon Overcoming Satan

I called on the LORD in distress; the LORD answered me and set me in a broad place.
Psalm 118:5

Distress manifests in different ways, including extreme anxiety, sorrow, or pain. The term carries various meanings. It can refer to the state of a ship or aircraft when it's in danger or difficulty and in need of assistance. It may also mean suffering caused by a lack of life's basic necessities. And, it can be used to describe a state of physical strain or exhaustion.

Despite these definitions, the scriptures stand firm in our *S.O.S.*: "*Who shall separate us from the love of Christ? Shall...distress...?*" (Romans 8:35). Certainly not! Jesus knows Morse code, and He's able to decipher any distress signal. Therefore, send out your *S.O.S.*, and He'll come and save you, no matter what dire circumstances you're in.

Rock of Escape

They called that place the Rock of Escape.

1 Samuel 23:28

Not only was David fighting every enemy of Israel, he also had to contend with Saul's death threats. He'd just defeated the Philistines, when Saul called all the people together for war and planned to surround David and his men. David and about 600 of his men fled to the mountains (see 1 Samuel 23:13). Although Saul sought him daily, God protected David. Then, another collaborator approached Saul with news of David's whereabouts; Saul blessed and thanked the informant for his allegiance:

25When Saul and his men went to seek him, they told David. Therefore he went down to the rock, and stayed in the Wilderness of Maon. And when Saul heard that, he pursued David….26Then Saul went on one side of the mountain, and David and his men on the other side of the mountain. So David made haste to get away from Saul, for Saul and his men were encircling David and his men to take them. 27But a messenger came to Saul, saying, "Hasten and come, for the Philistines have invaded the land!" 28Therefore Saul returned from pursuing David, and went against the Philistines; so they called that place the Rock of Escape (1 Samuel 23:25–28).

Like Saul, the devil relentlessly hunts us down and tries to undermine us. You've probably felt at times as if you were on one side of the mountain and Satan was on the other, encircling you. However, there's no other Rock like our Rock. God sent a messenger to Saul to distract him from pursuing and harming David.

David's key to success was that he sought the Lord's advice. To ensure victory, consult your Commander in Chief. God, your Rock of Escape, has an exit strategy for every battle and foe you face.

Human Inabilities, God Abilities

…you are loosed from your infirmity.

Luke 13:12

Scripture records, *"…behold, there was a woman who had a spirit of infirmity"* (Luke 13:11). The word *infirmity* depicts "feebleness (of body or mind)... disease...weakness."[1]

Having dug deeper into its definition, it was as though I discovered gold! The root meaning of *infirmity* refers to "an inability to produce results."[2] How many times have you tried to "overcome" a weakness with no results?

Verse 11 makes a profound statement: she *"could in no way raise herself up."* Likewise, in our own strength and ability, there's no way we can raise ourselves up. But, with God all things are possible (see Matthew 19:26).

Then, in verse 12, Jesus *"saw her."* There's no mention of the woman first seeing Him or crying out. He loved her first, He saw her first, and then He called her to Himself and healed her saying, *"Woman, you are loosed from your infirmity."*

In verse 14, observing this woman's healing, a ruler of the synagogue was angry that Jesus healed her on the Sabbath. Addressing his wrong thinking, Jesus said, *"ought not this woman, being a daughter of Abraham, whom Satan has bound—think of it—for eighteen years, be loosed from this bond on the Sabbath?"* (Luke 13:16).

Satan, not God, bound this woman for eighteen years! As long as we live in our earthly bodies, we'll battle infirmities that affect our spirit, soul, and body. But with Jesus, we don't have to stay bound.

That is the love and power of Jesus! If Satan has you bound with physical, emotional, or spiritual weakness, know that Jesus had you in mind on the cross. He is drawing you to Himself and laying His hands on you, saying, "Son or daughter, you are loosed from your weakness."

Mystery of Marriage

This is a great mystery, but I speak concerning Christ and the church.

Ephesians 5:32

In the movie *Princess Bride*, Buttercup, coerced into marriage, stands before the clergyman with the evil Prince Humperdink by her side. With unexpected humor, the clergyman opens the ceremony saying, "Mawage. Mawage is wot bwings us togeder tooday."[1]

All joking aside, marriage is what brings us together today. Although many are familiar with God's words in Genesis 2:18, *"...it is not good that man should be alone; I will make a helper comparable to him,"* many are strangers to His deeper meaning.

We all know God designed woman from the rib of Adam's side and that He placed her back at Adam's side as helper and companion (see Genesis 2:22). Symbolically, from Christ's pierced side (see John 19:34), His Bride—the church—also came forth as a helper and companion. Now submitted to her Bridegroom, Jesus, through her, fulfills His heavenly vision for mankind, which is illustrated through the role of an earthly wife walking side by side with her husband, fulfilling God's kingdom purpose.

In Christendom, a man's love and pursuit of a woman, as well as the proposal of marriage to her, mirrors Christ's pursuit of mankind, proposing marriage and offering eternal life. The desire of Jesus, as is of every man who proposes, is for the woman to say yes. By saying yes to Jesus, we become born again and are joined to Him. By this we become one spirit with Him and enter into an eternal covenant marriage. In the same way, when a woman responds positively to the pursuit and proposal of a man, they too unite in holy matrimony; the two become one flesh and enter into a covenant relationship. As Christ remains forever married to us, *ideally*, those whom God joins together in marriage, are also to remain married.

I encourage you to study in Scripture God's perfect plan for Jesus' marriage to His bride, the body of Christ, as well as your personal marriage. Even if you're not physically married, know that, if you're born again, you're married to Jesus! Either way, by God's grace, He's enabled you to walk in your appointed role as a spouse.

Two Become One

I in them, and You in Me.

John 17:23

Today's writing is not for the shy of heart, as I speak frankly about the *physical union* between a man and a woman in a Christ-centered marriage. This physical relationship is God ordained as a type and shadow of the *spiritual union* between Christ and His Bride, the Church.

The body of Christ has little revelation of God's true intention for intimacy within an earthly marriage, let alone in a spiritual marriage to Christ. However, I hope what God shared with me brings clarity for you.

John 17 records Jesus praying to His Father, which illustrates the cry of His heart for oneness with those who believe and those who will believe. Jesus prayed, *"As You, Father, are in Me, and I in You; that they also may be one in Us"* (John 17:21). The oneness that the Godhead shares is the highest, holiest, most intimate, face-to-face fellowship in existence.

An even more amazing mystery, the sexual union between a man and a woman in marriage is the *sole* reflection of the Father, Son, and Holy Spirit's oneness. By divine design, the husband and wife fit together perfectly. In this reflective face-to-face act, the wife opens herself up to her husband, and he enters into her. He is in her, she is in him, and they are one.

In our spiritual marriage to Christ, we open our heart to receive Jesus. At this point, we become His Bride; and Jesus, as our Bridegroom, enters into our spirit and we into His. Christ's prayer then emerges: We are now one, just as He and the Father are one.

This face-to-face fellowship in your spiritual marriage with Christ is the most important factor of your life—oneness. John 17:3 tells us, *"And this is eternal life, that they may know You, the only true God."* Make it a priority to fellowship with the Lord every day. It is through this time of intimacy that you will truly get to know Him.

Heavenly Passport

For our citizenship is in heaven.

Philippians 3:20

A citizen, whether native or naturalized, is a member of a particular country. A sure way to be a citizen is to be born in that country. However, when a foreigner fulfills the requirements of the law by going through a legal process called naturalization, citizenship is also granted.

In order for a person to cross borders, legal documents are required. The passport originated as a medieval European document. Local authorities issued such papers to travelers, granting them permission to journey to other regions.

Today, this type of documentation is still in effect, which validates the holder's citizenship and allows that person to cross international borders. Within the pages of an American passport are stamps and seals unique to the United States, along with necessary information identifying the traveler's country of origin, name, date, and place of birth.

Our heavenly passport also includes identifying characteristics, namely, the blood of Jesus and the seal of the Holy Spirit as a guarantee. As born-again believers, our citizenship is sure because Jesus has fulfilled the righteous requirements of the Law.

Without legal earthly documents, travel outside our country is forbidden. Similarly, we can't pass into heaven without our saintly passport in order. We won't find Peter at heaven's pearly gates accepting illegal or stolen papers. Spiritually speaking, you can't be an illegal immigrant in heaven.

Passports include an expiration date, but your heavenly credentials do not. In the kingdom of God, once you become born again, you're a citizen forever!

Is your passport in order for your heavenly trip? Just as you must take steps to secure an earthly passport, you must also take a step to obtain your heavenly passport. The process is simple, yet profound: Believe on the Lord Jesus Christ, and you will be saved. Then, you can be assured that your trip to heaven is secure!

Framed

By faith we understand that the worlds were framed by the word of God, so that the things which are seen were not made of things which are visible.

Hebrews 11:3

While reading our opening passage, I saw a picture frame in my mind with several scriptures written inside. God said to me, "Your teaching ministry is framed by the Word of God." Immediately, I purchased a frame and filled it with scriptures dear to my heart concerning teaching.

Numbers 24:2–4— ²Then the Spirit of God came upon him, and this is the message he delivered: …³the message of the man whose eyes see clearly, ⁴the message of one who hears the words of God, who sees a vision from the Almighty, who bows down with eyes wide open (NLT).

Isaiah 50:4— The Lord has given me the tongue of the learned that I should know how to speak a word in season to him who is weary.

Matthew 7:29— … for He taught them as one having authority.

1 Corinthians 2:4–5— ⁴And my speech and my preaching were not with persuasive words of human wisdom, but in demonstration of the Spirit and of power, ⁵that your faith should not be in the wisdom of men but in the power of God.

2 Timothy 4:17— But the Lord stood with me and strengthened me, so that the message might be preached fully through me.

Because the Word of God framed the world, I sensed that God was telling me that this was a sure way to frame His teaching gift in my life. I pray these passages and others over myself whenever I teach and speak on God's behalf.

Today my hope is to inspire you to find truths that will frame your calling and prophesy your purpose through the Word of God! Frame them, meditate on them, and hide them in your heart. I believe that then you'll see the picture of His plans and purposes come into view.

Blood Transfusion

The life of the flesh is in the blood.

Leviticus 17:11

Once while taking communion, I heard these words: *"Because of My body and because of My blood you can receive a blood transfusion."*

As the life of our flesh is in our blood, the life of our spirit is in Jesus' blood. In regards to our physical body, various reasons may necessitate a blood transfusion, such as surgery, injury, infection, or disease.

A disease called sin corrupted our spiritual blood, and therefore, an incorruptible blood was required so that, spiritually, we would live and not die. Under the old covenant, it was *"not possible that the blood of bulls and goats could take away sins"* and make a person permanently clean (Hebrews 10:4). However, under the new covenant, the precious blood of Christ, as a Lamb without blemish and without spot, cleanses us from all sin (see 1 Peter 1:19; 1 John 1:7).

Human blood didn't course through Jesus' veins. In an article by Dr. M. R. DeHann, titled, "The Life Is in the Blood," DeHahn writes, "the blood which flows in an unborn baby's arteries and veins is not derived from the mother but is produced within the body of the fetus itself only after the introduction of the male sperm. An unfertilized ovum can never develop blood since the female egg does not by itself contain the elements essential for the production of this blood. It is only after the male element has entered the ovum that blood can develop." Because Joseph's blood was not involved in the Holy Spirit's conception of Jesus, it proves that His conception came about only by divine incorruptible blood alone.[1]

The flawless blood of Jesus is God's redeeming blood transfusion for mankind. Through His heavenly blood bank—the cross—Jesus provided His incorruptible blood. This blood heals your every need—spirit, soul, and body. If you haven't yet received this life-giving transfusion, I encourage you to meet with the Great Physician. In His presence, you'll come away transfused with the life that only He can supply.

Blessing Africa

So they all ate and were filled, and they took up seven large baskets full of the fragments that were left.

Matthew 15:37

A vision came to me during a time of worship while I was a first-year Bible college student. I saw myself standing near the ocean in a tropical place, which I understood to be Africa. After the worship service, the director of the school informed the students of an opportunity to travel to Ivory Coast, Africa.

With the trip confirmed, and at the director's instruction, we were asked to write support letters to help raise the necessary funds. During this time, the Lord led me into a period of prayer and fasting. One day as I read my Bible, this verse leapt from the page: *"They all ate and were filled, and they took up seven large baskets full of the fragments that were left"* (Matthew 15:37).

This verse indicated to me that not only would I have enough money for my travel and accommodations, but I'd have money left over! That was exactly what happened. The support I received amounted to $700 more than I needed. I knew I was to give the money to the African people, but I didn't know how to distribute it. I asked the director, "How many churches are we visiting in Africa?" When he said, "Seven," I knew that each church would receive $100.

While in Africa, I purchased fruit from a woman at a market. The Lord led me to have her keep the change. Reluctantly, she accepted. I told her God was a giver of good gifts and that He loved her so much that He gave Jesus, His only Son, for her salvation. She told me, "I've never heard the name of Jesus." Because of time constraints I had to end our conversation, but I knew God accomplished what He purposed.

God provides so that we can eat to the full of His love, His Word, His abundance, and His comfort. Whatever your need, God wants to fill you to overflowing with leftovers. These leftovers are not to be kept for ourselves, but rather used to bless those around us: *"Freely we have received, freely we give"* (Matthew 10:8).

Put Another Log on the Fire

And let us consider one another in order to stir up love and good works.

Hebrews 10:24

As a fire needs fuel or wood to continue to burn, so the love in our heart needs fuel; otherwise, it too can grow dim, smolder, or burn out.

It takes action to chop, collect, and put wood on a fire. The apostle Paul tells us to *"pursue love"* (1 Corinthians 14:1). It takes effort on our part to thoughtfully consider acts of kindness, or coals, which we then carry to the fire of love in our marriage or other godly relationships. Because *"God demonstrated His own love toward us, in that while we were still sinners"* (Romans 5:8), as Christ followers, we can also demonstrate deeds, which fuel love. A great fire starter is *"²²the fruit of the Spirit, [which] is love, joy, peace, longsuffering, kindness, goodness, faithfulness, ²³gentleness [and] self-control"* (Galatians 5:22–23, brackets added).

To keep a fire going we may need to get out the bellows. Additionally, we must stay with the process until the fire is burning bright and hot. By God's grace, we should do whatever He initiates to keep or reignite the flames of love burning, or better yet, bring that fire to the point where it crackles and the sparks fly! Fan the flames of your relationships, blow on them, or if need be, poke them! *"The Lord [will] direct your hearts into the love of God and into the patience of Christ"* (2 Thessalonians 3:5, brackets added).

Because God is love and not a feeling, to love is an act of the will. We must allow the Holy Spirit to love others through us. If the love in your heart smolders with self-centeredness, stoke the fire with logs of selflessness. If impatience has dampened your flames, fuel the embers with a few sticks of patience. If rudeness is smoking you out, fan the flame with kindness. The love of God will render you victorious in every situation.

The Work Horse

*Take My yoke upon you and learn from Me, for I am gentle
and lowly in heart, and you will find rest for your souls.*

Matthew 11:29

The large, powerful, striking Clydesdale horses pulled heavy loads long before the invention of tractors. These gentle giants' genetic make-up enabled them to work effortlessly.

I once heard a story about these amazing animals where the owner purchased two young males then sent them away for training. The trainer took his already submitted, trained, and mature stallion and yoked it with one of the younger colts. When initially tied to the stallion, the colt showed signs of apprehension at the commands he was given.

A picture of our walk, yoked with Christ, came into view. Jesus said in our opening verse, *"Take My yoke upon you and learn from Me, for I am gentle and lowly in heart, and you will find rest for your souls."* It wasn't until the colt was coupled with the stallion that the young horse began to learn. The stallion waited patiently for the colt to trust his lead and follow his example.

Restless and fidgeting, he attempted to break loose of the yoke, and stopped completely when the stallion led him to cross over streams or venture into unfamiliar territory. But, by the end of the day, the young horse was following without hesitation. Likewise, the only way we'll learn and find rest for our souls is by being yoked with Jesus.

Never having the confinement of a collar around his neck, the young horse encountered challenges. Yoked with Jesus, you too will be joined with things new or unfamiliar and will have to trust. Jesus has a proven and submitted track record. He'll never steer you wrong or take you places He hasn't already gone. His yoke is one of rest and not bondage. Accept Jesus' invitation to take His yoke today.

Testing One...Two

You shall not steal.

Exodus 20:15

As a new believer in the '80s, I was in a grocery store picking up a few essentials. Visualizing the contents of my wallet, I pictured a twenty-dollar bill. Realizing I had more items than cash, I placed an avocado in a nearby freezer as I approached the checkout line.

Arriving at the cash register, the Lord said, *"Sharon, you're stealing."* Shocked, I inwardly responded, "Lord, what did I steal?" He said, *"You're stealing by not putting the avocado back in the produce section, and the store will lose profit."* I had two choices: Leave the checkout line and return the avocado to its proper place, or ignore the Lord's words. I chose to put the avocado back. This test was a forerunner to the lesson that followed.

My next errand was to purchase supplies for a mailing project with a ten-dollar budget. Instead of purchasing the single sheets of paper needed, I bought a ream, thinking I could use the paper later. Sitting in rush-hour traffic on the way home, I heard the Lord say, *"I can show you how to get everything you need for your project for ten dollars!"*

I sat in traffic with yet another choice before me: I could go home and do things my way (after all, it's only ten dollars), or turn around in the gridlocked traffic. I passed the avocado test and wanted to keep up the good grades, so I braved the traffic and went back to the store. I returned the ream of paper and purchased only the amount I needed, along with stamps and envelopes—all for ten dollars.

Whether it is pleasing or displeasing, we will obey the voice of the LORD our God, that it may be well with us when we obey the voice of the LORD our God. (Jeremiah 42:6)

Does obedience in the seemingly minuscule and unseen things matter to God? The answer is YES! In the smallest or largest detail, whether it is convenient or inconvenient, there is great significance in our obedience to the Lord's voice!

Combat Communication

However, when He, the Spirit of truth, has come, He will guide you into all truth;
for He will not speak on His own authority, but whatever He hears He will speak;
and He will tell you things to come.

John 16:13

For all ranks—from privates to generals—communication is a key, life-saving role in a military campaign. Proper equipment, along with the ability to relay commands and other survival information, is vital, as lives depend on it.

From the onset, Bible battles included written or verbal communication by which people on foot or riding on animals relayed valuable intelligence. Most of us are familiar with America's fight for independence and the notorious ride of Paul Revere. On horseback, Revere warned of the invading British. Military operations have also employed homing pigeons to send messages. Today, soldiers use satellite technology to communicate.

Although implemented long ago, biblical communication technology never changes nor becomes out of date but continues to be life saving. God spoke with Adam and Eve, giving them specific instructions for their well-being, but they disobeyed orders. Deuteronomy 4:36 reads, *"Out of heaven He let you hear His voice, that He might instruct you, on earth."* My desire is to please the One who enlisted me as a soldier and comply with His life-giving orders (see 2 Timothy 2:4).

Jesus is the Messenger of the Covenant (see Malachi 3:1) and God's final courier, communicating the new covenant of His grace. Today, God, Jesus, and the Holy Spirit continue to communicate with us on earth, in everyday life, and in the battle to provide us with life-saving guidance!

As a spiritual soldier, become familiar with the various types of communication technology God has provided to keep you safe and informed. When you meet with God through prayer and Bible reading, you'll receive the most accurate information necessary for your spiritual battle. Also remember to keep the communication lines open in both your natural and spiritual families, which makes for a healthier, more cohesive family unit.

Beware of...

The priests did not ask, "Where is the LORD?"
Those who taught my word ignored me.

Jeremiah 2:8 (NLT)

A s one who teaches God's Word, I don't hesitate to ask, "Where are You, Lord?" Moreover, I didn't ignore God while writing this book. Therefore, reading Jeremiah 2:8 came as a surprise to me! Who are those who teach His Word without seeking Him or who ignore Him?

The title of "priest" applies to one who serves the people on behalf of God. This doesn't only include those who wear robes or collars or those with a title or position. Nor is it only for those who hold Divinity degrees. All who call Jesus Lord and Savior are a royal priesthood and ministers of God (see 1 Peter 2:9).

Jeremiah 2:8 serves as a warning. Beware of false teachers, prophets, brethren, apostles, and witnesses. We heed warning signs such as "Beware of bears," "Beware of the Red Tide," or "Beware of dogs." Obeying these signs can save our lives, as will our compliance with the forewarning of Scripture.

"Beware of the leaven of the Pharisees" (Luke 12:1). This refers to those who proclaim a false doctrine centered in works to be made right with Christ, when it's not by works of righteousness but by His mercy that He saved us (see Titus 3:5). We have peace with God because of Jesus Christ alone; not because of one solitary good thing we do (see Romans 5:1).

"Beware lest anyone cheat [you] through philosophy and empty deceit according to the tradition of men, according to the basic principles of the world, and not according to Christ" (Colossians 2:8, brackets added). We, who are redeemed of the Lord, shouldn't fall for the tradition of men or the philosophy of the world.

Be aware of whom and what you listen to. It's important to read and know your Bible for yourself and to listen to what the Holy Spirit is saying to you. He'll confirm His words of truth. Allow Him and not those who ignore the Lord to lead you.

Ten Days

Is this not the fast that I have chosen…?

Isaiah 58:6

Fasting gets a bad rap by some, but as children of God, we should welcome the Lord leading us into times of fasting and prayer.

I sensed my New Year fast of 2008 would be unlike others. God asked me to prepare by eating only vegetables from Thanksgiving to Christmas. Then, during the first ten days of January, I was to drink only water.

My intentions with the fast leaned toward prayer for Mark's work, direction for the new year, and our family. However, as the fast progressed, the Lord's plan emerged as I began praying specifically for our nineteen-year-old daughter. For three weeks, she attended the college church group and social events accompanied by a certain young Christian man. All of this was normal and innocent, however, as a spiritual warrior mother, I was alert and engaged, pondering the matter in my heart.

The day my fast ended, my daughter called to say that she and the young man weren't going to be a suitable fit. Instantly I heard the words, *"How to lose a guy in ten days"* in reference to the movie with the same title. Who says God doesn't have a sense of humor? He used a movie title and a ten-day fast to remove this young man from Sasha's life.

By putting faith in God and not the fast, your Father, who is in the secret place, sees in secret, and rewards openly (see Matthew 6:18). Personally, God's reward was His revealed wisdom for Sasha and a set path for Mark's work. The sacrifice of this fast outweighed any fleeting passions of my flesh. What were ten days out of my life to pray for my daughter to acquire the husband of divine design?

Stick to Jesus' advice—*"Do not labor for the food which perishes, but for the food which endures to everlasting life, which the Son of Man will give you"* (John 6:27)—and you too will see God move miraculously in your life.

The King's Chambers

...the communion of the Holy Spirit be with you all. Amen.

2 Corinthians 13:14

Most believers are familiar with the Greek word for communion, which is *koinonia*. The word describes fellowship, partnership, participation, or social intercourse.[1] To me, these characteristics echo intimacy.

Although Adam and Eve severed God's original design of relationship in the Garden of Eden, Jesus reconciled us back to God at the cross. With Jesus now at the right hand of the Father, He hasn't left us as orphans but has sent His Spirit to live in us and through us. Individually as children of God and corporately as the body of Christ, we can participate in continuous companionship with the Spirit of God.

In a time of prayer, God shared with me personal examples of individual and corporate fellowship. Koinonia exists when the Holy Spirit and I come together to share thoughts and emotions, communicate verbally and nonverbally, and simply enjoy each other's presence. He and I are in fellowship as one would be with a dear friend or, deeper still, in a marriage between a man and woman. When my husband and I have intimate fellowship, the door to our bedroom is closed. That is a time shared *only* between the two of us. No guests allowed!

Spiritually, there's also a hidden place belonging *exclusively* to the Holy Spirit and me, in which even my husband's presence is barred. Then, there are times at church, worship services, or Bible studies where I relish in His fellowship corporately with my family in Christ.

In the Song of Solomon, the Shulamite bride says, *"The king has brought me into his chambers"* (Song 1:4). A chamber is a type of bedroom or inner room, portraying intimacy.

Allow the Holy Spirit to usher you into the secret place to talk with Jesus. There, He'll comfort and refresh you, and believe it or not, simply enjoy your presence. Once you come into the King's chambers, you'll never be the same.

Heavenly Home Going

For I know the thoughts that I think toward you, says the LORD,
thoughts of peace and not of evil, to give you a future and a hope.

Jeremiah 29:11

It was a typical spring morning in Colorado—invigorating temperatures accompanying a fleeting snowstorm. The day held an air of quietness, as my husband worked in his shop, I in my home office, and our daughter at a local coffee shop; my prayer time was also unusually hushed. As I later reflected on my journal entry from that day, I was disheartened as there was no warning of what lay ahead. The only thing recorded was, *"I know the thoughts that I think toward you, says the LORD, thoughts of peace and not of evil, to give you a future and a hope."*

Our son, who was traveling back from the Colorado mountains, kept in touch with us with his estimated time of arrival. My husband and I prayed specifically for God to send legions upon legions of angels to protect Levi. This prayer was unlike any other, as I felt my spirit move within me, arresting my attention. I quietly pondered this peculiar experience.

Later that afternoon, my husband received a phone call. I could tell by his ashen face that it was serious. Our son and the young men he was traveling with had an automobile accident. Our family immediately began the three-hour trek to Eagle, Colorado.

Twenty minutes into our journey, we received a call from a coroner, with inconceivable news. Our beloved son had died instantly when a faulty tire exploded on the vehicle in which he was a passenger. The weight of our grief became heavier with each approaching mile marker to our destination: the morgue. I couldn't believe what was happening. How did this coincide with God's earlier impression of peace, a future, and a hope?

I don't know that it's possible to be prepared for the worst day of your life. However, responding to Christ's call of salvation thirty years earlier prepared me to walk through this anguish. *"You do not know what will happen tomorrow. For what is your life? It is even a vapor that appears for a little time and then vanishes away"* (James 4:14).

The best preparation for any crisis is to know Jesus. Don't be caught off-guard. Get to know Him today. *"Whoever calls on the name of the LORD shall be saved"* (Acts 2:21).

Shiloh

...the house of the LORD in Shiloh.

1 Samuel 1:24

Hannah prayed to God, *"¹¹If You...will give Your maidservant a male child, then I will give him to the LORD all the days of his life.... ²⁰Hannah conceived and bore a son, and called his name Samuel"* (1 Samuel 1:11, 20).

In Hannah's day, there was an annual sacrifice at the house of the Lord in Shiloh. After weaning Samuel, she took him there where he was to remain and left him at the tabernacle in Shiloh for the Lord's purposes (see 1 Samuel 1:22, 24, 27).

Living thousands of years apart, Hannah and I possess striking similarities. We bore sons and dedicated them to the Lord forever. They both lived in a place called Shiloh, and there they grew from young boys into young men. In their early years, they learned to hear the voice of God and worship Him. Like Samuel, my son saw some of his leaders profess godliness, yet live without conviction. Both young men addressed their overseers and encouraged them to live godly lives. Samuel and my son, Levi, both *"grew in stature and in favor both with the LORD and men"* (1 Samuel 2:26).

Hannah weaned her son, gave him to the Lord for His service, and left him at Shiloh. My son's transition from a young boy to a young man was also a type of weaning. Dedicating our son to the Lord as an infant, I had no knowledge of what surrendering him truly meant. Later, living on a ranch called Shiloh, like Hannah, I surrendered our son there as he passed on to be with Jesus at nineteen.

When you, as a Christian parent, dedicate your children to the Lord, you're committing them into the hands of their Creator for His plans, purposes, and safekeeping. If you haven't done this yet, declare, "Lord, they are Yours all the days of their lives." If you're pregnant, pray over your womb. You'll find no hands safer or stronger than Christ's nail-pierced hands.

Resurrection and Life

Jesus said to her, "I am the resurrection and the life."

John 11:25

Arriving at the Eagle County Morgue, my steps were slow and hesitant as I went in to identify my son's body. We acted upon our authority in Christ and cried out to the Lord to bring his spirit back to us. Our hearts so longed for a different outcome.

Three days later while taking a shower, I cried out, *"Jesus, why didn't You raise Levi back to this earthly life? In the Bible You raised the only son of the widow of Nain."* Suddenly, I heard a powerful voice full of majesty say, *"I am the resurrection and the life. I raised Levi from the dead at the cross. Levi's resurrection from the dead came about when he became born again by My Holy Spirit. He is alive and well, and forever more with Me. I am telling you this in the shower because I am giving you Living Water."*

God's love flowed over me like a steady gentle stream, temporarily refreshing my broken heart. I later opened my Bible to read John 11. Jesus spoke to Martha regarding her brother, Lazarus, saying, *"'25I am the resurrection and the life. He who believes in Me, though he may die, he shall live. 26And whoever lives and believes in Me shall never die. Do you believe this?' 27She said to Him, 'Yes, Lord, I believe that You are the Christ, the Son of God, who is to come into the world'"* (John 11:25–27).

Jesus asked me the same question He asked Martha, "Do you believe this?" She and I believe in the Resurrection. However, Jesus really drove the point home for me concerning Levi, as the Holy Spirit illuminated the scriptures. *"Levi, who believes in Me, though he may die, he shall live. And because Levi lived on the earth and believed in Me, He shall never die."* Spiritually, Levi lives!

In the hope of His resurrection, Jesus made a promise to you, and He'll keep it. His grace is available for you to believe in Him. Today, like Martha and me, declare, "Yes, Lord, I believe that You are the Christ, the Son of God!"

Homecoming King

He is Lord of lords and King of kings;
and those who are with Him are called, chosen, and faithful.

Revelation 17:14

Only days after Levi's death, I passed by a photograph on my mantle. The picture, taken five months earlier, was of Levi and a young woman when they were crowned homecoming king and queen. At this time the Holy Spirit whispered, *"Levi was Homecoming King in high school, but he has met 'The' Homecoming King, Jesus Christ."*

As children born again of God, heaven is the homecoming we all anticipate and where our true citizenship lies (see Philippians 3:20).

Often, a distinguishing item for a king and queen is a crown. King Jesus wears a golden crown (see Revelation 14:14). He also wore an earthly crown—one no human would desire or be able to bear. The soldiers twisted thorns and placed them on His head. They bowed their knee before Him, mocking His true status and saying, "Hail, King of the Jews!" He *willingly* took the crown of thorns that we deserved, and in exchange gave us His crown of righteousness.

As a gifted athlete in track and football, Levi received earthly awards in the form of trophies. First Corinthians 9:24–25 refers to running races and receiving prizes. Earthly runners run to obtain a perishable crown. In our heavenly race, we run to receive an imperishable crown. *"If anyone competes in athletics, he is not crowned unless he competes according to the rules"* (2 Timothy 2:5). By God's grace, Levi ran in such a way that he received the prize. Disciplined in grace, he fought the good fight. He kept the faith and finished the race.

Are you running in the heavenly race? Jesus gives you grace to run and strength to finish, no matter if you lag behind or run steadily. If you haven't yet entered the race, Jesus welcomes you to join at any time. Then, like Levi, upon entering the kingdom of heaven, you'll receive imperishable crowns of eternal life and righteousness.

The Unveiling of a Prayer

It is good for a man not to touch a woman. Nevertheless, to avoid fornication, let every man have his own wife, and let every woman have her own husband.

1 Corinthians 7:1–2 (KJV)

When Levi was three years old, the Holy Spirit led me to fast for him. Aligning with his age, I refrained from food for three days. As he lay asleep for his afternoon nap, I placed my hands on him and began to pray in tongues and then in English. The prayer of interpretation which began to flow from my spirit was our opening passage, 1 Corinthians 7:1–2. This surprised me because of his young age. My request was that Levi would not touch a woman sexually before he was married.

First Corinthians chapter 6 speaks of the body being the temple of the Holy Spirit, which is not to be given to fornication or sexual immorality—sex outside of God's kind of marriage between a man and a woman. Because of the incredible moral battle that rages in society and even among Christ followers, I prayed tenaciously for the purity of my children. Bathed in prayer and now a teenager, my son had a God-given fondness for young women, but he also had godly respect.

Only a few days after Levi's passing, the Lord spoke to me saying, *"Levi married the Lamb. He never touched a woman before he married the Lamb of God."* God now reminded me of my fasting prayer in a way that I never could have imagined. I was thankful that the Lord answered my prayer and that He comforted me with these words.

Parents, your children's lives matter. Parents, your prayers matter, and they change things. Grandparents, your grandchildren need your prayers! Prayers to God on behalf of children protect them spiritually from the onslaught of the enemy and temptation. Will you join with me in fighting to have no child left behind enemy lines?

Perfect Paradise

Jesus said to him, "Assuredly, I say to you,
today you will be with Me in Paradise."

Luke 23:43

Six weeks after Levi's death, my family and I were invited to rest at the home of our friends, Gary and Donna. Palm and fruit trees, along with a warm gentle breeze, surrounded us in the backyard. The waterfall's sound soothed my broken, grieving soul. The swimming pool's temperature felt perfect for a fair-weathered woman. It was heavenly! The home and its surroundings, inside and out, gave me the impression that I was in paradise.

When we departed our friends' home, a wave of grief hit me. It was time to return to reality, to our unknown future of living life without our son. I had tremendous anxiety on our plane ride home, but Jesus held me close and filled me with peace.

The following morning in prayer, God reminded me of one of the thieves on the cross. He had asked Jesus to remember him when he came into His kingdom. Jesus said, "Today you'll be with Me in Paradise." What a precious word from Jesus to that thief. Then, the Lord prompted me with an analogy: Our friends' home, located in Paradise Valley, Arizona, is the wealthiest part of Scottsdale. Jesus told me, *"From an earthly perspective, your friends' backyard is paradise. However, My heavenly Paradise, with its wealth, beauty, and perfection, cannot be described in earthly terms. Even as pleasant and refreshing as everything was to you, My heavenly Paradise is beyond comparison, and right now, beyond your comprehension."*

Paradise in Greek means "a park, an Eden."[1] I'm guessing it's like the first Eden, perfect in every way until the serpent came along! All of our family and friends who have put their faith in Jesus and departed this life are in that perfect Eden. They abide in Paradise—at peace and at rest, safe and secure in their Maker's presence for all of eternity.

"To him who overcomes I will give to eat from the tree of life, which is in the midst of the Paradise of God" (Revelation 2:7). If you're an overcomer, having trusted in Jesus' sacrifice on the cross, one day you too will be with Him in Paradise.

While You Are Sleeping

In a dream, in a vision of the night, when deep sleep falls upon men, while slumbering on their beds.

Job 33:15

Struggling with faith after Levi's death, God showed me my heart in a dream. Walking, I stooped through a filthy corridor precisely fifteen feet long, four feet wide, and five feet high; the corridor's end, a four-by-four-foot square opening, was approximately three feet off the ground.

Looking through the opening, I noticed a man standing in front of a feeding trough, mundanely stirring what looked like slop to feed pigs. The walls, along with his apron and boots, were covered in the filth.

Unaware of my presence, he took a pail, filled it with the slop, and hurled it through the opening where I stood. Coming toward me, the substance looked edible. I held out my hand to catch it, but realizing it wasn't fit for human consumption, I quickly withdrew my hand.

Suddenly, a herd of pigs came running at me from my right side. I jumped through the opening and into the room where the man once stood. Heading outside, I came into a fenced pasture feeling the relief of escape. Then from my left, another herd of pigs came at me. I ran for my life, leaping over a three-and-a-half-foot-tall fence. Only then was I truly safe!

When I awoke, I didn't remember the dream. As I checked my computer later that morning, my home screen showed a piggy bank, and I suddenly remembered: I dreamt of pigs!

Instantly, the Lord revealed the meaning of the dream, saying, *"You were in a pigpen in your thoughts, thinking I'm not your friend, since Levi is now with Me. The man was the devil, and the slop was his lies. Because he continually stirs and slings slop, what mattered was where you were standing. Standing in the truth of My Word and My love for you, you're less likely to be hit with his slop."*

God lovingly chose to reveal my wrong thinking in a dream, not because I was distracted or not listening while awake, but because He does what He pleases. If you're open to God communicating with you while you're sleeping, He'll speak to you this way as well.

Combat Vision

For You will light my lamp; the LORD my God will enlighten my darkness.
For by You I can run against a troop, by my God I can leap over a wall.

Psalm 18:28–29

A weighty concern on the battlefield is vision, as it's vital to survival. In daylight and darkness, soldiers wrestle unseen forces. For daytime maneuvers, soldiers receive government-issued, protective, ballistic eyewear, along with binoculars to scope out the enemy. With diminished or no visibility, warfare in the dark affects a soldier's ability to observe the terrain and enemy or friendly troop movements. Therefore, soldiers are equipped with highly sophisticated night vision goggles, enabling them to see in lowlight or nighttime operations.

For spiritual troops, God has also provided appropriate eyewear for 20/20 vision in the battle. He promises to sow light for the righteous (see Psalm 97:11), and He provided His Word as a lamp to our feet (see Psalm 119:105). Spiritually speaking, in my military campaigns, I pray God's Word against the enemy and his demons. I pray that *"they grope in the dark without light,"* and that God will make *"them stagger like a drunken man"* (Job 12:25).

I don't know of anyone who doesn't enjoy his or her eyesight, or who isn't thankful for it. Natural vision is of great importance, and we should do all we can to protect our eyes from injury and our sight from damage. Militarily, since vision is the most significant factor in defensive and offensive maneuvers, we must put on our Spirit-issued eyewear and remember, as optometrist Colonel David Hilber says, "To be vision ready, is to be mission ready!"[1]

With prayer and Bible reading, we can protect our spiritual vision from becoming blurred, diminished, or even blinded. Jesus said, *"I am the light of the world. He who follows Me shall not walk in darkness, but have the light of life"* (John 8:12). As you follow the voice of Jesus, clear vision is a guarantee on any battlefield that you find yourself.

Forewarned and Watchful

Take heed; see, I have told you all things beforehand.

Mark 13:23

Living on the northwest side of Colorado Springs, my backyard is a rocky cliff where rattlesnakes also reside. Overlooking my deck to a garden area below, I once saw the head of a rattler! Not a fan of snakes of any kind, now I only venture into the garden in winter or after it has rained.

Posted a couple of blocks from my home is a city ordinance sign that has a photograph of a rattlesnake and reads, "Watch out for rattlesnakes." Each person will react differently to this sign, but personally, I'm always on the lookout for them and won't enter that camouflaged, rocky, grassy terrain, having been forewarned that they're there.

An analogy came to me in regards to that sign and our spiritual life, in which God says, "Watch out for..."

Jesus *"40came to the disciples and found them sleeping, and said to Peter, 'What! Could you not watch with Me one hour? 41 Watch and pray, lest you enter into temptation. The spirit indeed is willing, but the flesh is weak.'"* (Matthew 26:40–41). By God's grace, throughout each day I pray and pay attention to protect myself from the weakness of my flesh, and from snakes—both spiritual and natural.

In the Bible, the ordinances of God are numerous in regards to watching or taking heed to His commands. Jesus said, *"Take heed that no one deceives you"* (Matthew 24:4). *"False christs and false prophets will rise and show great signs and wonders to deceive, if possible, even the elect"* (Matthew 24:24). If you have received Jesus and His atoning work, consider yourself "the elect."

Paul wrote, *"I do not write these things to shame you, but as my beloved children, I warn you"* (1 Corinthians 4:14). The Holy Spirit's desire is for us to "watch out" and not follow or give way to that which He forewarns us about—things that can harm us. As you study God's Word, you'll find these warning signs posted from Genesis to Revelation. Don't ignore them, but heed them—it's for your own good!

God's Comfort

Blessed are those who mourn, for they shall be comforted.

Matthew 5:4

All of us have experienced sorrow at one time or another. I can personally offer clear evidence that God comforts those who mourn. Even after receiving the call about Levi's car accident, and then the call from the coroner, although my heart and mind swirled with confusion, God's presence, peace, and comfort filled my innermost being.

After the initial shock of Levi's passing subsided, it was as if God's comfort also wore away. Faced with reality and completely crushed in spirit, I said to God, "Everyone else is comforting me. Where are You?" Then, during my devotional time one day, I read, "*[3]Blessed be the God and Father of our Lord Jesus Christ, the Father of mercies and God of all comfort, [4]who comforts us*" (2 Corinthians 1:3–4).

Through that verse, God turned the light on for me. His comfort *was* coming from every direction. The word *comfort* means "to console."[1] Its root meaning is "to call near."[2] God consoled me through my family who flew in from every corner of the country. Charis Bible College gave abundantly in so many ways, we could never repay their incredible kindness. New Life Church blessed us beyond what we could imagine. Messenger International also came to our aid in an incredibly kind way. It's a Grind, a local coffee shop, held a candlelight vigil, which comforted us and many others in the community.

Additionally, others who had children pass also came to our rescue. The local news reported our story and portrayed our son, as he was, an upstanding Christ follower. Each time I received a call, a card, a gift, a hug, a prayer, a soothing word, a text, an email, or a message on social media, God was calling me near to Himself. Once again, in the fog of my grief, my heart softened.

If you find yourself in the midst of pain, grief, or sorrow today, recognize that receiving comfort in any form is comfort from God Himself, because He is the God of *all* comfort. The blessing in our mourning is the presence of our Comforter.

Job's Comforters

*Job answered and said, "…miserable comforters…I also could speak
as you do, if your soul were in my soul's place. I could heap up words
against you, and shake my head at you."*

Job 16:1–2, 4

Yesterday I spoke of God's comfort during my grief process. Today, I'd like to discuss what Job refers to as "miserable comforters." My family and I encountered similar types of people as Job did—those who voiced opinions regarding our loss and suffering and brought only misery.

"Job was blameless and upright, and one who feared God and shunned evil" (Job 1:1). Yet, we find him in the midst of grief unspeakable. Because of the righteousness of Jesus Christ, my family and I, as born-again believers, are blameless in spirit. We too fear God and shun evil, yet faced unspeakable grief.

Some assumed that I feared as Job did, so my son's death came upon me, yet I never once feared for my children. Then, based on the writing of Moses in Psalm 90:10, *"The days of our lives are seventy years; and if by reason of strength they are eighty years,"* we were told the devil stole our son. Because God never planned for anyone to die—spiritually or physically—could it then be said that the devil steals everyone who dies, no matter what age? The statement "The devil stole your child" doesn't bring comfort to grieving families. It is one made by a miserable comforter.

Job basically said, "If your soul was in my soul's place—if you were in my shoes—I could heap up words against you." But then he said, *"I would strengthen you with my mouth, and the comfort of my lips would relieve your grief"* (Job 16:5). In bringing comfort to others, it's best to take the words of Paul deeper to heart: *"Rejoice with those who rejoice, and weep with those who weep"* (Romans 12:15).

We can choose to be vessels of God's comfort and relieve someone's confusion in grief. Or, we can follow in the footsteps of Job's comforters. Allow the Holy Spirit to use you to be the former.

Silent Comforters

A time to keep silence, and a time to speak.

Ecclesiastes 3:7

For the last two days, my purpose in writing about God's comfort and Job's comforters was to encourage and equip you as Christ followers, ministers, friends, or family members when encountering a grieving heart. I'd now like to share with you another type of comfort—silent comfort.

Upon our return from the Eagle County coroner, our longtime friends and business affiliates, John and Jan, arrived at our home with Mexican food. John sat quietly at the counter, while Jan, with an aura of peace about her, prepared the meal. Upon Jan's invitation to eat, my husband and I nibbled as we poured out our hearts as to the "why" of it all. John and Jan offered no Christian clichés or opinions, nor did they speak merely to cover their own discomfort. Instead, they listened to our every word with little or no response, speaking only when spoken to, and at times, not even then. Their silence was "golden" in our grief. Little did we know that their impression would be everlasting.

In Levi's passing, family and friends filled our home to capacity, expressing their condolences. Occasionally John would stop in, and among the crowd he continued to be a strong silent presence. It was as if he was saying, "I'm sorry for your pain. I don't understand either, but I love you, and I'm here for you." Body language speaks, and John, in his silence, was shouting. His silence was both deafening and comforting.

With the exception of the Holy Spirit and my family, conversation in grief sounded to me like the static of a radio. I can't speak for other grieving families, but I can be sure that they too struggle with processing conversation in the thick of grief.

In my conversations with God, there are many times when He's silent, but His presence is loud and powerful. When you comfort those who are grieving, consider the example that John and Jan, and the Lord Himself have offered. Sometimes, silence is exactly what is needed most when comforting a grieving heart.

Shock Absorbers

Have mercy on me, O LORD, for I am in trouble;
my eye wastes away with grief, yes, my soul and my body!

Psalm 31:9

Within a few days of Levi's passing, my husband and I determined it was time to get out of the house, and we agreed to venture out for coffee. As we traveled down the dirt road near our home, in my mind I began to see the undercarriage of my husband's Dodge Ram truck. Since his truck was not at all at the forefront of my mind, I understood that God was revealing this to me. Hidden away underneath the truck, the shock absorbers protected the truck from the brunt of the road's rough terrain and allowed it to encounter fewer jolts and vibrations from the washboard road.

The thought came to me: *The shock that my family and I met with when we heard the news of Levi's accident actually protected our physical bodies from the punishment that grief threw at it.* It protected us from absorbing grief's impact, which had the ability to cause our hearts to stop beating.

Personally, the shock didn't end with the memorial service; it lingered for a long while afterward. It wasn't until the second year that the numbness began to wear off, and the effects of grief became more distinguishable.

King David confessed that he was in trouble and that his eyes, soul, and body wasted away with grief. The grief my family and I experienced, although not without hope, also affected us—spirit, soul, and body. God is faithful. He rescued David years ago, and today He saved our lives.

There are countless things in life that can deliver the "shock" effect, such as news of a divorce, the loss of a job, or a diagnosis. Even if you're upset and confused about God in your circumstances, He'll still come to your aid, no matter what level of grief you're experiencing. Allow Him to carry you, and the brunt of your suffering will be absorbed.

The Spirit's Lead

For as many as are led by the Spirit of God, these are sons of God.

Romans 8:14

Befriending me, a woman invited me to go hiking with her and her friends. I jumped at the chance because prior to her invitation, the Lord told me, *"She's a new believer. She needs healing, and she hasn't yet received her Spirit language (or tongues.) As a gift for her, I want you to purchase a Willow Tree angel."* Then, strolling with a friend in a shop where it was unlikely to find these hand-crafted figurines, I found some. Elated, I said, "Lord, which angel would You like to give her?" He said, *"The one with a flame on her head, as it will be a memory of her Pentecost and receiving her gift of tongues."*

The following morning for His purposes, God downsized the group to three! I waited for the Lord's lead as we walked and chatted. Approaching a bench on the trail, I heard, *"Now's the time. Sit on the bench."* As I shared with her what God had spoken to me, He manifested tremendous healing in her soul as we prayed. Now praying for the gift of tongues, it was as if something was blocking her voice, when the Lord said, *"Fear is blocking her spirit language from flowing forth. Command fear to go."* In Jesus' name, I commanded fear to go, and immediately she began to pray in her Spirit language!

Back at the parking lot, giving her the angel gift, I shared Acts 2:3–4: *"³There appeared to them divided tongues, as of fire, and one sat upon each of them. ⁴And they were all filled with the Holy Spirit and began to speak with other tongues, as the Spirit gave them utterance."* Today, the Pentecost angel sits on her mantle, as the woman continues to enjoy her gift of tongues.

"For as many as are led by the Spirit of God, these are sons of God" (Romans 8:14). If you're a son or daughter, led daily by the Spirit of God, the Lord has much to accomplish through you. Let Him lead you so His purposes will be accomplished for His eternal good.

Tears in a Bottle

You number my wanderings; put my tears into Your bottle;
are they not in Your book?

Psalm 56:8

Have you ever felt like King David, wandering about aimlessly with no direction or purpose? One day while walking and talking with Jesus, I said, "Lord, I feel so lost." He responded, *"You're not lost; I'm your compass."*

I felt lost because within a two-year period, Levi went to heaven, my daughter married, my husband worked in another country, and I resigned from a position that brought me divine fulfillment. It *seemed* as though I had lost my bearings. On the other hand, maybe I should say the changes in my life made it appear as if I had fallen off-course. I found the words of Jesus reassuring. Since He gave the waters boundaries, He also knows the parameters of our destination from beginning to end.

David talks to God about his wanderings and his tears, which, at times, had been *"his food day and night"* (Psalm 42:3). From sunrise to sunset, I too cried a river of tears; so much so that I said to God, "I hope You have a lot of bottles, because I have a lot of tears." God assured me, *"I knew the number of your precious tears before the foundation of the world. I also have the correct number of bottles to collect them."*

David isn't the only one who had tears. Paul had many tears and trials (see Acts 20:19). Jesus also offered up prayers to God with vehement cries and tears (see Hebrews 5:7). I'm sure you've also had tears of both joy and sorrow.

Once, while praying for a widower, I began to feel warm drops falling on my hands. Wondering what it was, I opened my eyes. I realized the widower's tears were falling from his cheeks onto my hands. In that moment, the Lord spoke, saying, *"His tears are liquid gold to Me."*

Don't hold back your tears. God's waiting with His bottle in hand to catch every one of your precious golden droplets.

Blessed, Not Bitter

Looking carefully lest anyone fall short of the grace of God; lest any root of bitterness springing up cause trouble, and by this many become defiled.

Hebrews 12:15

One morning as I met with God, I sensed a barrier in our communication. He spoke to me, saying, "There's something blocking our relationship…it's bitterness.

But…You are not bitter, you are My Beloved. You are not bitter, you are Becoming.
You are not bitter, you are Blessed. You are not bitter, you are Beautiful.
You are not bitter, you are Bountiful. You are not bitter, you are Bathed in My love.
You are not bitter, you are My Betrothed. You are not bitter, you are My Bride, and I am your Bridegroom."

God shifted my focus from the bitterness that attempted to enslave me to my identity in Christ.

Two weeks later while in church, the impeding bitter spirit lurked once again. As we took communion, Jesus told me, "Because of My body and because of My blood, you are not bitter."

At times, bitterness grips everyone. Hannah, because of an empty womb and the provocation of Peninnah, experienced bitterness in her soul (see 1 Samuel 1:2–10). Job, having a rough go of life, said, "I will complain in the bitterness of my soul" (Job 7:11). I can relate to Job's anguish and the loss of one son. The apostle Paul told Simon, who previously practiced sorcery, "For I see that you are poisoned by bitterness" (Acts 8:23).

I'm certain that the demonic spirit of bitterness thought it got the best of me. Maybe you feel that way at times as well. Have you ever heard, "What God reveals, He heals"? Through communion, God exposed this bitter spirit and began manifesting my healing and deliverance. During the following three devotionals, I'll share the miraculous way in which God demolished the bitterness that had its hooks in my heart.

Maybe you're not dealing with bitterness today but another barrier that's hindering your relationship with the Lord. As you read my testimony, ask the Lord to reveal and heal any such blockage in your own life.

Overcome

Oh come, let us worship and bow down.

Psalm 95:6

Two weeks after my encounter with God during communion, I was walking across my living room when His unmistakable power and presence suddenly covered me like a cloak. I fell face down on the carpet and began weeping, while prayers and songs of worship in both English and my spiritual language of tongues rose from the depths of my inmost being. I lay there allowing the Holy Spirit to pray through me as He pleased. I didn't know what He was doing, but His presence was proof of Him working something miraculous.

The hour that passed seemed like minutes when I perceived the Holy Spirit's work end and His invisible but evident presence lift. Believing that God would speak, I scanned the room for pen and paper, but before I could find them, I heard, *"Gather around My throne. I'm about to do something mighty."* At this time, His purpose remained hidden.

Maybe you've had similar experiences as mine, or perhaps you feel you've been left out of such encounters. Know that God is eager to meet you personally.

My first memory of recognizing God's invisible but evident presence, besides my salvation experience, happened while sitting with my husband and watching a fire in the fireplace. Suddenly, I sensed the presence of Jesus, but I didn't see Him. I said, "He's here!" My husband asked, "Who is here?" I replied, "Jesus!" Mark responded, "Jesus is always here."

He meant, of course, that Jesus is omnipresent, which is true; but at times He makes His presence evident. *"He who loves Me will be loved by My Father, and I will love him and manifest [or reveal] Myself to him"* (John 14:21, brackets added).

When I recently sensed the presence of the Lord in my living room, I couldn't help but bow in worship. It wasn't until one month later that God revealed His purpose for this encounter. As I share more of this story tomorrow, ask the Lord to stir your heart of faith in order to experience a deeper, more personal relationship with Him.

God Levels Our Mountains

*This is the word of the L*ORD *to Zerubbabel: "Not by might nor by power, but by My Spirit," says the L*ORD *of hosts. "Who are you, O great mountain? Before Zerubbabel you shall become a plain! And he shall bring forth the capstone with shouts of 'Grace, grace to it!'"*

Zechariah 4:6–7

A few days after meeting God on the carpet, our opening scripture came alive to me when I distinctly heard, *"This is the word of the Lord to Sharon Rose: 'Not by might nor by power, but by My Spirit,' says the Lord. 'Who are you, O great mountain of bitterness? Before Sharon Rose, you shall become a plain.'"*

Not only did God's words penetrate my heart, they rang true because bitterness had been a thorn in my side since my childhood.

Further study led me to Jeremiah 51:25–26, which was like water breaking through a dam and flooding my heart:

*"*25*Behold, I am against you, O destroying mountain, Who destroys all the earth," says the Lord. "And I will stretch out My hand against you, roll you down from the rocks, and make you a burnt mountain.* 26*They shall not take from you a stone for a corner nor a stone for a foundation, But you shall be desolate forever," says the Lord.*

Although Jesus delegated to us His power and authority, God showed me through this verse that He was taking charge and that He would destroy the mountain of bitterness in my heart, leaving it desolate forever. Unknown to me, He had His own plans to level the mountain. In my defense, He told me He'd speak to the mountain and tell it what He was going to do, and in turn, tell me what I would do because of His intervention.

By personalizing Jeremiah 51:25–26, the mountains in your life will also become level plains, just as mine have. As His powerful arm rises against the mountains in your life that are bound for destruction, they won't be able to stand in His mighty presence. Tomorrow, I'll share the finality of God's miraculous, mountain-leveling ability.

God's Fire Path

*Therefore understand today that the LORD your God is
He who goes over before you as a consuming fire.
He will destroy them and bring them down before you.*

Deuteronomy 9:3

A month passed following my encounter with the Holy Spirit. The Canadian government employed my husband, and in his absence, Mark asked that I deliver an envelope to his friend Paul, the founder of Operation Restored Warrior, a ministry in which veteran warriors help restore wounded warriors—spirit, soul, and body.

In fulfilling my husband's request, I had no idea it would also provide me with a measure of restoration. With delivery complete, Paul prayed for me. As he prayed, a vision came to me of an earthly mountain looming large in front of me. Jesus stood with me at the foot of this mountain. Soaring upward, it went through the galaxies and stopped at God's throne where He sat and the Holy Spirit stood. Then Jesus reminded me, *"I said I'm going to stretch out My hand against this mountain of bitterness and make it a burnt mountain."* Unexpectedly, with a vial in hand, the Holy Spirit poured one drop of oil onto the top of that mountain, and the mountain became a heap of ash at our feet.

I now understood the work that the Holy Spirit did through me in my living room, and I remembered God's words: *"Gather around My throne. I'm about to do something mighty!"* The mountain stopped at the foot of His throne because the bitterness was toward Him for creating me. Jesus reminded me that it wasn't by my effort but by His Spirit that He'd speak grace to that bitter mountain, which became ash.

During this time, Colorado Springs was experiencing extremely destructive wildfires. The mountains directly behind my home remain charred from this inferno. God utilized the burnt environment as an analogy to the work He was doing in the Spirit.

Our God is personal. He *"is a consuming fire"* (Hebrews 12:29), and what He did for me, He'll do for you—but *only* in a way that best suits you. Come boldly to His throne of grace where you'll obtain mercy and find grace to help in your time of need (see Hebrews 4:16).

Combat M.A.S.H.

"For I will restore health to you and heal you of your wounds," says the LORD.

Jeremiah 30:17

M obile Army Surgical Hospitals, otherwise known as M.A.S.H., are vitally important facilities near the battlefield. M.A.S.H. units were used to provide life-saving surgery to injured troops and were strategically placed in combat zone locations during a war.

In war, there's another expression called a *dust off.* This simply refers to evacuating casualties from a war zone where the wounded are transported by medical personnel via ground or air to better-equipped, critical-care medical facilities.

As saintly soldiers, we also need a dust off or casualty evacuation from time to time. For instance, when my son passed away, I was severely wounded and in need of life-saving attention. Jesus evacuated me from the battlefield, transporting me to His very own "loving arms" unit, which was located under His healing wings. This godly action was the *only* thing that saved my life. *"The eternal God is your refuge, and underneath are the everlasting arms; He will thrust out the enemy from before you"* (Deuteronomy 33:27).

Today in spiritual battle, many purposely or unintentionally run into the arms of the enemy—the wrong people—or even into the prosthetic arms of false comfort. Tempted at times during my grief to run from God instead of to Him, He reached for me with His mighty outstretched arms that are safe, secure, and saving.

As the Great Physician, Jesus is always on call and fully operational in your battle, even if you're barely breathing and holding onto life. *"God is our refuge and strength, a very present help in trouble"* (Psalm 46:1).

In the armed forces, the combat medics' ears are trained to hear the voice of those crying out, "Medic!" Likewise, Jesus is always listening intently for your cry for help. Wounded or in need, just call out to Him, and He'll come running.

Communion Poetry

*Now in Christ Jesus you who were once far off
have been brought near by the blood of Christ.*

Ephesians 2:13

While meditating on our opening scripture, I thought that, because it cost Jesus everything, there should never be a day that we hesitate to draw close to God and enjoy His fellowship.

Looking to the famous biblical sisters, Mary and Martha, Martha was distracted with much work and complained to Jesus about serving alone, while Mary sat at His feet. Jesus answered her, *"41Martha, Martha, you are worried and troubled about many things. 42But one thing is needed, and Mary has chosen that good part, which will not be taken away from her"* (Luke 10:41–42). Mary sitting at the feet of Jesus is a prophetic picture of the closeness that Jesus provided through His blood on the cross and His indwelling Spirit.

Because the blood of Christ brought us near, as Christ followers in a society saturated with busyness, to neglect drawing close to God is to slight the priceless sacrifice of Jesus. However, His mercies are new every morning. Each day you can begin anew. Since Jesus never leaves you, you only need to turn to Him and He'll respond to you, drawing you closer and closer to His heart for intimate fellowship beyond your imagination.

Receive the following poem from the inspiration of the Holy Spirit:

Thank You
Thank You for Your body on the tree, which reconciled me.
Thank You for Your blood, which bought and brought me near.
Thank You for Your stripes that bled, which raised me from the dead.
Thank You for Your crown of thorns in which the veil was torn.
Thank You for Your nail-pierced hands and feet, which freed me from defeat.
Thank You for Your lance-pierced side, which allowed me to cross over to the other side.
Thank You for Your body and Your blood on the tree…for me.

Take time today to personally express your gratitude to Jesus for providing a way for you to draw near to Him.

Encounters of a God Kind

Does He not see my ways, and count all my steps?

Job 31:4

I had been volunteering with Courtside Ministry only a few months when an invitation to their annual barbeque arrived. A lawyer founded the ministry after witnessing much unrest in courthouse appearances. In order to ease the tension, he began offering prayer for any willing participant who approached the courthouse. I had hesitated to attend the barbeque not knowing many volunteers but ultimately decided to step out and meet other team members.

At the close of the evening, I met Kathy, who was fully convinced she knew me. We exchanged ideas of where our meeting may have occurred. Finally, I asked, "My nineteen-year-old son, Levi, recently passed away. Do you know me from the media coverage?" "No," she answered, "but please tell me about your son." I shared my story, to which she replied, "I can't believe you still love God!"

"God is good," I said. "He heals the brokenhearted and the crushed in spirit."

As I was leaving the party, the woman found me and asked, "How about we have coffee sometime?" And, additionally, "Let's be friends on Facebook." She was kind, and a person I would like to know, but I was still hiding underneath God's healing wings and guarding my time carefully. We parted with the intention of connecting soon.

The following morning at Courtside's office, the host said, "Kathy's daughter died last night." In disbelief, I questioned him, making sure we were talking about the same woman I had just met fewer than twenty-four hours before.

I phoned her, and she said, "I was telling my husband your story, when I received a call saying that our daughter had passed away. Immediately, I heard your voice and our conversation, and it softened my heart toward God."

The Holy Spirit is on the move, going before us and orchestrating each divine encounter. Jesus continually said, "Follow Me." Take a step of faith, and boldly follow Him wherever He leads. You'll be glad you did.

Julie's Persuasion

Preserve me, O God, for in You I put my trust.

Psalm 16:1

My friend Julie is an inspiration to me when it comes to faith. Whenever I'm around her, I wonder, *Where is my faith?* That's not necessarily bad, and it's not that she makes me feel that my faith is small. However, I can't rub elbows with her and not feel compelled to believe God in greater ways.

Julie and her family came from the Congo. War erupted, forcing them from their country. While refugees in Kenya, Julie's husband, Isaac, fled the country under extremely dangerous circumstances, temporarily leaving his family behind. Unfortunately, the boat that he managed to escape the country in lost power and drifted directly into enemy hands, armed with machine guns. Standing in the boat, Isaac declared to the gunmen, "God didn't bring me this far to kill me!" In the face of death, his faith stood tall! Miraculously, the guerillas allowed the men to go free.

A few days after his Bible college graduation in America, Isaac fell ill and within hours went to be with the Lord and their firstborn son who had died in Kenya. Heartbroken and widowed with six children under the age of fifteen, Julie stood at her husband's grave. I know this kind of loss would rock anyone's world. To this day, Julie continues to cling to God, while she and her children experience firsthand His unfailing love and faithfulness.

After Levi's death, I visited with Julie. She told me, "There are some things I can't do, but I can trust God!" Her statement of faith will resonate in my heart forever. The apostle Paul wrote, *"Imitate me, just as I also imitate Christ"* (1 Corinthians 11:1). As the body of Christ, we are to be living epistles before each other and the world. Because Julie imitates Christ, I believe that I can imitate Julie in her example of trusting in God in a time of loss.

We need to seek out those around us whom we can imitate and follow as they follow Christ. Allow the Lord to lead you to such believers so that you may grow in faith and Christ likeness.

My First Fast

But the days will come when the bridegroom will be taken away from them, and then they will fast in those days.

Mark 2:20

In 1986, my pastor introduced me to a life of prayer and fasting, both of which have played a major role in my Christian walk. Looking back on my first fast is comical now, but we all start somewhere. As a new disciple, I brought a filthy cigarette habit with me into God's kingdom. With God's Word now planted in my heart, it was a good time to rid myself of this practice.

Despite Matthew 6:18's instructions, *"Do not appear to men to be fasting, but to your Father who is in the secret place,"* I did the exact opposite and told everyone, "I'm fasting." By noon on the first day, I thought I'd starve. I began to eat but continued to tell myself and others I was fasting. By dinner, I ended my so-called fast.

Although naïve in my fasting attempt, God answered my prayer through a vision. I saw the Father, Son, and Holy Spirit silently standing around my physical heart, as if it were a smoky campfire. When I inhaled on a cigarette, they were choked by the smoke and began coughing. Jesus said, *"You're smoking Us out!"*

Smoking doesn't cause God to depart from us; Jesus simply shared a picture with me that I'd understand. With Father, Son, and Holy Spirit now living within my spirit, I'm to keep my body, which is their temple, free of pollutants, like cigarette smoke. With God's grace, I did quit smoking!

Because biblical fasting is hardly exciting to our carnal nature, we must embrace God's help to both begin and end a fast victoriously. Pray and commit the time to Him, otherwise you won't reap the many benefits of fasting. It's only those who hear the Word of God and do it that are blessed (see James 1:23).

Whether this is your first time fasting, or you're mature in the process, God rewards those who diligently seek Him (see Hebrews 11:6). Keep in mind, however, your faith is not in the fast, but in God *through* the fast! I encourage you to fast as often as God leads you, as the benefits are numerous.

Me, Insane?

For it is the land of carved images, and they are insane with their idols.

Jeremiah 50:38

When I read this passage, I visualized the earth as a land filled with carved idols. Idolatry is when someone gives extreme admiration or attention to someone or something. Whether our idols are physical "carvings" or only found in our mind, knowingly or unknowingly, throughout time mankind has been insane with its idols.

You've probably heard the saying, "Insanity is doing the same thing over and over again and expecting a different result." How often do we entertain recurring, idolatrous thinking with the expectation of a different outcome?

Most of us are familiar with *insanity* being defined as "a state of serious mental illness."[1]

However, before you think I'm confessing madness over you, here are some definitions from the Old Testament Hebrew language: "(clamorously) foolish," and "to rave."[2] If one acts foolishly, does that deem that person certifiably insane? What about causing a commotion? We've all seen young and old alike rave in fits of anger. Do we regard them as unsound because of it? Does this aptly describe humanity at times?

Long ago, two idols in my heart were anger and envy. From my youth, year after year, these idols spoke delusion to me (see Zechariah 10:2). After repeatedly listening to and acting upon those lies, I expected different results but always received the same outcome: troubled relationships.

As God continued to draw me to Himself, He showed me that I was giving those idols more attention than I was giving Him. Lovingly, little by little, day by day, He revealed to me His truths, and as I applied them by grace, I achieved different results.

The Lord says, *"It shall be in that day…that I will cut off the names of the idols from the land, and they shall no longer be remembered"* (Zechariah 13:2). Jesus cut them off at the cross so you could serve the living and true God. Whether physical or imaginary, idols no longer have power over you. That means that today you can turn to God from idols once and for all.

I Am...Because He Is

Finally, my brethren, be strong in the Lord and in the power of His might.

Ephesians 6:10

While attending fitness classes at YMCA, the instructor played a secular song with the following lyrics: "I'm sexy and I know it."[1] Hearing this line, a thought came to me: *Because the Holy Spirit dwells within us, we are powerful and we know it, and the signs and wonders show it.*

Believing God works through us is not pompous thinking. God chooses to manifest His power though people. Although not one of the Twelve, Stephen, *"full of faith and power, did great wonders and signs among the people"* (Acts 6:8). Apart from Jesus, we can do nothing. As born-again believers, *"we have this treasure [His Holy Spirit] in earthen vessels, that the excellence of the power may be of God and not of us"* (2 Corinthians 4:7, brackets added).

In Acts 8:18–19, we read, *"[18]When Simon saw that the Spirit was given when the apostles laid their hands on people, he offered them money to buy this power. [19]'Let me have this power, too,' he exclaimed, 'so that when I lay my hands on people, they will receive the Holy Spirit!'"* (NLT). The same Holy Spirit who made His power visible through the apostles makes His power tangible through believers today.

My heart's cry comes from 1 Corinthians 2:4–5: That *"[4]...my speech and my preaching [are] not with persuasive words of human wisdom, but in demonstration of the Spirit and of power, [5]that your faith should not be in the wisdom of men but in the power of God"* (brackets added). I don't want people to see me but rather God's Spirit working through me.

In Christ, "We are powerful and we should know it; and the signs and wonders should show it!" Be open to God wielding His power through you. After Jesus was received into heaven and sat down at the right hand of His Father, the disciples *"went out and preached everywhere, the Lord working with them and confirming the word through the accompanying signs"* (Mark 16:20). He wants to do the same with you!

Relationships' Contender

He said to them, "All too well you reject the commandment
of God, that you may keep your tradition."

Mark 7:9

The Greek word *commandment* is defined as "an authoritative prescription"[1] or God's written Word, which trumps *tradition*, or "the handing down" of customs or beliefs from generation to generation.[2] When it comes to relationship with God, I consider *tradition* to be a contender.

You've probably heard it said, "You can't teach an old dog new tricks." I have good news. We are not dogs, and we can learn new ways of the Spirit.

The Pharisees asked Jesus, "Why do Your disciples not walk according to the tradition of the elders?" Jesus responded, "Because you make the Word of God of no effect through your tradition, which you have handed down" (see Mark 7:13). Steeped in the rituals of men, the Word of God has no effect in people's lives. This grieves and limits the Holy Spirit to do the marvelous things He desires to do (see Ephesians. 4:30).

Many believe water baptism is required for eternal security. If held to tradition, what hope was there for the thief on the cross who believed but was not water baptized? Jesus *alone* was his hope, not a ceremonial bath. As Jesus told the man, *"today you will be with Me in Paradise"* (Luke 23:43). God's prescription for salvation is not a physical act of water baptism, but a spiritual baptism, which comes *only* as the Holy Spirit washes and renews our unregenerate spirit (see Titus 3:5). In this washing, we become born again, and our immersion in water symbolizes our baptism into Christ and into His death.

I'm a firm believer in water baptism, but only after following God's prescription found in Romans 10:9–10, *"9If you confess with your mouth the Lord Jesus and believe in your heart that God has raised Him from the dead, you will be saved. 10For with the heart one believes unto righteousness, and with the mouth confession is made unto salvation."*

Ask the Lord to search your heart to see if you're holding onto age-old customs that are contrary to Christ and His Word. If so, exchange those traditions today for His true commandments so you can boldly follow Christ in His power.

Tongues and Interpretation of Tongues

I will pray with the spirit, and I will also pray with the understanding.
I will sing with the spirit, and I will also sing with the understanding.

1 Corinthians 14:15

Unless we act on the instruction of our opening passage, we won't experience its truth. Our spirit language of tongues, especially if spoken publicly without interpretation, leaves others without understanding of what's being spoken.

Having prayed in tongues since 1986, the Spirit has worked many wonders through me for the benefit of others (see 1 Corinthians 12:7). Once, while at a cabin, I was fasting and praying in tongues for my Bible college class, when this interpretation came forth: *"There is a spirit of suicide in the second-year classroom."* Two days later, I shared this experience in class, and a student came forward with a visitor, who told me, "The very day you were praying, I had a gun to my head with the hammer down," meaning his finger was on the trigger. The day the Spirit prayed through me and gave me the understanding was the very day God spared that man's life.

On another occasion in the classroom, God had me pray for a student whom I was meeting for the first time. Praying for her in tongues, suddenly, in my spirit, I saw Hawaiian hula dancers wearing coconut cups and grass skirts. Their hips swayed as gently as palm trees in the breeze. The scene, although extremely peculiar, wasn't sensual but pure and peaceful. I had to stop praying and ask her, "Does this make sense to you?" She said, "Yes, I'm new in town from Hawaii, and I lead Hawaiian worship dance at my church." God lovingly reassured her that He was with her.

God desires to meet people in ways unique to them. By allowing the Holy Spirit to pray through you, through tongues and their interpretation, the Spirit reveals hidden mysteries (see 1 Corinthians 14:2, 4).

If you pray in tongues, never stop! If you haven't yet experienced this gift, simply ask Jesus to fill you with His Spirit and His language. In Acts 2, all 120 people in the Upper Room received the gift of tongues, not just a select few. This gift is available to every born-again believer, including you!

The Learning Curve

Do not become sluggish, but imitate those who through faith and patience inherit the promises.

Hebrews 6:12

For years, I rode with my husband on his Harley Davidson. However, things changed when I met a group of churchwomen who rode motorcycles cross-country without their husbands. I'd never heard of this among churchwomen! Next, I met a female veteran motorcyclist of forty-five years. Then, while at a Harley dealership, I noticed a poster that read: "I Ride." I asked an employee, "What does 'I Ride' mean." She said, "You can learn how to ride a motorcycle." I signed up!

My written test went better than my field test. When the instructor said, "Start your engines," I thought, *So soon?* Instruction then came to shut off our engines and dismount the bike. Knowing absolutely nothing about a motorcycle, and doing as instructed, suddenly I had 400 pounds of steel on top of me! He failed to say, "Put down your kickstand." This incident sent me over the edge to where I couldn't continue the class. Thankfully, the opportunity was available to take the class as many times as needed to pass.

Have you ever stepped out to learn a new skill? Did you find the learning curve steep, overwhelming, or fearful? God said, *"Behold I will do a new thing"* (Isaiah 43:19). We can learn new techniques in the natural as well as in the spirit. It took time for me to grasp the mechanics of a motorcycle. It also took patience, humility, testing, mistakes, and tenacity to learn how to handle larger bikes.

Discipleship is a similar process when it comes to learning the unknown ways of the Spirit. It takes time, and although rewarding, it's not without challenge. The longer I ride a motorcycle, the easier maneuvering the bike becomes. The longer we walk in tandem with the Spirit's grace, the easier it is to make the necessary adjustments to stay in step with Him.

For me, the third time was a charm in passing my field test. Jesus will offer you ample opportunities as well to learn to follow in His footsteps. Just be prepared to be patient, determined, and sometimes humbled.

Designated Chair

Please, let us make a small upper room on the wall;
and let us put a bed for him there, and a table and a chair and a lampstand;
so it will be, whenever he comes to us, he can turn in there.

2 Kings 4:10

Although our opening passage refers to a Shunammite woman who prepared a room for Elisha, the holy man of God, we can take this passage for ourselves in preparing a room, or a space within our home, with a chair to sit and rest awhile and visit with God.

What a great invention: the chair! Regardless of our mood, we all enjoy a comfortable chair. God sits on a throne and speaks of His mercy seat (see Revelation 7:10 and Exodus 25:22). In addition, *"We have such a High Priest* [Jesus], *who is seated at the right hand of the throne of the Majesty in the heavens"* (Hebrews 8:1, brackets added).

Babies have high chairs. Mothers and grandmothers often rock in rocking chairs. We're all familiar with the "Time Out" chair! Others may sit in a wheelchair. Kings and queens sit in chairs known as thrones. The courtroom also boasts of a seat. Pilate, as judge, brought Jesus out and sat down in the judgment seat (see John 19:13). A witness has selected seating, known as the "witness stand."

From the beginning of my Christian walk, I intentionally designated a chair to spend time with God. However, over time, I bought a specific chair at a thrift store for ten dollars. Although we're free to commune with God at any place and time, each day after greeting Him when I awake, I sit with Him in my prayer chair, committing my day to Him and asking, "Lord, what's on Your heart?"

Do you have a designated prayer chair? If the three bears can have individual chairs, I believe that God can have a chair that fits you perfectly. Maybe it's already in your home. Or, maybe it's waiting for you at your local thrift shop. Perhaps your prayer chair is the seat in your car! Ask the Lord where your designated chair is, then use it to draw close to the Father's heart.

Good Nutrition

Listen carefully to Me, and eat what is good, and let your soul delight itself in abundance. Incline your ear, and come to Me. Hear, and your soul shall live.

Isaiah 55:2–3

God stirred my heart with what seemed to be firm, fatherly advice: *"Listen carefully to me, Sharon Rose. Eat what is good, and your soul will delight in abundance. Incline your ear, come to Me, hear, and your soul shall live."* Truly, the Lord is calling us to feast at the banquet table of His presence.

At that time in my life, I had developed some bad spiritual "eating habits." Instead of my well-balanced diet of the Word of God, I had acquired a taste for junk food, which manifested in negative confessions. Nutritionally, junk food or food that perishes, is as good as dead. Thinking about this, John 6:27 came to mind: *"Do not labor for the food which perishes, but for the food which endures to everlasting life, which the Son of Man will give you."*

Unlike junk food, living food has all the nutrients needed for a healthy body. Father, Son, and Holy Spirit are living, and feeding on them fortifies us with the proper nutrients our spirit craves. Jesus said, *"55For My flesh is food indeed, and My blood is drink indeed. 56He who eats My flesh and drinks My blood abides in Me, and I in him. 57As the Living Father sent Me, and I live because of the Father, so he who feeds on Me will live because of Me"* (John 6:55–57).

In the natural, I know that when I eat unhealthy food, I'm not able to function at the level that I do when I make healthy choices. Spiritually speaking, unless we feed on Jesus in prayer meetings, church gatherings, at work, and in our family, we're eating things void of the nutrient-rich life that He alone provides.

Today, cling to the words of Jesus, and follow the diet of Jeremiah the prophet. He found God's words, ate them, and they were a joy and a rejoicing to his heart (see Jeremiah 15:16).

Night Visions

I have had a dream.

Daniel 2:3

My first dream of Levi came nine months after his heavenly departure. The scene involved a home, in which we previously lived as a family. When I opened the front door to go onto the porch, Levi stood before me; my husband and daughter were sitting on a swing to the left of us. Knowing Levi is a heavenly resident, I wondered what he was doing on the porch. Dumbfounded, I stood about twelve inches from his face and studied him intently, not having seen him in quite some time.

Oddly, there was no touch or conversation between us, yet his presence spoke volumes. His body pulsated with an energy that was otherworldly, which I believe was the life of the Spirit of the living God. Love radiated from him like thermal energy emanating from the sun's surface. Peace, too, was a pulsating, living presence, as was a silent, yet audible joy. I sensed I was seeing and experiencing Levi clothed in his heavenly garments, which made him more alive than when he lived on the earth.

Throughout the Bible, we read how God comforted and warned His people through dreams. Today is no different. I would call Joseph's dream pure solace. Not only was his fiancée, Mary, pregnant, but he wasn't the father! *"While he thought about these things, behold, an angel of the Lord appeared to him in a dream, saying, 'Joseph, son of David, do not be afraid to take to you Mary your wife, for that which is conceived in her is of the Holy Spirit'"* (Matthew 1:20). God not only set Joseph free with the dream, He released Mary from any judgment Joseph *may have had* toward her being with child before marriage.

Always be open to how God desires to speak to you, and be careful not to limit the Holy One from speaking audibly; through His written Word; or through a dream, vision, trance, or circumstances. If you don't experience heavenly dreams, ask Jesus to share His heart with you in this way.

Combat GPS

Direct my steps by Your word.

Psalm 119:133

Location is paramount on the battlefield. Knowing your position in relation to the enemy is a key to survival. Since the beginning of time, the stars have been the source of navigation. Today, we still use space to guide us, but it's through satellite technology.

For God's heavenly troops, He is our GPS—God's Positioning System. Through His Holy Spirit, He transmits essential information to us to safeguard us in the fight.

In wartime, an enemy map of any type is coveted booty. Without accurate maps in the combat zone, I can only imagine a soldier's unrest. Lacking these, troops are vulnerable to ambush. In my battles, I crave the Holy Spirit's reconnaissance and mapping intelligence with regards to adversarial troop movement, hidden ammunition and fuel depots, or obtaining any information that would provide victory.

Before the foundation of the world, God mapped out His plan and purpose for each of our lives in great detail. We read about this in Psalm 139:16, *"Your eyes saw my substance, being yet unformed. And in Your book they all were written, the days fashioned for me, when as yet there were none of them."*

When we lack knowledge of God's strategies, destruction follows (see Hosea 4:6); however, by adhering to His life-giving coordinates, victory is secure.

For the modern world, GPS is standard technology, but it's not perfect technology. It may've caused you to get lost, or if you're familiar with the area, you may know of a better route than the GPS does.

Because of this, you may think you don't need GPS because you know where you're headed. You also may think you have a handle on the enemy's position, and he can't get you off your course. Think again! If he can get Adam and Eve off-track in a perfect Garden, don't think you're safe traveling without God's Positioning System. He knows every square inch of the map!

Good Things

Can anything good come out of Nazareth?

John 1:46

S itting with Jesus is a daily practice for me, no matter how I feel. Is it that way for you? We *"walk by faith and not by sight,"* or feelings (2 Corinthians 5:7). One particular time of prayer was neither a cakewalk nor a faith walk, but a grace walk due to my immense grief.

A short while after Levi's death I met with additional life-altering circumstances when my daughter married. Two weeks after that my husband took a temporary job in northern Canada. All I knew and loved was gone in a matter of two short years. Disoriented in my circumstances, I said, "Father, I have nothing to offer You, not even praise." God didn't condemn me for the grief and uncertainty I was experiencing. Nor did He scold me for living out of my soul and not my spirit, where praise is readily available and plentiful.

As I sat silently before the Lord, He asked me a rhetorical question: *"Can anything good come out of Nazareth?"* No sooner had I thought His question strange, He continued, *"Can anything good come out of your son, daughter, and husband being gone?"* He asked, not seeking my opinion, but to state His point. He went on, *"Something very good came out of Nazareth: love, healing, provision, protection, forgiveness, reconciliation, deliverance, and much more. All that is good came out of Nazareth because Jesus came out of Nazareth, and everything good is in Jesus. Sharon, everything good is going to come out of your son, daughter, and husband being away from you."*

Because God is good, we now have Emery Rose, our first grandchild. My husband no longer travels extensively, and God has filled my heart to overflowing, meeting me day after day and year after year to write this book. And, the best part, because Someone good came out of Nazareth, I will see Levi again. As you trust in Jesus, be encouraged that God will bring good to you despite your circumstances.

Psalm 73:1—*Truly God is good.*
Psalm 143:10—*Your Spirit is good.*
John 10:11—*I am the good shepherd.*

Friendship Undercover

He who covers a transgression seeks love,
but he who repeats a matter separates friends.

Proverbs 17:9

Going into my marriage as a new believer, I acted like a Pharisee, continually reminding my husband of his past. I would've done well to follow the instruction of Luke 6:42, *"How can you say to your brother, 'Brother, let me remove the speck that is in your eye,' when you yourself do not see the plank that is in your own eye? Hypocrite! First remove the plank from your own eye, and then you will see clearly to remove the speck that is in your brother's eye."*

During this time, the Lord revealed our opening passage to me: Proverbs 17:9. It only took seconds for me to understand what God was saying. By covering any imperfections I perceived my husband had, I was actually loving him. If I continued to acknowledge perceived faults, I was separating our friendship.

Unfortunately, my metamorphosis didn't happen overnight. Years later, my husband reminded me that the past is behind us. The following day, God, in His fatherly approach, illuminated Psalm 103:12—*"As far as the east is from the west, so far has He removed our transgressions from us."*

"So, Sharon," asked the Lord, *"why do you continue to remember your husband's?"*

With our sinful slate wiped clean, why do we continue to allow Satan to remind, remember, and accuse others and ourselves of the past? My husband and I still miss the mark, and, as in any healthy relationship, we discuss those issues that foster division and unrest and take action to change our ways. But, the past is the past.

If you find that you're reliving the past with yourselves or others, take hold of Philippians 3:13, which says, *"Brethren, I do not count myself to have apprehended; but one thing I do, forgetting those things which are behind and reaching forward to those things which are ahead."*

Prisoners!

Return to the stronghold, you prisoners of hope.
Even today, I declare that I will restore double to you.

Zechariah 9:12

After Levi's physical death, hope *appeared* to be a thing far on the horizon. It *seemed* as each day dawned, it became less and less visible. In truth, it was the opposite, as I am one who grieves but not without hope. I turned to the Lord, but my broken heart wavered. It was as though I was pulling the petals off a daisy while foolishly saying, "He loves me; he loves me not."

My heart leaped for joy when I read the words of Zechariah, as God beckoned prisoners, which includes me. The definition of *prisoner* refers to being bound or captive. If imprisonment is necessary for hope, then being a cellmate with Jesus, who is our hope, would be my preference.

Scripture encourages the prisoners of hope to return to the stronghold. Nahum 1:7 tells us, *"The Lord is good, a stronghold in the day of trouble; and He knows those who trust in Him."* Unknowingly, in my sorrow, I veered at times from my fortified place in God and my anticipation of anything good yet to come. However, the too-good-to-be-true news is that God's unfailing love never allows us to stray far. He knows our whereabouts at all times.

The word *hope* is described as "a cord (as an attachment)" or "thing that I long for."[1] The God of hope has yoked Himself with us. Further meaning of the word *hope* is "to bind together (by twisting)."[2] Linked and intertwined with God, He encourages us to set our heart and mind on the expectation of His good.

If you're a prisoner of hope, be encouraged today. One of the most endearing passages in my grief process was Romans 15:13—*"Now may the God of hope fill you with all joy and peace in believing, that you may abound in hope by the power of the Holy Spirit."* Now that's amazing grace for you and for me.

Prizes Await

I will give your life to you as a prize in all places, wherever you go.

Jeremiah 45:5

Although we were living in a rural area, my husband's desire was to raise our children in an even smaller community. After eleven years of marriage, and after occupying eleven different homes, the prospect of moving again didn't appeal to me. Then, I came across Ezra 8:21 and 23, which read, *"²¹I proclaimed a fast there at the river of Ahava, that we might humble ourselves before our God to seek from Him the right way for us, our little ones, and all our possessions.... ²³So we fasted and entreated our God for this and He answered our prayer."*

I understood that it was God's will for us to fast, humble ourselves, and seek His plan for our family and our possessions, as my husband was self-employed. In agreement, we petitioned God for these things and waited expectantly to hear from Him. The hour we broke the fast, my husband said, "We are moving." I was upset, as the Lord had not yet confirmed anything in my heart!

The following morning when I woke up, the Lord spoke to me, simply saying, *"Jeremiah 45:5."* I sat on the edge of my bed and opened my Bible to see what the scripture had to say. To my amazement, I read, *"I will give your life to you as a prize in all places, wherever you go."* God answered my fasting prayer as He did Ezra's. Right or wrong, I was moving, and God was going to make my life a prize, not only in this move but also in any unforeseen moves.

The prizes from this move included the honor of God working through me to lead a young woman to Jesus. It also settled my husband's heart in regards to moving, and gave me a deeper faith in God.

You can trust the Lord as you commit everything to Him in prayer. He *will* bring the answer to pass. It may not be what you expect, but everything He does works for your good, as He works to conform you into the image of His Son (see Romans 8:29).

A New Creation

Do not marvel that I said to you, you must be born again.

John 3:7

On May 3, 1986, in the Colorado mountains, I withdrew from a drug party and went deeper into the woods by a pond. Looking up at the star-filled spring sky, I began to experience a vision, which I knew was not from the drugs. Before me was a Hebrew-like scroll, rolled open with some of my sins written on it. With my heart now exposed, I fell to my knees. Realizing I was trashing my life, I asked Jesus to be the Lord of it.

Weeping, I felt the presence of God overwhelm me and wash me clean of every sinful thing I had ever done. Forgiven and forgotten, I perceived the filthiness of my sin completely removed.

Back at the party, now sober and looking past the bonfire at the people opposite me, I understood the eternal change; I had just passed from death to life. I had no doubt that I had just met the Savior of the world, Jesus Christ. In the Bible, Jesus describes this change as being born again. Because all of mankind is born in sin and separated from God, we must be born again by the Holy Spirit from above into God's original sinless design. Jesus, in His death, burial, and resurrection, made the way for this birth to be possible.

From that day forward, my life changed dramatically. By God's grace, or ability, many things too numerous to mention became new. I never did another drug. A love flowed from me that I had not previously known. This love was willing to give and forgive more freely. *"If anyone is in Christ, he is a new creation; old things have passed away; behold, all things have become new"* (2 Corinthians 5:17).

You, too, can become a new creation and eternally secure, born again by the Holy Spirit of God from above. You may not be in the same pit I was, but apart from Christ, you're still in a pit. Turn to Jesus, and receive what He has so graciously provided for you in His death, resurrection, and ascension: eternal life, knowing Him, forgiveness, healing, and hope.

A Raging River

When you pass through the waters, I will be with you;
and through the rivers, they shall not overflow you.

Isaiah 43:2

Within eight hours of being born again, a couple of male friends and I decided to go canoeing with an overweight dog down the Colorado River. It was springtime. The water that splashed on my hands and face, although hypothermic, was invigorating. Approaching a fork in the river, we unanimously chose the most turbulent path. Pacing from one side of the canoe to the other, the dog in his excitement plunged the three of us into the frigid water.

I sensed overwhelming peace and assumed the current would sweep me down river. However, things didn't go as I had envisioned. At the bottom of the river, unseen boulders held me captive by trapping my foot. The force of the raging water drove me face down so that I couldn't rise above the surface.

Beneath the rapids, I prayed, "Jesus, I'm so happy I met You last night; otherwise, right now I'd be headed to hell. Thank You for saving me. I can't wait to meet You face to face." All of a sudden, whether I was in heaven or in a vision, I don't know, but I saw blades of green grass, which I didn't recognize as earthly. I also saw a form of brilliant light with a red sash, which I clearly understood to be Jesus.

Above the water, one of my friends (now my husband) was also talking to God. He swam the rapids several times in an attempt to successfully free me. Exhausted, he prayed, "God, if You don't save her, she'll die." Under the water and still before His brilliant presence, Jesus spoke to me, saying, *"It's not time for you to come home. I have work for you to do."* Instantly, the boulders miraculously released their grip on my foot, and I washed downstream onto the riverbank.

His word is true in my life and yours. When you pass through waters—natural or spiritual—He'll be with you. Just call out to Him in your time of trouble.

Knit Together

That their hearts may be encouraged, being knit together in love.

Colossians 2:2

Throughout this book you'll see that I've dedicated certain parts to family and friends. Today's message is devoted to our friends Paul and Maaike, whose second-eldest son went to high school with Levi. Both Maaike and her son attended Levi's memorial service, but it wasn't until six months later that we met when we received a call from them. They wanted to meet our family because their eldest son had passed away, and they needed to talk to people who understood. With our hearts knit together in Christ and in grief, our friendship blossomed.

A rare and special treasure, these two benevolent hearts gave generously. Both motorcycle enthusiasts, Maaike was my female inspiration to ride. They not only loaned me a motorcycle, paying fees and insurance, but also a car.

Some time later, I received another call from Maaike, saying that her youngest son had passed away. There were no words to describe their heartache. We never know what a day holds in store, but our assurance is that no matter what the day holds, Jesus will be holding us.

Our friends needed God's comfort more than ever. I prayed to the *"Father of mercies and the God of all comfort, who comforts us in all our suffering"* (2 Corinthians 1:3), asking God to overwhelm them with His unfailing love and peace.

Recently, Maaike's husband, Paul, passed on. Her heart was once again grief stricken. God knits things together, namely hearts, for the sole purpose of creating something beautiful. For our grieving families, God took strands of yarn in the form of comfort, tears, and at times, laughter, in order to handcraft a beautiful bond. Unless intentionally cut with scissors, or unraveled, the interwoven stitches of something knit together remain intact. I encourage you to regard God's eternal knitting process in your relationships as rare and valuable, like a priceless work of art.

The Great Deception

The God of heaven Himself will prosper us.

Nehemiah 2:20

Christian mothers with pre-kindergarten children often say, "My husband wants me to work because he doesn't make enough money." Feeling obligated to obey or help, mothers leave the care of their children—even newborns—to family, daycare, or worse…strangers. Today, among Christ-professing parents, this is the "Great Deception."

"Jesus Christ is the same yesterday, today, and forever" (Hebrews 13:8). What God did for our parents yesterday, He can do for parents today and beyond, which is to provide—His way. It's best not to tamper with divine DNA: fathers provide, and mothers nurture and care for the family.

The "Great Deception" involves many things, including fear. Trusting God for provision can be frightening, and when the going gets rough, many panic and turn to self-effort. Husbands mistakenly think, *Why should I be the sole provider?* Or, disregarding Scripture, *My wife can do as she pleases.* Alternatively, wives say, "I need, I want" or, "I can have both kids and a career."

Men, in committing your wives to the workplace, you might ask yourself, "Is God my source or my wife?" Women, by taking matters into your own hands, you might ask, "Am I trusting God? Am I shirking my divine design of nurture in providing my children the love, attention, and security that only I can give?"

God has individual family plans, but He never contradicts His covenant policy. As an older woman, I'm to *"⁴encourage the young women to tenderly love their husbands and their children, ⁵to be sensible, pure, makers of a home [where God is honored]"* (Titus 2:4–5, AMP).

Young believing parents, you're not of this world. God has limitless "how-to" ideas for cutting costs and supplying income in ways that won't interfere with your child's God-given right to your personal parental care.

God's Kind of Mother's Day

Open for me the gates where the righteous enter,
and I will go in and thank the LORD.
These gates lead to the presence of the LORD, and the godly enter there.
I thank you for answering my prayer and giving me the victory.

Psalm 118:19–21 (NLT)

Six weeks after my son's death, Mother's Day arrived. As much as I dreaded the day, it came. Opening my eyes with my head still on my pillow, these words resonated in my heart: *"¹³Enter by the narrow gate; for wide is the gate and broad is the way that leads to destruction, and there are many who go in by it. ¹⁴ Because narrow is the gate and difficult is the way which leads to life, and there are few who find it"* (Matthew 7:13–14).

Then the Lord spoke to me: *"Sharon, thank you, for not only raising Levi to love Me at a young age but to meet Me face to face at nineteen. There are ninety-year-olds who are not even ready to meet Me. Levi entered by the narrow gate and is eternally secure. Good job, Mom."*

Well aware of my broken heart, instead of greeting me with, *"Happy Mother's Day,"* God said, *"Good job, Mom."* True to His character, *"He rejoices with those who rejoice and weeps with those who weep"* (Romans 12:15).

Later that morning as I read Psalm 118, I sensed God telling me it was Levi's prayer. God not only opened the gates of heaven where Levi entered, but He answered his prayer that He'd do something mighty in the hearts of the teachers, staff, and students at the high school he attended. Like a prophet to the nations, he was crying out for others to put their faith in Jesus. God gave Levi the victory, as hundreds came to Christ in his passing.

Now five years down the road, with regard to my son, I'm once again a happy mother. On Mother's Day, God reassured me, *"Levi is not only praising Me, but he's praising God that his mother's fear of the Lord led him to that narrow gate, which few find."*

Mothers (and fathers), don't believe the lie that being a parent isn't a rewarding life. The value of your worth and your fear of God is eternally priceless! As much as it depends on you, don't let your kids leave home without Jesus.

Dreams, Visions, and Trances, Oh My!

And it shall come to pass afterward that I will pour out My Spirit on all flesh;
your sons and your daughters shall prophesy, your old men shall dream dreams,
your young men shall see visions.

Joel 2:28

The *Wizard of Oz* characters Dorothy, Tin Man, and Scarecrow fearfully walked through the forest, singing about lions and tigers and bears…oh my! Today in the body of Christ, many are fearfully singing a similar song: dreams, visions, and trances…oh my! But these forms of biblical communication are nothing to fear. From Genesis 15 to Revelation and our present day, God speaks to people in such ways.

I've heard statements that misrepresent the truth of our topic, such as: "I live by faith and not by sight, so I don't need outside influences such as dreams, visions, or trances." Does that mean if you experience one of these, you're not living by faith? That's absurd! As spiritual beings, we have spiritual eyesight, which enables us to see things in the spirit world. When it comes to dreams, visions, and trances, it's not an outside job, but an inside job of the Holy Spirit. He's the treasure within our earthen vessel speaking to our spirit as He chooses, whether through a revelatory word in Scripture, or through spiritual or visual means.

Another idea contradictory to Scripture is that God speaks in these ways *only* because people aren't paying attention to His voice. Daniel, Peter, Cornelius, and Paul were paying attention. They were in fervent prayer when they experienced these forms of dialogue.

I also don't agree that simply because we have the Bible, the Holy Spirit no longer speaks in these ways. No doubt, the written Word is God's gift, and He often speaks to us though that. But because the Holy Spirit and the Word are one, He does lead and guide us as He chooses, in any form of communication. Jesus Christ is the same yesterday, today, and forever (see Hebrews 13:8). Through these avenues, God spoke and continues to speak to believers and unbelievers alike.

I encourage you to pray and expect God to speak to you through dreams, visions, and trances—or any other method He chooses. There's nothing to fear if God is behind it.

Dream On

Daniel had a dream....Then he wrote down the dream, telling the main facts.

Daniel 7:1

Not all dreams are from God. Some come from the devil, our own subconscious desires, or, as we've heard it said, from pizza! As for God's dreams, they accomplish what He pleases, and like His words, they never return void. If you do have a dream, I encourage you to write it down as Daniel did, and unless the Holy Spirit gives you the immediate interpretation, continue to pray about it. Over time, the Lord will reveal if you should hold onto it for later, or if it wasn't from Him, perhaps let it go.

Joseph's brothers, speaking about Joseph, said to one another, *"Look, this dreamer is coming"* (Genesis 37:19). Are you a dreamer who is mocked and criticized by others? I've never believed that Joseph was premature or arrogant in telling his dream. The problem was with his brothers, who hated him. God had a purpose for Joseph prophetically foretelling the dream that was later revealed in the midst of the famine and that affected his family and nation years later. In my life, the foretelling dreams of Levi's death also came years later, which eternally affected me and my family.

The wise men and Joseph also had life-altering dreams: *"¹²...being divinely warned in a dream that they [the wise men] should not return to Herod, they departed for their own country another way. ¹³Now when they had departed, behold, an angel of the Lord appeared to Joseph in a dream, saying, 'Arise, take the young Child and His mother, flee to Egypt, and stay there until I bring you word; for Herod will seek the young Child to destroy Him'"* (Matthew 2:12–13, brackets added).

We can see God's specific instruction of warning, guidance, and comfort in each of these dreams. Through dreams, God restrains from evil, reveals His will, encourages, reveals the future, and offers instruction. With the Lord's strong desire to communicate with His people, He uses all means possible to connect with us, including dreams. Never discount your dreams but talk to God about them. He may be trying to get a message to you!

Visions of Sugarplums?

I will come to visions and revelations of the Lord.

2 Corinthians 12:1

Don't you love the boldness of the apostle Paul? I agree with his confidence of receiving from the Lord: *"I will come to visions."* As I read the Bible, I envision God as a visual being. After all, with everything He created, He *saw* that it was good. Since we are created in His image, we have the same spiritual DNA, including spiritual eyesight.

According to *Vine's* dictionary, a vision is "a spectacle."[1] And, Noah Webster's original 1828 dictionary defines a vision as "…a revelation from God; an appearance or exhibition of something supernaturally presented…"[2] Numbers 24:4 reads, *"Who sees the vision of the Almighty, Who falls down, with eyes wide open?"* Different from dreams, visions happen while you are awake.

Although we're not discussing visions of sugarplums, the topic of visions is vast throughout the pages of the Bible. From Genesis through Revelation, we find the word *vision* recorded eighty times in the Old Testament and seventeen times in the New Testament. God conversed with Abram in a vision (see Genesis15:1–21). Ananias, a New Testament believer, had a vision in regards to ministering to Saul (see Acts 9:10). And John, on the Island of Patmos, had a vision concerning the end of the age (see Revelation 9:17).

The ancient prophet Habakkuk writes, *"²And the LORD answered me: 'Write the vision; make it plain on tablets, so he may run who reads it. ³For still the vision awaits its appointed time; it hastens to the end—it will not lie. If it seems slow, wait for it; it will surely come; it will not delay'"* (Habakkuk 2:2–3, ESV).

A vision was so important to God, He told the prophet to write it on tablets! Today, visions are as important as they were thousands of years ago. Sit with the Lord with pen in hand, and like Habakkuk, get ready to write!

A Soul-Saving Trance

Now it happened, when I returned to Jerusalem and was praying in the temple,
that I was in a trance and saw Him saying to me, make haste.

Acts 22:17–18

Entering Sam's Club with my husband and two children, we ran into an old friend. When I looked into her eyes to say hello, I suddenly fell into a divine trance. When I did, I had no awareness of my earthly surroundings, including the people around me—my friend, my family, and those in the store. I heard Jesus say, *"Make haste, Jane is going to hell."* Just as quickly I then came out of the trance. I realized that Jesus and I were the only two who knew what had just happened. The woman said, "We should have coffee sometime." I agreed!

The *Vine's Complete Expository Dictionary* describes *trance* as "A condition in which ordinary consciousness and the perception of natural circumstances are withheld and the soul is susceptible only to the vision imparted by God."[1] The apostle Paul, when in a trance, *saw* Jesus speaking to him (see Acts 22:17). Peter, also, while praying on the rooftop, was in a trance, and he *saw* heaven opened. Therefore, a trance involves sight (see Acts 10:1–11).

Two days later, in my friend's home, everything seemed ordinary to the natural eye, but nothing could have prepared me as she described her rafting trip down the Colorado River through the Grand Canyon. She said, "When I sat on the side of the raft, terror gripped me, and I saw the swirls in the water go down to hell." I responded, "I have something to share with you. Jesus sent me here because He told me you're headed to hell."

My friend considered her life, which included church attendance and teaching Sunday school, good enough for God. However, she'd never heard, *"you must be born again"* (John 3:5). She accepted the salvation Jesus offered her that day.

I am living proof that trances, just like dreams and visions, have not ceased with the disciples. God chose to reveal Himself to me in this way to accomplish His work. Don't be afraid to ask Him to use you in similar ways, and then get ready for the adventure!

Two Mothers

The angel said to her, "Rejoice, highly favored one,
the Lord is with you; blessed are you among women!"

Luke 1:28

The angel Gabriel shares wonderful things with Mary, such as: *"[28]Blessed are you among women"*; *"[30]You have found favor with God"*; and *"[31]You will conceive and bring forth a Son"* (Luke 1:28, 30–31). Sounds like many blessings are about to overtake Mary!

In Luke 2:22–35, we find Mary, Joseph, and the Child, Jesus, with Simeon in the temple. Simeon blesses the Child, then directs his words to His mother, saying, *"[34]Behold this Child is destined for the fall and rising of many in Israel, and for a sign which will be spoken against [35](yes, a sword will pierce through your own soul also), that the thoughts of many hearts may be revealed."* At this time, I don't believe God revealed the severity of the sword, which was to pierce Mary's soul. Nor do I think a picture came to her heart of her Son hanging on a cross, bloodied beyond recognition.

I can only imagine that Mary was a mother like me. She tucked those prophetic words into her heart. Like Mary, I too pondered in my heart the Lord's foretelling words regarding my son: *"Levi will leave you and Mark at a young age. Cling to him and embrace him, for your days with him will be short."*

In John 19:25, Mary, a human mother in anguish at the foot of her Son's cross, looked intently at Jesus, while the sword prophesied by Simeon painfully pierced her soul. My soul's piercing came when I found myself at the morgue, identifying Levi's body after his fatal car crash. There, I remembered God's words, *"Levi is going to leave you…."*

Perhaps you're in the midst of a soul-piercing circumstance right now. Without God revealing the meaning of Simeon's prophetic words, Mary could only speculate about their interpretation. But you can be at peace knowing that your heavenly Father is fully aware of every situation that you face. The secret things belong to your loving, all-knowing God.

Modesty Matters

…in like manner also, that the women adorn themselves in modest apparel.

1 Timothy 2:9

Calling all saints: fathers, mothers, husbands, wives, brothers, and sisters. We're not of this world, nor are we to dress by its standards. With the world's rapid infiltration of the church, the call to modesty within the body of Christ is essential. Modesty isn't a topic for women only, as men also bear the privilege as leaders in the church and family to instruct in this area.

It's been said that God looks at the heart, so clothes don't matter; however, for Christ followers, modesty matters. Well aware of the fallen status of the world, God covered Adam and Eve's nakedness with animal skins. Paul penned God's heart on this matter, which isn't Old Testament Law to eliminate, but a directive to embrace by grace. Jesus is pleased when we don't put other gods before Him, commit adultery, or dress immodestly. As God's chosen people, the Israelites were peculiar to the foreign nations surrounding them. As children of God, we too, are to stand out as a peculiar people to the world.

Once Mark and I attended an event believing we could make an impact for God's kingdom; however, the stiff-necked culture shocked us, and the blatant immodesty of the women stirred heated conversation. I was told that men go without their shirts, so what's the difference if women do as well? God shared His opinion with me, saying, *"When men go without a shirt at inappropriate times, it's immodest; when women do, it's immoral."*

Chatting with two women, one said, "My brother's a nudist," and added, "I think nudity is an art form." The other chimed in, "Our state has an acclaimed nudist parade." They were speechless when I shared God's opinion.

Granted, believers aren't coming to Sunday service naked, but it's evident that the love of the world and its fashion are affecting the church. Ladies, you can be modest and lovely. Men, you can be modest and also dashingly handsome at the same time. Make the right choice to glorify Christ instead of your flesh.

Combat Weapons

You are My battle-ax and weapons of war.

Jeremiah 51:20

In modern-day warfare, there are large varieties of choice weapons, each used for various military maneuvers. A soldier's personal arsenal includes a gun, a knife, and grenades. Corporately, resources may consist of substantial caliber guns and many other lethal devices.

Resembling earthly foot soldiers, as God's mighty ground troops, we also have weapons. Our weapons differ in form but deliver with identical force. They include swords, hammers, and fire—all of which refer to the Word of God. *"For the Word of God is living, powerful, and sharper than any two edged sword, piercing to the division of our soul and spirit, and of joints and marrow, and it discerns between the thoughts and intents of our hearts"* (Hebrews 4:12). And, Jeremiah 23:29 calls God's Word *"a hammer that breaks the rock in pieces."* To me, rocks can be lies and strongholds in my life.

Another weapon used on the battlefield is the flamethrower. As spiritual soldiers, we possess a combustible heat source like a flamethrower—the fire of God's Word and the fire of His presence by which our enemies are consumed. His Word is like a fire, and He is a wall of fire all around us (see Jeremiah 23:29; Zechariah 2:5).

A heart of praise and thanks toward God is another powerful weapon, although sometimes not thought of as destructive. And, wielding authority in the name of Jesus stops the devil in his tracks. Jesus calls you and me, as He *"called His twelve disciples together and gave them power and authority over all demons, and to cure diseases"* (Luke 9:1).

Become familiar with the spiritual arsenal you possess, and gain experience in handling these weapons and others, such as prayer and God's Word. You may want to consider joining other spiritual soldiers in prayer groups or Bible studies, where as a unit you can gain weaponry knowledge and experience. Continue to use His weapons as needed, as they are the source of your fiery ammunition, which carry a devastating payload to the enemy!

Willing and Able

Do you believe that I am able to do this?

Matthew 9:28

How do you see Jesus in your circumstances: able, but not willing? Or, willing, but not able? The truth is that Jesus is both able and willing to come to our aid.

Matthew 9:27–28 tell us, *"27…two blind men approached Jesus asking, 'Have mercy on us.' Jesus said, '28Do you believe that I am able to do this?' They said to Him, 'Yes, Lord.'"* As I read these verses, a hidden link in my relationship among God, my dad, and me came to mind. In my early twenties, I befriended a young woman who repaid my kindness by stealing money from me. Low on funds, I called my dad for help. For whatever reason, my always well-meaning dad chose to deny my request. Subconsciously, I attached this memory of my earthly father to my heavenly Father.

Although persuaded that God is *able*, at times I questioned His *willingness*. God was *able* to keep our son safe, but he died in a car accident. He was *able* to bring Levi back to life on earth, but he now lives in heaven. I've never doubted God's ability, but at times I've doubted His willingness.

In Mark 1:40, *"a leper came to [Jesus], imploring Him, kneeling down to Him and saying to Him, 'If you are willing, You can make me clean'"* (brackets added). Reading Jesus' response was like He was speaking to me face to face, saying, *"I am willing…be cleansed"* (v. 40). I believe His words were as much of a relief to me as they were to the leper. Jesus wasn't only able but also willing!

Because of my dad's choice and the imprint it left, I had wrongly associated God with being able, and *only* in certain cases willing, especially after Levi's passing. Jesus brought me peace, as I pray He does for you, in revealing His ability and also His willingness through the lives of the blind men and the leper.

Jesus has already moved toward you with compassion at the cross. Now, in your earthly circumstances, He's stretching His hand toward you, touching you, and speaking to you, saying, *"I am not only able, My child. I am willing!"*

Beginner Believers

Receive one who is weak in the faith.

Romans 14:1

Once while riding my bicycle on a city path I encountered an oncoming cyclist approximately thirty feet ahead of me. As I reached for my water bottle I swerved ever so slightly into a miniscule portion of her roadway. With the intent to show my apologies, I smiled as we passed, but she scowled back at me. I had barely crossed the line, and I veered back in ample time for her to continue her racing pace. I assumed the "look" I received stemmed more from our interaction causing her to slow her momentum than from any threat of injury.

At that moment, other roadway scenarios came to mind. Whether on a bicycle, motorcycle, or in a car, we can all be naturally self-centered at times. When motorists encounter something causing them to slow down, the temptation to become impatient can arise. The agitation reveals itself in following too close, passing aggressively and plunging into oncoming traffic, or generally driving in an unsafe manner, causing oncoming traffic to yield to the temper of those drivers. With cyclists and motorcycles, you'd think extreme caution would apply. However, that's not always the case. When I ride my bicycle, I wear a hot pink shirt; and when I ride my motorcycle, I wear a neon green vest with the words: "Beginner Motorcyclist."

Considering the concept of ill-mannered motorists, I thought, *How great would it be if new believers wore a high-visibility shirt or vest, identifying them as "Beginner Believers."* My hope is that other motorists along the highway to heaven cut them some slack and show lots of patience by granting them the divine right of way of grace as they daily put on their new man. It takes patience to be around infants in their developmental stages. How much more perseverance should we exercise with a spiritual newborn?

It's good to instruct our newborn friends and help them learn the ways of the road. If you have newborn friends, cheer them on in their learning process by sharing God's promises, helping them to have a safer, more enjoyable trip.

David & Jonathan

The soul of Jonathan was knit to the soul of David,
and Jonathan loved him as his own soul.

1 Samuel 18:1

With the head of Goliath in hand, David made a notable impression on Saul's son, Jonathan, as the two men pledged their friendship toward one another that day.

My son, Levi, met Austin in kindergarten. Since then, the boys were virtually inseparable. Their life together included father-son campouts, birthdays, youth retreats, X-Box gaming, sports, guns, and girls (in a godly way). Paintball fights consisted of heroic re-enactments of 'Nam or Normandy, along with their victory cry: "Freedom!" And, in worship, they experienced the presence of God together.

David and Jonathan experienced similar life events as Levi and Austin. However, their campouts were strategic hideouts, as tormented Saul hunted David continually, with intent to kill him. Jonathan, until his death, risked his own life protecting David from those threats.

Second Samuel 1:26 records David's grieving words upon hearing that Jonathan was slain in the midst of battle: "*I am distressed for you, my brother Jonathan; you have been very pleasant to me; your love to me was wonderful, surpassing the love of women.*"

Austin also spoke lamenting words in Levi's passing: "I loved Levi so much...more than a brother...I miss him so much. But I'm excited for the day that I'll get to see him again." As friends, brothers, and warriors, David expressed a bond with Jonathan that ran deep. By divine plan, Levi and Austin, like David and Jonathan, were covenant friends who loved, protected, and encouraged one another.

If you don't have an earthly covenant friend, know that you have a heavenly One in the Father, Son, and Holy Spirit. Although temporarily separated, the friendship Levi and Austin pledged in kindergarten remains. Likewise, the covenant relationship Christ promised you at the cross also remains.

Dance with Me

A time to dance...

Ecclesiastes 3:4

Some of us are familiar with the contemporary Christian worship song, "Dance with Me." While praying today, a vision emerged in my mind of a man and woman dancing. Then something familiar occurred. A man walked up to the couple, and tapping the man on the shoulder, he "cut in" and began dancing with the woman. Surprisingly, Jesus was the One cutting in. To my amazement, when the man turned his head, it was the devil dancing with the woman. God was showing me that at times, we spiritually find ourselves "dancing with the devil," or the wrong company.

For me, having got off on the wrong foot today with discouragement—even though it appeared to be a small thing—God showed me that because I was discouraged, I was dancing with the devil! Seeing the Lord "cut in," I understood perfectly what He wanted to convey.

Discouragement depicts a lack of hope. Because Jesus is our hope, there's no discouragement in Him. Isaiah 42:4 reads, *"He will not fail nor be discouraged."* And, in 1 Corinthians 15:33, *"Do not be deceived: evil company corrupts good habits."*

When a man cuts in on a man and woman dancing, the matter is between the two men who are competing for the woman's affection and attention. For those of us who have made Jesus Lord of our lives, as our spiritual Husband, Jesus has every legal right to cut in and protect His bride, the body of Christ, from the devil's false and misleading smooth moves and deceptive intentions. Even if we're in good company, I still sensed the Lord's desire was to cut in and dance cheek to cheek with us, relishing in our uninterrupted gaze, affection, and attention.

I'm sure as the bride of Christ you would agree with me that we'd all prefer to cut a rug with Jesus. He's an excellent dance partner, and by dancing with Him we're dancing with "The Star"—*"...the Bright and Morning Star"* (Revelation 22:16). Don't hesitate to let Him "cut in" on your disappointments, hurts, and negative emotions. After your dance, your hope will be restored.

God's Green Acres

In all your ways acknowledge Him, and He shall direct your paths.

Proverbs 3:6

Eighteen months after Levi's passing, we moved from our country home into a house in the city. Set on a hill overlooking Colorado Springs, my backyard consists of thousands of acres bordering a national forest, which makes for amazing hiking. For the most part, I can say, "I have God's green acres all to myself." However, although rare, occasionally I run into people on the trail.

One day I saw a man approaching and began to pray, "Jesus, please keep me safe and allow me an opportunity to vocalize Your goodness." Stopping, we exchanged small talk regarding where we lived in location to the trailhead. As I shared about our recent move, he asked, "Why did you move from the country into the city? Most people are doing the opposite." I said, "With our son having passed away, living in that house was painful." Kindly expressing his sympathy, I began to share my story when he said, "I remember hearing about that accident on the local news. Wasn't it during spring break?" I replied that it was.

His next statement came as a surprise. "When watching the newscast, my heart broke for that mother, and I thought that I'd like to meet her one day. I couldn't imagine the pain, and I wanted to know how someone goes through that and lives."

As we conversed, I remembered committing my day to the Lord and asking for divine encounters, because without them, my life has significantly less meaning. Whenever I have opportunity to share the Good News of Jesus Christ and the cross and to tell others of His compassion in my son's passing, it brings me tremendous fulfillment.

God's faithfulness shined in both of our hearts like the sun burning on that hot August day. The Lord answered both of our prayers right there on God's green acres in the middle of the wilderness.

If you don't already, start today to daily commit your steps to Jesus. Ask Him for divine opportunities to be a blessing to those you encounter on your daily paths. I guarantee you, He'll take you up on it!

Speak Up and Speak Out

The righteous are bold as a lion.

Proverbs 28:1

If you're not already roaring as bold as a lion, I encourage you to do so. The Lord once told me, *"Speak My word boldly in love because the god of this world is voicing his vulgarities."*

We know by the very words of Jesus that not everyone put out a welcome mat for Him or His disciples: *"If the world hates you, you know that it hated Me before it hated you"* (John 15:18). The god of this world hates the truth of Jesus Christ.

In Acts 5, the leaders were filled with indignation and imprisoned the disciples for performing miracles. However, an angel of the Lord opened their prison doors and brought them out, saying, "Go, speak to the people all the words of this life." This caused quite a stir, as the instruction was contrary to the very demands of their captors: "Did we not strictly command you not to teach in the name of Jesus?" Peter spoke boldly, saying, "We ought to obey God rather than men."

Christ followers, we need this attitude! The council wanted to kill the disciples, but after discussing the matter, the authorities decided to let things run their course. They called for the men, beat them, and commanded them again to not speak in the name of Jesus. The disciples departed from the presence of the council, rejoicing that they were counted worthy to suffer shame for His name. Daily in the temple and in every house, they didn't cease teaching and preaching Jesus as the Christ! (See Acts 5:42.)

With the Bible already under attack in today's culture, I have no doubt the events of the apostles will come full circle. *"If you are reproached for the name of Christ, blessed are you, for the Spirit of glory and of God rests upon you. On their part He is blasphemed, but on your part He is glorified"* (1 Peter 4:14).

In the name of the Father, the Son, and Holy Spirit, speak up and speak out to people "all the words of this life." It's time to hear you roar!

Mama Bear

It shall come to pass that before they call, I will answer;
and while they are still speaking, I will hear.

Isaiah 65:24

I wrestled a demonic spirit of fear in my mind while praying and fasting at a cabin in the mountains. I took authority over fear, saying, "In Jesus' name, fear go!" (see Mark 6:17). However, in this extended and fierce battle, the demon did not relent. Then I heard Jesus say, *"Just call out My name."* I blurted out, "Jesus!" and that spirit's oppression left me.

"Whoever calls on the name of the Lord will be saved" (Romans 10:13). In this fight, new revelation came to me with the term, *will be saved.* It applies to salvation for eternal life but also salvation for every moment of every day.

Free from fear, I immediately saw my daughter in a vision. It seemed odd, as she wasn't in the spiritual position that God revealed to me. In the vision, I saw myself looking out of my kitchen window, when I noticed my daughter lying in a fetal position on the driveway with demons surrounding her. The moment she began to open her mouth to call on me for help, and before an audible word came forth, I bolted out of the house in a fury to help her. Like a ferocious mother bear protecting her cubs, I unleashed with my mouth the power and authority of Jesus Christ over those devils, and they cowered, fleeing instantly.

Through this picture, God showed me that like a mama bear, He comes to our aid before we call. Before an audible sound passes our lips, He's there, protecting us from demonic forces, seen or unseen. *"He understands our thoughts; He comprehends our path, and is acquainted with all of our ways. He knows every word on our tongue"* (Psalm 139:2).

Although fear can be relentless, Jesus is more so. Demonic spirits may intimidate you, but Jesus defeated them at the cross. And because God is your refuge, strength, and present help in trouble (see Psalm 46:1), when you call on Him, victory is sure!

Obscurity

*And those members of the body which we think to be less honorable,
on these we bestow greater honor.*

1 Corinthians 12:23

One day as I was driving, an elderly man caught my attention in the distance. With Bible in tow, he pressed the button to enter the crosswalk. A prayer and compassion welled up from my spirit, as the man's age and devotion to God were apparent. As my light turned red, the man clutched his Bible, cautiously crossing the street. God showed me two enormous angels, opaque in appearance, floating alongside him, then said, *"I fiercely protect all of My children, but I especially protect My elderly children."*

Ecstatic, I pulled alongside him to share my experience. Before I could fully lower my window to tell him, the man said, "You're an obedient woman. I only live two blocks away." Unexpectedly, the stranger opened the door and sat next to me! Startled, but not sensing any danger, I told my story. He also shared things with me—things which God only knew.

Reaching our destination, he expressed his gratitude, got out of my car, and headed toward the house. I put down my window and asked, "Sir, what's your name?" Responding, he leaned over, and then added, "When you preach to the people, make sure they get born again, baptized in water, and in the Holy Spirit." He knew nothing of the Bible course I had just developed, titled "The 3 B's," referring to the very statement he made.

To my astonishment, he didn't enter the house but a camper in the backyard! Immediately, I thought, *This wasn't of God after all. He lives in a camper; he's a transient!* God dealt with me concerning my hasty judgment, then said, *"I have people all over the world just like My son in this camper—children living in obscurity who are praying and interceding on behalf of My kingdom. I work wherever, however, and through whomever I please."*

Perhaps you've also formed opinions at one time about others based on their circumstances or appearance. Or, maybe other people have done this to you. Just as God looks on our heart and not our appearance, we need to do the same (see 1 Samuel 16:7).

Red Carpet

He made Himself of no reputation, taking the form of a bondservant,
and coming in the likeness of men.

Philippians 2:7

After speaking to me about the elderly man living in obscurity in his camper, the Lord immediately gave me another vision in which a plethora of ministers—men and women dressed in fine clothes, some well-known television personalities, and popular names shepherding mega-congregations—walked a red carpet, while other members of the body of Christ were their adoring fans. The scene was identical to Hollywood's red carpet, where movie stars pose for photos and to savor the praise of their admirers, with fans held at bay by velvet-roped barriers.

The epistle of James reads, *"²For if there should come into your assembly a man with gold rings, in fine apparel, and there should also come in a poor man in filthy clothes, ³and you pay attention to the one wearing the fine clothes and say to him, 'You sit here in a good place,' and say to the poor man, 'You stand there,' or, 'Sit here at my footstool,' ⁴have you not shown partiality among yourselves. And become judges with evil thoughts?"* (James 2:2–4). God showed me that because I considered this man a transient, unknowingly, I concluded that he had little if any value in God's kingdom plan.

God then revealed a much different view of the all-too-familiar Hollywood red carpet, which some in the body of Christ mimic, either by proudly walking the red carpet, or as misguided admiring fans. God showed me the only "red carpet" a Christian should be concerned about walking is the "red carpet" stained with the blood of Jesus. He *alone* is worthy of *all* glory, praise, honor, and unending admiration!

If you're on a spiritual Hollywood red carpet, you can get off at any time. Simply repent, turn from the false fame and adulation of people and to the "red carpet" of Jesus Christ. His is the only "walk of fame" we should ever concern ourselves with. If you're an adoring fan, you can also leave the scene and turn your face to the One who is worthy to receive glory and honor (see Revelation 4:11).

Details, Details

What is man that You are mindful of him,
or the son of man that You take care of him?

Hebrews 2:6

It's amazing that God, the Creator of heaven and earth, the One who rules and reigns supreme, cares about that which concerns us, from the least to the greatest.

Generous supporters, including my husband, financially paved the way for me to take several mission trips to Russia. Many of the native people we spent time with didn't have material extras, so I rarely wore my nicer jewelry. For whatever reason, though, when I traveled to Saint Petersburg, I wore my anniversary diamond ring. While in the country, I didn't have any incidents while wearing the ring—or so I thought.

On my first night home, experiencing jet lag, my bed called my name earlier than usual. That night I dreamt I was in the backseat of a Russian taxi. Upon reaching my destination, I exited the taxi, and as I did, my diamond ring loudly collided with the steel doorframe. Looking at the ring, two of its six prongs had incurred damage to the point where the stone was knocked out of place. Waking up after this vivid dream, I looked at my ring, and to my astonishment, two prongs were bent, and the stone was loose.

In another more recent incident, I was swimming at a campground in South Dakota. I had placed my wedding ring and cell phone in a zipped plastic baggie. As I left the pool and headed toward the cabin, I noticed my ring wasn't in the baggie. My heart sank. This ring was handcrafted for our renewal vows, which Mark presented to me at the Wailing Wall in Jerusalem. I prayed fervently all the way back to the pool, searching diligently as I crossed over grass and pavement. When I came to the pool, relief overtook me when I saw my ring under a lounge chair.

These are but two examples of just how mindful God is of us and how well He takes care of us. We're His children, loved and kept by Him. God chose to protect these gifts not because I'm materialistic, but because they're important to me. If something is dear to you, it's dear to God.

Bought Back

In Him we have redemption through His blood, the forgiveness of sins.

Ephesians 1:7

While preparing for a time of communion, a thought came to me: *"Because of My body and because of My blood you were bought back."*

Once, as slaves of sin, Satan owned us. Thank God, *"¹⁷…though, [we] were slaves of sin, yet [we] obeyed from the heart…. ¹⁸And having been set free from sin by the blood of Jesus, [we] became slaves of righteousness"* (Romans 6:17–18, brackets added).

In the Garden of Eden, God commanded Adam, saying, *"¹⁶Of every tree of the garden you may freely eat; ¹⁷but of the tree of the knowledge of good and evil you shall not eat, for in the day that you eat of it you shall surely die"* (Genesis 2:16–17). Given free will, Adam didn't choose wisely in the Garden and sold mankind into slavery to sin and to the devil.

Will and choice also accompanied Jesus in the Garden of Gethsemane. Praying, He said, *"Father, if it is Your will, take this cup away from Me; nevertheless not My will, but Yours, be done"* (Luke 22:42). It was in the Garden where Jesus chose of His own will to emancipate us from the slavery of sin and death. Both Adam and Jesus were tempted in the Garden, but only Jesus overcame.

The word *redemption* in Ephesians 1:7 denotes a ransom in full. *Redemption's* root definition means "something to loosen with, i.e. a redemption price."[1] First Corinthians 6:20 tells us, *"you were bought at a price."* It was *"not with the blood of goats and calves, but with His own blood"* that Jesus ransomed us from sin and Satan, and back to God. *"…He entered the Most Holy Place once for all, having obtained eternal redemption"* (Hebrews 9:12).

Faith in God alone will not suffice; you must have faith in Jesus Christ, because He paid the price. When you turn to God and receive His ransom price in Jesus Christ, you *"are a Holy People, the Redeemed of the LORD"* (Isaiah 62:12). If you haven't yet placed your faith in Jesus Christ, today is your day of salvation! (See 2 Corinthians 6:2.)

The Coming One

We give You thanks, O Lord God Almighty,
the One who is and who was and who is to come.

Revelation 11:17

It's been Prophesied — It's been Promised —
It requires Patience — It requires Purpose — It will be Powerful

Angels *"prophesied…this same Jesus, who was taken up from you into heaven, will so come in like manner as you saw Him go into heaven"* (Acts 1:11).

"³Scoffers will come in the last days, saying, ⁴'Where is the promise of His Coming?'" As believers, we are to be *"¹²…looking for and hastening the coming of the day of God"* (2 Peter 3:3–4, 12). Let's not be mockers but watchers. Jesus said, *"I say to you all: Watch!"* (Mark 13:37). God fulfilled the appointed time for Jesus' first appearing (see Galatians 4:4). Be assured the Second Coming of Jesus is *pending,* but certain.

A prerequisite for awaiting His return is patience. *"⁷Be patient, brethren, until the coming of the Lord. See how the farmer waits for the precious fruit of the earth, ⁸…you also must be patient. Establish your hearts, for the coming of the Lord is at hand"* (James 5:7–8).

His coming requires purpose. Psalm 90:12, a prayer of Moses, reads: *"Teach us to number our days, that we may gain a heart of wisdom."* Lord, please mold our hearts each day with eternal intentions.

His coming will be powerful! *"Then they will see the Son of Man coming in the clouds with great power and glory"* (Mark 13:26). *"Therefore you also be ready, for the Son of Man is coming at an hour you do not expect"* (Luke 12:40).

Jesus is coming back. Are you ready to greet the Coming One? If you're uncertain, simply believe that Jesus is the Christ, the Son of God. Then, when He does return, assurance is yours of ruling and reigning with Him for all of eternity.

Wrestling for Fun

A Man wrestled with him.

Genesis 32:24

Our family considers Levi's passing a holy day, and each year we do something special. In 2015, on his fifth heavenly birthday, we traveled to Mt. Vernon, Washington, which accommodates the largest producers of tulips in the world, yielding more flowers than the Netherlands.

I asked God for extra strength and to write a special devotion relating to Levi. Reading Psalm 100:1–2, 4, gratitude overflowed my spirit for all God has done and continues to do in our lives since Levi's departure.

"¹Make a joyful shout to the Lord...."
I gave a *joyful* shout that Levi is safe with Jesus.
"²Serve the Lord with gladness; come before His presence with
singing." Gladness filled my heart, knowing one day we'll be
together forever. I was *singing* at the thought of our reunion.
"⁴Enter into His gates with thanksgiving, and into His courts with
praise. Be thankful to Him, and bless His name." Thanksgiving
and *praise* overwhelmed me with Jesus having
kept His promise to heal my broken heart.

Then, as if watching a movie, I saw Levi and Jesus, laughing and wrestling in endless tulip fields. They wrestled for fun, not minding the flowers they were crushing around them. I sensed that the flowers, which possessed the divine ability to spring back unscathed, were delighted with their guests.

I thought the vision was perhaps all in my mind because of our plans to visit the tulip fields, although I'd never seen these fields. When we arrived, the fields were as I saw in the vision—vibrant and endless.

The following day, I saw a Bible footnote about Jacob wrestling with God. I chuckled. Only God could confirm the picture He placed in my spirit and reaffirm His love for me on this bittersweet day. If you need God to do something special for you, be open to however He wishes to speak to you and wherever He chooses to take you—even to the tulip fields!

Rock Energy

For their rock is not like our Rock.

Deuteronomy 32:31

Preparing for my day, I heard the words, *"There is only one Rock that gives energy."* Smiling, I understood what God meant. That one Rock is Jesus Christ (see 1 Corinthians 10:4).

Some people are convinced that stones possess metaphysical properties. A book titled *Love Is in the Earth*, is considered the encyclopedia for crystal and mineral enthusiasts. It boasts a myriad of qualities, which they believe rocks hold: strength, courage, protection, wealth, forgiveness, spiritual understanding, peace, fidelity, love, clarity, healing, creativity, and many more.[1]

Never exposed to this philosophy, the fallacies to which people cling puzzle me. In regards to rocks and stones, the book mentions attributes that are those of the Living Stone, Jesus Christ (see 1 Peter 2:4). An inanimate object, such as a rock hanging from the neck or worn in clothing, holds no energy to save, heal, or deliver as proclaimed.

Clear quartz crystal is the foundation for these believers. In truth, Jesus is the *"Chief Cornerstone, elect, and precious, and whoever believes on Him will not be put to shame"* (1 Peter 2:6). Amber, a fossilized resin, is believed to purify body, mind, and spirit, when in fact, the blood of Jesus alone purifies one's spirit, soul, and body.

David knew his Rock when he said, *"The LORD is my rock and my fortress and my deliverer; My God, my strength, in whom I will trust"* (Psalm 18:2). Another exaggeration is that these rocks communicate, but only the Rock of Israel speaks (see 2 Samuel 23:3).

In biblical times and today, Jesus continues to be a stone of stumbling and a rock of offense for some. Please don't reject the true Cornerstone with the false hope of looking to rocks to save you. If you're not a believer in the Living Stone, hear what God is saying to you today from Isaiah 44:8, *"Is there a God besides Me? Indeed there is no other Rock; I know not one."*

Who's the Judge?

Behold, the Judge is standing at the door!

James 5:9

As a teenager, I formed a negative opinion about my mother's Catholic devotion. Observing people kneeling at her funeral, my aged and critical heart couldn't hide from God, who asked me, *"What's wrong with this posture?"* My heart responded, *"Nothing, Lord; it's a reverent attitude."* Seeing a cross spanning from floor to ceiling with a sculpture of Jesus hanging on it, I heard, *"What do you think of when you see this cross?"* I responded, *"It makes me think of Your sacrifice for us."*

With the pianist seated, I was sure Charismatic worship would begin, but instead we opened a hymnal. Then I heard, *"Don't you have a hymnal called the overhead?"* Correction silenced my heart. As the priest read scriptures on love, God spoke again, *"Don't you read these same scriptures in your Bible college class?"* My sheepish answer was, *"Yes, Lord, I do."* At the foot of my mother's casket, God's rebuke pierced my heart. It was so gentle, I had to I ask, *"Lord, are You correcting me?"*

Days later, asleep in my bed at 3:00 a.m., I awoke to a loud, audible knock on my bedroom door. Startled, I sat straight up. "Come in!" I said, thinking it was one of my children. There was no response. Then I heard, *"Behold I stand at the door and knock."* I understood that the knock was from the Lord Himself, but He spoke no further.

That morning, preparing to teach my Bible college class, I read James 5:9, *"Behold, the Judge is standing at the door!"* Confirmation was sure. Then the Holy Spirit opened Hebrews 12:9 to me: *"We have had human fathers who corrected us, and we paid them respect. Shall we not much more readily be in subjection to the Father of spirits and live?"* God lovingly told me He was the Father of my mother's spirit, and I had no place to judge her faith.

Perhaps the Lord has been knocking on the door of your heart in regards to prejudices or preconceived judgments. If so, freely allow Him to deal with those thoughts, opinions, or actions that weigh your heart with judgment instead of mercy.

MGM

Blessed be the Lord, who daily loads us with benefits.

Psalm 68:19

Once, when accepting an invitation to speak at a Bible college, I asked the Lord for a Missile Guided Message. My desire was for God to give me something that would hit the "bull's eye" in the hearts of those attending. Forgetting this detail, a couple of months later as I prayerfully prepared, I sensed God say, *"I am going to give you an MGM."* I questioned, "An MGM?" I realized that our Father has a sense of humor, as the thought came to me, a *Missile Guided Message!*

After this prayer conversation, I began to think of how a heat-seeking missile operates. The infrared homing device requires a heat source as its target, and once locked on, there's no escaping contact. With this illustration, I thought of the Holy Spirit as an infrared homing device and mankind as His target. With mankind as a heat source, we're the target onto which He can lock and launch His love and blessings.

"The eyes of the Lord run to and fro throughout the whole earth" (2 Chronicles 16:9). Like the pilot of a fighter jet flying to and fro in the sky seeking heat targets for destruction, God goes to and fro seeking hearts, or targets hot with anticipation—onto which He can launch His blessings, as He *"daily loads us with benefits."*

No matter how difficult life's circumstances get, God's only desire for us is good. I personally don't know of a single parent whose desire is not to daily load their children with love and benefits. We feed, clothe, house, protect, and counsel our kids, and then provide extras to help them on their way with all God called them to be.

God's desire is to bless everyone, including the unthankful and evil, who are cold targets that resist those blessings. Don't be a cold target, but instead an expectant red hot one that will receive all of God's benefits and blessings provided by Jesus.

Lord...Please!

O LORD God...please give me success this day.

Genesis 24:12

When Abraham's servant sat at a water well, wife hunting for Abraham's son, Isaac, he prayed our opening verse, *"O LORD God of my master Abraham, please give me success this day...."* As the women came to draw water, the servant said to God, *"14Let it be that the young woman to whom I say, 'Please let down your pitcher that I may drink,' and she says, 'Drink, and I will also give your camels a drink'—let her be the one You have appointed for Your servant Isaac. 15And it happened, before he had finished speaking, that behold, Rebekah...came out with her pitcher on her shoulder"* (Genesis 24:14–15).

God answered his prayer! Like Abraham's servant, I needed God's guidance during my grief process. Otherwise, I'd still be in a fetal position today on my bed. Reading our opening passage of Scripture, like Abraham's servant, I prayed:

"O Lord God...please give me success this day. What should I do? Please be my guide." Before I finished speaking, God answered my prayer by illuminating the words of Jehoshaphat in 2 Chronicles 20:12, *"God...we do not know not what to do, but our eyes are upon You"* (NIV).

"O Lord God, I'm confused. Please lead me into truth." Instead of confusion, they shall rejoice (see Isaiah 61:70). *"The Spirit of truth, has come, He will guide you into all truth"* (John 16:13).

O Lord God, I'm angry. Please be my peace. *"Be angry, and do not sin"* (Ephesians 4:26). *"These things I have spoken to you, that in Me you may have peace"* (John 16:33).

For me, these emotions were a part of a healthy grieving process. As I walked through the different stages of my grief with the Lord in prayer, He gave me success. If you're grieving today or need success in any area of your life, don't be hard on yourself. Turn your heart to God in prayer like Abraham's servant did, and He will grant you success.

Divine Housing

Paul dwelt two whole years in his own rented house.

Acts 28:30

For two years as we prayed for the sale of our home, it seemed as if the heavens were brass, meaning our prayers weren't getting through. Then one week after Levi passed away, the Lord spoke to me, *"When the house sells, look to live on the west side of the city."* Great comfort overwhelmed me and my husband, as we were incapable of making decisions of any kind. I assumed the house would be selling any day, but God had a different plan.

We continued to live in our home for another year and a half. When we received an offer, the Lord led me to Acts 28:30 to show me that Paul lived in a rented house. We agreed that God's direction was for us to rent.

Reminded of God's words, we rented a house on the west side of town that was suitable for our family. I heard the Lord say, *"This is the home you prayed for."* I asked the realtor if we could rent for more than one year, because I knew I wouldn't be able to move again after all I'd been through. "Actually, this home is available with a two-year lease," she answered. Then in my heart, I heard, *"Paul dwelt two whole years in his own rented house"* (Acts 28:30).

As I drove from the house, within two blocks in a city of 500,000 people, I noticed a vehicle with the bumper sticker made in memory of our son. It read: "Remember Levi, live like Jesus." The love of God flooded my heart, and I knew that, at least temporarily, I was home.

When we receive Christ, the promise of John 14:2 is ours: *"In My Father's house are many mansions; if it were not so, I would have told you. I go to prepare a place for you."* But, He also has places on earth prepared just for us. Be sure to pray and receive God's direction before making any moves, and He'll lead you to your perfect spot.

Combat Armor

Put on the whole armor of God...having girded your waist with truth, having put on the breastplate of righteousness, and having shod your feet with the preparation of the gospel of peace...taking the shield of faith with which you will be able to quench all the fiery darts of the wicked one...take the helmet of salvation, and the sword of the Spirit, which is the word of God.

Ephesians 6:11, 14–17

Because of Jesus, the war for us to become in right standing with God is over. Although Jesus disarmed Satan at the cross, the devil is in continual attack mode; therefore, our conflict with this defeated foe continues.

You've heard the expression "dressed for battle." The dress code for soldiers, otherwise known as "battle rattle," consists of several different elements. For example, one piece of body armor, in the form of Kevlar, is bullet-resistant chest protection from life-threatening projectiles. Saints also wear protective clothing, tailor made by Jesus, in the form of the breastplate of righteousness, which protects us from eternal death.

In earlier wars, soldiers carried necessary field equipment on a waist belt, such as guns, grenades, and ammunition. For believers, a spiritual belt of truth supplies us with strength in the battle. In regards to foot protection, combat boots are essential. Fellow soldiers, covering our feet with the gospel of peace is a must. We also wield a shield, called faith, which snuffs out all the fiery darts, or missiles, of the enemy. Since head protection in the fight is mandatory, we wear the helmet of salvation. To cut and gut the enemy, we swing an incredibly sharp two-edged sword, which is the Word of God (see Hebrews 4:12).

A soldier's uniform is not only for protection, but it also communicates affiliation. Like the dapper troops standing at attention, I am honored and aware that I'm well dressed in the armor God has provided for His Heavenly Armed Forces. You, too, are a part of this military parade, *if* you have received Jesus as the Lord of your life.

Are you standing at attention, dressed in God's spirit-issued battle rattle? Daily put on His grace, truth, and faith. In prayer, take up the sword of the Spirit, and you'll find yourself "dressed for battle" and ready for any war Satan tries to draw you into.

Greatest Wedding Ever

*Let us rejoice and give Him glory, for the marriage of the Lamb has come,
and His wife has made herself ready.
Blessed are those who are called to the marriage supper of the Lamb!*

Revelation 19:7, 9

As I prepared for my Christian covenant-wedding day, wanting everything to be just right, I took the smallest, seemingly unimportant details to God in prayer. Scripture promises that as we do this, God will direct our paths (see Proverbs 3:6).

When I thought about my bridal bouquet, Isaiah 1:18 came to mind: *"Though your sins are like scarlet, they shall be as white as snow."* At one time all of our sins were red like scarlet; however, God's plan for the blood of Jesus has made us all as white as snow. My spray of flowers, although not elaborate, consisted of one red rose, two white roses, and white baby's breath. The red rose represented the blood of Jesus, the two white ones symbolized my fiancé and me as *"white as snow,"* and the white baby's breath represented the Holy Spirit—the breath of the Almighty.

Some might consider this attention to detail unnecessary. However, like an earthly bride, Jesus also cares about wedding details. The heart of a woman with regard to her wedding day is the very heart of Jesus and the wedding He's preparing for you and me.

Friend, let me advise you, you cannot attend the wedding without the proper garment! Matthew 22:11–12 read, *"¹¹But when the king came in to see the guests, he saw a man there who did not have on a wedding garment. ¹²So he said to him, 'Friend, how did you come in here without a wedding garment?' And he was speechless."*

To acquire the proper garment, you must believe and receive Jesus' invitation of eternal life, to know Him and walk with Him. He clothes you with the garments of salvation and covers you with the robe of righteousness (see Isaiah 61:10), and with these you are invited in.

There is an RSVP included in your invitation to the "Marriage Supper of the Lamb." How will you respond to the greatest wedding ever?

The Twelve's Inheritance

For the children ought not to lay up for the parents,
but the parents for the children.

2 Corinthians 12:14

The monsignor officiating my dad's funeral referenced the gifts of wood my father had designed over the years for his twelve children. At the time, our opening scripture came to mind. Not only did my dad give earthly gifts to his children, but most importantly, our parents laid up for us spiritually, as they prayed for their children daily.

Because of my parents' prayers, they laid a spiritual foundation of salvation, which ushered in God's blessings for our taking—for me and my siblings, as well as our children, and our children's children. Jesus also laid up for His children. Not only did He pave the way, He paid the way, and He continues to pray the way for us to receive His inheritance, which He so lavishly provided.

The scriptures say, *"...as many as received Him, to them He gave the right to become children of God, to those who believe in His name"* (John 1:12). Not everyone is a child of God. In Acts 13:10, Paul spoke to Elymas the sorcerer, saying, *"...you son of the devil, you enemy of all righteousness, will you not cease perverting the straight ways of the Lord?"* In 2 Thessalonians 3:2, we also find Paul asking for prayer for deliverance from unreasonable and wicked men, for not all have faith.

In order to become a child of God, biblical instructions are clear: believe and receive the atoning work of Jesus. *"Repent, and let every one of you be baptized in the name of Jesus Christ for the remission of sins; and you shall receive the gift of the Holy Spirit"* (Acts 2:38). By repenting, we turn from sin to God.

Are you God's child? If so, continue receiving what He's freely given and laid up for you. But, if you find yourself in a spiritual orphanage, know that Jesus already signed and sealed your adoption papers at the cross with His blood. Being adopted is extremely special; it means Jesus hand picked you! His arms are open wide. Believe in Jesus as your Lord and Savior, and lay hold of your God-given right to become His child.

Forsaken?

My God, My God, why have You forsaken Me?

Psalm 22:1

In Psalm 22 David prophesies what Jesus would one day cry out to His Father on the cross: *"My God, My God, why have You forsaken Me?"* (Matthew 27:46).

Nine months had passed since Levi's entrance into heaven. No one can comprehend the utter anguish of separation that occurs with the death of a child or someone close and dear unless that person has personally walked that path.

With Levi living at home we were accustomed to his presence. My longing for him plummeted to depths of my being that I didn't even know existed. This feeling made me so uneasy; it was something that I couldn't comprehend, bear, or deal with. I thank Jesus that He carried our sorrow for us.

In my anguish, people who lacked experience with grief told me my sorrow was self-centered. "After all," they said, "your son is happy with His Savior." Fortunately, Jesus spoke life-giving words to me when He said, *"Sharon, as the Son of Man, I wasn't only separated from My Father as I bore the sins of the world, I also experienced the anguish of separation from My Father so I could bear witness with you, being separated from Levi in his physical death—a very real and very painful process."*

If you've experienced separation due to death, Jesus understands. Military families comprehend the pain. Holocaust victims understand, as they also endured horrific separation when families were pulled apart after exiting the rail cars. Others may endure geographical separation from loved ones.

When I think of my unbearable load with separation, I think of the help God provided for Jesus, such as Simon of Cyrene bearing His cross (see Matthew 27:32). As the Son of Man, Jesus had help carrying His load. Do you think He will do less for you? Ask the Lord for His help in your time of need. He'll never forsake you.

Intentional Acts of Kindness

The LORD will perfect that which concerns me.
Psalm 138:8

I n our grief process following Levi's heavenly departure, many months passed without my husband and me getting necessary things accomplished. With Mark living and working in Canada for several months and me feeling like I had assumed the role of a widow, important matters fell by the wayside.

I had planned to attend an Independence Day barbeque and fireworks celebration in a nearby city, and my only transportation at the time was our Dodge Ram truck that Mark left with me. Lying in bed before falling asleep, a picture of the license plate of the truck crossed my mind. I asked God, "Do You want me to look at that plate?" Sensing confirmation from Him, I headed to the driveway with a flashlight to check it out. To my surprise, the plate had expired six months earlier. God is a protector of women, and His favor obviously surrounds my husband, as authorities had not stopped or fined him!

This incident was a big deal to me. Not only did God show Himself once again to be up close and personal, but He also kept me from a fine that could've emptied my wallet. And, He prevented me from having to sit at the DMV, which in my estimation would've been greater punishment than a fine.

You've probably heard the phrase, "random acts of kindness." Random acts are undirected or casual acts. But, with calculated and deliberate "intentional" acts of kindness," God gives attention to both the smallest and the greatest details of our lives. Today's writing mimics what King David said about the Lord: "I remember the days of old. I ponder all your great works and think about what you have done" (Psalm 145:3).

What are some intentional acts of kindness that God has done for you? Because God is good to all, I'm confident you can think of at least one, if not many. Starting today, be on the lookout for God's acts of kindness toward you—both big and small!

Faith Requires Something

For as the body without the spirit is dead, so faith without works is dead also.

James 2:26

The news of my seventy-seven-year-old mother's death came unexpectedly. Her departure was my first experience of great personal loss. At her gravesite, earth bestowed a beautiful spring day. I could sense God's presence in every way. One thing I remember so vividly was the weather—a perfect seventy degrees with a gentle breeze and sunshine: *heavenly.*

With the casket set just above the dirt of the ground, my family and I stood reverently as the priest presided over my mother's burial. Beautiful pink roses, which my dad had selected, adorned the light-gray casket. Memories of her life as far back as I could think flooded my heart.

As I reminisced, I was staring at, but looking past, my mother's casket. God suddenly made His presence known to me, and said, *"As the body without the spirit is dead, so faith without works is dead."* In that moment a revelation came to my heart: My mother's spirit departed, and her earthly body would never move again; therefore, faith without action is as dead as her lifeless body!

Faith: We can't live without it, can't leave home without it, the just live by it, and it pleases God. But, faith requires action!

James 2:18 and 20 record, *"*[18]*...'You have faith, and I have works.' Show me your faith without your works, and I will show you my faith by my works....* [20]*O foolish man,...faith without works is dead."* With this example of faith and works, I tell those believing to have a baby, in order to conceive you have to put action to your faith! In addition, if I sat at my computer never taking action to type the words on the page, this book would not be in your hands.

"A man's heart plans his way; but the LORD directs his steps" (Proverbs 16:9). Your act of faith is stepping out and making plans, but the Lord is ultimately the one who directs your steps.

Life Is Not a Cake Walk, but a Faith Walk

…exhorting them to continue in the faith, and saying, "We must through many tribulations enter the kingdom of God."

Acts 14:22

You've probably heard the term, *cakewalk,* which refers to a surprisingly easy task. The kingdom of God is *not* a cakewalk! Through many tribulations we enter the kingdom of God. Matthew 11:12 promises, *"The kingdom of heaven suffers violence, and the violent take it by force."* This certainly doesn't sound like a surprisingly easy task!

Once, while listening to a preacher expound on James 1:2—*"My brethren, count it all joy when you fall into various trials"*—he said, "God brings trials to train us." As a new believer, this statement was like a dagger in my heart. I'd had it hard enough, and now God was going to bring trials? As I studied the passage, I saw something completely different.

In the Greek, the word for *fall* means "to fall into something that is all around."[1] *Various* means "diverse," and a *trial* is "putting to proof…by implication adversity, temptation."[2] Adversity equals misfortune—not God's handiwork! Living in a fallen world, the trials that surround us put us to the test. At times, we fall into them. Maybe we're not paying attention. Or, we could be involved in a spiritual drive-by shooting, caught in the devil's crosshairs of no fault of our own.

God doesn't tempt us, but He does test us. Revelation of His testing came to me with my daughter's approaching driver's test. For the purpose of testing her skills, I took her to unfamiliar territory. Coming to a four-way stop, she didn't see the sign. I scanned the intersection, and there were no cars in sight, so knowing no harm would come to her, I didn't tell her when she ran the stop sign. I used this test to reveal her need for improvement. I believe God works with us similarly.

Another definition of *cakewalk* is a "strutting dance, popularized by minstrel shows in the late 19th century."[3] Jesus sent His Holy Spirit so you can walk gracefully with Him in the midst of all of life's difficulties, dangers, and snares. Stick close to Him, and you'll also receive a prize: a deeper faith walk.

At Home with God

The cup of blessing which we bless, is it not the communion of the blood of Christ? The bread which we break, is it not the communion of the body of Christ?

1 Corinthians 10:16

As mentioned previously, I weaved the Lord's personal revelation of communion into the pages of this book. And, like the apostle Paul, what I received from the Lord in regards to communion, I'm delivering to you (see 1 Corinthians 11:23).

With the exception of one time, all of my communion moments written in this book took place in the privacy of my home and not in a church service with other believers. In this intimate setting, Jesus meets me personally and powerfully, as I remember the sacrifice of His body and His blood symbolically through crackers and grape juice: *"24And when He had given thanks, He broke it and said, 'Take, eat; this is My body which is broken for you; do this in remembrance of Me.' 25In the same manner He also took the cup after supper, saying, 'This cup is the new covenant in My blood. This do, as often as you drink it, in remembrance of Me.'"* (1 Corinthians 11:24–25).

Maybe the concept of taking communion at home is new to you. Maybe you've been instructed that, as a "lay person," the clergy must present you with the elements of the body and blood of Christ. But, if you're born again, God's Spirit lives within you, and you've been given the divine privilege of taking communion and meeting with your Lord anytime and anywhere. Corporate communion is biblical and beneficial, but it's not necessary to enter a building to remember the sacrifice of Jesus Christ. This is the beauty of the indwelling Spirit—continual fellowship with God.

By now, you may have read some of these communion writings. As you read how God met me personally through communion, extend your faith to believe that He'll meet you in real and personal ways as well.

Head to Toe

The whole head is sick, and the whole heart faints. From the sole of the foot even to the head, there is no soundness in it, but wounds and bruises and putrefying sores; they have not been closed or bound up, or soothed with ointment.

Isaiah 1:5–6

It's a beautiful thing when we become born again. In 2 Corinthians 5:17 the Bible refers to us as "new creations," reminding us that old things have passed away and all things have become new. In Christ, with our old man crucified (see Romans 6:6), our new man emerges. However, the old man of every believer shadows like a flatfoot—better known as a private investigator—and ditching him is a lifelong process. We can become *out of pocket,* meaning the watcher has lost sight of the subject.[1] In this case, as we renew our mind to the Word of God, as watchers of our new man, we lose sight of the subject—our old man!

As a new believer, eager to rid my life of old soul habits and not understanding that the Holy Spirit is the Counselor, I considered Christian counseling. Mulling the idea over with a friend, she blurted out, "Draw the bloodline and get over it!" I didn't care for her less-than-compassionate response. First, I didn't know how to "get over it." Second, I didn't know what "it" was. When she left my home, the Counselor Himself, the Holy Spirit, spoke our opening scripture to me.

God lovingly showed me that, as a new creation, I needed to live out of my new head. My old, un-renewed mind caused my soul to experience wounds, bruises, and putrefying sores not yet closed, bound up, or soothed with the healing ointment of the Holy Spirit's revelation. At the Lord's direction, I made an appointment for divine counseling, and through Him, healing manifested as He promised.

If you're hurting today, turn to the Healer. He applies His atoning work and the medicinal liniment of His Word to any afflicted area. What God did for me, He'll do for you. He's no respecter of persons (see Acts 10:34).

Fruitful Land

Joseph named his second son Ephraim, for he said,
"God has made me fruitful in this land of my grief."

Genesis 41:52 (NLT)

My heart skipped reading this scripture, as God spoke to me: *"I'm giving you the spiritual name of Ephraim, as I'm going to make you fruitful in the land of your grief."* Having walked through the land of unimaginable grief during the agonizing months and years following Levi's death, God's words were life to me.

At seventeen, most young men are looking forward to their future, but Joseph's future appeared to be stolen at the hands of his jealous brothers and his abrupt imprisonment. His grief, however, was the very vehicle God used to produce fruit.

God's plan emerged after He gave Joseph the interpretation of Pharaoh's dream. To implement the dream, Pharaoh positioned Joseph second in command over all of Egypt. The dream of severe famine happened just as Joseph said. When the people cried out to Pharaoh for food, he told them, "Go to Joseph." Joseph opened the storehouses and distributed grain to the Egyptians. People came from all of the surrounding countries to purchase grain (see Genesis 41:53–57).

The Lord spoke to me a second time, saying, *"Like Joseph, I've been filling your storehouse with the grain of My Word. The Egyptians represent the world, and My followers represent believers; both are coming to you for spiritual grain. I'm a type of Pharaoh, only I rule supremely throughout the land. Although the people don't realize it, they're crying out to Me for the Bread of Life as they cried out to Pharaoh for food. My Spirit will send them to you, as Pharaoh sent the people to Joseph."*

Jesus has already purchased grain for today's starving world. Born in the city of Bethlehem, or the House of Bread, Jesus is the Bread of Life. You also have barns that God has filled or longs to fill. There are people in your midst who are starving in the famine. God is able to make you fruitful, even in a land of immense grief, so that you can allocate the grain of His Word to them.

Three Monkeys

Depart from evil, and do good.

Psalm 37:27

This morning a picture came to me while taking communion. Jesus stood behind me with His nail-pierced hands and covered my ears. I sensed His hands protecting me from hearing evil. *"Take heed what you hear"* (Mark 4:24). From this same position, He sheltered my eyes to guard them from seeing evil. *"I will set nothing wicked before my eyes"* (Psalm 101:3). A third time, He gently placed His strong hands over my mouth so that I would not speak evil. *"Keep your tongue from evil, and your lips from speaking deceit"* (Psalm 34:13). I couldn't help but think of the three Japanese monkeys and the well-known proverb they embody together: see no evil, hear no evil, speak no evil.

Evil is something that's profoundly immoral and associated with the forces of the devil. Evil isn't limited to acts such as Hitler's or serial killers'. Closer to home, evil includes worthless, depraved, and injurious thoughts or actions that are harmful and undesirable, and that manifest in people.

Jesus said in John 17:15, *"I do not pray that You should take them out of the world, but that You should keep them from the evil one."* As Christians passing through this world, we don't have to look for evil; it surrounds us. Riddled with it, society manifests evil through billboards, media, movies, music, and fashion. If we're not careful to keep our heart with all diligence, we can be tempted by its pull. By covering themselves, the Japanese monkeys disassociated themselves from every evil. As parents, we at times have covered our children's eyes, ears, and mouths, protecting them from depraved behavior.

Remembering the nail-pierced hands of Jesus and the blood that covered them, He also provides protection, disassociating us with evil's tug and keeping our soul gates from the contamination of living in this world, which is *"under the sway of the wicked one"* (1 John 5:19).

Although you may be surrounded by evil, you don't have to be affected by it. As you spend time with God in communion, prayer, or Bible reading, you'll find His nail-pierced hands covering and protecting your heart, as well as your eyes, ears, and mouth.

Rotten Fruit

Mercy triumphs over judgment.

James 2:13

The Christian life doesn't consist of simply pressing the "Easy" button. During a time in my teaching ministry, I came against forces of darkness through some brothers and sisters in Christ. One morning in prayer, I sensed the Lord telling me that people would come against me at work. There, the Lord directed me to the very person who would betray me.

As I was walking down the hall to teach my class, I had an open vision. I saw the Holy Spirit and myself standing side by side at a podium in the middle of a public rodeo arena located in my community. Sand carpeted the arena floor, and there were grandstands located in the north and south sides of the arena. The north stands were teeming with people, but oddly, the south stands held no spectators. Suddenly, the people from the north bleachers began to throw rotten fruit at me. Before it could hit me, I disappeared. The Holy Spirit now stood alone. In the vision, I wondered where I went.

The Spirit said, *"You are hidden with Christ in God"* (Colossians 3:3), meaning I was under His protection from the rotten fruit being thrown. Standing tall at the platform, the Holy Spirit took all of the hits of rotten fruit that were meant for me, which were symbolic of judgment and criticism. He informed me, that when people—including me—engage in judgment and criticism, rotten fruit is being thrown.

In my vision, the north stands represented the graduates, and the south represented the undergraduates. Surprisingly, the upper classmen were the ones throwing rotten fruit, when they were supposed to be examples to the underclassmen.

Today, ask the Lord to reveal if you're throwing rotten fruit while you sit idly in the stands of criticism, or if you're the one working hard, and the rotten fruit is being thrown at you. Either way, keep your heart with all diligence, and with a Christ-like attitude, follow after mercy, which triumphs over judgment.

The Mentor

*Clearly you are an epistle of Christ…written not with ink
but by the Spirit of the living God.*

2 Corinthians 3:3

In my mind, there are two types of mentors: those from whom we learn excellence, and those from whom we learn what not to do, meaning they provide a bad example.

At the cave of Adullam, David trained a motley crew. *"Everyone who was in distress, everyone who was in debt, and everyone who was discontented gathered to him. So he became captain over them"* (1 Samuel 22:2). Jesus tutored the Twelve. Paul instructed the Gentiles. Peter taught the Jews. The Spirit of God, through the Word of God and relationship, mentors believers in Christ. As Christ followers, we're also called to mentor, or give of ourselves, in ways that we've freely received.

Although a friend of the family, my husband and I wondered how eighteen-year-old Alan and our ten-year-old Levi came to have such a strong bond. We trusted that God was ordaining the steps of righteous men (or, in this case, young boys).

Eli, an Old Testament priest, and Alan, of the royal priesthood of the New Covenant (1 Peter 2:5), both mentored young boys in the ways of God at Shiloh. In Eli's day, he instructed Samuel, and Shiloh was the house of the Lord. Alan guided Levi, and Shiloh was the name of the ranch on which we lived.

Alan was a living epistle of Christ to Levi: He led by example, and he encouraged Levi in an even closer walk with God through daily prayer, Bible reading, and godly living. Alan's expression of Christ further rooted Levi, preparing him to meet his Lord and Savior at such a young age. I pray that God will bless Alan richly. And for all that he poured into Levi, I pray that God would instill the same consistent love, instruction, devotion, and more into his three boys.

"My beloved brethren, be steadfast, immovable, always abounding in the work of the Lord, knowing that your labor is not in vain in the Lord" (1 Corinthians 15:58). You never know what God is working through you behind the scenes. Each moment of your life counts, so make your moments count for Jesus.

Temptation's Burn

Blessed is the man who endures temptation.

James 1:12

While participating in a muscle fit class at the YMCA, the instructor declared, "You're stronger than the burn in your muscles. You can make it through the exercise!" In that instant, a thought came to me: *We're stronger than the burn of the temptation, and we can make it through the pressure and not give into it.*

First Corinthians 10:13 is a barricade to self-pity: "*No temptation has overtaken you except what is common to mankind. And God is faithful; he will not let you be tempted beyond what you can bear. But when you are tempted, he will also provide a way out so that you can endure it*" (NIV). *Overtake* denotes something that comes upon us suddenly or unexpectedly, which fitly describes temptation's characteristics. Temptation is a hound of the human heart, always looking to overtake us.

When tempted, we're drawn away by the lure of our own desires (see James 1:14). God doesn't tempt us, nor will He allow us to be tempted beyond what we can bear. With the temptation, He'll provide a way out so we can endure it. Through God's Spirit, we have the ability or strength to walk through difficult circumstances with patience. Our escape is the footpath He opens for us to walk away from the temptation's confinement or control. Or, not as exciting, He'll provide the strength to endure under temptation's pressure.

What temptations have you been facing? They come to each one of us without fail. It's important that you "*Watch and pray, lest you enter into temptation. The spirit indeed is willing, but the flesh is weak*" (Matthew 26:41). To overcome, look to 2 Peter 2:9, which assures us that "*the Lord knows how to deliver the godly out of temptations.*"

There Is Life in the Desert

The desert shall rejoice and blossom as the rose.

Isaiah 35:1

Visiting my family in Arizona shed new light on my idea of the desert, which, as a non-desert dweller, I considered a lifeless place. God not only granted me rivers of new revelation concerning the desert, but insight came in regards to the *seeming* "desert experience" in connection with our spiritual life.

To my surprise, I found the desert animated in the springtime, just like any other region. I was fascinated, as cacti and fragrant multicolored flowers bloomed and wildlife greeted springtime. The first animal I encountered besides my family's lively dog was none other than a rattlesnake! Along nature's trail, other less intimidating animals included deer, rabbits, lizards, and various birds.

Because of the Israelites' wilderness journey, at times Christians have likened their relationship with the Lord to the desert: dry or void of His life and presence. Although at times it may *feel* this way, with the Spirit's indwelling presence we don't possess an arid relationship, but one like that of springtime—vibrant and thriving!

The Israelites' journey was anything but lifeless! God was present, supplying their every need, such as water, meat, and manna, which I consider to be a desert dessert: *"the taste of it was like wafers made with honey"* (Exodus 16:31).

Not without desert challenges, the Israelites encountered enemies—snakes and scorpions in the form of Egyptians. Still today, we're surrounded by a spiritually dry and fallen world. However, as we drink from the fountain of God's living water, and not the well of our soul, where water levels fluctuate with the seasons of our circumstances and moods, we'll continue to experience the very life of God in what feels like a desert.

When Jesus is in your desert, because of His life-giving water, you'll experience "life in the desert." As God led the Israelites, He leads you, providing and guiding along any *seeming* desert route and performing mighty miracles on your behalf.

Talkin' 'bout My Girl!

One pearl of great price…

Matthew 13:46

"My girl…talkin' 'bout my girl" are lyrics from a song by the Temptations.[1] Today, I would like to do just that. I have met pearls in my lifetime, but none compares to my daughter, Sasha, my firstborn: my earthly gem and treasure.

While pregnant, with prayerful consideration, we chose the name Sasha, which is of Russian origin, meaning "Helper of Mankind." I knew that "my girl" would one day love and serve Christ, and like Jesus, she would be a helper to mankind.

At the age of three, my daughter gave her life to Jesus and *she chose* to live for Him, which was something I didn't do when I was younger. Now a woman, having graduated college, married, and with a daughter of her own, she continues to fear the Lord and is a blessing to many. True to her name, she gives generously, helping with whatever is in her power to do, not only for our family, but also for those in her community and church.

Even with Sasha being my priceless pearl, after her brother's death, my desire to live diminished. One day, as I prayed for her, God's tangible presence overwhelmed me in the form of love and peace, which completely filled her car where we sat. Holding back tears, I asked, "God, what does this mean?" He responded, *"I'm revealing your reason to live. The love I'm pouring onto you now is the love I want you to pour into her."*

For grieving parents these feelings are common; however, we need God's help in our heartache to see the bigger picture with our surviving, priceless treasures. Still talking 'bout my girl, I am blessed beyond measure to have Sasha in my life, but even more blessed to know that part of my purpose on this earth still involves her and everything that pertains to her, including her husband and our first grandchild.

Now, "talkin' 'bout" your kids, I hope and pray they're as much of a blessing to you as mine are to me. Regard them and treat them in the same manner that God does—as priceless pearls.

Heartfelt Request

Be anxious for nothing.

Philippians 4:6

There was a time when my husband received an invitation to speak at a prayer conference. I was a bit anxious, as it had only been a year and a half since Levi went to be with Jesus. Change or separation of *any kind* was still unsettling for both of us.

During my prayer time, I brought this anxiety to the Lord, when the Holy Spirit quickened a well-known passage of Scripture to me: *"⁶Be anxious for nothing, but in everything by prayer and supplication, with thanksgiving, let your requests be made known to God; ⁷and the peace of God, which surpasses all understanding, will guard your hearts and minds through Christ Jesus"* (Philippians 4:6–7).

This scripture is likely as familiar to you as it was to me. However, the words, *"let your requests be made known to God"* pierced my heart in way they never had before. I understood perfectly what He was asking of me: *"What is your request in this present situation?"* Having read this scripture for years, God's question caught me off-guard, as He'd never asked me this before. I thought before responding, "I want to travel with my husband." Instantly, a tangible peace came over me. Jesus is peace. In His presence, my prayer request was granted, and the anxiety disappeared.

Exactly one year later to the day of my prayer, God spoke these words to me, *"I am faithful as promised. Remember the day I showed you Philippians 4:8? I asked for your request, and you said, 'To travel with my husband.' In that moment, I answered your prayer with peace, guarding your heart and mind. Today, your ticket to travel with your husband was booked!"*

There's not a human on the planet, including infants, who isn't affected by anxiety. Take all your unrest to Him, and pray Philippians 4:6–7. God will be faithful to grant you peace.

Heaven and Earth Working Together

Whatever the LORD pleases He does, in heaven and in earth.

Psalm 135:6

It had been eighteen months since Levi departed for heaven. Excitement wasn't at the forefront of my life. However, joy welled up in my heart when the opportunity to speak at a young adult conference arose.

When preparing in prayer for the meeting, a vision came to me where I saw an angel and my son in heaven discussing the plans for the meeting. God was up to something good, showing me how much heaven is involved with earth, and earth with heaven.

Although God's presence permeated the atmosphere of that meeting, there was no visible evidence of divine activity. This didn't discourage me, as I live by faith and not sight.

Three weeks later, after delivering a Sunday sermon, a man approached me and shared an amazing story. His family was hosting a female Korean high school exchange student. Although sharing Christ with her in word and example, they observed little response. The young woman came home from this meeting and told her host family that she had a vision of Jesus hugging me as I spoke about Levi. In this picture, she said, "Jesus revealed to her that the love He had for me was the same love He had for her." Because of the Holy Spirit's work through the vision, she gave her life to Christ that night.

Maybe heaven's residents discuss kingdom purposes in relation to earthlings' eternal destinies more than we know. God chose a young girl from Korea to attend a meeting He pre-ordained. Going a divine step further, I discovered the young woman was also a close friend with the family of Levi's best friend.

Heaven and earth may seem light years apart, and that may be true physically, but that day God chose to bring the two closer than I could've ever imagined. What ways have you experienced heaven invading earth when you pray? Maybe you've sensed the Holy Spirit actively working to bring salvation, healing, or revelation in ways that have touched you and those around you. Continue to pray, *"Your kingdom come. Your will be done on earth as it is in heaven"* (Matthew 6:10).

Don't Worry, Be Happy

Do not worry...

Matthew 6:25

One day I sensed God telling me that I wasn't experiencing joy to the degree that it's available to me. Unknowingly, I entertained worry, which tried to steal that joy. Because Job 5:17 reads, *"...happy is the man* [or woman] *whom God corrects"* (brackets added), I am therefore one happy woman!

At this time, Bobby McFerrin's song "Don't Worry, Be Happy" came to mind: *"Here's a little song I wrote/You might want to sing it note for note/Don't worry, be happy/ In every life we have some trouble/When you worry you make it double/ Don't worry, be happy."*[1]

Since my personality is on the serious side, a prayer of mine has been to stagger like a drunken man, intoxicated with the joy of the Lord, just as the disciples appeared drunk to onlookers when they were filled with the Holy Spirit of Promise (see Acts 2:15). God has answered my prayer to varying degrees. However, after all I've been through, I still anticipate a big, God overdose of "holy laughter." Hopefully, I won't be rolling out of control on the floor at a public meeting, but maybe in the privacy of my living room!

When our daughter attended Christian grade school, my husband and I went to a parent-teacher meeting. We were so full of the joy of the Spirit, the teacher asked, "Have you been drinking?" My heart screamed with laughter. Intoxicated with the joy of God, he thought we were drunk!

Have you seen the world that surrounds you lately? Who doesn't need a deluge of the joy of Jesus, including the world? Jesus told us in John 15:11, *"...I have spoken to you, that My joy may remain in you, and that your joy may be full."* Joy is important because it works like a medicine keeping the heart healthy, happy, and free.

Because of the new covenant, a merry heart is available to us. Let's take full advantage of it. Don't allow the devil or circumstance to steal your joy. There is power when you "laugh it up!"

It's Raining Bread

Behold, I will rain bread from heaven for you.

Exodus 16:4

After reading Exodus 16:4, I complained to God, "Where *is* Your bread from heaven?" Knowing God is good, I'm not proud of my disrespectful tone. He made the above scripture come alive to me, saying, *"Behold, I will rain bread from heaven for you."* When God spoke, faith erupted! I understood financial provision was a done deal. I didn't know how, but I believed He was going to rain bread from heaven for me by the close of the day.

At times, like the apostle Paul, I too feel pressed on all sides but not crushed (see 2 Corinthians 4:8). Are you encouraged as I am when reading Paul's words, *"I know how to live on almost nothing or with everything. I have learned the secret of living in every situation, whether it is with a full stomach or empty, with plenty or little"* (Philippians 4:12, NLT)?

Things happen. Do you think Paul's tent sales fluctuated? I do! Many glamorize those in biblical times, as if they were unlike us, but Paul also lived in a fallen world. My husband's art sales fluctuate. When unemployment is high, people purchase necessities, not artwork. The world's economic and financial systems may collapse, but our security as believers is found in Jesus.

During this time, my friend Diane called unexpectedly and asked me to meet for coffee. Upon my arrival she handed me an envelope, saying, "Lee and I want to bless you. This is what the body of Christ does; we help each other."

First John 3:17–18 read, *"17If anyone has material possessions and sees a brother or sister in need but has no pity on them, how can the love of God be in that person? 18Dear children, let us not love with words or speech but with actions and in truth"* (NIV). Our friends, emulating Christ, lived this truth to the fullest. When I opened the envelope, I found it contained $1000.

Do you need God to rain bread from heaven for you today? Be encouraged from my testimony of His faithfulness. He never fails at keeping His Word to His children.

Nailed It!

Having wiped out the handwriting of requirements that was against us, which was contrary to us. And He has taken it out of the way, having nailed it to the cross.

Colossians 2:14

N*ailed it* is an expression meaning, "to do something perfectly or successfully."[1]

When my husband and I drive around Colorado Springs, "nailed it" is a regular part of our vocabulary, meaning we perfectly and successfully hit another pothole! The city promises to deliver repairs to wipe out the potholes, but we've yet to see this promise kept.

God shared a comparison with me that isn't meant to demean what Christ did on the cross, but it revealed a modern-day analogy.

We can say that Jesus completely and perfectly performed the Law, or that He "nailed it" by wiping out the handwriting of requirements that was against us. These requirements, given at Mt. Sinai, were in the Law of Moses. They included the Law of sin and death and the Law of works, which contained bondage, curse, and guilt. Demanding righteousness, they exposed and remembered sin, and were powerless to save, redeem, or satisfy.

Faulty, weak, and unprofitable, the Law held no miracle power. The Law required numerous animal sacrifices and many priests to atone for sin. It was an old way, lacking mercy and possessing condemnation. Additionally, the Law also left no inheritance.

Unlike the city of Colorado Springs, Jesus delivered on His promise. As Eternal High Priest, and with one blood sacrifice, He "nailed it" perfectly and completely at Calvary. We no longer have to hit the potholes of the Law to be made right with God. We now have smooth access through Jesus, our new and living way to better promises. We live by the law of Christ, of righteousness, and of the Spirit, and by the law of grace and faith. Furthermore, Jesus left an inheritance in the form of eternal life—a free gift to all who believe in His name.

If you believe that Jesus "nailed it," you can also nail it by making the right choice to believe and follow *"the law of the Spirit of life in Christ Jesus [which] has made [you] free from the law of sin and death"* (Romans 8:2, brackets added).

Loose Lips

Death and life are in the power of the tongue.

Proverbs 18:21

"Loose lips sink ships" is an American English idiom that means "unguarded talk may give useful information to the enemy." This phrase was coined as a slogan during WWII as part of the U.S. Office of War Information's attempt to limit the possibility of people inadvertently giving useful information to enemy spies.[1]

Although ships are large and driven by fierce winds, James writes a about a very small rudder that turns them wherever the captain desires. He correlates the rudder with our tongue—so little a member, yet it steers our lives in one direction or another (see James 3:4).

For navy personnel, exercise-related activities can take place in just about any setting, from a state-of-the-art gym, to an open field, to the flight deck of an aircraft carrier. On the voyage of this sea of life, each of us must continually engage in daily exercise to tighten and tone our lips. We see results of this conditioning when we refuse to give the devil any place with negative or careless words. Psalm 34:13 also presents us with a navigational directive for our mouth: Steer clear of an evil tongue and your lips from speaking lies.

Through loose lips, the devil gains legal access to us and attempts to sink the dreams, plans, and purposes that God has for us. But today's good news from Proverbs 13:3 trumps any of his evil plans: *"He who guards his mouth preserves his life, but he who opens wide his lips shall have destruction."*

It's no wonder James wrote about the member that cannot be tamed: our tongue. We bless God with it and curse men with it. Out of the same mouth proceed blessing and cursing. These things ought not to be so, says James (see James 3:8–10). The Bible speaks of many different types of tongues—backbiting, false, wise, and gentle—and the choice is always before us as to how we will use ours.

Don't have loose lips! Think before you speak, and use your words for good and not evil.

Wonders of His Love

He went into a city called Nain.

Luke 7:11

Good things happen wherever Jesus walks, including in the ancient city of Nain. At its gate, Jesus encountered a funeral procession where a widow's only son was being carried in an open coffin.

Beginning with Adam, God's perfect plan of provision for a woman came through her family's male headship. Biblically, provision for a widow without sons was to come from any of her husband's surviving brothers. Apart from this, there was little hope for her livelihood.

As a defender of widows (see Psalm 68:5), Jesus was in the right place at the right time. Having compassion on this widow, *"He came and touched the open coffin, and those who carried him stood still"* (Luke 7:14). Then, Jesus spoke to her dead son, *"Young man, I say to you, arise"* (Luke 7:14). He sat up and began speaking, and Jesus presented the boy to his mother (see Luke 7:15).

Reading verse 15, the fire of heaven torched my heart. Although I'm not a widow, nor was my son physically raised from the dead, he *is* my only son, and I often think of my heavenly reunion with him.

As a mother, I once had more interest in seeing Levi in heaven than I did in seeing Jesus. For those of you in my shoes, you understand perfectly, and amazingly, so does Jesus! If the Lord tarries in His return, I've envisioned me greeting Jesus, all the while looking over His shoulder for Levi. Jesus gloriously changed this picture for me. He branded my heart with the idea that I won't need to look for Levi because, as Jesus presented the widow's son to his mother, Jesus assured me, He'll present my son to me.

If you've experienced someone dear to your heart passing on to be with Jesus, be hopeful and encouraged from Scripture that what Jesus did for the widow of Nain, He'll do for you. He'll either bring your loved one back to you, or, as He'll do for me, He'll present that person to you when you reach heaven.

Fish Food

Then Jesus said to them, "Children, have you any food?"
They answered Him, "No." And He said to them,
"Cast the net on the right side of the boat, and you will find some." So they
cast, and now they were not able to draw it in because of the multitude of fish.

John 21:5–6

As a first-year Bible college student reading this passage, I sensed Jesus speaking to me, saying, *"Sharon, do you have any food?"* Thinking He asked me about natural food, I responded exactly like the disciples, "No, Lord, I don't have any food; I'm in class."

Then He said, *"Do you have spiritual food to feed the people to whom I'm sending you?"* My inward response was, *I have some spiritual food because I was a student of the Word before Bible college.* Just like Jesus told His disciples to cast their net on the right side of the boat, He said to me, *"While you're in school, if you'll cast your net on the right side of the boat, you too will find food, so much that your net will yield a multitude of fish."*

God explained to me that the right side of my boat meant a right attitude. I was to cast my net, or attitude, by having the proper behavior toward the authority of the instructors. Only then would God fill my net to overflowing with the food of His Word.

Simon Peter fished all night and caught nothing (see Luke 5:5). Hypothetically, maybe he caught nothing because he cast his net on the left side of the boat in the "frog water" of complaints. "Frog water" is a fishing term referring to murky, slow-moving water where fishing is challenging. When the disciples did as Jesus instructed they weren't able to draw the net in because of the multitude of fish! This kind of haul is the hope of every fisherman. In our obedience, God will fill our net with the multitude of His Word, and in return, our nets will have an abundant quantity of fish in the form of human souls.

Do you have fish food? Is your net full? Or, are you in "frog water"? If the latter, ask the Lord what the proper attitude is that you need to have so your nets will burst at the seams.

Help!

God is our refuge and strength, a very present help in trouble.

Psalm 46:1

Has there been a day where *help* is the only word that rolled off your tongue? For me, today is one of those days. Within six months of this book's conception, I thought it would be complete. However, God had a different plan. A lot of life, healing, and significant changes have taken place since I began. Little did I know that two years later, I'd come to such unexpected turns. Thinking I was finished, I discovered I'd miscounted the number of devotions actually completed. Still needing sixty-five more, all I could say was, "Help!"

Thinking of my own plea, the Beatles' song, "Help!" came to my mind: *"Help! I need somebody…not just anybody…you know I need someone…. Won't you please, please help me?"*[1] Co-writer and Beatles' member John Lennon, said, "When 'Help!' came out, I was actually crying out for help. Most people think it's just a fast rock 'n roll song."[2]

Psalm 54:4 is also a reflection of someone who called for help. King and warrior David, unashamedly declared, *"God is my helper."* What a relief! God is our very present help for any trouble. We're never without it; all we need to say is, "Jesus, help!"

The lyrics to "Help!" continue: *"I never needed anybody's help in any way, but these days are gone."* Thank God, Lennon's independence ended. That to me is a scary place to be, especially if it's independence from God. Not only do we need His everyday help, but also apart from Him, there's no other help or hope for eternal life. Like David, everyone needs to cry, *"Help me now, O Lord my savior"* (Psalm 38:22, GNT)! *"Salvation can be found in no one else* [but Jesus]. *Throughout the whole world, no other name has been given among humans through which we must be saved"* (Acts 4:12, CEB, brackets added).

We can't be self-reliant, self-governing, or separate ourselves from God and win. Where does your help come from? If you're crying for help in all the wrong places, lift up your eyes, because your help comes from the Lord and Him alone (see Psalm 121:1–2).

Nathan David Samuel

Now there stood by the cross of Jesus...

John 19:25

Anger encased my heart, and within days of Levi's death, I said, "Lord, when a person loses a spouse, he or she can remarry. I can't have another son!" In that moment, the Lord said, *"I'll give you a son in Sasha's husband. He'll be an incredible blessing to you and your family."* At this time, our daughter wasn't married, nor was anyone in the forefront, but God calmed my heart with His words.

My husband played a large part in Sasha's choice for a husband, as many nights while I slept Mark prayed over my pregnant womb, not only with our daughter but also with Levi. We spent their lifetimes seeking God in prayer for the spouses our children would one day marry. Our son-in-law is everything we prayed for and more, especially with the name Nathan David Samuel, which means "prophet, king, and priest!"

Six months before their wedding day, God began to speak to me about a wedding toast, quickening John 19:25–26: *"25Now there stood by the cross of Jesus His mother...26When Jesus therefore saw His mother, and the disciple whom He loved standing by, He said to His mother, 'Woman, behold your son!' Then He said to the disciple, 'Behold your mother!'"* Jesus revealed to me that, like Mary, I was at the foot of the cross with the death of my son. The day Nate married our daughter, Sasha, was the day the Lord's word came to pass in my life: *"I'll give you a son in Sasha's husband."*

Through a lifetime of prayer, I trusted that God would guide my children. The decision was made when they were young that I'd love the man whom my daughter chose to marry and the woman my son chose. I love Nate as I love my own son, and I consider him and his family a special gift to us from God.

If your children haven't yet married, now's a good time to begin to pray for their future spouses. If they have already married, it's still not too late. Pray for God's wisdom and direction for them and their future families.

Surprise!

Hear now My words: "If there is a prophet among you, I, the LORD, make Myself known to him in a vision; I speak to him in a dream."

Numbers 12:6

Once in a dream, my husband and I approached the back door of a home unfamiliar to us, yet we lived in the home. Entering the kitchen, we saw Levi through the living room window playing in the front yard with our former family dog, Blackjack, who passed away one year after Levi. My heart leaped, thinking, *Levi's home!* I also wondered what this meant, since he had been a heavenly resident for five years.

Thrilled to see him, Mark and I walked toward the front door to greet him. As with any long, unwanted separation, we exchanged priceless hugs, kisses, and verbal greetings, and then made our way into the house. With continued excitement, I asked, "Levi, what is heaven like?" In the same tone in which he spoke to me when on earth, he said, "Oh, Mom, heaven is such a distraction." With surprise and curiosity, I asked, "How's heaven a distraction?" Then, my alarm woke me.

Later that afternoon, admiring a photograph of Levi, I realized the dream personified his character in ways that the photo could not. The dream, so alive, radiated his voice, his smile, his laugh, and his touch. In addition, considering my question and my son's response, I remembered how I used to send Levi to do something, but he became distracted along the path, and tasks often fell by the wayside. I wasn't sure how heaven was a distraction for him other than possible sights and sounds beyond imagination, or that God was merely comforting me with Levi's personality and tangible presence in a dream.

God isn't limited to human thinking. He does what He pleases. If He chooses to comfort us in ways we might not expect, that's okay. We can trust His ways because He loves us, and all of His ways are perfect. Be careful not to limit God in any guarded or fearful thinking about how He might choose to comfort or speak to you.

Pillow Talk

He was in the stern, asleep on a pillow. And they awoke Him and said to Him, "Teacher, do You not care that we are perishing?"

Mark 4:38

Having trusted in Jesus and His atoning work, we're disciples of Christ as much as these men in the boat were.

One morning, the perilous waves of the enemy overwhelmed me. I said, "Jesus, I feel as though You're asleep in the back of the boat on Your pillow! Don't You care that my boat is filling fast and in danger of sinking?" I heard the immediate response, *"I never sleep, nor do I slumber when it comes to the things concerning you. As the Son of Man in the midst of the storm on the sea with the disciples, I did require sleep, but the disciples approached Me and woke Me."* Jesus was telling me to come to Him even when it appeared He was unconcerned or "sleeping."

Jesus calmed the storm then asked His disciples, *"Why are you so fearful? How is it that you have no faith?"* (Mark 4:40). I've often thought Jesus was hard on the disciples when it came to faith. After all, until His coming, they hadn't encountered such wonders: healing the sick, raising the dead, seeing coins in the mouths of fish, or walking on water!

As born-again believers, we possess the faith *of* the Son of God (see Galatians 3:21, KJV). However, at times we exercise that faith in small amounts. Jesus wants us to take Him at His Word, which was, and still is today, *"Let us cross over to the other side"* (Mark 4:35).

I'm reminded of the song, written by Louisa M. R. Stead:

'Tis so sweet to trust in Jesus, just to take Him at His Word; Just to rest upon His promise, and to know, "Thus saith the Lord!"
Jesus, Jesus, how I trust Him!
How I've proved Him o'er and o'er Jesus, Jesus, precious Jesus!
Oh, for grace to trust Him more![1]

We've all felt at one time or another that Jesus was asleep in our boat. But you can trust your Captain. He's never lost a crew member or a ship to the storms of the enemy.

Wall of Fire

*"For I," says the LORD, "will be a wall of fire all around her,
and I will be the glory in her midst."*

Zechariah 2:5

Approximately five months after Levi departed for heaven, God called me back to a Bible teaching position. Although unsure of God's direction so soon after Levi's passing, He assured me that He'd take care of me.

One day in the classroom I sensed demonic forces working, but I couldn't pinpoint them. At this time, brokenhearted and in the thick of grief, I was incapable of defending myself, let alone taking authority over an enemy. I asked God what was taking place. Extremely fragile, I relied on Jesus for everything, including protecting and defending me from unseen forces.

The next morning I awoke at 3:00, sensing the presence of the Holy Spirit and feeling compelled to worship God. I went to my living room sofa and began singing quietly to Him. Soon, revelation came in the form of a vision about what I was experiencing in the classroom. God showed me that demons were coming at me through the students. I wasn't wrestling the students, however, as *"we do not wrestle against flesh and blood, but against principalities, against powers, against the rulers of the darkness"* (Ephesians 6:12).

In the vision, a ring of fire encircled me and the podium where I stood teaching. God showed me that demons were trying to attack me because they saw my vulnerability. In my grief, I was susceptible to them. The Lord said, *"I'll be a wall of fire all around you and the glory in your midst. Whenever those demons try to approach you at the lectern, they'll fall back because of the heat from the ring of My fire all around you."*

Are you feeling susceptible to attack? No matter what your circumstances, fighting evil forces in your own strength is impossible, but with the Spirit of Christ living in you, you can. *"In Him we live and move and have our being"* (Acts 17:28). Allow the Lord to surround you with His strength, and fight the good fight!

Weapons of Mass Destruction

No weapon formed against you shall prosper.

Isaiah 54:17

While reading Isaiah 54:17, the word *formed* leapt off the page. We know God formed man (see Genesis 2:7, 19), but how often do we consider today's passage and the weapon that is formed against us?

Until now, my focus has predominately been on the word *weapon* instead of the term *formed*. In the Hebrew language, *form*, mentioned in both Genesis and Isaiah, is the same word that describes "squeezing into shape" or "molding into a form."[1]

Global weaponry continues to be a top priority for nations. To safeguard citizens, military operations continually research and develop state-of-the tactical arms. Unfortunately, the devil is also hard at work, forging a single weapon of mass destruction, uniquely designed for each individual in an attempt to keep us from prospering in spirit, soul, or body. Although it may appear that he has an arsenal, he doesn't. He only has one weapon: deception.

Satan's intent with his weapon is to kill, steal, and destroy—physically, emotionally, and spiritually. But the good news is that, although he holds an ancient fabricated model, it's of faulty design and won't prosper.

As sons and daughters of God, the weapons of our warfare are not carnal but mighty in God. *"His Word is living and powerful, and sharper than any two-edged sword, piercing even to the division of soul and spirit, and of joints and marrow, and is a discerner of the thoughts and intents of the heart"* (Hebrews 4:12). Jesus wielded the sword and responded to Satan by saying, *"It is written"* (Matthew 4:4).

God hasn't left you weaponless. You're the one with an arms cache. You might not know where the armory is located, or maybe you don't think you have the key. But the armory is located in your spirit, and the Word of God is your key to utilize those arms.

Service and Worship

Then Jesus said to him, "Away with you, Satan! For it is written, 'You shall worship the LORD your God, and Him only you shall serve.'"

Matthew 4:10

In the wilderness temptation, *"⁸the devil took Him up on an exceedingly high mountain, and showed Him all the kingdoms of the world and their glory. ⁹And he said to Him, 'All these things I will give You if You will fall down and worship me'"* (Matthew 4:8–9). Satan covets worship.

As children of God, most believers don't think of themselves as serving Satan. However, when reading Jesus' words, *"Him only you shall serve,"* a light went on in my heart. I realized that by embracing anger and depression, even unintentionally, I was serving Satan. The thought of that alarmed me! But God, who is rich in mercy and truth, shared Numbers 15:28 with me: *"The priest shall make atonement for the person who sins unintentionally, when he sins unintentionally before the LORD, to make atonement for him; and it shall be forgiven him."* Jesus, our High Priest, made restitution for sin, intentional or unintentional!

The rich man who yielded plenty in Luke 12:19, said, *"I will say to my soul…."* Today, you and I also need to speak to our soul, saying, "Away with you, Satan, for it is written…." I personally need to declare, "Satan, it is written that God will give me the garment of praise for the spirit of heaviness" (see Isaiah 61:3). Endowed with joy, a fruit of the Holy Spirit, I should be dancing! Concerning selfish anger, I need to say, "Satan, it is written, I will put off anger" (see Colossians 3:8).

Thanks to the Spirit of Truth, who once again helps me get my eyes back on what is important: serving and worshipping Jesus only. Have you gotten off-track and started unintentionally serving Satan? If so, it's not a place where you want to pitch your tent. I encourage you to break camp immediately and return to serving God alone.

Dr. Jesus Will See You Now

However, when He, the Spirit of truth, has come, He will guide you into all truth;
for He will not speak on His own authority, but whatever He hears
He will speak; and He will tell you things to come.

John 16:13

My home office was always my place of prayer and fellowship—not only with the Lord, but also with my children. After Levi's death, I never returned to that office. Our living room couch became my new place of devotion, prayer, and fellowship with Jesus.

Morning by morning, I met with Him in prayer on the couch. With journal and pen in hand, I wrote, "Lord, here we are again, on the couch!" At that moment, He gave me a picture. I was lying on a chaise lounge with Jesus sitting beside me, as one would be in a patient-psychiatrist setting. Inwardly, I laughed at His analogy where I was the patient on the couch, and He was the Doctor of Psychology sitting next to me.

An attitude of gratitude overwhelmed me! I said, "Jesus, thank You for meeting me on the couch! Thank You for listening to me in all my moods, yet responding to me with truth instead of lies. Thank You for not charging me to talk with You! I'm grateful that You always leave me with hope. Thank You for getting to the matter of my heart and not merely medicating my symptoms. Thank You for being my Holy Spirit of Truth."

A psychiatrist deals with the mind and determines a cure. Jesus is the Shepherd and Overseer of our souls, our Great Physician, and His prescription for our cure is to be in health just as our soul prospers. His prescription is His presence, His power, and His truth. His truth is what sets us free, and whom the Son sets free is free indeed! (See John 8:32, 36; 1 Peter 2:25; and 3 John 1:2.)

There's no doubt that Proverbs 11:14 is true: *"Where there is no counsel, the people fall; but in the multitude of counselors there is safety."* However, the ultimate Counselor is the Lord, *"who is wonderful in counsel and excellent in guidance"* (Isaiah 28:29). Seek Him first for all your counseling needs.

Liberty Bell

Proclaim liberty throughout all the land to all its inhabitants.
It shall be a Jubilee for you.

Leviticus 25:10

In 1751, the Speaker of the Pennsylvania Assembly, Isaac Norris, chose a portion of Leviticus 25:10 as the inscription for the State House Bell, later dubbed by abolitionist societies as the "Liberty Bell."

The Israelites had their own Liberty Bell in the form of Jubilee. During the time of Jubilee, they forgave debts, freed slaves, and held a festival signaled by a blast of a horn. The American Liberty Bell signals our festival of independence from British rule. As born-again believers, we also have a Liberty Bell in Christ to celebrate our freedom from the slavery of sin.

As I write, the night I became born again and all that has transpired since that time comes to mind. God's love and goodness overwhelms me, as I meditate on how Jesus Christ liberated not only me but all of mankind from the law of sin and death. We celebrate a greater independence in Jesus because *"the Lord is the Spirit; and where the Spirit of the Lord is, there is liberty"* (2 Corinthians 3:17). Today and throughout eternity, we can ring our spiritual Liberty Bell as often as we like.

The Liberty Bell cracked on its first test ring. The Liberty Bell of Christ, however, has no flaws and will never crack. God is perfect. *"Jesus Christ is the same yesterday, today, and forever"* (Hebrews 13:8).

The Holy Spirit encourages us daily to ring our Liberty Bell and declare the promises of God. In doing so, we receive the freedom granted to us. *"If the Son makes you free, you shall be free indeed"* (John 8:36).

Ring your spiritual Liberty Bell, and enjoy the chimes of freedom, knowing that you're loved (see John 16:27), redeemed, and forgiven (see Colossians 1:14). Celebrate that God chose you before the foundation of the world (see Ephesians 1:4). And know that if you believe in Him, you won't perish but have eternal life (see John 3:15).

The Pool of Bethesda

After this there was a feast of the Jews, and Jesus went up to Jerusalem. Now there is in Jerusalem by the Sheep Gate a pool, which is called in Hebrew, Bethesda, having five porches.

John 5:1–2

Swimming is one of my favorite things to do, especially on a hot day when the cool water refreshes me. Today I'd like to talk to you about a different pool—one that can literally melt away the burden of your heart, refresh your entire life, and give you a hope and a future to look forward to. There was something unique about this Pool of Bethesda: Jesus was there!

If you find yourself by this pool, you'll either be in the water or lying poolside waiting for its stirring. For this is where you'll discover the refreshing water of the Holy Spirit and the warm touch of the Son of God.

In A.D. 1888, while the Church of St. Anne in northeast Jerusalem was undergoing a restoration process, a reservoir was discovered. The reservoir, cut from rock, measured about fifty feet long and twelve feet wide. It was a spring-fed pool, surrounded by five porches in Jerusalem. Approaching the pool, there was a flight of steep and winding steps. On a wall next to the reservoir, workers found a faded fresco depicting an angel troubling the water. Scholars believe this place best fits the description of the Pool of Bethesda mentioned only once in the Bible, in John 5. The Pool of Bethesda and its literal Greek meaning is "House of Kindness" or "House of Grace."[1]

After living an emotionally crippled life for thirty-eight years, everything changed when the Holy Spirit gave me a revelation that I was figuratively the crippled man at the Pool of Bethesda. Seeing Jesus at my own pool enabled me to walk in a newness of life like never before.

For the next nine days, I invite you poolside as I expound on the scriptures and revelations God gave to me to walk out my healing in a tangible way. I pray that you'd also experience Jesus by your Pool of Bethesda. He's your expert, all-knowing, all-seeing, ever-present Lifeguard.

Pool Loungers

In these lay a great multitude of sick people, blind, lame, paralyzed, waiting for the moving of the water.

John 5:3

While reading our opening passage, the Holy Spirit gave me a vision where a multitude of believers and unbelievers lounged by a modern-day swimming pool. The Lord showed me that these loungers were physically, emotionally, and spiritually sick. Some were blind because they didn't know the Word of God. Some knew the Word but were lame in walking it its truth. Paralyzed with fear, others were unable to move toward the pool. Some were lazy and chose not to move toward the healing waters, as many believed they were helpless.

Although rest and relaxation have their place, if we stay engaged in them for too long we can become complacent, even to the point of developing destructive life patterns instead of jumping into the healing pool. You might be lying by the pool blind right now, not knowing Christ and His Word. Be encouraged, as the man at the Pool of Bethesda didn't initially know Christ either.

Many of the people at the pool appeared to possess an attitude of complacency, as they passively waited for the stirring of the water, or figuratively, waited for God or others to do something for them. But God has already provided what we need to walk out our lives on earth through the Spirit of Jesus, and that is His Word in written form. As we turn our hearts to Him in prayer and Bible reading, the Spirit begins to stir our spirit with truth. This, in turn, enables us to step toward our pool of healing—for our spirit, soul, and body.

Spiritual blindness and fear, along with lameness and laziness, have hindered everyone at one time or another. If you need a helping hand into the pool, call on your friend, Jesus. He is poolside. Take His hand, and jump into the healing waters together.

The Pool's Angel

For an angel went down at a certain time into the pool and stirred up the water;
then whoever stepped in first, after the stirring of the water,
was made well of whatever disease he had.

John 5:4

In a modern-day swimming pool, activity is commonplace. Likewise, when an angel stirred the water in the Pool of Bethesda, there was also activity. Things happened! People came out of the pool healed and transformed.

When I was a four-year-old kindergartner, my school bus driver took a genuine interest in me by calling me to the front of the bus to sit with him. I felt extremely special.

One day, the driver summoned another little girl, Kim, to come and sit with him at the front of the bus instead of me. Deeply hurt, thinking that was my special place, my feelings toward him quickly changed. I was full of anger. I felt replaced. I believed that somehow she was more valuable than I was.

I was so enraged, I actually wished that Kim was dead. One week later, her brother accidentally shot and killed her while cleaning his gun. I remember feeling sad because selfishly, I hadn't wanted to share the bus driver with her. I also felt guilt, thinking that the accident was my fault because of my thoughts toward her. At the same time, however, I was happy because she'd no longer be able to sit by the bus driver.

I remember Kim not having a father present in her life. My father was present in my life, but he was a silent presence. Now I know that Kim needed the bus driver's attention also, maybe even more than I did.

At the time, I wasn't aware of the void that existed in my life, which was due to a lack of my earthly father's affection, and me not understanding my heavenly Father's love. Therefore, unknowingly, I looked to the bus driver to fill this crevasse.

Have you ever felt special and then replaced? Today, the Holy Spirit is stirring the waters of healing. If you're like me and enjoy the water, jump in! If you're leery of the water, step in slowly. Either way, you'll be transformed by the admiration, affection, and attention of Jesus Christ.

The Pool's Certain Bystander

Now a certain man was there who had an infirmity thirty-eight years.

John 5:5

I could sense the Holy Spirit's presence as I read John 5:5. I was stunned as He revealed to me that, figuratively, I was this man with the infirmity of thirty-eight years! I did the math and realized it'd been exactly thirty-eight years to the day since I experienced what I describe as the "school bus episode." Just as the man in this scripture was physically crippled, anger and jealousy had crippled me emotionally since that day. These sinful emotions became a filter through which I viewed myself and my relationships.

Most of us are aware of our weaknesses, but without God's revelation, the deeper issues can remain clouded from our view. I knew something was not quite right in my behavior, but only by the power of the Holy Spirit could I know the depth of those wounded emotions.

Two years after I gave my life to Christ, the Holy Spirit reminded me of the "school bus episode." I was an adult now and hadn't thought of the incident or talked to anyone about it since that fateful day. I remembered that day, but without God's further revelation, it was *only* a reflection.

Then three years later, during a time of prayer and fasting, the Holy Spirit revealed the school bus scene to me again in a vision. I was once again on the bus as a four-year-old girl, experiencing those vehement emotions of anger and jealousy. This reality startled me and shook me to my core. I could hardly believe that such a young girl could possess a heart with such strong, violent emotions.

Do you have an infirmity that God is asking you to release? You may think it's not a big problem. We don't often understand that tiny problems start as small seeds and grow into big trees. As God reveals, allow Him to deal with your issues. The sooner you can release your infirmity to Him, the sooner you'll be on your way to victory.

The Pool of Healing

John 5:6

When Jesus saw him lying there, and knew that he had already been in that condition a long time, He said to him, "Do you want to be made well?"

Jesus saw me lying by the pool for thirty-eight years. He was aware of my situation long before I even realized I was "stuck" beside the pool. I couldn't remember ever being anyone other than this jealous, angry person. I really believed God had created me this way, so there was nothing I could do to change. I used to tell God, "You're a jealous God. Apparently, I got it from You. Like Father, like daughter!" ("The LORD, whose name is Jealous, is a jealous God," Exodus 34:14.) I felt like it was up to God to do something. After all, He was my Creator!

Then the Holy Spirit asked me, just as Jesus asked this man, "Sharon, do you want to be made well?" He was giving me the choice. I was amazed! I said, "Lord, why would You ask me such a question? Of course I want to be made well." Then there was silence.

Although God was able to instantly zap the anger and jealousy from my life, suddenly, I had a revelation: I had to do something! To experience change, it meant me being obedient to His directives and taking steps by His grace, knowing that my heavenly Father would be with me all the way. Change can be frightening, even when it's good for us.

I also realized that I had identified for so long with the wrong thing (a lie), it'd take a concentrated effort of my will to choose to accept God's truth in this area of my life. It would take God's grace to get into the pool of healing.

Jesus is asking you today, "Do you want to be made well?" He gives us the choice to accept the healing He provided at the cross. Symbolically, He's inviting you into the healing waters of Bethesda. It's a great day for a swim! Come on in, the water is fine. In fact, it's divine!

The Pool's Victims

The sick man answered Him, "Sir, I have no man to put me into the pool when the water is stirred up; but while I am coming, another steps down before me."

John 5:7

"I'm a victim," the sick man seemed to be saying. "I have no one to help me, and when I do make a feeble effort, someone else takes my turn." Like this man, I too had excuses! My thoughts were, *God is my Creator. Let Him do something about this anger and jealousy. If so and so wouldn't do such and such, I wouldn't respond with anger and jealousy. What kind of person would I be if I chose a new way?*

Take a moment and think about these principles. Are you comfortable remaining a victim of excuses, or do you want to experience success and victory? This question can apply to every area of your life.

In 1986, I used to smoke cigarettes. I knew that smoking was bad for my health and that it contaminated my body, which God says is the temple of the Holy Spirit. However, I was afraid to quit this destructive habit because I thought I'd gain weight. Six months after I became born again, I gave my cigarette habit to the Lord in prayer, asking Him to help me quit. With His success, I did quit and didn't gain the dreaded weight. You could say I gained spiritual weight by giving up my fleshly desires!

In addition, the negative behavior of anger and jealousy that I was so familiar with was difficult for me to give up. At the time, change didn't come easily or overnight. It was challenging and difficult, but the rewards of positive change outweighed the pain in which I would have otherwise continued to live. As I grew in the knowledge of God's grace, I recognized it was His ability in my weakness that made change come about more easily.

Does the term *victim mentality* describe your attitude today, as it did mine years ago? The scripture says, *"the sick man answered Him."* In Christ and in your spirit, you're not sick. As a born-again child of God, you have everything within your spirit that you need to be an overcomer in your mind, will, and emotions! No more excuses!

Poolside Instruction

Jesus said to him, "Rise, take up your bed and walk." Immediately the man was made well, took up his bed, and walked.

John 5:8–9

Jesus said a similar thing to me as He did to the lame man at the pool: *"Rise, take up your bed, and walk away from this sinful anger and jealousy."* In order to receive the healing Jesus provided, I had to obey His instructions. I had to get off of my bed of sinful emotional responses, stop believing lies, and walk toward the newness of life that God provided in Christ. Jesus wasn't expecting me to do it by myself, as John 15:5 informs us, *"without Me you can do nothing."* Just as He did for the lame man, Jesus will come to your aid at the pool.

I'd been lying by the pool for so long that I never would've made it into the healing water without Jesus' help. Until the Holy Spirit revealed this to me, I didn't even know that I was by the pool, nor did I know how to get into the pool. No matter what kind of healing you need—whether physical, emotional, or spiritual—the Holy Spirit knows how to get you to the pool.

Healing and wholeness came to all whom Jesus touched. Many healings were instantaneous, while some occurred only after the person responded to Jesus' instructions. Jesus initiated this healing, saying to the man, *"'⁸Rise, take up your bed and walk.' ⁹Immediately the man was made well, took up his bed, and walked"* (John 5:8–9). The words of Jesus made the man whole and *then* he walked. Although healed, the man still had to take Jesus at His word by getting up and walking.

Like the lame man, obedience to the Holy Spirit's instructions is required to obtain the healing Jesus provided at the cross. The manifestation of the Spirit's healing is varied and uniquely individual for each of us. Rise, take up your bed, and walk away from any sinful lifestyle He's addressing in your life. I believe that if the lame man then—and I today—had ignored Jesus, we could still be lying by the side of the pool for another thirty-eight years.

Pool Pushers

The Jews therefore said to him who was cured, "It is the Sabbath;
it is not lawful for you to carry your bed.... Who is the Man who said to you,
'Take up your bed and walk'?"

John 5:10, 12

The Jews questioned the man as to why he was carrying his bed on the Sabbath. He told them that the Man who made me well said, *"Take up your bed and walk."* According to the Law of Moses, the Jews observed the Sabbath as a day of rest and worship. This made carrying the man's mat and Jesus' healing unlawful practices, when in truth, God can work on any day of the week, including the Sabbath.

Can you imagine the tone of the man's interrogator as he asked, "What is the name of the One who healed you?" I believe the accusers knew that Jesus was the Healer. However, the miracles and multitudes that followed Jesus only exposed the accusers' envious and fearful hearts in losing followers.

A happy-go-lucky pool party can sometimes turn ugly if people angrily begin pushing others into the pool. Likewise, today Satan and his "pool pushers" mock or attempt to drown out the authority of Jesus, which holds power to heal us. Satan will come to us maliciously through uninformed or even well-meaning people, saying, "Who says you can be different after thirty-eight years? Who says healing is for today? Who says the sick are made well without an earthly physician?" To Satan I say, "Be silent," and to those in need of healing, I would say, *"Jesus the Christ heals you"* (Acts 9:34).

The Pharisees, priests, and Jews slandered Jesus continually for performing miracles on the Sabbath. Jesus silenced them, saying, *"'Is it lawful on the Sabbath to do good or to do evil, to save life or to kill?' But they kept silent"* (Mark 3:4).

Part of the beauty in this story is that the man didn't know it was Jesus who had healed him. His touch is unconditional. There's nothing too difficult in your life that the Great Physician, Jesus, cannot heal. Jesus is present to help you with the demonic pool pushers intimidating you at the healing waters of Bethesda, and His power is present to manifest your healing now. What are you waiting for? Step into His healing water.

The Pool's Mystery Man

But the one who was healed did not know who it was, for Jesus had withdrawn, a multitude being in that place.

John 5:13

At this pool party, we remember the Jews approaching the healed man, asking, *"Who is the Man who said to you, 'Take up your bed and walk'?"* (John 5:12). I'm persuaded that these curiosity seekers *knew of* Jesus, but they didn't really *know* Him. If they had, they would've recognized Him and His work at the pool from the words spoken by the prophet Isaiah: *"He Himself took our infirmities and bore our sicknesses"* (Matthew 8:17).

There's more Sonshine at this pool than the natural eye can see. Amazingly, the man didn't know who had healed him. He didn't know Jesus, but Jesus certainly knew him and chose to approach him in the crowd. It wasn't a small crowd, but a great multitude that lay by this pool, yet we read of no other healing except this *one* man. To me, this represents a picture of the personal love and attention that Jesus has for each of us within the vast sea of humanity.

Jesus saw you before your substance was formed in your mother's womb (see Psalm 139:6). He knows *you!* Maybe you know Jesus as a Savior and Healer, which is wonderful! On the other hand, could you be like this man and not know Jesus as your personal Savior or your personal Great Physician?

Although this man lived before Jesus completed His redemptive work on the cross, Jesus revealed a foretaste of that divine work at the pool by healing him and fulfilling Isaiah's prophecy quoted in Matthew 8:17. Having fulfilled this prophecy at the cross, Jesus delivered us from sin and sickness. By His stripes, we were healed (see 1 Peter 2:24).

One minute, the man at the pool knew nothing of Jesus, and then in an instant Jesus revealed Himself as Savior, Healer, and Friend. Jesus is eager to reveal Himself to you as well. Do you hear Him asking, "Do you want to be made well?" Today, salvation, healing, and friendship are yours for the taking.

The Pool and the Modern-Day Church

Afterward Jesus found him in the temple, and said to him, "See, you have been made well. Sin no more, lest a worse thing come upon you." The man departed and told the Jews that it was Jesus who had made him well.

John 5:14–15

Applying the above verse to myself, I realized that Jesus found me not only by the pool, but also in the temple—our modern-day church. Although born again and attending church, I still struggled with these sinful emotional responses. You may also be a struggling Christian, or perhaps you're not yet born again; Jesus will meet you wherever you are.

See is a simple word, but profound when the Holy Spirit illuminates it. It means "to gaze (i.e. with wide-open eyes, as at something remarkable.)"[1] God wants us to "see" that in Jesus Christ we've been made well. The truth in my life is that I wasn't the angry, jealous person I had believed myself to be. According to 2 Corinthians 5:17, *"if anyone is in Christ, he is a new creation; old things have passed away; behold, all things have become new."*

The words of Jesus, *"Sin no more, unless a worse thing come upon you,"* don't mean that Jesus was going to cause worse things to happen to this man. Jesus is saying that if we continue along the path of sinful choices, we'll reap the natural but painful consequences.

Slowly, over time, God showed me the holes in my reasoning. He helped me realize that jealousy, not others, was the root of my problems. By spending time with God in His Word, He replaces our faulty ideas with His life-giving principles. As a result, we become more skilled at rejecting the lies of Satan and more able to stand firm in God's truth.

I'm telling you the same thing that the man in John 5 told the Jews, "It is Jesus who made me well."

If you want to be made well, your part is to believe and embrace His grace, which enables you to step into His healing waters. As you do so by faith, He'll be there, helping to pull you from your sin and into emotional wholeness.

He Walks with Me

…two of them were traveling that same day to a village called Emmaus….
…while they conversed and reasoned…Jesus Himself drew near
and went with them.

Luke 24:13, 15

One brisk and sunny spring day, looking out of my window, I noticed a man walking. I couldn't determine if old age or injury had impaired his gait, but he leaned heavily on a walker, while a woman held him securely from behind by a medical waist belt. At a snail's pace, they walked in perfect unison, occasionally conversing. They say a picture is worth a thousand words. This picture of the woman walking in tandem with the ailing man spoke volumes.

Riveted, I watched as the man led the way, and although the woman didn't touch him, the way in which they walked as one resonated in my heart. The woman personified the very character of Jesus, moving with compassion (see Matthew 14:14). As a servant-friend, she graciously walked and talked with this precious elderly man at his pace.

In this scenario was a recurring theme of the woman's love and patience. She never once rushed him. Her pace was his pace. Her selflessness was unmistakable. God's love was on display through her kindness, as she didn't behave rudely or seek her own way (see 1 Corinthians 13).

The two men in our opening passage encountered an unexpected guest while they were walking. That guest was Jesus, who began walking and talking with them, accompanying them on their way to Emmaus.

Just as Jesus was in step with these men, He's also in step with you. As Your Helper companion, He walks with you at your pace and your ability to keep in step with Him. Like this woman, He's patient and doesn't force or set a speed that you can't achieve.

One day, I had the strangest thought that I wasn't walking through grief properly. God showed me that, because He walked with me, I was walking through properly, and He was walking with me at my pace. If you feel you're out of stride with Jesus, remember that God is love. He's not demanding or overbearing; therefore, you can have peace in your pace because He walks with you.

Three Fathers

I am the God of your fathers.

Acts 7:32

was as surprised by this title as some of you might be. No matter what our circumstances, everyone has a father somewhere.

"I will be a Father to you, and you shall be My sons and daughters, says the LORD Almighty" (2 Corinthians 6:18). As Christ followers, God is our Father. I pray this is your standing, and if not, that it will be soon. *"For you did not receive the spirit of bondage again to fear, but you received the Spirit of adoption by whom we cry out, 'Abba, Father'"* (Romans 8:15).

The second father is our earthly father. Matthew 15:4 tells us to *"honor your father."* Depending on your story, you hold either fond or negative memories of this father. Some dads, in their own brokenness, are unable to reflect the image of our loving heavenly Father. Our Father asks us to forgive as we have been forgiven, and with Him, all things are possible. I don't say this lightly, as I have also plunged into the depths of forgiving as I have been forgiven—to a small degree with my dad, but to the ultimate degree with the death of my son.

Although created by God, the rebellious devil is our third and least of all fathers. The words of Jesus are shocking: *"You are of your father the devil"* (John 8:44). How often do we consider the devil as someone's father? Not everyone is a child of God. In Acts 13:10, Paul spoke to Elymas the sorcerer, saying, *"You son of the devil, you enemy of all righteousness, will you not cease perverting the straight ways of the Lord?"*

The scriptures say that as many as received Jesus, to those who believe in His name, He gave the right to become children of God (see John 1:12). In order to become children of God, we have to receive Jesus. Have you received Jesus? Are you a child of God? If so, continue to walk in the Father-child relationship He has freely provided. If not, tell Him now that you want to be His child.

Spiritual Atherosclerosis

Beware, brethren, lest there be in any of you an evil heart of unbelief in departing from the living God; but exhort one another daily, while it is called "Today," lest any of you be hardened through the deceitfulness of sin.

Hebrews 3:12–13

Atherosclerosis is a disease that attacks the heart. Arteries harden and narrow, gradually becoming blocked with plaque, resulting in restricted blood flow to the heart. Without intervention, heart attacks and strokes can occur.[1] We can experience a similar block in our spiritual arteries, as they too can become hardened and obstruct our relationship with God—not on His end but on ours.

Although atherosclerosis can be deadly, it is also preventable and treatable. Atherosclerosis, a natural enemy of our body, mirrors a certain spiritual enemy that many of us have encountered. For the natural heart, enemies include bad fats, smoking, and high blood pressure. A deadly enemy of the spiritual heart is the deceitfulness of sin. Doses of this enemy progressively harden our spiritual arteries.

The good news is that if this spiritual disease has already taken root in your heart, or if you want to take preventative measures, there's hope. To protect yourself against this preventable, treatable, and potentially fatal spiritual disease, you'll find the antidote is in the Great Physician Himself and His redemption. If this remedy is new to you, you only need call on Jesus, and He'll give you what you need. Begin to meet with Him, and receive His Word for your specific ailment as a medicine for as often and as long as He prescribes.

If you have previous experience with the medication of His Word (the Bible), continue in it as the Doctor orders until further notice. By doing so, you'll be hiding His Word in your heart, protecting yourself against spiritual heart disease: *"Your word I have hidden in my heart, that I might not sin against You"* (Psalm 119:11).

Combat and Fear

And the LORD said to Joshua, "Do not fear them, for I have delivered them into your hand; not a man of them shall stand before you."

Joshua 10:8

Unlike the brave men and women in the armed forces, I've never been on an actual battlefield. However, as a warrior in God's army, I fight on a spiritual battlefield and am therefore able to correlate some military principles.

On both battlefields, whether natural or spiritual, soldiers experience fear to a large degree. There's no denying that fear rears its ugly head, and each soldier copes in his or her own way. From the beginning of time to the end of the age, adversaries will continue to use terror tactics as weapons. However, to deal with fear's intimidation, tools have been provided for both units.

To strengthen themselves for battle, spiritual soldiers can look to Galatians 5:19–21. Because fear is a spirit, it's not listed among the works of the flesh. We can't crucify a spirit as we do the flesh, so we must deal with fear by casting it out. Jesus said, *"In My name they will cast out demons"* (Mark 16:17). Second Timothy 1:7 also records, *"For God has not given us a spirit of fear, but of power and of love and a sound mind."*

Equipped for battle, we possess the miracle power of the Holy Spirit to overcome threats. When anchored in God's love, fear is absent, and the result is power, love, and a sound mind, which are essential qualities for a soldier. Fear can be paralyzing and life threatening in a war zone. Because fear exists, it's best to train the troops to recognize it and overcome it as effectively and quickly as possible.

From time to time, fear attempts to overtake me when I preach. My weapon is 2 Timothy 4:17. Although this passage doesn't specifically mention fear, it speaks directly to my need, and when I speak it in faith, that spirit quits harassing me: *"The Lord stood with me and strengthened me, so that the message might be preached fully through me."*

Scripture references in regards to fear are too numerous to mention here. But if you're occasionally assaulted by fear, find a battle passage (or a few) from God's Word and begin wielding it against this enemy.

The Health Club

Exercise yourself toward godliness.

1 Timothy 4:7

Most people understand the term *workout*, whether it's chopping wood or being at the gym lifting weights. In my youth, for the sanity of our parents and my eleven siblings, each day held mandatory playtime in the open air, and because of this, today I'm still a fan of an active life.

As a member of a local gym, most days I'm eager to work out. At other times, however, participating in physical exercise is the last thing I want to do. With each drop of sweat and every grueling repetition, I wonder if all the hard work is worth it. When I temporarily moved out of state and had no health club access, and therefore no regular workout routine, I quickly realized that there were results to my previous fitness regime. With those consistent workouts, my strength and stamina held steady.

Exercise is an activity requiring physical effort to sustain or improve our body and mind. Spiritually speaking, believers oftentimes consider exercising spiritually through disciplines such as prayer, fasting, and reading the Word to be work. If you're one of those people, I have good news for you! By the grace of God, we can all live a spiritually disciplined life, which helps us produce great results that remain and keeps us steady in our faith.

I don't know about you, but some days my spiritual life is like the routine at the gym in which my flesh is not interested in my necessary spiritual conditioning. We can find the cure for this thinking in 1 Timothy 4:8, which tells us, *"bodily exercise profits a little, but godliness is profitable for all things."*

Let's pump a few spiritual repetitions of Scripture and *"not grow weary while doing good, for in due season we shall reap if we do not lose heart"* (Galatians 6:9).

Combat—Global Weapon

...pray without ceasing.

1 Thessalonians 5:17

Pray without ceasing. Is that too tall an order for the troops of God? Globally, prayer is a life-saving weapon for soldiers. What warrior do you know of—with the exception of Desmond Doss, the American pacifist combat medic from the movie *Hacksaw Ridge*, who engaged in combat with prayer alone[1]—who would refuse to pick up a gun? For most troops, entering the fight without fully loaded weapons means certain death. However, Doss, with faith and prayer alone, single-handedly rescued seventy-five of his fellow soldiers and came out alive, receiving the Medal of Honor.

Without prayer, God's troops are defenseless against the enemy, the devil. Jesus told us, *"In this manner, therefore, pray: Our Father in heaven, Hallowed be Your name"* (Matthew 6:9). Consider the soldier's ammo box "the privilege of prayer." With it, you praise God and take authority over enemies. In addition, you're free to talk with Jesus about anything and everything that's on your heart.

The soldier's military manual, the Bible, is chock full of prayer weapons. Some troops might be in the trenches as James 5:13 describes: *"Is anyone among you suffering? Let him pray."* Maybe you feel like a POW (Prisoner of War) in the devil's camp. Peter was kept in prison, but constant prayer was offered to God for him by the church (see Acts 12:5). Victory came when an angel of the Lord released Peter, and he came knocking on the very door of those praying for him (see Acts 12:7, 16).

Prayer touches the heart of our heavenly Father. It keeps the devil at bay, and it stops him in his evil tracks. Side by side in the fight, it protects the troops. *"Confess your trespasses to one another, and pray for one another, that you may be healed. The effective, fervent prayer of a righteous man avails much"* (James 5:16).

Is a battle raging in your life? Do you feel pinned down? Is the enemy displaying the upper hand? Brave believer, draw your weapon, wielding the words of Jesus spoken to every enlisted soldier, *"men always ought to pray and not lose heart"* (Luke 18:1).

Kingdoms Clashing

Of the increase of His government and peace there will be no end.

Isaiah 9:7

Two kingdoms are at work in the earth: the kingdom of God and the kingdom of darkness. Before our very eyes, the two are clashing like thunder!

Jesus said, *"Nation will rise against nation, and kingdom against kingdom"* (Matthew 24:7). And, *"My kingdom is not of this world"* (John 18:36). His kingdom is where the sovereign Godhead—the Father, Son, and Holy Spirit—rule and reign. Satan, although defeated, has his own synagogue of followers and sits on a throne. The heads of his domain are the dragon, the beast, and the false prophet (see Revelation 2:9, 13; 16:13).

Progressively, world government leadership with their choices are aligning themselves with the kingdom of darkness. Despite this, those of us who love Christ and live for Him count it all joy, as Jesus owns the victory over darkness! It's just a matter of time until He brings all things together.

As citizens of the kingdom of God, we have a mandate to arise and shine within the kingdom of darkness. It's our spiritual duty to tell others of the good news of the death and resurrection of Christ. We're also called to strengthen each other and exhort one another to continue in the faith as we enter the kingdom of God through many tribulations (see Acts 14:22). Can you hear the swords clashing in the battle? The antichrist and his kingdom of darkness are on the move throughout the world, attempting to draw people further and further from God, Jesus, and the Spirit of Truth.

Alone with a small group and His disciples, Jesus said, *"To you it has been given to know the mystery of the kingdom of God; but to those who are outside, all things come in parables"* (Mark 4:11). When it comes to the kingdom of God, are you an insider or an outsider? When you believe on the Lord Jesus Christ, you're transformed and made new on the inside. This is how you become an insider in the kingdom of God, *"for indeed, the kingdom of God is within you"* (Luke 17:21).

God of Hope

Now may the God of hope fill you with all joy and peace in believing,
that you may abound in hope by the power of the Holy Spirit.

Romans 15:13

On foreign soil with grief, holding onto hope after Levi's passing was something unattainable for me. I assumed that because of my lack of strength, all hope would be lost. However, in my brokenness, Jesus, my Savior and Friend, reassured me that hope continued to be a tangible part of my journey because *"with men this is impossible, but with God all things are possible"* (see Matthew 19:26).

Having lost its way, God redirected my heart by revealing Romans 15:13. His words became an instant source of relief. The God of hope would not only fill me with all joy and peace but also enable me to believe that I could even abound in hope. Any abiding or abounding in hope, joy, peace, or even faith, would come from the power of His Holy Spirit within me and not my strength; because apart from Him I had none. My bond with hope, or expecting things from God, waned; after all, we prayed for our son's safety, yet he died.

I'm grateful that God is love, which is always patient and kind. Now, after five years, although Levi resides with Jesus, my heart bursts with hope and eagerly desires the fulfillment of the works in which God created me to walk. I can truly say that once again I am abounding in hope.

As believers in Christ, Galatians 2:20 is essential: *"I have been crucified with Christ; it is no longer I who live, but Christ lives in me; and the life which I now live in the flesh I live by [the] faith [of] the Son of God, who loved me and gave Himself for me"* (brackets added). Because of this, you and I can do all things through Christ—even hope.

Blood Bath

To Him who loved us and washed us from our sins in His own blood.

Revelation 1:5

In my personal time of communion, I heard these words: *"Because of My body and because of My blood, I have washed you in a blood bath. You are bathed in My blood."*

The term *blood bath* in our modern language denotes a great and violent bloody slaughter, which is not a pleasant image to ponder. But neither is the bloody and savage crucifixion of Jesus. His definition of "blood bath" is life giving, as He cleansed our spirit, soul, and body with His own blood on the cross.

As a parent washes a child in a bath, Jesus washes us in His blood bath. As a parent wraps a child with a robe coming out of the bathtub, we too, emerge from our spiritual bath, and Jesus clothes us with the garments of salvation and covers us with the robe of righteousness (see Isaiah 61:10).

It's required for every person to take part in this blood bath in order to receive God's robe of righteousness. Righteousness is the character or quality of being *right* or *just* with God. In Romans 10:3, Paul said that Israel, *"being ignorant of God's righteousness, and seeking to establish their own righteousness, have not submitted to the righteousness of God."*

Like a child resisting the bath water for whatever reason, Israel, ignorant of God's right standing through Jesus, resisted His blood bath. By insisting on their own standard of cleanliness, they continued depending on the works of the Law and sacrifices to make themselves right.

In the end, it's *"⁵not by works of righteousness which we have done, but according to His mercy He saved us, through the washing of regeneration and renewing of the Holy Spirit, ⁶whom He poured out on us abundantly through Jesus Christ our Savior"* (Titus 3:5–6).

Don't be deceived and misled that your good deeds will be enough to make you right with God. The body and blood of Jesus alone cleanse us and bring us to righteousness. His blood bath was enough to make you clean!

The Panting Soul

As the deer pants for the water brooks, so pants my soul for You, O God.

Psalm 42:1

As I emerged from sleep, I didn't *feel* like meeting the Lord in our customary morning prayer. With the death of my son weighing heavily on my heart, it felt numb. Heading to my kitchen for coffee just before dawn, with discouragement bearing down on my soul, I saw a deer through the window.

Gazing at the deer, I stopped mid-stride as God's presence overwhelmed me. My heart stood still in awe as He impressed me with His Word: *"As the deer pants for the water brooks, so my soul pants for You, O God."* I sensed Him telling me that even though I didn't *feel* like meeting with Him, in truth, my heart was panting after Him like a deer pants for water. Panting depicts a longing for something. With God's picture of me like the deer panting for water, His unconditional love and encouragement led me straight to the prayer closet where we had a sweet, priceless time of intimate fellowship.

At times, our soul speaks loudly to our mind, will, and emotions, but God's voice overrides those voices or feelings. Mark 14:38 tells us that *"The spirit indeed is willing, but the flesh is weak."* But, in our weakness, He is strong.

It's been said more than once, and it's true, that we are to live by faith and not feelings. Aren't you glad that God is so good to us? If you're anything like me, some days my feelings speak louder than my faith. However, the faith of Jesus Christ comes to the rescue and speaks louder than my feelings.

In what ways do you need for God to override your feelings? As the deer pants for the water, your soul longs for Him as well. Circumstances and feelings may have clouded your view to this truth. Know that Jesus loves you so much, He'll do for you what He did for me.

Unfailing Love—Part 1

Surely your goodness and unfailing love will pursue me all the days of my life, and I will live in the house of the LORD forever.

Psalm 23:6 (NLT)

Our families were neighbors with John and Paige until we moved after Levi's passing. Sixteen months later we heard that John and Paige's only son, Jason, had died. Later meeting with Paige, we shared our stories, triumphs, and tears. *Awe* is the only word to describe their testimonies, as Paige and John were grieving parents that hadn't yet received Jesus as their Lord and Savior.

After Jason's funeral, John had a dream that he shared with us. "I dreamt I was in a beautiful open field, and a dark-haired man with a holy presence was at the field's edge. I was talking with some friends but noticed this man immediately. He spoke to me without opening His mouth. I could hear His voice; it was full of love, compassion, and grace. He told me that I was doing well for now, but He'd be here for me when I needed Him. The man looked familiar, like I'd always known Him. I woke up at 3:00 a.m., as did my wife. I described to her what had just happened. She'd also been dreaming of a dark-haired man."

Paige dreamt, "I was in a store and arguing with the salesclerks about something I needed that they couldn't help me with. I yelled out, 'No one understands; I'm all alone!' As I was leaving, I dropped my purse and everything fell out. I started crying. The store's door opened, and a tall, dark-haired man entered. He said to me, 'You're not alone,' and He began to help me pick up the contents of my purse. He opened His arms for me to hug Him. The feeling I experienced wrapped in His arms is inexplicable with our vocabulary. The serenity, peace, comfort, and contentment settled deep into my soul."

For both John and Paige, their dreams revealed an identical dark-haired man—in height, weight, and hairstyle, along with facial features and age. They concluded that the man was Jesus. At this time, John made a commitment to Christ, but Paige didn't. Their miraculous story continues in tomorrow's devotional, as you'll see that you're never out of God's watchful eye or loving reach.

Unfailing Love—Part 2

But I trust in your unfailing love. I will rejoice because you have rescued me.

Psalm 13:5 (NLT)

Several days after John's first dream, he experienced another defining one. "I was in a small town," John began, "which appeared to be in the Middle East. It was a beautiful day. I was on a roof of a building with my wife. An evil, black blob appeared, and we began to run together. We ran to the edge of the roof and jumped to the next roof, as the buildings were only two feet apart.

"We approached another edge. This time, the buildings were four feet across. We jumped but barely made it. Then we approached another edge, with the buildings now eight feet across. I started to jump but didn't think my wife could make it. I decided I wouldn't leave her behind, and we needed to do this together. I grabbed her hand, and we jumped. We made it across, and the evil blob couldn't make the jump, so it stopped following us."

At the same time, Paige had her own experience. "I woke up in a completely paralyzed state," she recalled. "I couldn't move a single part of my body. A cold, dark, malevolent presence wrapped around me. It felt as if my soul was being raped. It took every ounce of energy I could muster to kick my right foot from underneath the covers and escape the evil presence. I said aloud, 'I believe Jesus Christ is my Lord and Savior!' Instantly, the evil presence lifted from my body. I wasn't a practicing Christian by any means, and these words weren't in my daily vocabulary. How I knew what to say to save my soul was a gift from God!"

This is the power of God unto salvation. Equally yoked ever since, John and Paige are committed to and serving Christ. Are you living, as John and Paige were, without Jesus as your Savior? There's hope available to you! God knows who you are, where you are, and how to reach you, no matter how distant from Him you might feel. If you're away from God, reach out to Him now through His Son, Jesus, and you'll never be alone or hopeless again.

Levi's Covenant

"Then you shall know that I have sent this commandment to you,
that My covenant with Levi may continue," says the LORD of hosts.
"My covenant was with him, one of life and peace, and I gave them to him
that he might fear Me; so he feared Me and was reverent before My name.
The law of truth was in his mouth, and injustice was not found on his lips.
He walked with Me in peace and equity, and turned many away from iniquity."

Malachi 2:4–6

One morning with my first waking thought being, *"healing in His wings,"* from Malachi 4:2, God began setting the stage for a healing He was about to manifest. Then, sitting in my prayer chair, a song written by Julie True titled, "Healing in His Presence" came to mind. Soaking in worship and preparing my communion elements, I sensed the power and presence of the Lord's love overwhelm me.

Then, what I thought was me accidentally transposing Malachi 4:2, was instead God's divine leading. Opening my Bible to read Malachi 4:2, I instead read Malachi 2:4: *"that My covenant with Levi may continue…."* I then heard God say, *"My covenant with Levi continues."*

As only God can do, He opened the scriptures to me, informing me that His covenant with my son continues in heaven. It was, and continues to be, a covenant of life and peace. God sent many people to our young Levi, and as a witness for Jesus, he feared God. Levi was and remains forever reverent before the Lord's name at His throne. As his feet walked on earth and now in heaven, the law of truth still proceeds from his mouth.

In Christ, Levi was and is blameless and holy, and no injustice is found on his lips. He walked on the earth with the Father, Son, and Holy Spirit in peace and equity. In his witness for Jesus, many turned from sin, coming forward with the pastor's invitation for salvation at Levi's memorial service.

God does what He pleases. Today He showered me with His unfailing love and rendered yet another tender occasion at His communion table. Take time to draw near to Him through the communion covenant, and bask in His healing presence. It affords more than you can comprehend.

Awesome God

Come and see what our God has done,
what awesome miracles he performs for people!

Psalm 66:5 (NLT)

In 2001, with blueprints in hand, Mark and I began building our rustic, yet luxurious, custom log dream home. Our goals were for it to be a place where our children could feel safe and secure and have room to roam. Another desire was that it would be an enjoyable place where family and friends could relax. Shiloh Ranch in Black Forest, Colorado, became just that place.

During the building process, the house, a work of art in itself, intrigued strangers to the degree where they came to our door asking for tours. These requests were unusual to me. First, because its location was on a dirt road in the country; and second, I found it odd that people would ask for a tour of a stranger's home. These curiosity seekers made me think of Psalm 66:5—*"Come and see what our God has done, what awesome miracles he performs for people!"*

Some might be hesitant to invite strangers into their home, and for good reason. However, this was God's project! What better way to show off His handiwork, brag on His name, and tell others how much He loves them and desires to do magnificent things for them too.

People coming to the front entrance of our home illustrates how Jesus is the Door for His sheep. Upon entering, the home becomes a dwelling place, a sanctuary for many. At the completion of our home, God illuminated Isaiah 65:10, *"Sharon shall be a fold of flocks…a place for herds to lie down."* Just as this passage begins with my name, our home also became a resting place—not only for our family but for God's sheep, including those not yet of His flock.

Jesus said, *"Behold, I stand at the door and knock. If anyone hears My voice and opens the door, I will come in to him and dine with him, and he with Me"* (Revelation 3:20). When we open the door of our home for others, we open the door to Jesus (see Matthew 25:40). Practice opening your home to others, so they can see what your God has done for you.

Identity Theft

*For whom He foreknew, He also predestined to be
conformed to the image of His Son.*

Romans 8:29

I recently came across the book, *Safeguard Your Identity*, by Maris J. Frank, which is about avoiding and recovering from identity theft. An analogy came to me regarding spiritual identity theft: It's big business, and the devil continually attempts to steal our identification in Christ.

Our identity as disciples should imitate that of Jesus Christ. Some are secure in this truth, yet others hold a mistaken identity in wealth, physical appearance, career, or family. The list of false identities is endless.

Because God thinks well of Himself, we should also think well of ourselves, having been created in His image. He plainly and confidently declares His identity when He asked, *"Is there a God besides Me? Indeed there is no other Rock; I know not one"* (Isaiah 44:8).

Some of Frank's ideas correlated with my thoughts concerning spotting and protecting oneself from spiritual identity theft:[1]

The tricks impersonators use: Satan is an impersonator; it's no wonder he transforms himself into an angel of light (see 2 Corinthians 11:14).

How are you a target for identity theft? Marked by the blood of Jesus, you have a bull's eye on your back. Satan's plans are to steal, kill, and destroy.

Tools for guarding yourself from identity theft: Useful tools to safeguard your spiritual identity are the Word of God, grace, prayer, and gathering with other believers. With these straightforward, positive steps, you'll gain peace of mind and secure your most valuable asset—your identity in Christ!

God also has a book that safeguards against identity theft. It's the number-one bestseller of all time, and the information in it is like gold. The Bible is our personal survival guide, giving us an emergency plan that spells out easy-to-follow steps for both avoiding and recovering from spiritual identity theft. Take time to read this valuable resource to help protect yourself from the lies and deceit of the enemy.

This Book Is Alive!

Awake to righteousness, and do not sin; for some do not have the knowledge of God. I speak this to your shame.

1 Corinthians 15:34

Two weeks after responding to Christ's invitation of salvation, I was alone in the woods in the early morning hours reading my Bible when my thoughts wandered to an old boyfriend and his headstrong lifestyle. When I read our opening passage, with my hidden thoughts now laid bare, I removed my hands from the Bible in sheer amazement, thinking, *This book is alive!*

At that point, I had no knowledge of Hebrews 4:12, which states, *"For the word of God is living and powerful, and sharper than any two-edged sword, piercing even to the division of soul and spirit, and of joints and marrow, and is a discerner of the thoughts and intents of the heart."*

For the first time, God made His Word alive to me. Commanding and effectual, it pierced my thoughts about my former boyfriend. As a new believer, the Lord showed me I was to awaken to the right standing that I now had in Him. He made it known to me that some people, like my old boyfriend, don't have knowledge of God. He didn't scold me or humiliate me saying, *"Shame on you!"* In Greek, *shame* denotes turning inward. God didn't want me to turn inward or be introverted, but to speak up to my friend about the gospel.

My heavenly Father's first directives from His Word were perfectly timed and skillfully spoken. I did awaken to righteousness in the woods that day, and I approached my old boyfriend with the gospel. He turned his life around, and I married him!

Since my first encounter with God's Word, it's been my firm foundation, my plumb line, my anchor, my light, my strength, my hiding place, my compass, and my comfort. If this isn't your experience, ask the Lord to open your eyes anew as you read His Word today.

Delegated Authority

And Jesus came and spoke to them, saying,
"All authority has been given to Me in heaven and on earth."

Matthew 28:18

To protect my day, I began praying against any kind of approach the devil might attempt to make toward me, when a vision came to me. Jesus, with His back to me, His right arm outstretched, and His nail-pierced hand held up, He signaled as one would for someone to come to a halt. It appeared we were at a border crossing equipped with a gate and guard shack. Standing directly behind Jesus, I moved slightly to see what was happening because the gate was up, and there were no guards present.

Approximately twenty feet away was the devil, and he was aiming for me. Jesus, as mediator, didn't need to speak to the devil. Satan knew that all-too-familiar, powerful nail-pierced hand, which indicated, "You'll go no further." Without hesitation and cowering, the devil stopped immediately. The vision ended.

When it comes to the power and authority of Jesus Christ, nothing compares! *"For with authority He commands even the unclean spirits, and they obey Him"* (Mark 1:27).

Jesus is *"²¹far above all principality and power and might and dominion, and every name that is named, not only in this age but also in that which is to come. ²²And He [God] put all things under His feet, and gave Him to be head over all things to the church"* (Ephesians 1:21–22, brackets added).

Jesus also *"called His twelve disciples together and gave them power and authority over all demons, and to cure diseases"* (Luke 9:1).

When you put your life in those nail-pierced hands, you become a disciple, or learner of Jesus. As the disciples of yesterday, so are you today: authorized to represent Jesus in tasks or responsibilities here on earth. By putting up your spiritual hand, you're putting up the unmistakable nail-pierced hand of Jesus, and with His delegated authority and power, you're saying to the devil and his demons, "Halt in the name of Jesus. You will go no further."

New Shoes!

Every place that the sole of your foot will tread upon I have given you.

Joshua 1:3

Because my husband spoke often of *possible* employment in Washington, I didn't think the day would arrive. Then, one day our church's youth pastor said, "Sharon, I don't know if this makes any sense to you, but God said He's giving you a new pair of shoes." I knew then I was headed to Washington. Later, I questioned, "Lord, for months I've looked to You for an answer to that request." I sensed His response to be, *"I am free to answer prayer in whatever way I please."*

Although Washington was beautiful, arriving in the winter months offered nothing but the ocean with rain and more rain. As a Colorado girl, I was comfortable in my well-worn, sun-dried, leather cowboy boots. However, with the natural climate change also came a spiritual one, as I sensed God now spiritually fitting me with that new pair of shoes.

They were a pair of waterproof rubber boots known as *wellies*, or Wellingtons, which are excellent for wet conditions. Spiritually disgruntled with the fit of living in Washington, I told God I wanted to return the wellies, meaning I wanted to go back to Colorado. He assured me, *"Once broken in, they'll fit perfectly."* This meant that after I'm settled, the environment will be a perfect fit. I reminded God, "You can purchase new shoes that fit comfortably with no need of break-in." He reminded me, *"blessed are you who sow beside all waters"* (Isaiah 32:20), or wherever He places me I am blessed.

In this misty, mossy place, I was about my Father's business, as it wasn't only natural water that surrounded me but also the living water of the Holy Spirit. I felt as if I was walking in the shoes of the disciples in the book of Acts. Led by the Spirit, I went about preaching the Good News of Jesus, praying for the sick, and rebuking demons.

Perhaps spiritually or in the natural, God has called you to an initial uncomfortable change of climate. Trust that He knows your shoe size and type of footwear you'll need for your journey. He'll find the perfect fit!

In *That* Day

*"But I will deliver you in that day," says the L*ORD*, "and you shall not be given into the hand of the men of whom you are afraid."*

Jeremiah 39:17

Has the tormenting spirit of fear ever waged war against you? Unfortunately, it still knocks at the door of my heart from time to time; only now, I'm better at recognizing it.

I don't fully recall the scenario, but in 2007, the spirit of fear badgered me. It was most likely with thoughts of abandonment, since that seemed to be the area that fear attacked me the most. I'll never forget that day: Jesus showed up and cut that lying spirit with the sword of His Word—the two-edged knife that conquers our spiritual enemies.

With regards to fear, the words of Jeremiah became branded on my heart when God spoke to me as if He was standing in front of me in the flesh, saying, *"'I will deliver you in that day,' says the L*ORD*." That* day for me was that present moment! Jesus disarmed principalities, powers, and fear at the cross; however, He's still the God of the present day, manifesting rescue and deliverance.

Jesus was fighting for me! He promised me that I wouldn't be given into the hands of the men of whom I was afraid—these weren't human men, but demonic spirits that harassed me. Jesus also said, *"'For I will surely deliver you, and you shall not fall by the sword* [that fear wields]; *but your life shall be as a prize to you, because you have put your trust in Me,' says the L*ORD*."* (Jeremiah 39:18, brackets added). *That* day, the Lord did in my life exactly what He said He'd do.

Although fear is relentless with intimidation, with Jesus as your Savior, Defender, and Friend, He delivers a promise of rescue that rings true again and again.

Because fear introduces itself to everyone, if you don't have a plan of escape, God does. Call on Him in the moment, and He'll lead and guide you in each individual situation where fear rears its ugly head. He'll deliver you because you put your trust in Him.

No Spitting?

He spat and touched his tongue.

Mark 7:33

Do you remember the days when spitting in public was considered a vulgar and ill-mannered practice? I remember watching movies from the '30s and '40s where signposts read: "No Spitting in Public." Today unfortunately, anything goes, including spitting in public.

It's true there's nothing new under the sun, as we read in Luke 18:32 concerning the Son of Man: *"He will be delivered to the Gentiles and will be mocked and insulted and spit upon."* With this statement, can you imagine spitting in public being an acceptable custom in biblical times?

In Mark 7:32–33 Jesus took aside from the multitude a deaf man with a speech impediment. Surprisingly, Jesus put His fingers in the man's ears, and He spat and touched his tongue. Imagine this scene then, and picture yourself today, attending a healing conference. First, the preacher separates you from the crowd. That alone should be a red flag! Then to manifest healing, he spits on his hand and touches your tongue!

As I read this passage and others, I was a bit repulsed. *Spit* in the Greek language means "spit."[1] When I read this, I see Jesus spitting, not on the person but on the demonic force behind the infirmity. Although spitting disgusts me, if I were going to spit on anyone, it would be on the devil with the Word of God!

Jesus did things contrary to the social rules of the day, but never contrary to His heavenly Father. *"The Son can do nothing of Himself, but what He sees the Father do; for whatever He does, the Son also does in like manner"* (John 5:19).

Don't limit God as to how He wants to manifest healing in your life. Be open, and allow Jesus to be Lord no matter how strange His methods. Hanging out with Jesus, the disciples were *"all amazed, and they glorified God and were filled with fear, saying, 'We have seen strange things today!'"* (Luke 5:26).

Combat Snipers

For the LORD your God is He who goes with you,
to fight for you against your enemies, to save you.

Deuteronomy 20:4

The perception of the sniper world is that of a lone camouflaged gunman, such as a Navy SEAL. Marines, however, are also highly skilled military personnel sometimes operating in teams of two—a spotter and a shooter—who act as *one* to kill enemies from a concealed location.

The spotter is the more experienced senior member. His responsibility is to give the sniper coordinates of their enemy along with other vital components, such as wind velocity and bullet trajectory. Based on this information, the sniper aims, then pulls the trigger to kill the enemy.

As believers, our design is also to operate in a unified team of two that act as one, with the Holy Spirit being the spotter, and you and I, the sniper. Through this design, we're able to take the devil at any distance. As the spotter, the all-seeing Holy Spirit looks through His field glasses and detects all enemy activity. No location of the devil at any distance escapes Him, and *"He will tell you things to come"* (John 16:13). If your enemy, strife, is in His sights, He'll relay crucial information allowing you to fire your weapon of truth at precisely the right moment.

I recently watched a television program recognizing American snipers. One team eradicated an enemy at a range of 1.5 miles, which I found amazing. Another story included two snipers stalking each other in jungle warfare. Facing off through their scopes, the American spotted a flash of light reflecting from his enemy's scope. Reacting quickly, he shot the enemy sniper through his own riflescope, and through his eye.[1] That's what I call marksmanship!

As spiritual warriors, your enemy the devil is also hunting you through the eye of his scope. However, by staying in close communication with your spotter through prayer and Bible reading, the Holy Spirit relays the devil's coordinates, allowing you the assurance of the kill shot.

Spiritual Baggage Fees

*Stand fast therefore in the liberty by which Christ has made us free,
and do not be entangled again with a yoke of bondage.*

Galatians 5:1

As we walked, my delightful new friend, Tammy, and I discussed the negative things people experience in childhood and how that baggage, unless checked, is often carried into adulthood. I said to her, "I had a lot of baggage. In fact, my bags were overweight with fees."

Reflecting on our conversation, I considered airline luggage policies. When it comes to fees and regulations, everyone has faced the baggage police. Thankfully, we can choose our preferred carrier.

Spiritually speaking, we're also free to choose with whom we travel: Jesus or the devil. Those jet-setting with Satan will sadly be charged plenty in baggage fees. On the return flight (if there is one), they'll end up paying astronomical fees for overweight luggage due to bondage. Even worse, they may encounter a fatal, eternal crash. The enemy's jingle may be, "Come fly with me," but *we* will always pay the price!

An American Airline slogan once read: "Something Special in the Air." Because Jesus is Someone indescribably special, flying with Him is definitely first class. When we board with Jesus as our Captain, the only luggage requirements are that His abundant blessings overflow our suitcases. Unlike some baggage regulators, Jesus understands that everyone boards with overweight bags. Through His death, burial, and resurrection, He paid our penalties, and He'll assist us in every way so we don't continue to lug these heavy items around.

Our journey only requires a one-way ticket, as Jesus alone is the Way, the Truth, and the Life. We won't arrive at our destination, which is the Father, except through Him (see John 14:6). Although we'll encounter many lovingly thought-out layovers, Jesus' flight path for us is always the best. It may not be the shortest, but it will be safe and sure.

If you feel you've boarded the wrong plane and have carried on old, overweight luggage, feel free to change planes at any time. Jesus will be waiting for you with suitcases filled with new and better promises.

By Comparison

*For we dare not class ourselves or compare ourselves with those
who commend themselves. But they, measuring themselves by themselves,
and comparing themselves among themselves, are not wise.*

2 Corinthians 10:12

Comparison affects everyone, even from an early age. Watch infants as they play; it's game on when they spot a toy that another child possesses. It's the same with adults. Comparison nips us all.

The scriptures reveal numerous examples of people comparing themselves with others: Saul compared himself with David when the women sang about his thousands and David's ten thousands (see 1 Samuel 18:7); Rachel envied her sister, Leah, and her fruitful womb, while hers lay empty (see Genesis 30:1); the older brother in the parable of the prodigal burned with anger, as he compared himself with his younger brother's blessings, despite his unfaithfulness (see Luke 15:28–30); and the disciples argued among themselves who should be considered the greatest (see Luke 22:24).

Coming from a family with eleven siblings, as Saul eyed David, I too eyed my parents' treatment of my siblings, as well as the gifts they granted to my brothers and sisters. Regrettably, I continued a lifestyle of comparing myself with others. Because comparison happens, what matters is how we deal with it when it does. As with any area of temptation, it's best to look to Jesus, as He alone provides the way of escape.

Jesus steered clear of evil as He set His face like flint in what He had to accomplish (see Isaiah 50:7). With blinders on, Jesus, as the Son of Man, resisted every temptation that assailed Him: temptations within His own soul, His earthly ministry, and those leading up to His death.

Keeping our eyes on Jesus instead of the blessings of others will keep us on track with God and all that He has for us personally. Proverbs 4:27 encourages us to *"not turn to the right or the left,"* but to remove our feet from evil. Just as Jesus resisted temptations, we can also resist the temptation to compare ourselves with what others may have or not have when we keep on the blinders of God's Word.

What Can Separate

Who shall separate us from the love of Christ? Shall... famine...?

Romans 8:35

With our son's passing, our hearts lost their get-up-and-go. In these circumstances, some lose themselves in work, while others can't work at all. Although my husband had the grace to work, after twenty-five years of being a successful artist, sales were now sporadic and scarce, which led him out of the country and into working the oil fields, where he was employed prior to our marriage.

In all my years of walking with the Lord, He never once spoke to me about famine, until now. Genesis 12:10 popped into my heart like a cork popping from a bottle. This passage explains how there was a famine in the land, so Abram went to live in Egypt. I saw that my husband was experiencing the same thing as Abram. Mark was forced into Canada, where he would live as a foreigner. God also reminded me of the history of the Irish potato famine, which wiped out entire crops, causing starvation, death, and immigration.

In Genesis 45, God didn't remove the famine, which affected the entire world. Instead, He led Jacob and his sons to Joseph in Egypt, providing for them there. What God did for righteous Jacob, he did for Mark and me.

In Acts 11:28–29, the Holy Spirit showed Agabus that there would be a great famine throughout the entire world. The disciples, each according to his ability, determined to send relief to the brethren dwelling in Judea. This is a beautiful picture of the body of Christ coming to the aid of one another.

God kindly revealed to me that famines happen, and they don't always result from one's stewardship, but rather because we live on an economically unstable planet.

Although famine came as a surprise to my husband and me, it wasn't a surprise to God; nor was the famine in Egypt, as God set Joseph in place years in advance to manage the situation. Don't fear if you find yourself in a famine; Jehovah Jireh is your Provider. What God did for Joseph's family and mine, He'll do for you and yours.

See Us Soar

God created man in His own image; in the image of God He created him; male and female He created them.

Genesis 1:26–27

Once, while in a worship service with hands raised to the Lord, in my heart I heard this peculiar statement, *"I am woman, hear me roar."* Then I heard the lyrics from the song, "I Am Woman," by singer songwriter Helen Reddy, written in the 1970s.[1] God spoke to me, saying, *"My daughters need not declare, 'I am woman, hear me roar,' but, 'I am woman, see me soar.' When a woman understands her identity in Me and is surrendered to Me, she can't help but soar like an eagle in all the plans and purposes that I have for her."*

The following morning I woke at 2:30, and in my mind I saw the famous ship, the *Titanic*, in a vertical position, split in two, with people sliding to their deaths. God showed me that, like the *Titanic*, there are people all around us sliding to their deaths spiritually, physically, and emotionally.

Then another song, "It's a Man's Man's Man's World," written in the 1960s by James Brown came to mind. A portion of those lyrics are, "This is a man's world/But it would be nothing, nothing/Without a woman or a girl."[2] From the beginning, God had a divine plan for both men and women. Side by side, Adam and Eve were to be fruitful and multiply to bring about His kingdom purposes.

Adam Clarke, a Bible scholar who lived from 1762–1832, said this about women: "Under the blessed spirit of Christianity, they have equal rights, equal privileges, and equal blessings; and, let me add, they are equally useful."[3] Thank you, Adam Clark!

Men and women, although uniquely different, have similarities. Yes, we each have specific God-ordained roles, yet in Christ, *"there is neither male nor female; for you are all one in Christ Jesus"* (Galatians 3:28).

Referring back to the *Titanic*, the Lord told me He needs *"all hands on deck."* People who are falling to their deaths aren't concerned with your gender. They're only concerned with your lifesaving hand. So, ladies (and gentlemen), put out your hand and allow God to rescue someone through you!

Pay Check Possibilities

It is the Spirit who gives life; the flesh profits nothing.
The words that I speak to you are spirit, and they are life.

John 6:63

One evening in 1998 while chopping chicken for dinner and singing to the Lord in English and in tongues, a vision appeared to me. In the vision, I had been working extremely hard at a task, and by the end of the day exhaustion overwhelmed me. Tired, I went to receive my paycheck. To my disappointment, the check contained only zeros! I thought, *That was a whole lot of hard work for nothing!*

The second day I went to work again, but this time my labor produced peace and productivity. And my paycheck totaled $100. I said to myself, *This is more like it!* Immediately, the Lord spoke to me, saying, *"It is the Spirit who gives life; the flesh profits nothing. The words that I speak to you are spirit, and they are life. Sharon, the first day on the job you were working in your own strength, or your flesh, which profits you nothing. The second day you were working with My Spirit, which yielded one hundred fold."*

When God speaks, things happen! He revealed to me that I had been walking out my marriage in my own strength. He encouraged me to move in tandem with His Spirit, who gives life, and to be obedient to His life-giving words. When I did, I would experience His abundance in that area of my life in a greater way.

Each of us has walked out a portion of our lives apart from Christ, or in the flesh, for a variety of reasons. For me, as a young Christian, it was due to a lack of knowledge. If you find yourself worn out, maybe it's time to pause and ask Jesus, "What is it that I'm working so hard at and earning nothing for in return?" Then, begin cooperating with His Spirit, and watch your efforts produce much fruit for His glory.

Forgiveness

Who can forgive sins but God alone?

Mark 2:7

A Catholic English poet named Alexander Pope once said, "To err is humane; to forgive, divine."[1]

Knowing and understanding that *forgiveness* implies ceasing to harbor resentment or pardoning someone is beneficial and lifesaving. In addition, we find a hidden word within *forgiveness*, which is *give*. When forgiving an offender, we usually move toward reconciliation by giving something, such as a gift, a smile, a hug, a kiss, or a handshake.

Throughout these next few devotionals, I'd like to inspire you to appreciate forgiveness in four significant ways: 1) the purpose of forgiveness; 2) God's forgiveness toward mankind; 3) forgiving one another; and 4) forgiving ourselves.

First, what is the purpose of forgiveness? With Adam and Eve's choice to eat from The Tree of the Knowledge of Good and Evil, mankind was separated from God and inherited a sin nature. Leaving us self-centered, prideful, and capable of bitter grudges, this nature leads to an unforgiving heart. In view of this, God pardoned mankind. Having reconciled us to Himself through Jesus Christ, He gave us the ministry of reconciliation (see 2 Corinthians 5:18).

When we reconcile with someone, we restore friendly relations with that person. Not only are we now friends with God, but as believers we're ambassadors for Christ, encouraging others to also make peace with God. And, we are to be friends with one another, forgiving others as Christ forgave us.

The answer to forgiveness can only be found at the cross of Jesus Christ, where *"…God was in Christ reconciling the world to Himself, not imputing their trespasses to them"* (2 Corinthians 5:19). Moving toward reconciliation with you and me, God *"gave His only begotten Son, that whoever believes in Him should not perish but have everlasting life"* (John 3:16).

We can choose to live without forgiveness, but I don't recommend it. By doing so, we will reap the consequences of a miserable earthly life, or worse—an eternal death. Let's now look deeper into the most significant aspect of God's forgiveness and His all-encompassing solution.

God's Forgiveness

In Him we have redemption through His blood,
the forgiveness of sins, according to the riches of His grace.

Ephesians 1:7

When considering forgiveness and its solution, we must turn again to the cross of Christ, wherein lies the only true source of forgiveness: *"To the Lord our God belong mercy and forgiveness, though we have rebelled against Him"* (Daniel 9:9).

There's an old expression, "You can't give away what you don't have." We can't grant an offender or understand lasting forgiveness apart from first having received God's forgiveness for ourselves. During our lifetime, you and I will either be granting or receiving forgiveness.

Most of us are probably acquainted with Mel Gibson's movie, *The Passion of the Christ*. The title of the movie illustrates its theme, which is the passion of God—reconciling mankind to Himself for relationship through forgiveness of sin. Remember, *forgiveness* is a word within a word. When Jesus forgave us, He gave us His right standing with God and pardoned all of our past, present, and future unrighteousness, or sin.

My experience with God's forgiveness came in 1986. While gazing up at the night sky, I experienced a vision. I saw a scroll resembling a Hebrew Torah that had three of my many sins written on it. At that moment, Jesus revealed His forgiveness toward me, and by His grace, I received it.

The ability to forgive ourselves and others is nonexistent without first understanding that God has already forgiven us. Apart from this, our pathway is likely paved with guilt, shame, and blame. But it doesn't have to be!

Before you join me tomorrow in looking at an often-difficult aspect of forgiveness, which is forgiving others, I'd like to ask if you've received the forgiveness that God has offered you. Because He's the God of reconciliation, His forgiveness is available to you. Simply call on the name of Jesus, receive His gift, and be forgiven and free. Then, you can turn the page, and begin your journey in forgiving others.

Forgiving Others

...bearing with one another, and forgiving one another, if anyone has a complaint against another; even as Christ forgave you, so you also must do.

Colossians 3:13

When considering personal injustice, forgiveness can be a hot topic. After her release from Ravensbruck concentration camp, Corrie ten Boom, a Dutch Christian who protected Jews from the Nazis in World War II, traveled extensively, sharing her testimony. At one point, she came face to face with the guard who beat her sister Betsy, accelerating her death.

The former guard approached ten Boom, saying, "Miss ten Boom, I'm glad to see you. Don't you know me?" Suddenly, [ten Boom] saw that man that was one of the most cruel overseers at the concentration camp. [He] said, "I'm now a Christian. I found the Lord Jesus. I read my Bible. I know that there's forgiveness for all the sins of the whole world; also for my sins. I have forgiveness for the cruelties that I have done. But then I have asked God's grace for an opportunity that I could ask one of my very victims for forgiveness. And, Fraulein ten Boom, will you forgive me?"[1]

Ten Boom couldn't forgive. In her mind, she could only hate him. But then, she thought of Romans 5:5, *"the love of God has been poured out in our hearts by the Holy Spirit who was given to us."* She said, "'Thank You, Father, that Your love is stronger than my hatred and unforgiveness.' That same moment I was free, and I could say, 'Brother, give me your hand,' and I shook hands with him. And it was as if I felt God's love stream through my arms." Recalling this story, she said, "You've never touched so the ocean of God's love as that you forgive your enemies. Can you forgive? No! I can't either, but He can."[2]

Although Christ heals the *pain* of memories, some memories remain. I doubt that ten Boom forgot Ravensbruck. However, by allowing Christ to forgive through her, the darts of pain and resentment no longer possessed the power to pierce and poison her heart. Today, you too, can be free, allowing Jesus to forgive through you.

Forgiving Ourselves

And Peter remembered the word of Jesus who had said to him, "Before the rooster crows, you will deny Me three times." So he went out and wept bitterly.

Matthew 26:75

Can you imagine how Peter felt? With the Master apprehended, chaos prevailed in the city and among the disciples. As twenty-first century Christians in America, we haven't experienced such frightening, life-threatening circumstances as Peter. However, most of us can remember a time, when in the company of others, although not having blatantly denied Christ, we have kept quiet that we knew Him.

Forgiving ourselves is part of the earthly experience; we're human! Even though pardoned memories can linger, with true forgiveness, we won't incur the guilt and shame often associated with those memories.

Until Peter met with Jesus after His resurrection, I can imagine him struggling with persistent guilt and shame because of his denial of Christ. The scriptures tell us, while people associated Peter with Jesus. *"⁶⁰...Peter said, 'Man, I do not know what you are saying!' immediately, while he was still speaking, the rooster crowed. ⁶¹And the Lord turned and looked at Peter"* (Luke 22:60–61). How heartbreaking it must have been for Peter when Jesus caught his gaze in the midst of his denial.

When the women had gone to the tomb and seen that the stone had been rolled away, a young man inside the tomb, clothed in a long, white robe said to them, *"⁶...You seek Jesus of Nazareth, who was crucified. He is risen! He is not here... ⁷But go, tell His disciples—and Peter..."* (Mark 16:6–7). I believe God's love, compassion, and forgiveness toward Peter was the angel's mention of him by name.

By not forgiving ourselves, we deny the power of the body and blood of Jesus. Psalm 103:12 reads: *"As far as the east is from the west, so far He has removed our transgressions from us."* I can only imagine that great gap!

Because God has removed your sins from you, there's no need for you to dwell on them. As you renew your mind to the Word of God, you can move on with, and in, your new man, which is forgiven and free! It's time to let bygones be bygones!

Unbelief and His Faithfulness

For what if some did not believe?
Will their unbelief make the faithfulness of God without effect?

Romans 3:3

After thirty years of hiding God's truth in my heart, I encountered a deadly heart disease called unbelief. It happened after Levi departed for heaven. The prayers we prayed for the one most precious to us appeared unanswered, so why would I continue to believe God for anything more? In its relentless pursuit, this spirit of unbelief almost captured my heart until Jesus broke through, saying, *"Because of My body and because of My blood, you can believe."* In this spoken treasure, God's unfailing love melted my heart like wax.

In Scripture, Jesus complimented and marveled at the faith of certain people. Matthew 15:28 records Him saying to one woman, *"O woman, great is your faith! Let it be to you as you desire."* And, to another, *"According to your faith let it be to you"* (Matthew 9:29). I believe that Jesus was referring to their natural faith, in that, before the cross, people heard of and saw miracles He performed. This produced faith in His ability. It was not yet the faith *of* the Son of God, deposited into a born-again spirit that we have access to today. This could only come about after Jesus' death and resurrection.

As Christians, we've been crucified with Christ. It's no longer we who live, but Christ lives in us, and the life which we now live in the flesh we live by the faith *of* the Son of God, who loved us and gave Himself for us (see Galatians 2:20, KJV). What a relief! If I looked to *my* faith and not the faith *of* the Son of God in my brokenhearted condition of anguish and grief, I can't say that I would be alive and believing today.

Are you like me, or like the father in Mark 9:24, who said with tears, *"Lord, I believe; help my unbelief!"* I'm not advocating unbelief, as it carries deadly potential. However, as a child of God, even if you think or feel faithless, you're never without an antidote, which is "His faith" living through you. It produces every time, in any situation, even during times of unbelief.

We Are Family

…but made Himself of no reputation, taking the form of a bondservant, and coming in the likeness of men. And being found in appearance as a man, He humbled Himself and became obedient to the point of death, even the death of the cross.

Philippians 2:7–8

My biological family consists of my father, mother, myself, and eleven brothers and sisters. I have often thought of my family much like Jesus' earthly family. Growing up, there were chores, animals, and arguments, along with laughter, sorrow, celebrations, church attendance, and sibling rivalry. Bystanders amazed at the wisdom and miraculous works of Jesus, questioned, "*55Isn't this the carpenter's son? Isn't his mother's name Mary, and aren't his brothers James, Joseph, Simon and Judas? 56Aren't all his sisters with us?*" (Matthew 13:55–56, NIV). Can you picture the earthly family of Jesus somewhat like your own family?

God made flesh—Jesus, the Son of Man—come in the likeness of humans, yet He was without sin. Because Jesus had to be made like us (see Hebrews 2:17), He was born into an earthly family, reared by and subjected to mortal parents, Joseph and Mary (see Luke 2:51). I can imagine His parental instruction including manners, social skills, rabbinical training, and attending synagogue and mandatory Jewish festivals.

His brothers didn't believe in Him until after His resurrection; therefore, I can also envision sibling rivalry (see John 7:5). Much like you and me, Jesus had a cousin. His name was John the Baptist. He also had friends, such as Mary and Martha; their brother, Lazarus; and, of course, John (see John 11:5; 13:23). Jesus wept (John 11:35), He experienced anger (see Mark 12:15), and He had joy (see Psalm 45:7). Jesus dwelt humanly, like us, as a son, carpenter, minister, brother, and friend.

To read the Bible in light of our humanity, its characters and their life events should encourage us in our family life and our role in that family. Granted, until the return of Jesus, dysfunction will affect the family unit. But, by looking to His Spirit, as much as depends on us, we should live peaceably with one another and enjoy the blessings God has designed for us within our family.

God's Reward Card

Do not be afraid, Abram. I am your shield, your exceedingly great reward.

Genesis 15:1

As I was driving my husband's truck, a Best Buy rewards card sitting in the console caught my attention. In that moment, God began to show me an analogy of the card and Jesus. He wasn't diminishing the value of His Son to a bonus prize, but merely offering a comparison to which I could relate. Businesses with reward cards grant various benefits and perks to their customers. God's message to us is that Jesus is His reward card to mankind, and He daily loads us with benefits (see Psalm 68:19).

Reward often denotes payment of a contract, compensation, or benefits. *Vine's Expository Dictionary* explains it as "to give back."[1] The card's purpose is to give back something in return; it affords rewards in advance for participation and recompense for damages in time of need. Airline cardholders may receive free air miles, seat upgrades, or compensation for lost or damaged luggage.

In Christ, God has compensated us in full with blessings and comforts in exchange for the damage that sin brought. As believers and joint heirs with Christ, we now receive these rewards: eternal life, forgiveness, healing, deliverance, peace, hope, joy—and my favorite—never being abandoned. God's advantages are endless.

Oftentimes in the Bible, we see the following phrases: "in Me," "in Christ," "in Him," and "in Jesus." As born-again believers, we are "in" Christ. Jesus the *"I Am"* means "I am everything you need." As God said to Abram, He says to you and me today: *"I am…your exceedingly great reward."*

Do you hold God's reward card in your heart? Remind yourself daily of all His wonderful benefits. He has forgiven all your sins, healed all your diseases, redeemed your life from destruction, and crowned you with lovingkindness and tender mercies (see Psalm 103:2–4).

Crown of Thorns

God has not given us a spirit of fear,
but of power and of love and of a sound mind.

2 Timothy 1:7

While taking communion, a picture came to my mind of soldiers, forcefully pressing the crown of thorns deeply into Jesus' head, penetrating His skin and skull to the point that His brain swelled. With His blood flowing from His head, brow, and face, symbolically, I considered the bleeding to represent His sacrifice to give us a sound mind.

Jesus thought of our mind long before Arthur Fletcher, former head of the United Negro College Fund, coined the phrase, "A mind is a terrible thing to waste."[1] A sound mind is a coveted asset, and the brain a vital key organ.

In Mark 5:1–20 we read about a man with an unclean spirit and a troubled mind. No one could bind him with chains, nor could he be tamed. Always, night and day, he was in the mountains and in the tombs, crying out and cutting himself with stones. In today's society, a straightjacket and a padded cell would be this man's lot. With the sin of Adam and Eve, mental illness—demonic possession of the mind—plagues our society.

Nevertheless, with Jesus on the scene, healing and deliverance arose for this man: "*8...He said to him, 'Come out of the man, unclean spirit!' 9Then He asked him, 'What is your name?' And he answered, saying, 'My name is Legion; for we are many'*" (Mark 5:8–9). After this, the demons asked to enter into a herd of two thousand swine, which then plunged to their death in the sea. The local townspeople "*15came to Jesus, and saw the one who had been demon-possessed and had the legion, sitting and clothed and in his right mind*" (Mark 5:15).

Because of Jesus, the demon-possessed man was found sitting and clothed and in his right mind. My encouragement to you is that, because of the blood of Jesus, you also have access to a sound mind, therefore "*do not be conformed to this world, but be transformed by the renewing of your mind [through reading God's Word], that you may prove what is that good and acceptable and perfect will of God*" (Romans 12:2, brackets added).

Strong Arm

Nor did their own arm save them; but it was Your right hand, Your arm, and the light of Your countenance, because You favored them.

Psalm 44:3

know that you and I have the same enemy, the devil, and hopefully the same God, Jesus Christ, who defends us.

The following is an excerpt from my journal. As you read, take for yourself God's strong arm, power, and favor, which defend you, and not your own mighty arm. Figuratively, *arm* is a force, a help, power, a shoulder, or strength.

"Tightly, this is how I am hanging onto you. My arm is strong, stronger than that of any action hero's. You need not fear. I will never let you go. You are always safe and secure with Me.

"I am hiding you from the enemy. He is searching diligently for you. He is relentless in his pursuit of you; however, I am more relentless for you than he could ever dream of being. He is incessant to kill, steal, and destroy. Yet, I am in red-hot pursuit of you, only to continue to lavish My unfailing love and blessings on you.

"I am all power over the adversary who stalks you. When they came for Me in the Garden, I spoke saying, 'I am He.' And because of My power, the people drew back and fell to the ground. Therefore, when the enemy comes for you, he is also powerless and falls back because of My power."

As the enemy holds no power over Christ, as born-again children hid in Him, the enemy has no claim on us. Do you sense the devil attempting to flex his seemingly strong, but in reality, flabby arm in your life? Buff with pride, he's sure he'll gain the victory over you. However, Jesus has done marvelous things; His right hand and His holy arm have gained Him the victory (see Psalm 98:1). His victory over the enemy *is* your victory!

"Have you not known? Have you not heard? The everlasting God, the LORD, the Creator of the ends of the earth, neither faints nor is weary" (Isaiah 40:28). God's strong arms never tire. Will you allow them to be your strength today? They are open wide!

Pure Gold

And the gold of that land is good.

Genesis 2:12

The wildfires of 2012 burned hundreds of homes to the ground in several subdivisions near my house in Colorado Springs. To respect the homeowners who were experiencing grief and loss, I didn't venture into the burned area; however, I saw the devastation on the news, and I prayed for them.

One day while praying, God gave me a vision. I saw the foundations of these houses that had burned. To my amazement, beneath the ashes I saw a gold heart that glistened like a gold wedding band in the sun. Then, a second gold heart shining through the ash appeared. Finally, I saw a third gold heart shimmering through the ash directly above the first two hearts. The Lord revealed the vision to me, saying, *"The first heart is your heart. The second heart is your husband's heart. The third heart, which was above both of your hearts, is My heart, and I am bringing your hearts up out of the ash."*

The Lord was referring to the foundation of our hearts, buried in ashes, in the aftermath of Levi's death. One glistening gold heart represented the Son of God shining in our ashes; the other two symbolized God bringing gold out of the ash in our circumstances. Jesus has and is continuing to restore the foundation of our hearts.

If you're in a situation that has scorched your heart and all that remains is a heap of ashes, turn to the God whose eyes are on you, ablaze with the fire of His unfailing love. *"His eyes [are] like a flame of fire"* (Revelation 1:14, brackets added). Through His everlasting love and arms, He'll rebuild the foundation of your heart. His desire is to encourage you today. There's no devastation too overwhelming for Him. No matter the pain or loss, comforting those who mourn, He gives you His beauty for your ashes (see Isaiah 61:3).

Sitting Ducks

My enemies without cause hunted me down like a bird.

Lamentations 3:52

My husband and I temporarily lived in a home on a golf course smack dab on the Washington-Canadian border. We had incredible views, including that of a pond on the eleventh hole. From this position, I'd watch as many as forty ducks fly in every morning to swim, feed, and playfully bob in the water.

While enjoying this scene, I noticed an incredibly large bird perched in a tree overlooking the water. As an out-of-state resident, I didn't immediately recognize the bird as a bald eagle. My thoughts were that the eagle is duck hunting, and the ducks were unsuspecting "sitting ducks," so to speak.

As I pondered this scenario, I thought about the devil's roost and how we are sometimes sitting ducks for him. We're not to look around every corner for spiritual predators, but we are to be aware of our enemy, who *"walks about like a roaring lion, seeking whom he may devour"* (1 Peter 5:8).

Instinctively, these feathered fowl know they are prey. I hadn't witnessed it, but I'm sure if the eagle opened its wings and swooped down, there would be duck mayhem. Although we have Jesus as our Protector, we need to understand that we are spiritual prey for the devil. We still have a role in staying alert and keeping from the enemy's talons of deception.

Does the devil have his eagle eye on you, or are you the one doing the bird watching? Stay close to God, and *"He shall cover you with His feathers, and under His wings you shall take refuge; His truth shall be your shield and buckler"* (Psalm 91:4). Through prayer and communion with His Holy Spirit through the Word of God, you can avoid being a "sitting duck."

Worthless Idols

They served their idols, which became a snare to them.

Psalm 106:36

Throughout the Old and New Testaments, we see God on the pages of the Bible as a living God. Two scriptures that resonate this are Jeremiah 10:10, *"He is the living God,"* and John 6:69, *"We have come to believe and know that You are the Christ, the Son of the living God."*

In Athens, Paul's *"spirit was provoked within him when he saw that the city was given over to idols"* (Acts 17:16). Today, little has changed. People still believe and trust in all sorts of dead gods that offer nothing. Some worship statues, other people, material goods, or fame above God.

These gods are like that of Psalm 115:5–8—useless. *"⁵They have mouths but cannot speak, and eyes but cannot see. ⁶They have ears but cannot hear, and noses but cannot smell. ⁷They have hands but cannot feel, and feet but cannot walk, and throats but cannot make a sound. ⁸And those who make idols are just like them, as are all who trust in them"* (NLT). They have no resemblance to something living, which can breathe and awake from sleep.

I enjoy reading 1 Kings 18:24, 26–29, where Elijah mocked the Baal worshippers, saying, *"'²⁴You call on the name of your gods, and I will call on the name of the Lord....' ²⁶...from morning even till noon [they cried], 'O Baal, hear us!' But there was no voice; no one answered.... ²⁷...Elijah mocked them and said, 'Cry aloud, for he is a god; either he is meditating, or he is busy, or he is on a journey, or perhaps he is sleeping and must be awakened.' ²⁸So they cried aloud and cut themselves... until the blood gushed out on them. ²⁹...But there was no voice; no one answered, no one paid attention."*

In the end, God spoke to Elijah, but the Baal worshippers never heard a peep. This is always the case for those who look to false gods for help. King David said, *"In the day when I cried out, You answered me"* (Psalm 138:3). God is not dead, but alive and well. When you call, He will answer you!

Grasp on Grace

*And He said to me, "My grace is sufficient for you,
for My strength is made perfect in weakness."*

2 Corinthians 12:9

Knowing Jesus since 1986, although not having arrived, I felt I had a grasp on the sufficiency of His grace. Then, the day my son departed for heaven, further revelation emerged, which only solidified that understanding.

Walking toward the door of the Eagle County Coroner where Levi's body lay, I couldn't even comprehend what was happening, let alone possess the strength to cross that threshold. It was as though nothing was left of me; I was an empty shell. However, as a born-again child of God, with the Spirit of grace indwelling me, I felt God's Spirit, tangibly and completely overtake me from within. It was as if He filled every molecule of my body from head to toe with Himself. It was then Him living and moving within me. His grace, or His divine influence upon my heart, is what walked me through that doorway.

The apostle Paul continued our opening passage: *"9...most gladly I will rather boast in my infirmities, that the power of Christ may rest upon me. 10Therefore I take pleasure in infirmities, in reproaches, in needs, in persecutions, in distresses, for Christ's sake. For when I am weak, then I am strong"* (2 Corinthians 12:9–10).

Helpless, brokenhearted, confused, crushed, and *lifeless* are the words that described me on the day my son died. The word *weakness* implies an incapacity or powerlessness. Unlike Paul, most people prefer to expound on strengths rather than weaknesses. I wholeheartedly agree with Paul. When I am weak, Christ in me is strong. His grace not only enabled me to face the coroner but to also enter the room where Levi's body was.

Have you ever felt unable to do something? It may not be crossing the threshold of the morgue, but certainly, difficulty can come to us in a way that we're without natural strength. The grace I experienced is the same grace available to you: God's life, ability, and power working through you. It *is* sufficient for you at any and all times.

God's Good News Plan

The LORD make His face shine upon you, and be gracious to you.

Numbers 6:25

Has location or poor cell phone or internet service ever cut you off from family and friends? The adjustment of living out of state was hard enough. And with the thought of being severed from cyberspace relationships, I called Verizon Wireless to add data capacity.

While doing business, the young agent and I chatted. I said, "I prefer Colorado to the place where I am." He, too, was living out of state and preferred home. Continuing, I said, "My son passed away, and now I'm living away from my only daughter." I also shared with him how Jesus held me together in all of this.

After heartfelt condolences he said, "Ms. Patrick, I'm going to give you two free gigabytes per year." Surprised, I expressed my gratitude. Then he added, "I'm also giving you a one-time discount of 50 percent off your bill."

Holding back tears, it was as if God Himself was on the other end of the line, loving me and letting me know that He's not only with me in my new community, but He's also taking care of me.

The young operator asked, "Can you hold for a moment?" Returning to the line, he said, "Because you've been a long-time customer with us, your total bill for the duration of your time with us will be seventy-five dollars a month." Again, I couldn't contain myself. I responded, "You have the good news of Verizon, and I have the Good News of Jesus Christ!"

I heard God say, *"Ask if you can pray with him."* Losing the battle with tears, my voice cracked as I prayed with the man. God's loving kindness and presence overwhelmed me, as the agent's final words to me were, "Ms. Patrick, I talk to a lot of people, but you've changed my life. I'm getting married soon, and I'm going to find a church this week and start my marriage in the right way."

God always has good news for us—either to bless us, or to bless others through us. Just tap into the plan that He has for you, and receive all of His benefits.

Living Godly

Yes, and all who desire to live godly in Christ Jesus will suffer persecution.

2 Timothy 3:12

Reflecting Levi's life of evangelism and Christ-like character, a scholarship fund was established in his memory. The annual award is presented to one young man and one young woman, not only for their academic achievements, but more importantly, for their unwavering commitment to Christ.

Prior to this award ceremony, while reading Levi's Bible, I came across Matthew 5:11–12, which he had underlined: *"¹¹God blesses you when people mock you and persecute you and lie about you and say all sorts of evil things against you because you are my followers. ¹² Be happy about it! Be very glad! For a great reward awaits you in heaven"* (NLT). Because Levi lived his godly life openly, he experienced persecution in the halls and on the athletic fields of his school. Despite this, with God's help he stayed strong in his faith, and after his death, the very faith for which he was persecuted was now acknowledged.

At the ceremony, I encourage the graduating recipients to continue to live like Levi—following Christ and fearlessly speaking the name of Jesus. In addition, I remind them that as the world grows darker, Christian persecution will grow stronger. But, through it all, God is with them, and great rewards await them in heaven, which Levi himself is now receiving.

Although different forms of persecution exist, it's only when you are *"reproached for the name of Christ,* [that you are blessed], *for the Spirit of glory and of God rests upon you. On their part He is blasphemed, but on your part He is glorified"* (1 Peter 4:14, brackets added). Brought before the council for speaking the name of Jesus, the disciples were beaten. But they rejoiced, *"that they were counted worthy to suffer shame for His name"* (Acts 5:41). Being persecuted for the name of Jesus isn't pleasant, but it's a privilege!

To suffer persecution for Christ is a good, not a bad thing. Step out and be bold. Share the Good News of Jesus Christ. As you do, consider yourself highly favored and blessed of God.

Alumni Dinner

The godly will crowd around me, for You are good to me.

Psalm 142:7 (NLT)

After graduating from Bible college, I make it a point to attend the annual alumni dinner. One year, my son's high school graduation and the dinner fell on the same day and time. Of course, his celebration took precedence over the alumni dinner, as this was his big day! We were overjoyed for him and the future God had in store. After years of diligent hard work, he was about to receive his reward—his high school diploma. Everything was coming together as we proceeded with the customary planning.

Five weeks *before* his graduation, he died in a car accident. Five weeks *after* his death, I was to attend the alumni dinner. Having been involved with the college for many years, I consider the faculty and students like family. But the thought of joining my fellow classmates in my fragile condition caused me great uneasiness.

I assumed that my college family would crowd around me, wanting to show their love and condolences. Not knowing if I was emotionally stable enough to handle the attention, I gave the situation to the Lord in prayer. He impressed my heart with Psalm 142:7, "*...the godly will crowd around me, for you are good to me*" (NLT). I had my answer; I would attend the dinner.

My college family did surround me with love and affection, but God was good to me. They didn't throng me, but instead gave me space, which diffused any anxiety in my broken state.

Years ago, while singing in my spiritual language of tongues and then in English, I heard in my spirit, "*My heart is at rest because Father knows best.*" Father God truly knows what's best in every situation. It's wise to commit everything to Him, as He works it all out for our good.

Due Season

Those too lazy to plow in the right season will have no food at the harvest.
Proverbs 20:4 (NLT)

When my children started school, I became a full-time social butterfly. Despite good, godly activities, God had a bigger plan. Considering my lifestyle, which also included helping in my children's classrooms, I looked at attending Bible college. To commit this plan to God, I spent time in the mountains to pray and fast.

Returning home, I passed through a small town and stopped at a Christian bookstore to purchase the *New Living Translation* of the Bible. Back in my car, I opened the book to look at its text, and my eyes fell on our opening scripture. God answered my fasting prayer! This scripture confirmed to me that I was to attend Bible college.

Before Bible college, I was a "student of the Word"; however, God needed me at the right place and time, or the right season, to receive what He wanted to deposit into my life. It was time to clear my social calendar, plow new spiritual ground, and prepare my heart for the spiritual food, or the Word of God, which He wanted to plant.

From 1998 to 2012, my roles at the college included student, graduate, alumnus, intern, teacher, and Dean of Women. During this time, digging into the soil of my heart, God uprooted things that He didn't plant, and He cultivated more than I could've ever dreamed. Those years were preparation not only to withstand Levi's death, but to also bring the Bread of Life to a lost and dying world.

God created natural and spiritual seasons with specific purposes, such as spring plowing and planting, summer growing and maturing, fall harvesting, and winter rest. It's important to be cognizant of God's seasons and to be in step with them. Pray and ask God what season you're in and what you are to do during this season. Then, you can reap the reward promised in Psalm 145:15—*"You give them their food in due season."*

The Author and Finisher

Looking unto Jesus, the author and finisher of our faith.

Hebrews 12:2

While in a worship service, these words came to my heart, which I believe came by the inspiration of the Holy Spirit: *"My son, Levi, will be gone all the days of my earthly life. What will I keep my eyes on: Levi being gone or Jesus, the author and finisher of my faith? Jesus is my Alpha and Omega, my Beginning and my End, my hope, my salvation, and my eternal Father."*

At the onset, one of the hardest things for me in Levi's death was my continuous questioning, "How long, Lord? How long will I have to live without my son?" Although these were perfectly *normal* thoughts to have during my time of grief, they caused me distress. After all, I wouldn't see my son again until the fulfillment of my days or at the Lord's return. Would that length of time be six months, one year, ten years, twenty years, or even more? Levi went into glory in 2010. Although many years have passed, I feel as though I'll probably have many more to go.

God doesn't speak idly or at inappropriate times. For those of us who have had children pass, focusing on them in the grieving process is normal. However, *only* Jesus can tell grieving mothers or fathers when it's time to shift their focus. His words in that worship service breathed life into my heart.

No matter what your earthly journey or length of days, God promises that He'll keep us in perfect peace when our mind is stayed on Him, because we trust in Him (see Isaiah 26:3).

By His abounding grace and not my effort, Jesus led me little by little to focus more on Him instead of Levi. I'll never forget my son, but with my redirected focus, I found peace instead of distress.

Have your circumstances become your focal point instead of Jesus? Has divorce, the loss of children through custody battles, or sickness distressed and distracted you? Whatever your situation, you can be led of Jesus as He led me, and that is to center on Him once again.

Don't Fear the Dark

Indeed, the darkness shall not hide from You, but the night shines as the day; the darkness and the light are both alike to You.

Psalm 139:12

You've probably heard the English proverb, "The early bird catches the worm." I say, "An early bird catches the Word." Everything about the morning delights my heart: the colors that paint the sunrise, the fresh air, and the stillness that accompanies the dawn. Anticipation is also heightened as I sense the Spirit's presence, inviting me to prayer.

One pre-dawn hour, I rose from my bed to a room filled with darkness. Typically, I don't turn a light on, and like a church mouse, I quietly head for my prayer closet. This particular morning, without a hitch, I put my right foot into my slipper and then my left. Oddly, my feet went into those slippers as if I were in a room filled with light. I said, *"Lord, I can see in the dark!"* He responded, *"Yes, we see in the dark."* Instantly, I understood. Because His Spirit indwells born-again believers, we can see demonic forces in the dark.

David has a straightforward talk with the Lord regarding his enemies. He said, *"The proud have a hidden a snare for me, and cords; they have spread a net by the wayside; they have set traps for me"* (Psalm 140:5). For you and me, the proud are demonic forces who oppose us. David's words describe hidden entrapment. The enemy may think he's invisible; but, Jesus said, *"...there is nothing hidden which will not be revealed"* (Mark 4:22).

Once, a female co-worker of my husband's, even after hosting her in our home, strangely avoided me. I asked the Holy Spirit what was going on. He allowed me to see in the dark, saying, "This is a vulture attempting to attack your marriage. Shoo it away."

God, through His Spirit, has given us a gift that allows us to see in the dark, which is the discerning of spirits (see 1 Corinthians 12:10). This enables us to identify "hidden things" or traps that evil sets in our path, or unseen things that go bump in the night. So, don't fear the dark. With Jesus by your side, you'll see perfectly!

Trash Talk

A wise person is hungry for knowledge, while the fool feeds on trash.
Proverbs 15:14 (NLT)

Reading this scripture, I prayed, "Jesus, please help me to not be like the fool, who feeds on trash, but instead help me to feed on the truth of Your Word." As wise people of God, we're to be hungry for knowledge. My hope is that our longing would be for *"revelation in the knowledge of Him"* (Ephesians 1:17) and not just understanding apart from Christ.

Every person, at some point, engages in trash talk in the way of gossip, slander, or statements contrary to the truth of God's Word. God's kingdom frowns upon unwholesome language. This demoralizing speech gives way to boasting and insults, with the intent of intimidating opponents. The devil is a bully, and like the fool, his mouth is full of slander.

In the wilderness, Satan trash talked Jesus, saying, "If you are the Son of God… do this or that" (see Matthew 4:3). In modern-day terminology, the devil's libel would sound something like, "Jesus if You think You're the Son of God, let's see what You've got." Jesus responded to the devil's trash talk with: *"It is written…"* (Matthew 4:10).

God imparted the written Word to us for numerous reasons, but one purpose is to escape the liar's verbal abuse. With the devil's lowdown character, we'd do well to tune into the truth of God's Word, as Jesus did. By speaking, "It is written," we defy the oppression of the enemy's trash talk.

The Bible has a lot to say about our tongue and how we use it. I don't know about you, but after reading Proverbs 18:20, *"You will have to live with the consequences of everything you say"* (GNT), I need daily doses of God's Word to keep my heart and mouth in check.

Choose to be on the winning team of truth, which pummels your opponent's trash talk. Speak God's truth in love. It will set you free and protect you and those around you. *"When He, the Spirit of truth, has come, He will guide you into all truth"* (John 16:13).

God's Love Note

...the LORD delights in you.

Isaiah 62:4

We often hear it said, but we can't hear it enough: God loves us. The following is an excerpt from my journal. Please take God at His Word for yourself, because His love for you is great.

"It's okay that you need to hear the words, 'I love you' from Me. I made you to be the object of My affection. I created you with needs, such as the desire to be cherished and secure in My unfailing love. It's okay to be in need of Me! In My everlasting love, consumed with devotion for you, My love never fails, and My deep tenderness never ends. My love for you flowed through My Son's blood on the cross. I find it more blessed to give than receive. I experience joy beyond measure to bestow My kindness to you, not only through undivided attention and friendship, but in many more amazing ways. Having created you for My pleasure, I delight in you."

Love, Papa God

In a world where showing emotional need or desire is sometimes viewed as weak and needy, God openly reveals how natural it is for us to be in need of Him.

In general, with relationships, because of pride or fear of appearing weak, many hesitate to voice emotional needs. Oftentimes, "I love you," is not spoken or demonstrated enough, and being valued or helping others feel secure sometimes falls by the wayside.

These longings are not strictly feminine. Having five brothers and being married, I understand men need respect and admiration. And *most* don't shun the attention of doting females. Men also enjoy security in marriage. What man wants to feel as though his wife would abandon him at any given moment? Down deep, if we are honest, we're all needy.

Children openly and unashamedly ask for affection and affirmation. God loves you more than you can comprehend, and He knows your every need. Be childlike and tell God, "I need to hear," or, "Please tell me again," or, "Lord, I need...." He doesn't mind at all!

Mining Operations

A man's steps are of the Lord; how then can a man understand his own way?

Proverbs 20:24

You've heard of the "Mother Lode" when it comes to mining gold. Spiritually, for the full haul of the "Father Lode," some nuggets of gold would never see the light of day or come forth out of the mine of our heart unless we allow God to enter those shafts to mine that gold.

Suddenly repositioned in Washington, I sensed that God was mining gold from my heart for His good, as He went deeper into the shaft of my marriage, our finances, and my overall trust in Him.

A mining claim grants the owner the right to extract the valuable minerals within the claim for uses such as prospecting, exploration, and development. If we have allowed Jesus to be Lord, He holds claim to our lives and their development. God ordered the steps of my husband and me to Washington to mine gold on His claim.

As God extracted this heavenly ore, there was resistance from the "Claim Jumper," the devil. He attempted to steal my peace in all God was doing. Although having once laid claim to our lives, he continues his attempts to jump our God-given claim of promises. Despite this, through Jesus, we hold full legal rights of peace, provision, and security throughout all of God's mining operations in our lives. I can say, having submitted to God's mining operations, my "Father Lode" is priceless.

If God seeks to enter the various shafts of your relationship with Him, allow Him to. Don't board up areas where He wants to take core samples. Maybe you feel lost or trapped or consider the shaft too deep for rescue. Don't panic! The Holy Spirit, with His mining head lamp, will find you. Allow Him His rightful claim to mine the gold in your heart, and you'll be amazed at your eternal fortune.

Angel on Assignment—Part 1

The LORD, before whom I walk,
will send His angel with you and prosper your way.

Genesis 24:40

One day, as I read our opening passage on my couch, an angel manifested its presence on my left side. Although I didn't see it, its presence radiated masculinity. Sensing its enormity and power, I knew it was a fierce being that I wouldn't want to contend with.

For the next five days, the angel stayed at my left side—in a church service, walking the dogs, and teaching a Bible class. On the fifth day, the angel was still there when the enemy brought adverse circumstances into my life. It was also close to Levi's first heavenly birthday.

After lifting my circumstances in prayer, I still felt restless and decided a workout at the YMCA would do me good. Leaving my driveway and nearing the main road, the Holy Spirit spoke to me with firm yet gentle urgency, *"Sharon, things aren't right."* I understood that He wanted me to return to my couch to discuss the situation further. After more conversation with God, and doing all He'd asked, I headed out again, not sensing any remaining caution from the Lord.

While driving, I suddenly felt a violent crash and sensed the powerful angel holding me securely within my seatbelt. I had driven straight through a flashing red stop sign—the other driver couldn't avoid T-boning me at 65 miles per hour. Coming to my car, the driver asked, "Are you okay?" He had no idea that my sobbing wasn't due to the accident but because I was still alive and not in heaven with my son and Jesus, where I longed to be.

Because of my grief at thinking about Levi's first heavenly birthday, and the anxiety of my current circumstances, it wasn't until impact that I even realized I was driving. However, God knew where I was, and He sent His angel to protect me. Because of the angel's presence on my left side, I wasn't crushed between the one-ton truck and a steel lamppost!

God knows exactly where you are today and what's going on in your life. Reach out to Him as your ever-present help in trouble, regardless of what that might be. This angelic testimony continues tomorrow.

Angel on Assignment—Part 2

The angel of the LORD encamps all around those
who fear Him, and delivers them.

Psalm 34:7

Minutes after the accident I spoke of in yesterday's devotional, surprisingly, my daughter stood at my car window. Soon my husband arrived. First responders helped me out of my crushed, 4000-pound steel Volvo. Nothing on me was bruised, broken, or in pain. Amazed at my condition, the emergency medical technician said, "Your heart rate isn't even elevated." I walked away from my totaled car as if I had parked it.

Returning home and standing in my kitchen, I was livid that I wasn't in heaven. With a compassionate tone and knowing that I mistakenly believed I knew what was best, Jesus said, *"You were bought at a price; you're not your own. You don't decide when My plan for you on earth is done and when you will enter into glory."*

Later that afternoon a vision came to me. In heaven, I saw an angel walking up to Levi, saying, *"Your mother will be in trouble at Highway 105 and 83. I'm being dispatched to earth to rescue her."* Because there are no sorrows or tears in the heavenly city, I believe the heavenly family observes earthly happenings through our victory in Jesus.

That evening, as I lowered my head onto my pillow, another vision occurred in which Levi wore a brilliant smile. Jesus said, *"Levi is smiling because he's happy that you're not in heaven with him. He sees the fruit yet to come for the kingdom of God because of his mother."*

Revelation came that, although heaven and earth seem separated, they're not entirely. The heavenly family is working on behalf of God's kingdom on earth, while the family of God on earth is working on His behalf for the kingdom of heaven!

Today, are you in the midst of trusting God and His mysterious, unseen ways? You too have eternal fruit yet to produce. Know that not only is heaven on your side, heaven is working with you. Trust in the Lord and His ways. They are always for the best.

What Signs? These Signs!

*And these signs will follow those who believe: In My name
they will cast out demons; they will speak with new tongues.*

Mark 16:17

Reading our opening scripture, a revelation came to me. The signs mentioned won't necessarily follow all those confessing Jesus as Lord, rather only those who believe. Today, many who profess Jesus as Lord don't regard these words in our twenty-first century. Personally, I'm convinced of His truth, no matter what day or year it is. Therefore, because of faith and its ability to increase, my desire is to come to a greater persuasion of all that the Holy Spirit is able to do.

Since Jesus is the same, yesterday, and forever, why would He change His mind on this topic? People are still demon possessed and in need of deliverance today. In fact, with the days growing darker, the devil's assaults are becoming stronger against believers and unbelievers alike.

Another sign said to follow believers is the Spirit-given ability to speak with new tongues, which is a spiritual language not naturally learned or acquired. It was God's idea for His children at the fullness of Pentecost, and it's His will for His children today. This beautiful, yet mysterious language of the Spirit, according to Scripture, is available to all who believe.

Living with God means living by faith. Let's take Galatians 2:20 to heart: *"I am crucified with Christ: nevertheless I live; yet not I, but Christ liveth in me: and the life which I now live in the flesh I live by the faith of the Son of God, who loved me, and gave himself for me"* (KJV). We can do all things through Christ's faith in us.

As born-again children of God, believing Him and taking Him at His Word is essential. Live unselfishly, allowing the Holy Spirit within your earthen vessel to move through you as He pleases. If you let Him, He'll set captives free and pray through you with a language that brings Him glory and benefits you as well.

Trusting Him in Your Tent

You complained in your tents and said, "The LORD must hate us."

Deuteronomy 1:27 (NLT)

I n Deuteronomy 1:31–33, we read the continued saga of the Israelites and their preference for Egypt. Moses reminded them, "³¹*You saw how the LORD your God cared for you all along the way as you traveled through the wilderness, just as a father cares for his child. ³²...But even after all He did, you refused to trust the LORD your God, ³³who goes before you looking for the best places to camp, guiding you with a pillar of fire by night and a pillar of cloud by day*" (NLT).

I had a rough time getting back on track after Levi passed away. Well-meaning people told me to get back into the race, but the Lord kept the location of the race a secret.

Unfortunately, like the Israelites, God heard me complaining in my tent. I thought, *Lord, You must hate me! Can't You see I'm waiting? Don't You know I'm ready to run again?* Tears of repentance burst forth from my heart as He expounded on the words of Moses, saying, "*Sharon, all along the way that you've traveled through the valley of weeping with Levi's passing, I've cared for you as a father cares for his child. Even after all I've done, you refuse to trust My timing. I even went looking for the best places for you to rest along the way. In your darkest times, with the fire of My love, I've been your guide. I also gave you shade to rest.*"

Does this sound like a familiar parent-child conversation? At times, we too have reminded our children of the good we've done for them, as our parents did with us.

The word *refused* saddened my heart. It implies not being willing to do something. I didn't intentionally refuse the Lord. My broken heart clouded my way. I sensed His parental disappointment (not condemnation) in my lack of trust with His timing.

If you've been complaining in your tent, know that Jesus is the Lord of your process. Rest in His plans, His purposes, and His timing. He alone knows the road ahead.

Your Lifeguard Is on Duty

He sent from above, He took me; He drew me out of many waters.
He delivered me from my strong enemy, from those who hated me,
for they were too strong for me.
Psalm 18:16–17

C ontemplating David's life in Psalm 18, does your life ever appear similar? Mine has. Pangs of death, floods of ungodliness, sorrows, and snares all confronted me just as they did David.

In 1998, not certain I would make it though this one spiritual storm, I phoned my friend Teri. While praying for me, she saw me drowning in a raging sea of anger and bitterness. Fighting for my life, I bobbed on the turbulent waves of these negative emotions. Then Jesus came into view, standing on the seashore, with a life preserver in hand. Tossing it to me, His loving gaze pleaded with me to grab hold of His offer of help. Thankfully, in the vision, I clung to His lifeline. He then pulled me onto shore, covered me with a white robe, and set me on a rock. Then the vision ended.

Later that afternoon, while reading Psalm 18, I realized that the pangs of death, which confronted me, symbolized the waves of negative emotions. In my distress, I called upon the Lord, by calling on my friend to pray with me. God heard our voices, and our cries came before Him. Although ungodly emotions confront us, the Lord is our support, and He sets us in a broad place. Had I not taken His life preserver, He would've jumped in after me. Who, in the natural, wouldn't jump in to save someone who's drowning? How much more would God jump in after us?

The cries of David's heart go hand in hand with mine, and maybe yours. The specific moment we cry out, God sends His help from above. He draws us out of those life-threatening waters, delivering us from our enemy who is too strong for us.

Apart from Christ, your enemies have the ability to take you out. However, you're not alone in this sea of life. You have a competent lifeguard on duty twenty-four hours a day, seven days a week, ready to throw you His life preserver. Don't be afraid to cry out to Him.

Reely, Sharon?

Lord, I will follow You, but…

Luke 9:61

Although I'm not a fan of dining out, I am a fan of Chick-fil-A, notably for their family values, waffle fries, and advertisements.

Once, while watching television, an "Eat Mor Chikin" campaign had me in stitches. A cow was on scaffolding used to wash windows. Moving up the building, the cow came to a window where she watched with grave disappointment as a male office worker sat at his desk eating a hamburger. Sheepishly, the man observed the cow use her hoof to stick a piece of paper onto the window that read "Reely, Kevin?" In other words, "Eat Mor Chikin," not beef! With laughter like medicine, I had a large dose of it that day.

While in the Pacific Northwest, God, solitude, and writing were my constant companions. Then one day, while visiting the Chamber of Commerce, a young woman handed me her phone number after a brief conversation, and said, "I walk every day; you're welcome to join me."

Heading home, my mind spun with reasons for not responding positively to her invitation: First, walking was something I did alone; second, the morning was too early and too cold. There were other lame excuses as well, but God changed all of that when I remembered the cow's note. I heard God say, *"Reely, Sharon? I'm working here, doing a new thing, and you can't be flexible?"* No one can tell me the Godhead doesn't have a sense of humor…they created it.

I texted the young woman and agreed to meet with her. For the next four months we walked four days a week, talking about God, life, and everything else under the sun. Is God saying *"Reely"* to you in some form or another? Are you saying, Lord, I will follow You, but…. Our selfish nature may challenge us in not doing what God would have us do, but, *"Reely,"* you can't lose following God!

Predators

*Be sober, be vigilant; because your adversary the devil
walks about like a roaring lion, seeking whom he may devour.*

1 Peter 5:8

Drawn in by the stunning portrayal of Alaska's beauty and amazing wildlife, I enjoyed watching a television show called *Alaska, the Last Frontier*. The series depicted a group of fourth-generation, homesteading families.[1]

One episode focused on Alaskan predators in springtime. After hibernation or a sparse winter's food supply, most are ravenous. Alaskans are on high alert as these hungry animals attack from every direction. One particular scene left me both startled and at a loss for words, having never lived in a remote wilderness among these types of carnivorous creatures. As the homesteader's cow was giving birth, and with the calf's head crowned only to its eyes, a raven swooped down and began to peck at its eyes. As I watched, the Spirit showed me a correlation between these predators and the devil.

Just as the hungry Alaskan predators search for prey, and just as the calf was attacked at its birth, we also find at our spiritual birth, a ferocious devil lying in wait to kill, steal, and destroy the plans and purposes God wants to bring forth in our lives. Natural predators are similar to spiritual forces of prey, as they attack young and old alike. Satan stalks all people, but like a raptor, he especially targets the defenseless.

To prevent destruction by predators, the homesteader had to be watchful before, during, and after the birthing process of the calves. God also vigilantly keeps His eye on both the young and the old—before, during, and after the spiritual birthing process, to protect His own from the demonic predator.

God is ultimately in control, but like Alaskans, we have a responsibility through the Spirit's lead to be on guard, taking authority over spiritual predators. Jesus has given us *"authority to trample on serpents and scorpions, and over all the power of the enemy"* (Luke 10:19). Don't let this spiritual predator attack. Stop him in his tracks with the power of Jesus, which is the Word of God.

Saint Sympathizer

For we do not have a High Priest who cannot sympathize with our weaknesses, but was in all points tempted as we are, yet without sin.

Hebrews 4:15

While taking communion this morning, I wept thinking of God's kindness toward me.

One of the many reasons for Jesus—God Himself—coming in the likeness of man was to sympathize with our weakness. *Strong's Concordance* defines *sympathy* as: "to experience pain jointly" or "suffer with."[1] It's unimaginable, but you've heard the term "Nazi sympathizers." More incredible, Jesus is a "Saint sympathizer!"

In my grief, anger had wrongfully gripped my heart toward my heavenly Father. But Jesus completely lifted me out of the mud, saying, *"I, too, was tempted to be angry with My Father in heaven. However, as a faithful High Priest—holy, harmless, undefiled, and separate from sinners (see Hebrews 7:26)—I never yielded to that temptation because I knew no sin. I am a Saint sympathizer"* (see 2 Corinthians 5:21). It never occurred to me that Jesus would be tempted to be angry with His Father! However, because Jesus revealed how He could sympathize with me, I was instantly free of that anger.

We often hear it said that the Spirit has no emotion. Yet, the *King James Version* translates our opening verse as, *"For we have not an high priest which cannot be touched with the feeling of our infirmities"* (Hebrews 4:15). Clearly, Jesus is touched with the feeling of our weakness.

On occasion, the devil dishes up a plate of lies about us and our heavenly Father. Jesus wants to reassures us that the sin isn't in being tempted, but in giving in to the temptation.

Do you know Jesus as sympathizer? He understands you perfectly. He understands the temptations you face, and He's willing to come to your rescue. When you call on the name of Jesus in the midst of your weakness, He'll be there.

Unseen Protection

Good people pass away; the godly often die before their time. …No one seems to understand that God is protecting them from the evil to come.

Isaiah 57:1–2 (NLT)

Within hours of Levi's passing, a friend of his arrived at our home. The young man surprised us by addressing Isaiah 57:1–2, which only brought encouragement and comfort to our broken hearts.

In my grief process, meeting people who experienced the death of a child was important to me. Sadly, I met with many parents who've had children pass. We all possess a common core of grief, having few, if any concrete answers.

God speaks to grieving parents in ways that He doesn't speak to those who haven't experienced such heartache. Because God is at the very core of our comfort, what He reveals to us through Scripture, dreams, visions, or impressions can't be discredited.

One seventy-year-old Christian mother stands out. Her forty-year-old son loved Christ, yet was unable to rise above a vicious cycle of drugs. Prompted by God to pray in tongues one evening, she obeyed. Later, she realized that her prayer ushered her son into heaven. God spoke to this mother through Psalm 118:23–24: "*23This was the Lord's doing; it is marvelous in our eyes. 24This is the day the Lord has made; we will rejoice and be glad in it.*" She understood that although the drug overdose wasn't the Lord's doing, the outcome was. It was God's mercy saving her son. This mother possessed more peace than most.

There's rarely, if any, adequate preparedness for death. Young or old, God never meant for people to die, but until Jesus returns, we'll continue to do so.

For those of you in the thick of grief, or having walked through grief, take comfort that your eternal Father knows what evil our sons and daughters, who depart *seemingly* before their time, have been spared. If you're a bystander to this type of grief, please know that "*The secret things belong to the Lord our God, but those things which [God has] revealed belong to us,*" the grieving, and trust that God remains in control (Deuteronomy 29:29, brackets added).

Song & Dance Deliverance

I will praise You with my whole heart;
before the gods I will sing praises to You.

Psalm 138:1

Before I came to Christ, there were many gods in my life that I admired daily by serving them. Even after becoming a believer, I continued to serve some of those former gods. However, as I grew in God's love and grace, those clay deities began to crumble.

Most of us don't erect statues and worship them as the Old Testament saints did, but we can certainly give our time and attention to modern-day gods, such as the internet, television, smart phones, or sports; the list is endless.

God desires our undivided attention and affection because He loves us, and because He knows that following other gods can harm us and hinder our relationship with Him. Psalm 81:9 reads, *"There shall be no foreign god among you; nor shall you worship any foreign god."* Whenever I sense idols vying for my attention and affection, I'll turn to the Lord. With His help, I'll sing praises to the God of gods with my whole heart. As my song rises, those graven images don't stand a chance.

Praise is an effective weapon, which causes things to fall, including the walls of Jericho (see Joshua 6:20). I'm reminded of a very tall, large, fascinating, curly red-haired man, whom I observed in a worship service. As the music began, he started to sing and dance, and spin and twirl with all of his might. His sheer size and freedom spoke volumes! At the time, pride controlled my heart from taking part in any *seemingly* outlandish acts of worship. Many times, we may not feel like singing, but it works. Remembering the exuberant worshipper, by singing, and sometimes dancing, the many gods who clamor for my attention are silenced.

If you need the clay gods in your life to fall to pieces, sing and dance your way to freedom.

Psalm 136:2—*"Oh give thanks to the God of gods!"*
Psalm 86:8—*"Among the gods there is none like You, O Lord."*
Psalm 135:5—*"...our Lord is above all gods."*

Devocean

Command those who are rich in this present age not to be haughty, nor to trust in uncertain riches but in the living God, who gives us richly all things to enjoy.

1 Timothy 6:17

While riding my bicycle along the ocean shore in the Pacific Northwest, I noticed a posh boat with the name, *Devocean*. At the time it made me smile, as I was in the process of writing this devotional book.

Everyone is devoted to someone or something. The word depicts one who has love, loyalty, or enthusiasm for a person, activity, or cause. Personally, I'm devoted to God, my husband, family, and friends.

The boat, *Devocean*, so aptly named, lacked no opulence or amenities. Its name also revealed the posture of the owner's admiration, which was that boat on the ocean. I first considered the affection of the ship's owner misappropriated until God reminded me of our opening scripture. God *"gives us richly all things to enjoy."* He wants us to take pleasure in our lives here on earth.

Fun was a foreign concept to me after having walked through Levi's departure to heaven. However, thinking about the boat, its name, and its captain, I thought, *He has the right idea! He takes pleasure in his boat!* I don't know if he's rich or arrogant, or if he puts his trust in riches instead of the living God, but that boat was for him to enjoy, and he was doing just that.

As of late, a new devotion has surprisingly caught my attention, which is riding a motorcycle. You could say I'm a motorcycle enthusiast. I'm taking God at His Word and am freely enjoying my motorcycle. In fact, I relish almost every minute of it, while still fully devoted to God, family, and friends.

We've heard the saying, "All work and no play makes Jack a dull boy." All work and no play isn't good for the soul. Kick up your heels and have some fun, for *"Every man should eat and drink and enjoy the good of all his labor—it is the gift of God"* (Ecclesiastes 3:13).

Coat of Many Colors

Israel loved Joseph more than all his children....
But when his brothers saw that their father loved him more than all his brothers,
they hated him and could not speak peaceably to him.

Genesis 37:3–4

The Holy Spirit opened these scriptures to me in a way that one would open a gift. *"When Sharon saw [perceived] that her Father [God] loved her husband more than He loved her, she hated him [Mark] and could not speak peaceably to him."* Twice in my life I've slammed my Bible shut. This was one of those times!

Gifts from God often come to us in unusual packages with various deliveries, but when opened, they reveal truth. On this day, the Indescribable Gift Himself gave me a gift of revelation.

Like Jacob, my parents also had a quiver full of children—twelve to be exact. And like Joseph's brothers, in my estimation, I believed my parents loved my siblings more than me. Competing for the love and affection of my parents, sibling rivalry also played a role in my childhood. Unknowingly, I took this misconstrued competitive mindset into my marriage and directed it toward my husband.

Like Joseph's brothers, I was also full of hostility, believing that God presented Mark with a coat of many colors—or talents and opportunities—while ignoring the desires of my heart. At times, when living out of this ancient lie, I couldn't speak kindly to him.

Joseph's brothers stripped him of his coat. When I felt overlooked, I used criticism to attempt to strip my husband of his God-given coat. Disbelieving their father's love, Joseph's brothers brimmed with anger and hatred. Eaten up with jealousy, they stained their brother's coat with goat's blood and sent it to their father, saying, "We've found this. Is this your son's tunic?" (See Genesis 37:31–32.) This was a cruel act rooted in insecurity, as were some of my actions.

God your Father and Creator made you one of a kind. He loves you individually and has tailor made a coat of many colors to fit you perfectly. Don't compare yourself to others, but instead, put on the coat He's given you, which was created to uniquely wrap you in His love.

Dinner with Sinners

Why does your Teacher eat with tax collectors and sinners?

Matthew 9:11

In the Gospels of Matthew, Mark, and Luke, we read where Levi the tax collector gave Jesus a great feast in his house. A motley crew sat at this dinner table, which included God Himself. Observing this scene, the scribes and Pharisees complained against Jesus' disciples, saying, "Why do You eat and drink with tax collectors and sinners?"

To the Pharisees who considered others "sinners" and not themselves, Jesus said, *"Woe to you, scribes and Pharisees, hypocrites! For you are like whitewashed tombs which indeed appear beautiful outwardly, but inside are full of dead men's bones and all uncleanness"* (Matthew 23:27). Jesus reprimanded them for their facade of a well-polished exterior when their own hearts were anything but.

"The Scripture has confined all under sin" (Galatians 3:22), but the way out of that confinement is through faith in Jesus. To sin simply means to miss God's mark. The Bible classifies a "sinner" as one who hasn't yet believed he or she has been washed by the blood of the Lamb. Those who believe this truth still have the ability to sin, but the Bible calls them saints, not sinners.

Jesus' response to the complaining dinner guests needs no explanation. *"31It is not those who are healthy who need a physician, but [only] those who are sick. 32I did not come to call the [self-proclaimed] righteous [who see no need to repent], but sinners to repentance [to change their old way of thinking, to turn from sin and to seek God and His righteousness]"* (Luke 5:31–32, AMP).

Jesus, by sitting with sinners at dinner, was revealing a foretaste of Him calling all sinners to Himself at the cross, where *"God demonstrates His own love toward us, in that while we were still sinners, Christ died for us"* (Romans 5:8). If you're spiritually sick and in need of the Physician, simply repent. Turn to Jesus, and receive His medicinal treatments of salvation. You'll then have a new title: "A sinner saved by grace."

Secret Code of Combat

For if I pray in a tongue, my spirit prays.

1 Corinthians 14:14

Secret weapons are a handy advantage on the battlefield. Who doesn't covet the element of surprise in a military campaign? As I thought about combat, the Lord irresistibly drew me into a profound analogy using a true story and praying in tongues.

In 1941, the surprise attack on Pearl Harbor allowed Japan to gain the upper hand in the Pacific. Educated in the U.S., Japanese-American soldiers spoke English fluently and were able to intercept and decode American military messages. The U.S. was in need of an impenetrable code.

Philip Johnston, a World War I veteran, had an idea. He considered the possibility of America's military forces using the Navajo language as the basis of a secret code. Johnston's parents were missionaries to the Navajo people, and he had spent most of his life on or near the reservation. He was one of about thirty non-Navajos who could speak the unwritten, extremely difficult language. Within months, these men, known as "Navajo Wind Talkers," used their language to develop a code that was never broken during the war. Because of their effort, America was able to take Iwo Jima.[1]

The Holy Spirit also made a significant contribution to the war effort when He gave us a classified code in the form of spiritual tongues. This good and perfect gift, divinely distributed, is available to every soldier who'll receive it by faith. I'm very grateful for my "Wind Talking" language of the Spirit. In Scripture, the Holy Spirit is symbolic of wind, notably, the mighty, rushing wind during Pentecost (see Acts 2:2).

Privately or corporately, in distress or in praise and worship, we can engage in our secret prayer language. We don't have to fear interception or decryption by the enemy, as our mysterious dialect is God's impenetrable secret code!

Have you believed God for this secret code for yourself? Just believe, ask, and receive. Jesus delivers the payload He promises! *"And these signs will follow those who believe: In My name…they will speak with new tongues"* (Mark 16:17).

You Are Chosen

You did not choose Me, but I chose you.

John 15:16

We've all experienced the thrill of being chosen, the heartache of being the last selected, or the pain of not being picked at all. When Jesus called His disciples, they all experienced the joy of selection. From those, He then picked twelve to name apostles (see Luke 6:13).

We can't manipulate our opening scripture, nor should we attempt to. God is straightforward: *"You did not choose Me, but I chose you."* Some say we choose Jesus when we become born again. If this were true, who did the choosing, you or God? Ephesians 1:4 says, *"[God] chose us in Him before the foundation of the world"* (brackets added). Long before you encounter Jesus, you were chosen. The point of your salvation is your response to His choosing.

If Jesus can find me, He can find you, even if you're hiding. He revealed Himself to me at a drug party in the woods. I wasn't looking for Him, nor did I have a clue that He had His eye on me. In the natural, I was intoxicated and hallucinogenic, incapable of choosing anything. I had no faith; I didn't even know what faith was!

That night, Jesus endowed me with His faith and grace. His divine influence came upon my unregenerate spirit, permeated my will, and the reflection of this grace revealed itself when I said yes to His salvation invitation. *"By grace, you have been saved through faith, and that not of yourselves; it is the gift of God"* (Ephesians 2:8). Today, I continue to live my Christian life through His grace and His faith, which never fail.

Do you hold the special feeling in your heart that you are chosen by God? No matter what life has thrown at you in the area of acceptance, these passages of Scripture are just as much for you as they are me. Today you can experience the "thrill" of having been chosen. Thank Jesus, and accept the truth that you didn't choose Him, but that He loved you enough to choose you.

Angels on the Trail?

Do not forget to entertain strangers,
for by so doing some have unwittingly entertained angels.

Hebrews 13:2

While hiking with a friend who shared differing beliefs about Jesus, we came across two young men in a remote area on the trail. One man, walking a puppy, wore a T-shirt referencing Jesus. The four of us chatted briefly, and when an opportunity arose, I reached out my hand to shake his. "I noticed the message on your shirt; I'm also a believer in Jesus Christ," I said. Both men smiled and nodded in agreement, and we went our separate ways.

A short time later, we encountered the young men again, and a nod was exchanged. As we passed by them, my friend and I heard a bell ring. With surprise, we looked at each other. Immediately, I said to her, "That bell reminds me of the film, *It's a Wonderful Life,* and its association with angels."

The following morning, I awakened suddenly with Hebrews 13:2 imprinted in my mind's eye: "*...some have unwittingly entertained angels.*" I immediately wondered if the men we saw on the trail could've been angels. I believe so. Maybe God sent them specifically for my friend. After all, angels are ministering spirits sent forth to minister for those who *will* inherit salvation (see Hebrews 1:14).

In the movie, *It's a Wonderful Life,* each bell ring signified an angel receiving its wings for assignments accomplished.[1] Although far from truth, I don't fault the writer's fanciful imagination. Today, heaven and God's angels are rarely referenced, honored in film, or even mentioned in most churches.

Today, because the Holy Spirit indwells believers, many believe that the role of angels in our lives has diminished. While we're not to worship angels, they still have important roles in our lives, which are the same that God gave them from the beginning: protect mankind, act as God's messengers, and direct earthly activities. So, be on the lookout—you never know when you might be entertaining angels!

Foolish Heart Revealed and Healed

Do not hasten in your spirit to be angry, for anger rests in the bosom of fools.

Ecclesiastes 7:9

Wandering like the children of Israel, my family moved often. Before settling into our new custom log home, we inhabited eighteen houses. However, just when I thought we would finally begin to establish stability and routine in our new home, Mark was in a motorcycle accident and suffered extensive injuries. With our peaceful routine interrupted, selfish anger exploded in my heart.

At this time, our daughter had become involved with horses, so I thought I should develop some horse sense for everyone's safety. Two days before the first training lesson, my husband arrived home from the hospital.

Driving home from that lesson and feeling ill equipped for my new role as a nurse, anger was still present. Then I heard the words of Psalm 37:8—*"Cease from anger, and forsake wrath; do not fret—it only causes harm."*

Later that day, while dressing Mark's open wound and thinking about his scheduled surgery, Philippians 4:13 came to mind, *"I can do all things through Christ who strengthens me."* God did strengthen me by His grace to help my husband. However, God also had qualified medical professionals to take exceptional care of him after surgery.

Watching my husband sit in a wheelchair during his recovery, the compassion and mercy of God suddenly welled up in me and overflowed my heart. I placed my hands on his chest, and as I began to pray for him, I felt the power of God like a bolt of electricity surge through my hands and into his heart. I could sense the Holy Spirit releasing both of us—but mostly me—from the weight of my sinful, angry heart.

Be on guard; the enemy will attempt to imprison you with anger as he did me. When the Spirit reveals this anger, release it to God as quickly as possible. He longs to set you free and replace any destructive emotions with His peace. As *"the Lord is gracious and full of compassion, slow to anger and great in mercy,"* so should we be (Psalm 145:8).

All-Sufficient God

Now to Him who is able to do exceedingly abundantly above all that we ask or think, according to the power that works in us.

Ephesians 3:20

The power that works in us as believers is that of the Holy Spirit. As we prepared for Levi's memorial service, one of the ways God's goodness overtook us was through sympathy cards. We appreciated everyone's support as family, friends, and strangers from all around the country conveyed their condolences. One card, however, caught my attention because it wasn't a typical sympathy card. Embossed on the cover was Ephesians 3:20–21, and the following inscription was inside:

When you can't…He can.
When you are the neediest, *He is the most sufficient.*
When you are completely helpless, *He is the most helpful.*
When you are the weakest, *He is the most able.*
When you are the most alone, *He is intimately present.*
When you feel you are the least, *He is the greatest.*
When you feel the most useless, *He is preparing you.*
When it is the darkest, *He is the only Light you need.*
When you feel the least secure, *He is your Rock and Fortress.*
When you are the most humble, *He is the most gracious.*[1]

At the time, feeling only anguish, I was incapable of many things, including thinking clearly. Communicating was a wearisome task. Reading my Bible was difficult unless the Holy Spirit lead me to certain passages. This card, however, was alive with the Word of God, and brought me great comfort; so much so that I carried it from room to room and in my purse whenever I left the house.

Receive these words for yourself today, and allow the Lord's love and peace to quiet your heart, whatever you may be facing. And remember, when you can't He can.

Winning Souls

The fruit of the righteous is a tree of life, and he who wins souls is wise.

Proverbs 11:30

While standing at the bank teller's window, I noticed an employee across the room sitting at her desk. This employee and my son had been acquaintances, and when I saw her, memories flooded my heart of a story she once told me about Levi. Then a voice, in the form of a whisper, spoke to my heart: *"He who wins souls is wise."*

As Katie rose from her desk and approached me from across the room, tears flowed down my cheeks. After my son's death, in our complete brokenness, my husband and I had the distressing task of closing his bank account. Katie, with the utmost respect, quietly said, "If it makes it any easier for you, I want tell you that your son is the reason that I read the Bible and attend church with my daughter." She recounted how Levi would come into the bank and talk about how much he enjoyed his Bible and the things he learned from it.

After closing Levi's account, Mark and I agreed to purchase a Bible for Katie and gift one of our son's childhood Bibles to her daughter. In our sorrow, God met us with a testimony of joy.

By God's grace, Levi's wise choice to follow Christ led to the winning of souls. This was the trademark of his young life. I don't know about you, but I ask God for divine soul-winning opportunities nearly every day. I'd say that's what makes me tick!

The Holy Spirit in us gives us the ability to be bold and strong, so we can be witnesses and make a difference for Christ. As we are led by Him, we never know what our words or acts might accomplish in drawing others toward Jesus. Every day, ask the Holy Spirit to guide your steps for His eternal purposes.

Our Individual Road

Watch the road!

Nahum 2:1

S ince God has a path for the thunderbolt (see Job 28:26), He certainly has an individual path or road, complete with signs and companions, designed specifically for each of us.

Fifteen hundred miles from home, I came across a road sign while riding my bicycle that read "Sharon Drive." I got off my bike and took a "selfie" by the sign. I immediately heard God say, *"Spiritually, I have an individual road sign for each of My children."* Today, some of you might be on His path, but others might need God's Positioning System (GPS). Understand that He comprehends your path (see Psalm 139:3).

Written in the Bible for our example are people's lives and the individual roads they traveled. The most widely known is Jesus' road to Golgotha, where His destination was His crucifixion. Another well-recognized route is Saul's road trip to Damascus, where he personally encountered Jesus (see Acts 9). Abraham's path led to the land of Moriah, where his son was to become a burnt offering (see Genesis 22:2). And who can forget Balaam's outlandish road trip with his donkey? (See Numbers 22:23–35.)

None of us walks our road alone. God saw to it that a man from Cyrene helped Jesus carry His cross (see Matthew 27:32). When Saul fell to the ground blinded, his travel companions came to his aid. Servants accompanied Abraham on his difficult path. Two men traveled the road to Emmaus (see Luke 24:13), and in the same way that Jesus was present with these men, so He is with you.

God will post signs along the way for our guidance and protection. Job 21:29 asks, *"Have you not asked those who traveled the road? And, do you not know their signs?"* For the godly, a wealth of knowledge abides with those who have trekked before us.

If you don't yet know your individual path, begin to seek the Lord for it. Then, as you follow your course, pursue the counsel of those familiar with the signs and road conditions that lie ahead so your road will be smooth.

Song Bird

He has put a new song in my mouth—praise to our God;
many will see it and fear, and will trust in the LORD.

Psalm 40:3

Are you a songbird? I don't consider myself to have a singing voice, but I believe God enjoys it when I sing to Him anyway.

Before my great sorrow, songs easily radiated from my spirit, but after my sudden tragedy, I couldn't bear to sing. I was brokenhearted beyond description after Levi passed away, yet I'm confident God would rather hear a song out of tune from a broken heart than hear no song at all. Being crushed in spirit, all hymns, whether in corporate worship or in my personal prayer time, only resulted in tears gushing forth.

After nearly five years of innumerable tears and fragmented songs, everything changed when I asked my friend Sue, "What does a typical day look like for you?" At the young age of eighty-five, she responded, "I start my day singing to the Lord for about an hour and a half." In awe, I asked, "Do you listen to a worship CD?" She replied, "Oh no, I just sing quietly to the Lord." I remembered a day when I too had a song in my heart to the Lord. *"How shall we sing the LORD's song in a foreign land?"* (Psalm 137:4). Or, in my case, a land of grief.

All this time, I thought my voice box was broken because in my attempts to worship God, I always broke down weeping, and my song ceased. While temporarily living in the Pacific Northwest, I remembered the words of my precious friend, and as I headed into prayer, I slowly began singing again. Although the tears continue, the songs remain. I'm now daily singing a new song to the Lord (see Psalm 33:3).

If extreme circumstances have damaged the voice box of your heart, know that God understands. Sit with Him awhile, and trust Him to give you a new song to set your heart free.

It Wasn't Me!

It is no longer I who do it, but sin that dwells in me.

Romans 7:17

We have two kinds of flesh: our physical body and our sin nature. The problem isn't with our physical body but the carnal nature of our flesh.

A vision once appeared to me in which something came out of me and stood beside me. I had the distinct impression that the thing next to me was sin that dwells in my flesh. Paul wrote, *"17But now, it is no longer I who do it, but sin that dwells in me. 18For I know that in me (that is, in my flesh) nothing good dwells.... 20Now if I do what I will not to do, it is no longer I who do it, but sin that dwells in me"* (Romans 7:17–18, 20).

Although sin dwells in our flesh, it's separate from our spirit—our true nature in Christ. With this picture, any crippling guilt of wrongdoing evaporated. "It wasn't me!" Not that we disregard responsibility for taking part in the fleshly actions recorded in Galatians 5:19–21, such as, adultery, envy, or drunkenness, but the sooner we disassociate ourselves with the sin nature, the quicker we can relate to our identity in Christ.

Sin is more powerful than we are, but sin isn't more powerful than Jesus Christ. He condemned sin in the flesh, calling "it" guilty (see Romans 8:3). Instruction to overcome the sin in our flesh is found in Galatians 5:16–17: *"16But I say, live by the Spirit and you will not carry out the desires of the flesh. 17For the flesh has desires that are opposed to the Spirit, and the Spirit has desires that are opposed to the flesh, for these are in opposition to each other, so that you cannot do what you want"* (NET).

Following this instruction requires a relationship with Jesus. If Christ already has a place in your heart, ask Him to show you how to "live by the Spirit" and thereby conquer the flesh. If He doesn't, allow Him to make His home with you. The Holy Spirit will help you resist the sin nature and avoid doing what the flesh demands (see John 14:23).

The Implant

Receive with meekness the implanted word, which is able to save your souls.

James 1:21

You've probably heard that you have to read the Bible in order to get God's Word on the inside of you. Otherwise, God can't bring the scriptures you need for a particular situation to your memory.

John 1:1 tells us that *"In the beginning was the Word, and the Word was with God, and the Word was God."* And John 1:14 says, *"And the Word became flesh and dwelt among us...."* In addition, Revelation 19:13 proclaims, *"...His name is called The Word of God."* Do you agree that Jesus is the Word of God? Would you also agree that the Godhead made its home within your spirit when you became born again? Because of this, you now have the implanted Word—Jesus—operational within your spirit.

After becoming born again, Scripture came to my mind when I hadn't yet read the Bible or put the scriptures in me. I later realized that it was the implanted Word within my born-again spirit that spoke to my heart and mind.

God's written Word is His priceless gift to you to help you renew your mind, not your born-again spirit. *"Complete in Him,"* your born-again spirit, having *"the mind of Christ,"* needs no renovation (1 Corinthians 2:16; Colossians 2:10). However, your natural mind does need restoration. Romans 12:2 instructs us, *"do not be conformed to this world, but be transformed by the renewing of your mind, that you may prove what is that good and acceptable and perfect will of God."*

Even if you've never had access to the written Word, because you have the indwelling Word, Jesus, He's able to communicate the entire written Bible from your spirit to your mind. Keep reading your Bible, as it's your blueprint and plumb line to reconstruct your mind! In addition, receive the implanted Word, Jesus, who is able to save your soul.

Foxholes in Combat

Listen to Me, you who follow after righteousness,
you who seek the LORD: Look to the rock from which you were hewn,
and to the hole of the pit from which you were dug.

Isaiah 51:1

On the battlefield, soldiers dig critical defensive fighting positions known as foxholes. These are places of refuge or concealment. The troops can "hunker down" and use them as firing points or positions.

While in a worship service, I looked at the congregation surrounding me, and I sensed the Lord say, *"The church you hunker down in will be the foxhole in which you and your brothers and sisters will fight against the enemy."*

Encouragement comes to us from Hebrews 10:25, *"And let us not neglect our meeting together, as some people do, but encourage one another, especially now that the day of his return is drawing near"* (NLT). As the Lord's return approaches, the heat of the battle will intensify. The gathering of the saints is not necessarily in a building, since as believers *we* are the church—those whom God has called out from the world. Whether He summons us to a church family that meets in a building, a home, or a coffee shop, we should obey His orders because that's where we'll join together to fight against the enemy in the foxhole of life.

For twenty years, my family and I hunkered down in one church. Those years included positive aspects, and then extreme challenges, through which many left the church. Nevertheless, God led us to stay. Then, when Levi passed away, God provided everything needed to sustain us in that foxhole with our fellow companions.

The people of God—not the government—are the answer to humanity's needs. In a foxhole of God's leading, plan, and design, emotional, physical, financial, and spiritual needs are met in varying degrees. In Acts 2:45, the New Testament church, from their foxhole, *"sold their possessions and goods, and divided them among all, as anyone had need."* That's a clear picture of looking out for one another!

We all need a safe and secure foxhole. There we'll find provision, accountability, comfort, and companionship. If you don't yet have a foxhole where you can gather with other believers, make finding one a mission priority!

The Blacksmith

The proud have forged a lie against me.

Psalm 119:69

One morning, light years ago—in the '80s—as I awoke, the Holy Spirit spoke to me, *"Psalm 119:69."* I took my Bible from my nightstand and opened it to that verse. I read, *"The proud have forged a lie against me."* I asked God, "What is the lie?" He responded, *"The lie that I don't love you as a woman."*

Immediately, I had a vision of a blacksmith forging metal. By putting the steel into a hot fire and then into water, he pounded and molded the iron with his hammer. He repeated the process until he finally had the desired result: a very hard piece of sculpted metal. The devil was the blacksmith!

God showed me how the devil hammered at my heart with a lie, like a blacksmith, until he fashioned a false image of a woman who wasn't loved by God. In this deception, I had also unknowingly played a part by choosing to believe the lie that God didn't love me as much as He loved others. It seemed real to me growing up within a family of fourteen that there were favorites. As a young girl, and then as a young woman into my journey as a new believer, I had allowed my heart to harden and didn't even realize it.

In James 2:9 we read, *"If you show partiality, you commit sin."* Because I understood that God never sins, He couldn't possibly show partiality or favoritism. Believing that He loved other people more than me, I was, in effect calling Him a sinner. Wow! Coming out of the world as a new Christian, I may've had some misconceptions about God's character, but I knew He wasn't a sinner!

This scripture was foundational for me, as it helped me reject the lie that God had favorites. If at any time you've been fashioned into a make-believe image, turn to the fire and the hammer of the Word of God. Through it, He'll turn you away from the devil's lies and mold you into something beautiful.

For Heaven's Sake

I say to you, there is no one who has left house or brothers or sisters or father or mother or wife or children or lands, for My sake and the gospel's, who shall not receive a hundredfold now in this time.

Mark 10:29–30

After years of marriage and raising a family, I complained to God, "Mark experiences the adventures, while I'm left behind." Temporarily moving to Washington, I became part of a divine adventure! Little did I know that in God's vocabulary, the words *adventure* and *surrender* go hand in hand.

Moving to Washington wasn't "all the rage" I'd imagined. For the first week, the turmoil in my heart was rougher than the ocean water I watched through my window. I reminded God of how I left my homeland and my beautiful daughter and wonderful son-in-law. I also left friends—including my best friend, Sandy—and my church; and it seemed to all be for nothing! Isolated, I was writing while my husband worked.

Encouragement came to me through a phone call when my friend Mary Lou prayed our opening passage. She reminded me that God promised one hundredfold in this life. Then God revealed to me that I left everything for His sake and the gospel's, and I heard these words, *"I died for you; can you live for Me in Washington?"* His words pierced my heart.

The greater picture came into view as we moved into a home with an unsaved man. After a few weeks, we moved again; this time into a condominium on the beach, whose owners also needed spiritual guidance.

During these moves, I thought Mark was either out to sea adrift, or God was truly leading us. Then, assurance of my bearings came from Jeremiah 10:23 like a buoy, *"the way of man is not in himself; it is not in man who walks to direct his own steps."*

Corrie ten Boom said, "Every experience God gives us, every person He puts in our lives, is the perfect preparation for the future that only He can see."[1] The Lord is a Promise Keeper in this life and the next. My one hundredfold wasn't things, but a deeper, more intimate relationship with Him than I could've ever imagined.

Be bold and forsake all for Christ's purposes, knowing that you can't out-give God. He'll bring back to you more than you can imagine!

A Kiss from Heaven

You meet him with the blessings of goodness.

Psalm 21:3

Greeting me at work, the receptionist said, "I have a message for you. A woman found a note from your son." I wondered how that could be since Levi had been in heaven for eighteen months. I was anxious to learn what this note was.

Emotions ran high as my husband and I called the woman later that evening. She told us how she was shopping at Goodwill, tried on a pink fleece jacket, and found a note when she slipped her hands into the pockets. She said, "Having three boys, I knew I had to find this mother, so I 'Googled' your name that was on the envelope."

After hearing the events that led her to the note, I responded, "After the death of our son I took many things to Goodwill." With concerned surprise, she said, "Your son is dead?"

"Yes," I said. "It's been exactly one and a half years ago today."

She then remembered hearing Levi's story in the news. She told me she'd put the note in a plastic bag for protection. Although she and I lived in two different cities, miles apart, she promised that her husband would deliver the note the following day.

God's goodness overwhelmed us as a kiss from heaven. It was as if Levi was speaking to us directly from his eternal home as we read the card:

Hey Mom and Dad,

I want to thank you for everything you guys have done. I love you so much. I am so blessed by having you as my parents. You both have really showed me how to be a godly young man. You are really showing me how to live a Christian life. So thank you for everything. Thanks for coming to all my games and everything else you came to. Thank you for supporting me. I love you so much!

Levi P.

If you're having problems seeing and believing that God is good and on your side, trust in Psalm 52:1, *"The goodness of God endures continually."* Ask Jesus to open your heart and spiritual eyes so He can reveal His goodness to you.

The Importance of Action

Be doers of the word, and not hearers only, deceiving yourselves.

James 1:22

Years ago, I had an odd experience while teaching a Bible college class. The Lord gave me a vision of the students, in which their physical bottoms were hanging over the sides of their chairs. I sensed the interpretation was that the overflow represented them being spiritually overweight.

After eating too much, our physical body can feel full, and if there isn't an outlet to burn the calories consumed, we'll become overweight. Likewise, when we hear the Word of God and don't act on it, we can feel full and become spiritually overweight.

This was a common saying among the first-year Bible college students: "I'm so full of God and His Word, if I don't give it away, I'm going to explode!" Our counsel from James 1:22 is to be *"doers of the word, and not hearers only,"* deceiving ourselves. Just as our body gains weight when more calories are consumed than expended, our spirit can gain spiritual deception as we hear but don't act on God's Word.

Physically, it's best to stop eating before our stomach fills to the brim to avoid discomfort. Likewise, continually feeding on Scripture without acting on it causes deception. For example, the Bible tells women to respect their husbands. If a woman merely reads this portion of Scripture, yet continues to disrespect her husband, she'll likely be miserable. It's only as she begins to show respect for her husband that she finds relief and rids herself of deception.

Instead of merely saying we're going to lose weight or spiritual deception, we should take steps toward doing it in order to succeed. Be careful not to only read the Bible but to act on it. As earthly food sustains your physical body, the Word of God, as your spiritual food, fuels your spirit. When you consume God's Word then act on it, you'll stay spiritually fit.

Mercy Seat

I will have mercy on whomever I will have mercy,
and I will have compassion on whomever I will have compassion.

Romans 9:15

Two weeks after Levi's first heavenly birthday, I received a call that my youngest sister's nineteen-year-old son was in an accident in Japan, where his car went over a cliff.

Forty-five minutes after the wreck, emergency workers found him in the bottom of a ravine, unresponsive. They removed him from the vehicle with the Jaws of Life and revived him. After driving him to a nearby hospital, they discovered that the trauma unit wasn't advanced enough to meet his medical needs, so they transported him to another facility via helicopter. His heart stopped once again on the operating table, but he was resuscitated. He flatlined a third time in ICU, yet was brought back again. Although I was happy for the preservation of my nephew's life, I was also angry that my own son's life wasn't spared.

One day as I was walking my dogs and talking to the Lord, I asked, *"God, You could spare my nephew not only once, but three times, yet You couldn't spare my Levi?"* God responded immediately, *"I had mercy on them both. I will have mercy on whomever I will. I had mercy on Levi, and I had mercy on your nephew."* King David said, *"Who can tell whether the Lord will be gracious to me, that the child may live?"* (2 Samuel 12:22). With me, God always has the last word!

God knows our beginning from our end, but *"we see in a mirror, dimly"* (1 Corinthians 13:12). You and I might have a few answers about what goes on in our lives, but in Christ, we have a God who sits on His mercy seat pouring out the multitude of tender mercies whenever needed.

"Whatever the Lord pleases He does, in heaven and in earth" (Psalm 135:6). My prayer is that you can rest in His love for you, which He demonstrated on the cross. This is where you'll find peace for your heart for the questions to which you have no answers.

Silent Rain

*The LORD will open to you His good treasure, the heavens,
to give the rain to your land in its season.*

Deuteronomy 28:12

Feeling sorrow in my son's passing, in my quiet time and with pen in hand, God began to express His heart to me, saying, *"I long to bless you, to open the windows of heaven for you. I'm opening these windows, as showers of blessing of every kind are raining down on you. I give you your rain in season—the early rain and the latter rain—the showers of the living water of My Holy Spirit. I am a Master Gardner. I know exactly when to let it rain and how much of it you need for your heart to grow in Me, in My presence, and in My love for you.*

"In natural rain, you put up an umbrella to prevent from getting wet. Please don't put up your umbrella when My rain comes. Look up! Turn your face upward, toward My heavens, and let Me pour My rain on your face and refresh your countenance. Let it soak and permeate you as a natural rain soaks a person through and through. My rain won't give you a chill; it's soft and gentle upon you, not pelting and painful to the touch. It brings an abundance of life. Look at the results of the natural rain: everything blooms and turns green. Everything's more lush and beautiful. Then there's the rainbow, the seal of My covenant. You're sealed by My Holy Spirit; sealed for the day of Redemption."

Have you ever seen a picture of a person looking upward toward the sky, enjoying the rain on his or her face? This picture came to me when God asked me to turn my face upward. As I did, His rain washed and refreshed my sad countenance, because *"by sorrow of the heart the spirit is broken"* (Proverbs 15:13).

If your circumstances have altered your countenance, look to Him. You'll be washed and refreshed as He showers you with His love and blessings. All you need do is look up!

It Must Be Heaven

*How awesome is this place! This is none other than
the house of God, and this is the gate of heaven!*

Genesis 28:17

Until we cross over, we can only imagine heaven. Considered a place of tranquility, most people, for peace of mind for themselves and for those they love, accept heaven's existence.

Each person holds his or her own belief or image of heaven. With my black and white personality, I take the Bible as truth, so heaven exists. There's no doubt in my heart that God, Jesus, and the Holy Spirit dwell there. Innumerable angels also inhabit the heavens, as well as horses. And certainly, *All Dogs Go to Heaven*, as this Don Bluth film suggests! Another reason for my firm persuasion is that all departed persons believing in Jesus reside there, including my son. I'm convinced that to be absent from the body is to be present with the Lord in heaven (see 2 Corinthians 5:8).

Amazing things surround God's throne, such as four living creatures with wings full of eyes in front and back, and a rainbow in the appearance of an emerald. (see Revelation 4:3, 6). I believe worship in the form of adoration, song, and dance is perpetual (see Revelation 4:8). Rewards, crowns, and a marriage supper await those whose names are written in the Book of Life. Can you imagine the streets paved with gold, and each individual gate, a single pearl (see Revelation 21:21)?

Although Scripture reveals a miniscule glimpse of this inexpressible place, when I pass by a city park and see people relaxing, and kids running, playing, and laughing, I get the distinct impression that Levi is involved in the same activities among the heavenly residents.

Unlike earthly families, the heavenly family has no tears. *"God will wipe away every tear from their eyes; there shall be no more death, nor sorrow, nor crying. There shall be no more pain, for the former things have passed away"* (Revelation 21:4). Complete in every way, they're forever face to face with God—Creator, Savior, and Friend—along with believing family and friends.

I encourage you to read about heaven and look forward to the day when you get to stand face to face with Jesus in this amazing paradise!

True Intercession

He always lives to make intercession for them.

Hebrews 7:25

My husband and I believe one of God's gifts to us in marriage is our coming together in the prayer of agreement, which we take from Matthew 18:19, where Jesus said, *"if two agree on earth concerning anything that they ask, it will be done for them by My Father in heaven."* However, with the anguish of Levi's passing, there were days when we couldn't pray in this capacity.

Because grief can be extremely unpredictable, one day I approached my husband asking that we agree in prayer for the peace of Jesus to quiet our hearts; in his sorrow, he declined. The Lord impressed on me that I was asking something of Mark that he couldn't give under the circumstances.

In that moment, the Spirit gave me a vision. At God's throne, Jesus sat at the right hand of the Father making intercession for me. I stood before Jesus on what appeared to be a marble floor. With His head turned toward the Father, it was apparent they were discussing my prayer request. As I stood before Him waiting, He turned His face to me and said, *"Now this is the confidence that you have in Me, that if you ask anything according to My will, I hear you. And if you know that I hear you, whatever you ask, you know that you have the petitions that you have asked of Me"* (see 1 John 5:15).

This powerful truth altered my thinking in light of the prayer of agreement in marriage and with others. A weight lifted off me, which in turn lifted from my husband when I quit looking to him for what he was understandably not able to give in the moment.

Unity in prayer is godly and good, but ultimately, Jesus is our true intercessor (one who prays on behalf of another). What do you need agreement for today? The prayer of agreement with the Lord Jesus Christ is complete! You can come to Him with any request according to His will, and He'll hear and fulfill that prayer. He's always ready to agree with you.

Blinded by Doubt—Blinded by the Light

The Spirit of the LORD is upon Me,
…to proclaim liberty to the captives and recovery of sight to the blind.

Luke 4:18

One day, as I took communion and meditated on the truth that Jesus is our Physician, I looked back on all the countless ways He had manifested healing to me. Reading the words of Luke 4:18, "… *recovery of sight to the blind,*" I heard Jesus say, *"Because of My body and My blood, you are not blind."*

At that moment, Revelation 3:18 came to mind, and it became my prayer: "*anoint your eyes with eye salve that you may see.*" As I physically anointed my eyes with oil, Elisha's prayer for his servant also came to my mind, "*'LORD, I pray, open his eyes that he may see.' Then the LORD opened the eyes of the young man, and he saw*" (2 Kings 6:17).

After Levi's death, the truth of God's Word through my eyes of faith became blurred. With our prayers for his safety, death never once entered our minds. Then, suddenly, without warning, we received a call from a coroner. The anguish affected every molecule of my spirit, soul, and body.

Jesus the Great Physician, who gives recovery of sight to the blind, healed my eyes of faith in the secret place of His presence, through prayer and communion. During this time, I couldn't help but think of Saul on the road to Damascus. The light of Christ physically blinded him, but through that, he received his spiritual eyesight, as Jesus revealed Himself to him. Then in a vision, Jesus instructed a man named Ananias to go and lay his hands on Saul that he may receive his sight (see Acts 9:12). Through this act, Jesus healed Saul's physical blindness.

Maybe you feel like you're groping in the dark. Maybe you're like Saul, having not yet met the Light of the world. Or, perhaps you're like me, a believer temporarily blinded by extreme circumstances. It should bring you great comfort to know that you're in the hands of a bona fide optometrist! Thank the Lord that He has given recovery of sight to the blind—spiritually and physically—and receive it from Him now.

Combat Mines

Let a cry be heard from their houses,
when You bring a troop suddenly upon them;
for they have dug a pit to take me, and hidden snares for my feet.

Jeremiah 18:22

Most of us have heard of land mines, which are explosive charges concealed just under the surface of the ground and designed to be detonated by pressure. Another lethal device used by insurgent and terrorist groups is the Improvised Explosive Device, or IED. These are "homemade bombs, that despite being crude in design, can be highly destructive and deadly. ...Typically, IEDs are buried on the side of a road or disguised to look like innocuous junk. They are detonated by remote control as a military vehicle passes."[1]

Like an insurgent, the devil also secretly places land mines along our pathway with intent to destroy God's soldiers. Living in this world, we sometimes take a hit. But with God on our side we can't lose, as no device of the enemy is unseen by Him. *"He uncovers deep things out of darkness"* (Job 12:22). God is always with us and walking us through the enemy's landmines.

If we were on a natural battlefield filled with known or hidden explosive devices, our steps would certainly be cautious and calculated. We'd do all we could to seek out and stick close to those who held the map to the minefield. The same is true for the spiritual battlefield.

The key to avoiding contact with enemy IEDs is to stay in step with our Supreme Commander. We must acquire the mindset that says, *"My soul follows close behind You; Your right hand upholds me"* (Psalm 63:8). When you and I acknowledge Him in all of our ways, He directs our paths, and He makes known to us the hidden dangers that lie ahead (see Proverbs 3:6).

He promises to hide you from the secret plots of the wicked (see Psalm 64:2). Don't be caught in enemy territory without the One who holds the map! Stay close to Jesus, and He'll clear a path for you.

The Pearls of Birch Bay

*Again, the kingdom of heaven is like a merchant seeking
beautiful pearls, who, when he had found one pearl of great price,
went and sold all that he had and bought it.*

Matthew 13:45–46

For centuries, natural pearls have been highly valued as objects of beauty. Because of this, they're considered gemstones, and the word *pearl* has become a metaphor for something very rare and valuable.

Birch Bay is a picturesque, seaside town in Washington. Although oysters are plentiful there, not all contain a pearl like the pearls of Birch Bay. These are the women God hand picked to grow in my heart during my brief stay there. Just as an oyster holds a genuine, one-of-a-kind pearl, these uniquely individual women are the real thing and not imitations.

The first pearl, Brenda, is a realtor and friend. As a stranger in Washington, I wanted to run back to Colorado, but this gem invited me into her home and encouraged me to stay. The second pearl, Tammy, didn't approach me to be served, but to serve. This beauty and gem of a tour guide daily served me with friendship. The third pearl, Helene, reflected pearls of wisdom in her iridescence. She was full of creative ideas for my book distribution.

The fourth and final pearl, but certainly not the least in value, is Melanie. Although having never met me, Melanie opened her home to me. Because of her great kindness, I rested in utter solace during the bittersweet time of Levi's fifth heavenly birthday.

To Jesus, every pearl is of matchless worth, including you. He's the merchant seeking you. *"Our great God and Savior Jesus Christ"* (Titus 2:13) bought each pearl at a price (see 1 Corinthians 7:23). That great price was His crucifixion at Calvary for you (see Luke 23:33).

Who are the pearls that God has set in your life? In His goodness, He'll give us gems to help us along our way. As you view others as God's gemstones for your life, never forget that you're also a pearl of great price to Him.

Dry Bones

*The hand of the LORD came upon me and brought me out in the Spirit of the
LORD, and set me down in the midst of the valley; and it was full of bones.
Then He caused me to pass by them all around, and behold, there were very
many in the open valley; and indeed they were very dry.*

Ezekiel 37:1–2

I sensed I was Ezekiel himself, as God also drew me by the Spirit into a vision and
set me down in the midst of a valley full of dry bones. God not only set Ezekiel in
the midst of the valley, He caused him to walk all around the dry bones. Strikingly
descriptive, there were scores of bones, and they were, indeed, dry and lifeless.

In my vision, the Lord also walked me around my own valley of dry bones and said,
*"The bones in the valley represent you and all of the people whom I desire to touch
through you. These will stay dead if you, like Ezekiel, don't breathe the breath into
them which I breathe into you. The valley is full with many dry bones from abortion,
divorce, and suicide, along with spiritual and emotional death."*

Oddly, the Hebrew root meaning of the word *dry* is "to be ashamed, confused, or
disappointed."[1] I was confused and disappointed in my son's seemingly short-
lived life.

In our natural body, osteoporosis dries the bones. In our spiritual body, *"A broken
spirit dries the bones"* (Proverbs 17:22). God's desire is for our bones, and the bones
of those around us, to live.

Most of us have probably suffered from spiritual osteoporosis, resulting from a
broken spirit, at one point or another. The important thing is that we don't remain in
this condition, and we don't allow those around us to remain there either.

God has set each one of us in a particular valley or sphere of influence. Can you see
the dry bones in your valley, and if so, do they mirror the characteristics of those
described in Ezekiel 37:1–2? Imagine how the life-giving breath of God can change
them and raise them up through you! Ask God what He would like to breathe
through you into the dry hearts of those around you, then be expectant with the
opportunities He provides.

Can Dry Bones Live?

And He said to me, "Son of man, can these bones live?"
So I answered, "O Lord GOD, You know."

Ezekiel 37:3

God spoke to me again, as He did to Ezekiel concerning these dry bones, saying, *"Sharon Rose, can these bones live?"* I said, "Oh, sovereign Lord, only You know! Can my heart live again after the death of my son?"

Since God spoke it to Ezekiel, you and I can take it for ourselves and for those in our valley of influence: *"Prophesy to these bones, and say to them, 'O dry bones, hear the word of the LORD'"* (Ezekiel 37:4).

The definition of *prophecy* signifies "the speaking forth of the mind and counsel of God."[1] Not only did my broken heart need to hear the word of the Lord, but so did the people in my valley of influence. These people don't need opinions or eloquent speech. Jesus said it perfectly: *"It is the Spirit who gives life; the flesh profits nothing. The words that I speak to you are spirit, and they are life"* (John 6:63). Jesus alone has the words of eternal life for each dry bone in the valley.

Since God gives life to the dead and calls those things which do not exist as though they did (see Romans 4:17), we too, through His Spirit, have the ability to speak the Word of God over our lives and over the dry bones of others. As we do, the things that are dead or nonexistent will then come to life. One example of this is praying for the unsaved. As we pray God's will and Word over them, their once-dead spirit will eventually come to life and be born again.

I like our opening passage: *"O Lord GOD, You know."* God knows your needs, and the needs of your family and those of your valley of influence. Turn to Him and His Word, as it is the only life-giving source for dry bones. Fearlessly speak that Word to yourself and to believers and unbelievers alike. Jesus did, and the result was life!

Dry Bones Breathe

*Thus says the Lord GOD to these bones: "Surely I will cause breath
to enter into you, and you shall live. I will put sinews on you
and bring flesh upon you, cover you with skin and put breath in you;
and you shall live. Then you shall know that I am the LORD."
So I prophesied as I was commanded; and as I prophesied,
there was a noise, and suddenly a rattling;
and the bones came together, bone to bone.*

Ezekiel 37:5–7

Breathing on people is a trait of the Godhead. Father God *"breathed into [Adam's] nostrils the breath of life; and man become a living being"* (Genesis 2:7, brackets added). Jesus breathed on His disciples and said, "Receive the Holy Spirit" (see John 20:22). The Hebrew word for *spirit* is *ruwach* (roo'-akh), which literally means "wind, breath," or "breathe."[1] The Spirit manifested Himself symbolically in Acts 2:2 *"as a rushing mighty wind."*

Ezekiel's vision not only revealed the breath of God, but fibrous tissue in the form of tendons and ligaments that began connecting the dry bones together. Just as these bones came together when Ezekiel spoke God's Word over them, God also speaks over our lives, and His kingdom plans and purposes begin to come together. Part of God's plan after Levi's passing was to resurrect my dry and broken heart, and in turn, I'd rise up and speak life to the dry bones around me.

Like Ezekiel, we too, have a role in prophesying as God commands us. Depending on our circumstances, that prophecy will be different for each of us. In my morning prayer time, just hours before Levi passed away, God said, *"Sharon Rose, I know the thoughts I think toward you, thoughts of peace and not of evil to give you a future and a hope."* Even though it was difficult for me to believe at the time, a while later God asked me to begin to declare: "God has good plans for me after Levi's passing."

God's Spirit and His Word cause breath and life to enter our dry bones and the dry bones of others. Our words matter. They have power. Prophesy as the Spirit leads you. There will be a noise, a sudden rattling, and like these bones, God-designed dreams and visions will begin to come together for you piece by piece.

Dry Bones Change

Indeed, as I looked, the sinews and the flesh came upon them, and the skin covered them over; but there was no breath in them. Also He said to me, "Prophesy to the breath, prophesy, son of man, and say to the breath, 'Thus says the Lord God: "Come from the four winds, O breath, and breathe on these slain, that they may live."'"

Ezekiel 37:8–9

After Ezekiel prophesied as God commanded, he looked for and anticipated change. He saw for himself the fruit of his words, which in the vision were sinew connecting muscle to bone, flesh and fat appearing, and then skin covering the bones. Although there was notable activity among the bones, the *fullness* of his words had not yet revealed itself, as still there was no life in them. We may strive in speaking forth the desires of our heart, but His plans and purposes for our lives remain dead visions, or dry bones, unless the Spirit breathes life into them. *"There are many plans in a man's heart; nevertheless the Lord's counsel—that will stand"* (Proverbs 19:21).

At times, we don't see things going the way we're believing and speaking. But, ours is not a name-it-and-claim-it life in Christ. It's a relationship. First John 5:14–15 reads, *"14Now this is the confidence that we have in Him, that if we ask anything according to His will, He hears us. 15And if we know that He hears us, whatever we ask, we know that we have the petitions that we have asked of Him."*

About a year after Levi's death, our daughter approached us, requesting to date with purpose, meaning to have a relationship that would lead to marriage. My husband and I prayed and prophesied daily, "Lord, let the nice young man disappear." Frustration was our lot, as circumstances continued contrary to our prayers! Then, one day, the Holy Spirit breathed life into me and said, *"Grief is clouding your view of My will for your daughter's life."* Instantly, I accepted the young man who is now my son-in-law, whom I love as my own departed Levi.

Ask God what He wants you to speak to those slain areas in your life and in the lives of others. Then, just as Ezekiel looked with expectation after he prophesied, *"devote [yourself] to prayer with an alert mind and a thankful heart"* (Colossians 4:2, NLT, brackets added), and you'll see dry bones live.

The Dry Bone Army Walks

So I prophesied as He commanded me, and breath came into them, and they lived, and stood upon their feet, an exceedingly great army.

Ezekiel 37:10

Ezekiel was a lone man with God, who, in a vision, raised an exceedingly great army. As one with Christ, by prophesying as He commands, our bones and the bones of those lying in our valley of influence will also rise as a multitude of souls for the kingdom of heaven.

God further unveiled Ezekiel's vision in verse 11: *"These bones are the whole house of Israel. They indeed say, 'Our bones are dry, our hope is lost, and we ourselves are cut off!'"* An impression came to me from the Lord, *"These bones represent your broken heart and your crushed spirit. You lost hope after Levi's heavenly arrival. You say, 'My bones are dry. I too have died, and my hope is lost for any kind of earthly future. My life has been cut off. What reason is there to continue?'"* But God is telling me, as well as you, no matter what has dried your bones, according to the scriptures, *"Prophesy as I command, and you will live!"*

Chances are you've experienced dry bones of lost hope. Look around! Dry bones surround you. There are armies of souls, marriages, families, and relationships that God wants to raise to life. We see these bones walking, but we can't hear them breathing. With the breath of God's Spirit, raising the hearts and souls of people are a part of the good works noted for us in Ephesians 2:10, *"For we are His workman-ship, created in Christ Jesus for good works, which God prepared beforehand that we should walk in them."*

"The Spirit of God has made me, and the breath of the Almighty gives me life" (Job 33:4). As the body of Christ, it's important to breathe in rhythm with the Holy Spirit, only then can we rise as an exceedingly great army. What's the Lord saying to you today? Speak it out, and watch those dry bones stand to their feet! As Ezekiel's army walked, so will the army God is raising through you. God has places for these bones to go, and things for them to do!

Dry Bones and Their Graves

Then He said to me, "Son of man, these bones are the whole house
of Israel. They indeed say, 'Our bones are dry, our hope is lost....'
Therefore prophesy and say to them, 'Thus says the Lord GOD:
"Behold, O My people, I will open your graves and cause you
to come up from your graves, and bring you into the land."'"

Ezekiel 37:11–12

Reading this scripture, I received revelation as the Spirit said, *"I will open your grave of grief and cause you to rise again. Then I'll bring you into the land."* The grief, of course, was that of Levi's passing. I asked, "God, what is my land?" meaning, my purpose. I sensed this response: *"It's My purpose for you in the land of the living on earth and the kingdom work I have for you to do."*

Coming to the end of our journey through Ezekiel's vision, God said, *"Then you shall know that I am the LORD, when I have opened your graves...and brought you up from your graves"* (Ezekiel 37:13). Are you in a grave as I was? Although I haven't yet seen the bigger picture and the land that the Lord has for me, I'm persuaded that His promises are true for me and for you.

God continued in Ezekiel 37:14, *"I will put My Spirit in you, and you shall live, and I will place you in your own land. Then you shall know that I, the LORD, have spoken it and performed it."*

As born-again believers with the indwelling Spirit of God, we are alive. However, from time to time, a broken spirit dries the bones. No matter how dry the bones or how deep the grave, God is able reach us and do all that He promised!

If you find yourself in a type of grave, because Jesus conquered death and the grave, you too, have overcome. You can read about God's good plan for mankind throughout the Bible. However, He also has a unique and individual plan for you. He said, *"I will open your grave."* Your part is to embrace His grace and His leading. He'll open your grave of earthly circumstances and cause you to rise and live and come into the good land He's prepared for you.

When the Lord Prophesies

I, the LORD, have called you.

Isaiah 42:6 (NLT)

Reading the book of Ezekiel, I considered the prophetic words that God commanded Ezekiel to speak to those dry bones. It's one thing for Ezekiel, you, or me to declare the words of the Lord, but it's another when the Lord Himself, by His Spirit says, *"I, the LORD have called you."*

Four years into my healing rest with Levi's passing, I still sensed a shroud with God's plans for my life. Most of us would like to see the curtain of our future pulled back and get a sneak preview of some of the adventures God has for us. Maybe you feel as I do, as though you're waiting on God to draw the curtain for your next step. Despite divine obscurity, each day through grace and faith, we cling to Him, believing that He'll reveal and fulfill the works that He ordained for us before the foundation of the world (see Ephesians 2:10).

Today I saw the drapes open slightly, as I read God's words to Isaiah, which prophetically spoke of the Messiah. I felt as if God was speaking to me and to you, saying, *"6I, the LORD, have called you to demonstrate my righteousness. I will take you by the hand and guard you, and I will give you to my people…. And you will be a light to guide the nations. 7You will open the eyes of the blind. You will free the captives from prison, releasing those who sit in dark dungeons. 8I am the LORD; that is my name!… 9Everything I prophesied has come true, and now I will prophesy again. I will tell you the future before it happens"* (Isaiah 42:6–9, NLT).

With the Spirit of Jesus Christ living in you, He demonstrates righteousness through you. He takes you by the hand and leads you to those who need salvation for their spirit, soul, and body. The Lord Himself has called you, and what He declares shall always come to pass.

OCTOBER 13

No GMOs

...having been born again, not of corruptible seed but incorruptible, through the word of God which lives and abides forever.

1 Peter 1:23

Whether we're planting crops or having babies, we need seed to conceive. Amazingly, the Greek root translation for the word seed is "sperma."[1] There is no further need to define, as we all know about the birds and the bees.

In nature, fruit possesses the seed, and the dirt is its container. When planted, that seed, depending on the soil, produces a crop. In humans, the man carries the seed or the sperm, and the woman's womb is its receptacle.

The conception of Jesus didn't come about by human seed but by the incorruptible seed of the Word of God. Impregnation for Mary occurred through God's spoken word, as the messenger angel, Gabriel, told her, *"The Holy Spirit will come upon you, and the power of the Highest will overshadow you; therefore, also, that Holy One who is to be born will be called the Son of God"* (Luke 1:35).

The conception and birth of Jesus are similar to our spiritual birth process. Jesus said, *"You must be born again"* (John 3:7). This spiritual conception and birth come about as the Holy Spirit miraculously implants the incorruptible seed of the Word of God, which is not susceptible to corruption, death, or decay, into the receptacle of our unregenerate spirit. At this point, we become born-again children of God. God's seed is the real deal—incorruptible, no GMOs (Genetically Modified Organisms) or seeds here. Jesus, the Word of God, is that incorruptible seed (see John 1:1).

If you've not yet given God permission to till the spiritual soil of your heart, do so today. If your soil is dry and rocky, ask the Holy Spirit to help you remove any obstacles, which make way for better planting and harvest. We all want our heart to be good ground for the seed of God's Word, and as you continue to cultivate your relationship with Him, you'll see an abundant crop from your diligence—an increase of thirty, sixty, or even one-hundred fold (see Matthew 13:8).

The Lineup

Having been set free from sin, you became slaves of righteousness.

Romans 6:18

While praying, a vision came to me of people standing disheveled in what appeared to be an auction block lineup. One girl, looking as though she didn't belong, was in clean, brightly colored clothing. It wasn't until I saw Jesus come up to her and stretch out His hand that I realized I was that girl! Approaching me and taking my hand, Jesus pulled me out of the line, saying, *"I've bought you with a price; you've been set free from the slavery of discouragement."*

Having previously been in the public eye with ministry, and now writing a book and in obscurity, disappointment set in with my *seeming* lack of ministry opportunities. I didn't intentionally get back up on the auction block with the blues of my circumstances, but God showed me that I had.

Jesus was the only bidder purchasing mankind from the slavery of sin and death. I thought, *God, who doesn't experience lows from time to time?* But He reminded me that the lineup is no place—at any time—for a blood-bought, ransomed believer.

Romans 6:16 and 22 read, *"¹⁶Don't you realize that you become the slave of whatever you choose to obey? You can be a slave to sin, which leads to death, or you can choose to obey God, which leads to righteous living...²²But now you are free from the power of sin and have become slaves of God. Now you do those things that lead to holiness and result in eternal life"* (NLT).

Because Jesus personifies joy and not discouragement, we're not to obey downcast moods that attempt to sway us from the truth that we're slaves *only* to God and to holy living.

Even if there are times when you feel you're in shackles due to negative circumstances, know that Jesus has ransomed you. He's at the auction; just take His hand. Your new Master will pull you out of the lineup and help you off the block to begin, or continue, your new life of freedom in Him.

A Guest in the House

He has gone to be a guest.

Luke 19:7

Once as a houseguest, thoughts came to me of what occurred the times Jesus was a houseguest. One house he stayed in was Simon Peter's: *"14...when Jesus had come into Peter's house, He saw his wife's mother lying sick with a fever. 15...He touched her hand, and the fever left her. And she arose and served them"* (Matthew 8:14–15). As a guest, Jesus manifested healing in the house.

As a guest of Simon the leper's, a woman poured costly oil on Jesus' head. The disciples got angry, considering it wasteful. *"14Then one of the twelve, called Judas Iscariot, went to the chief priests 15and said, 'What are you willing to give me if I deliver Him to you?' 16...So from that time he sought opportunity to betray Him"* (Matthew 26:14–16). There was a thief and traitor in the house. As guests, we may encounter disagreement and betrayal.

Jesus saw the chief tax collector in a tree and summoned him, *"5...Zacchaeus, make haste and come down, for today I must stay at your house.... 7But when they saw it, they all complained, saying, 'He has gone to be a guest with a man who is a sinner'"* (Luke 19:5, 7). The presence and conviction of a holy God caused Zacchaeus, a sinner, to announce, *"8...if I have taken anything from anyone by false accusation, I restore fourfold.' 9And Jesus said to him, 'Today salvation has come to this house... 10for the Son of Man has come to seek and to save that which was lost'"* (Luke 19:8–10). Zacchaeus came clean because forgiveness and salvation Himself was present in the house.

"1It was heard that He was in the house. 2...And He preached the word to them" (Mark 2:1–2). As a guest, Jesus wasn't there to "chew the fat" or buddy up, or to be like minded or condone a sinful lifestyle. He sought and brought eternal truth to transform spirit, soul, and body. The next time you're a guest in the company of sinners, follow Jesus' example, and be a spiritual change agent for those around you.

Combat Rations

I am the bread of life. He who comes to Me shall never hunger,
and he who believes in Me shall never thirst.

John 6:35

Food and water are two commodities troops need to survive. MREs (Meals Ready to Eat) are fine dining for soldiers in a war zone. These individual, self-contained field rations in lightweight packaging are used in combat or other field conditions where organized food facilities aren't available.

As a battalion of believers, God prepares MREs through His Spirit, which provide us with stamina in combat. Whenever we compromise adequate nutrition, malnourishment or starvation sets in. God is a five-star chef in the mess hall, daily feeding and supplying fresh bread for His troops.

Since the human body is roughly 60 percent water, hydration is also vital to the life of the troops. As spiritual servicemen, without the pure living water of the Holy Spirit, we fall prey to the effects of dehydration, which can manifest in a myriad of ways. One of those is fatigue, which makes the fight of faith more strenuous.

In the most serious cases of dehydration, delirium or unconsciousness can also occur. However, Jesus invites each of us to stay nourished and strong, proclaiming, *"I am the bread of life. He who comes to Me shall never hunger, and he who believes in Me shall never thirst"* (John 6:35). Jesus is the living bread, and the Holy Spirit is the living water that sustains us.

I personally stay spiritually fed and hydrated by going to the One who is my portion. David, the mightiest of warriors, said, *"I cried out to You…'You are my refuge, My portion in the land of the living'"* (Psalm 142:5).

It's imperative in our military tour that we don't miss any mess hall meals. We must eat and drink daily of the only One who can sustain our life in battle—the Lord Jesus Christ. As a soldier receives allotted rations for each day on the battlefield, we also, as spiritual soldiers, receive the Lord's rations as we meet with Him through prayer and Bible reading. By doing so, we are fed, hydrated, and therefore prepared for the tasks ahead.

Bless the Lord

...to minister to Him and to bless in His name.

Deuteronomy 10:8

I met Alex when she crossed the ocean from Northern Ireland to America to attend a local Bible college. During a recent return visit, she mentioned a question her former classmates had asked: "What have you done with your Bible college education?"

Her response surprised those who inquired. Most were expecting to hear her report that she was now a pastor in a megachurch, or she had been evangelizing the world. Often, "big" in the Christian community equals success. Instead, she responded, "My calling is to minister to God. My desire is to bless Him and to daily learn what's pleasing to Him. Created to bless the Lord, what I do comes about only after His initiation. If He doesn't inspire and initiate, I won't move out just to be doing something for the approval of others."

How many of us could honestly respond like Alex did? Oftentimes, we find ourselves doing things "for" God just to be doing them for the approval of others. After the death of my son, although not concerned with ministry or the approval of others, my desire to bless God as Alex described fluctuated with my grief. However, God knew this about me and had compassion on me. During my conversation with Alex, God's love tangibly swept over me in such a powerful way that His manifest presence only resulted in my desire to worship Him more and more.

"Finally then, brethren, we urge and exhort in the Lord Jesus that you should abound more and more, just as you received from us how you ought to walk and to please God" (1 Thessalonians 4:1).

God knows the desire of your heart is to worship Him, even though that desire may be clouded with circumstances. Because you know this about Him and yourself, make it a point to first bless the Lord each day, and out of that will come the ministry or service He would have you carry out on His behalf.

Anxiety's Cure

Anxiety in the heart of a man causes depression.

Proverbs 12:25

From my youth, I was plagued with the questions, as some people are at least once in their lifetime, "Why was I born? What is my purpose?" As a babe in Christ, I read, *"And the LORD was sorry that He had made man on the earth, and He was grieved in His heart"* (Genesis 6:6). In my thoughts, I retorted, *God, You think You're sorry? I'm even sorrier that You made me!* It's apparent to me now that those words erupted from a wounded heart.

In the beginning stages of my walk with Christ, I turned to medication to calm my downcast soul, as depression was my constant companion. Then one day God quietly asked, *"Sharon, are you ready to deal with the real issue, which is that you're not fully trusting in My love for you? The medication is doing absolutely nothing for you."* His tone was serious but loving. In that moment, the time to embrace His grace clearly presented itself.

The following day, reading Proverbs 12:25, the words pierced my heart: *"…anxiety in the heart of a man causes depression."* The Lord spoke to me again, *"The real issue is anxiety and your lack of trust in Me; not depression."*

Despite the cause of anxiety, the cure is the Word of God. Philippians 4:6 reveals God's remedy, *"Be anxious for nothing, but in everything by prayer and supplication, with thanksgiving, let your requests be made known to God."* Because false evidence can appear real, we can receive His peace by giving every uneasy situation to Him. And His peace surpasses all understanding. While medication may be necessary at certain times, ultimately, it's God's peace that will guard the heart and mind of a believer through Christ Jesus.

If this is your situation, Jesus would like you to take hold of the freedom He provided for you at the cross. Seek Him today for His way out of despair and into a place of peace and rest. With Jesus, there's always hope!

Caught Up

*Take heed to yourselves, lest your hearts be weighed down
with carousing, drunkenness, and cares of this life.*

Luke 21:34

Once while preparing a Bible college teaching, the Lord said, *"Ask the students this question: 'Are you caught up in the Spirit, or are you caught up in the cares of this life?'"*

Strong's Concordance defines the phrase *caught up* in this way: "to seize...to catch (away, up), pluck...take (by force)."[1] Something that had previously escaped my attention in this passage now came alive: carousing, drunkenness, and the cares of this life are all inclusive.

Most believers wouldn't dream of carousing at loud parties or becoming intoxicated, but how many dabble in the cares of this life, which is listed alongside carousing and drunkenness? To me, these three ideas were never in the same category. Surely, drinking and carousing were more harmful than worrying.

During our journey, we've all embraced the cares and concerns of this life. For me, these have included anxiety, pressure in relationships, jobs, provision, or the need for direction.

One morning, long after my grief process, my tears flowed during a particular time of prayer. I thought this was odd, as I hadn't been weeping as much since God healed my broken heart. The Lord spoke to me in that moment, saying, *"Your tears are flowing from your cares. Cast your cares on Me, and I'll wipe away your tears."*

We're encouraged in 1 Peter 5:7 to cast *"all [our] care upon Him, for He cares for [us]"* (brackets added). To *cast* means "to throw something forcefully." As we cast our concerns on Him and trust in His unfailing love, our soul can return to its rest (see Psalm 116:7).

If you're caught up in the cares and concerns of this life instead of in the Spirit, freely and boldly cast all of your anxieties onto Him. He's waiting with His hands open wide to catch them.

The Fog

For there is nothing hidden which will not be revealed.

Mark 4:22

The following is an excerpt from my journal. Receive the words God spoke to me as your own.

"Oh, My child, I have things inexpressible for you; however, at this point they're cloaked, yet present. Fog covers the sky and the landscape, making them invisible to the natural eye, yet they both remain. My plans for you haven't vanished. I have good plans for you; plans of peace and not of evil to give you a future and a hope."

All My love, God

Living in Colorado, I believe the sun does shine three hundred and sixty days out of the year, and this makes fog somewhat of a foreigner. However, a deeper revelation of its meaning came to me while temporarily living in Washington, where it appeared the sun was gone from the earth forever! At this time, I couldn't help but think of the words God spoke to me. I'm encouraged even now as I write. As painstaking, yet joyful, as the process of writing this book has been, many dreams and desires continue to lie concealed within my heart by the fog of my seeming isolation.

Do you feel as though the fog of God or the fog of circumstances has covered your dreams? One day the Spirit told me, *"You have need of patient endurance."* Not only have I been in isolation with my writing, but also in isolation underneath God's healing wings with Levi's passing.

Because there's a time for every purpose under heaven, as you seek Him and are persuaded by His promises, the fog will lift at His leading, and in His timing you'll see the good plans He has for you. Although unseen through the fog, the sun and blue sky are still there, and as a child of God, *"your life is hidden in Christ"* (Colossians 3:3)—the plans that He has for you still exist and will soon be revealed. Hang in there! The clouds of your circumstances *will* break, and His Son *will* shine forth!

El Shaddai

I am Almighty God.

Genesis 17:1

In the weeks following Levi's heavenly home going, the only prayer that rose in my heart was an inaudible one. The words on the pages of my Bible were a blur. Only when the Holy Spirit prompted the scriptures could I find them. I could hear my heart beating out of rhythm with grief and anguish, but thankfully, I could hear the voice of God. He lovingly reminded me, *"I Am El Shaddai. I Am whatever you need."*

In Hebrew, *El* represents "God Almighty"; *shad* means "breast," and depicts or one who "nourishes, supplies, and satisfies"; and *dai* indicates "pours out." Together, *El Shaddai* means "the All-Sufficient One."[1] He is the God of all blessing, as we read the praise of David—*"You open Your hand and satisfy the desire of every living thing"* (Psalm 145:16).

God is true to His Word. Five months later, I returned to a Bible college teaching position. Still in grief, and incapable of reading or preparing my lessons, God would wake me at 3:00 a.m. and show me the lesson in a vision. I would fall back asleep, then, waking at my convenience, I went to my computer and typed out everything I saw earlier. This was how I taught Bible classes with El Shaddai.

When God sent Moses to free His people, Moses asked God, "What do I tell the children of Israel when they ask what Your name is?" *"14God said to Moses, 'I AM WHO I AM.' …You shall say to the children of Israel, 'I AM has sent me to you'"* (Exodus 3:14). God is not "I was" or "I will be," but He is "I AM." He is your All-Sufficient God, an ever-present help in any situation.

Although God brought me through my grief process, that doesn't mean I no longer need El Shaddai by my side, helping me every minute of every day. Do you need God as I do? Around the clock? I need all the help that I can get! And just by my asking, God performs wonders! I know if you ask, He'll perform wonders for you as well!

The Fire Within

...he took the fire in his hand.

Genesis 22:6

Once I heard a preacher expound on Genesis Chapter 22:6, which refers to when Abraham took his son, Isaac, to the altar of sacrifice as a burnt offering with *"fire in his hand."* The preacher's instruction was to take the fire in our hand, which is symbolic of the Holy Spirit in us and our relationship with Him, and be an example to our generation.

Calling his congregation to action, he suggested that if we considered the fire within us to be smoldering, we could come forward for prayer to reignite that fire. I watched amazed, as 95 percent of the congregation heeded his call. Immersed in a sea of humanity, the pastor couldn't move in any direction. I wondered how so many in the church ended up with their hearts in this condition.

Observing this scene, I sensed God was about to speak to me. I quickly grabbed a pen and paper and began writing as the Spirit spoke: *"See the multitudes, these are from one church. I have many different multitudes that need to be reached. I need you to carry the fire of the Holy Spirit placed within your spirit to the masses that I've prepared for you. Obey Me in sacrificial obedience, and along with the fire, you'll have the grain, the new wine, and oil for the multitudes that I have for you."* Through His statement, God revealed my underlying desire, which was to be as this man—reaching the wandering, smoldering, and hurting multitudes.

Within God's vast population, He has work for each of us to accomplish. Because the body of Christ is like a giant puzzle, each believer is God's key piece. Without each of us, His picture is incomplete, as *"God has set the members, each one of them, in the body just as He pleased"* (1 Corinthians 12:18). God alone knows how the finished picture looks.

Trust His hand in placing you within His puzzle, however He sees fit. Be encouraged that no matter where He places you, you'll be a perfect fit.

Knock, Knock, "Who's There?"

Behold, I stand at the door and knock.

Revelation 3:20

Assuming most homes possess an old-fashioned doorbell and not the new high-tech security systems, each time the doorbell rings, unless there's an intercom system or the door contains a window or peephole, the homeowner can't know who's ringing the bell.

Throughout our lives, we'll encounter numerous knocks at the door of our spiritual home, or heart. Believers, however, possess the most advanced security system in the person of the Holy Spirit. When we ask Him who's knocking at our door, He'll reveal to us who's there.

As Spirit-led children, unless we understand that we have access to God's spiritual peephole in our circumstances, answering the door apart from Him can be confusing or dangerous. Different spirits can come knocking, including the devil. Once we open the door, we give him a foothold.

When we answer the door and find challenging circumstances waiting to enter, know that it's not always Satan's handiwork. Jesus also knocks: *"Behold, I stand at the door and knock. If anyone hears My voice and opens the door, I will come in to him and dine with him, and he with Me"* (Revelation 3:20). The circumstances we face may be a delivery from God that He wants to use to work out negative issues in our soul and to conform us into the image of His Son.

If we rebuke the devil, yet our circumstances persist, it's oftentimes not the devil, but the Holy Spirit using circumstances in our sanctification process, setting us further apart for Christ.

Until my husband installed a peephole in our front door, I had no way of knowing who was on the other side. Now I have no concerns answering the door. I can see clearly "who's there."

No matter who knocks or what circumstances you find yourself in, it's best to ask, "Holy Spirit, who's there?" He'll not only tell you but give you specific instructions to either keep the door closed and rebuke the devil, or open the door and submit to Jesus.

Before Time Began

He chose us in Him before the foundation of the world.

Ephesians 1:4

One morning upon opening my eyes, I was immediately in a vision of what I understood to be God in the form of a cloudy, translucent figure. He took me backward at a very high rate of speed in what felt like a millisecond, then we came to a sudden stop. We stood in total darkness; nothing was visible except God and me.

Suddenly, Levi, who had already passed away, appeared in the vision with us. The three of us stood in total darkness, and God began to speak scriptures to my heart, starting with Genesis 1:2— *"the earth was without form, and void; and darkness was on the face of the deep."* I understood then that the three of us were in a time before the earth had its form.

God then impressed upon my heart a personalized version of Jeremiah 1:5 and Psalm 139: *"Before I formed Levi in your womb, I knew him. Before he was born, I set him apart. I ordained him as a prophet to Lewis Palmer High School. Levi's frame wasn't hidden from Me when I made him in secret. My eyes saw his substance being yet unformed, and in My book were written all the days fashioned for him, before one of them came to be. Levi is My workmanship, created for good works, which I prepared beforehand that he should walk in (see Ephesians 2:10). I chose Levi in Me before the foundation of the world. I created him for eternity."*

My son was part of God's plan before the earth had its form. Levi was God's—not mine—created by Him and for Him. Levi was, and is, living in the plan of his loving Creator.

God also had you in mind before time began. Forming you in your mother's womb, He knew His plan for you. Each day He has works planned and prepared for you to walk in. His plan is not only a good and perfect plan, but it's the best plan. Seek Him daily to discover all He has in store for you.

The Guiding Light

For behold, the darkness shall cover the earth, and deep darkness the people.

Isaiah 60:2

Gazing at the ocean in the pre-dawn hours, I spotted a miniscule dot of light shining from a lone ship on the horizon. The *only* evidence revealing the ship's presence was its light.

Because the Light of the world lives in us, I thought of us as believers. To the unsaved shrouded in darkness, we are to be a beacon in their midst. Led by the Holy Spirit in this sea of life, like a ship, we go to and fro, shining that light and giving aid to the ones passing by or those sending out a Mayday.

I often imagine the ocean liner *Titanic* and its survivors watching with disbelief. How tangible the darkness must have become after the ship's lights disappeared beneath the water. Symbolically, the world is like these survivors, floating in terror, fear, and darkness, putting out a distress signal. Like the ship, *Carpathia*, which came to rescue *Titanic's* survivors, we as believers, come to the rescue of those calling out for help.

"God... commanded light to shine out of darkness" (2 Corinthians 4:6). Isaiah 60:1 tells us, *"Arise, shine; for your light has come!"* Jesus Christ, our Light, has come, and we're to let His light in us shine before men (see Matthew 5:16). As we do, we become a beacon of rescue for others.

The telegraph officer of *Carpathia*, retiring from duty, was unlacing his boots when *Titanic's* call came. How many of us are just settling into our easy chair when we get a distress signal? *Carpathia*, designed to travel at a maximum speed of fourteen knots, was three and a half hours away from *Titanic*. Captain Rostron, *Carpathia's* commander, traveled at seventeen knots to *Titanic's* rescue!

People everywhere are sending out an SOS. Church of God, let's mimic Captain Rostron—ready and willing at a moment's notice, and full speed ahead! And, as much as depends on us, let's not allow a *Titanic* catastrophe on our watch.

God Cares for the Birds

Look at the birds of the air, for they neither sow nor reap nor gather into barns; yet your heavenly Father feeds them. Are you not of more value than they?

Matthew 6:26

I believe numerous people besides myself have received comfort from the words of Jesus regarding the birds of the air. During a temporary stay in the Pacific Northwest, my husband and I rented a studio apartment on the bay. Thankfully, the view was through a wall of windows facing the ocean's shore. There, I observed more birds than people. Every day, I watched a variety of birds, including ravens, bald eagles, and Western gulls, darting up and down the shoreline.

Like busy beavers, each day these birds gathered their goods and fought to keep them. Although they stayed busy finding food, according to our opening scripture, God is ultimately the One behind their provision. As I write, I'm receiving no monetary gain; my husband, on the other hand, is working, and due to unavoidable circumstances, paying for our homes in both Washington and Colorado. You could say we're on a financial tightrope!

While walking along the seashore during our stay, a bald eagle flew ten feet above my head with a seagull in its talons. Another bald eagle arrived on the scene to protect the bird carrying the prey. All three birds screeched nosily back to the eagles' nest.

Reinforcing His promise that humans are more valuable than the birds, God said to me, *"Not only do I take care of the little birds, I take care of the big birds, and I'm taking care of you."*

God, in His wisdom, left us with a powerful illustration in a common little creature. Day in and day out, God cares for the birds, which parallel His limitless love and provision. If the hand of God is so full for the birds of the air, how much more abundantly does it overflow to His very own children?

When you encounter seemingly sparse times, remember God's birds. They do not sow, nor do they reap, nor gather into barns; yet, your heavenly Father feeds them. And your value in God's eyes is far above the birds.

Precious Stones

The foundations of the wall of the city were adorned with all kinds of precious stones: the first foundation was jasper, the second sapphire, the third chalcedony, the fourth emerald, the fifth sardonyx, the sixth sardius, the seventh chrysolite, the eighth beryl, the ninth topaz, the tenth chrysoprase, the eleventh jacinth, and the twelfth amethyst.

Revelation 21:19–20

In the ninth month after our son's death, I thought I was going to die. With the agony of our separation, sorrow emerged from the depths of my being that I didn't know existed. For nineteen years, our son rarely left our side. He had a reason for that, saying, "I like being with you and Dad." That was a gift from God. Thoughts flooded my heart about Levi's current heavenly surroundings: *What does heaven look like? What does his mansion look like? Does he live by himself?* I cried out, "Father, please show me something from Scripture that describes Levi's heavenly habitation!" I had so many questions with so few answers.

God, in His mercy, heard my cries. He led me to read the book of Revelation. His love and compassion swept over me as I read, *"the foundations of the wall of the city were adorned with all kinds of precious stones…and the twelfth amethyst"* (Revelation 21:20).

Amethyst is significant to me. Through natural calculations, Levi was to be born in March, but to our surprise, he arrived in February, making his earthly birthstone amethyst.

The very day God led me to Revelation 21:20, was the very day I had to make a decision as to what kind of gemstone would go into a necklace I was having made in Levi's memory. After God's insight, the *only* stone that would suit the pendant was amethyst. God, in His unfailing love and compassion, answered my prayer by personally connecting me with my son in heaven through this gem.

Ask God to give you a glimpse of heaven and those things that await you. There are more gems to be seen there besides gold and pearls: There are jewels in the form of loved ones. And you can be sure, upon your arrival, you will be a dazzling one of a kind gem in His eyes.

The Weatherman

When it is evening you say, "It will be fair weather, for the sky is red."

Matthew 16:2

Weather forecasts are important to me because of my love of the outdoors and, living in Colorado, the weather can change at any moment. Technology offers weather apps with current meteorological conditions to help me see the weather live and plan for activities I enjoy.

Once as I checked my weather app, I thought of how God gives us a spiritual weather report. If we look to Him and His app—the Bible and prayer—we find that daily, from sunrise to sunset, He reveals as much of the forecast as is needed. It's not necessarily the detailed conditions of the day we'd like to have, but He's the weatherman! The sun doesn't always shine, but through sunshine or storms, with God, every cloud has a silver lining.

Here are some correlating natural and spiritual weather conditions:

Visibility—*"Stand and see this great thing which the LORD will do before your eyes."* (1 Samuel 12:16)

Wind—*"Suddenly there came a sound from heaven, as of a rushing mighty wind, and it filled the whole house where they were sitting."* (Acts 2:2)

Sunshine—*"The LORD God is a sun and shield."* (Psalm 84:11)

Rain—*"I will give you the rain for your land in its season, the early rain and the latter rain."* (Deuteronomy 11:14)

Flooding—*"When the enemy comes in like a flood, the Spirit of the LORD will lift up a standard against him."* (Isaiah 59:19)

Clouds—*"Then we who are alive and remain shall be caught up together with them in the clouds to meet the Lord in the air."* (1 Thessalonians 4:17)

No matter what kind of weather you're currently facing, turn to God first before taking action. With His Doppler Radar, He's able to weatherproof your day, allowing you to continually walk in the Son.

Hate Crimes

You love righteousness and hate wickedness.

Psalm 45:7 (NIV)

Many might be shocked to discover that God hates: *"The one who loves violence His soul hates"* (Psalm 11:5); *"The Lord God of Israel says that He hates divorce"* (Malachi 2:16); and Proverbs 6:17–19 list other things He hates, such as: *"[17]...A proud look, a lying tongue, hands that shed innocent blood, [18]a heart that devises wicked plans, feet that are swift in running to evil, [19]a false witness who speaks lies, and one who sows discord among brethren."*

"Love is all you need" are famous lyrics from a Beatles' song.[1] Many clamor in agreement with the Beatles. But the greater truth is that all we need is God, as God is love. But, love is not all that God is.

It's true that God is love, yet, *"Love does not delight in evil but rejoices with the truth"* (1 Corinthians 13:6, NIV). Loving as God loves, we aren't to delight in, but oppose evil spirits that rule this world and work within people who rebel against God's holy standards (see Ephesians 6:12).

King David, whom God called *"a man after His own heart"* (1 Samuel 13:14), prayed: *"[21]O Lord, shouldn't I hate those who hate you? Shouldn't I despise those who oppose you? [22]Yes, I hate them with total hatred, for your enemies are my enemies"* (Psalm 139:21–22, NLT). Today, David would be jailed for hate crimes!

Because, *"You who love the Lord, hate evil"* (Psalm 97:10), government laws and penalties cannot eradicate hate from the human heart. Another reason that hatred remains, stems from Jesus' words, *"... I chose you out of the world, therefore the world hates you"* (John 15:19).

All lives matter to God, and we're to love our neighbor as ourselves (see Matthew 19:19). But don't be surprised when the Spirit of Christ dwelling in you displays a righteous grief and dislike for beliefs that oppose and despise our God and King.

Brothers Breaking Bread

And when He had given thanks, He broke it and said, "Take, eat;
this is My body which is broken for you; do this in remembrance of Me."

1 Corinthians 11:24

Because the men at my church meet monthly for breakfast, which includes bacon, they've been dubbed "Brothers and Bacon."

At church, I've been given the privilege of sharing the communion messages. One morning in worship, the Spirit gave me a vision where I saw *only* men serving the communion elements. Then I heard the words, *"Brothers and Bacon; Brothers Breaking Bread."* Not certain of the Spirit's meaning, I shared my testimony with the congregation, and men came forward, offering to serve the elements the following week.

Preparing for the communion message and reading 1 Corinthians 11:24, the word *broken* leapt off the page. I've often wondered how Jesus' body was broken. Although the Bible says Jesus was pierced, that to me doesn't describe broken. Then a picture emerged in my spirit.

Jesus breaking the bread into pieces and offering it to His disciples was a symbolic act of Him giving Himself to His Bride, the Church. It was a foretaste of the living bread He was about to bring forth sacrificially through His body and blood on the cross. His living bread comes in the form of eternal life—forgiveness, healing, and so much more, which provides for our every need.

God had a purpose for the men serving the communion elements that day. Created in His image as providers, men, like Jesus, sacrificially go to work and bring back provision to their bride, breaking it into pieces and distributing it to the needs of their household.

These brothers are not only bringing home the bacon, they're participating in God's symbolism of Jesus: "Brothers Breaking Bread." The natural wife, representative of Christ's Bride, is to give thanks, appreciate, and appropriate wholeheartedly what her provider brings to the table.

Having received fresh bread from the brothers that morning, we remembered Jesus and His fresh bread of the New Covenant. As the Bride of Christ, give thanks. Appreciate and appropriate all He brings and has brought to the table for you.

Demons Speak

Demons also came out of many, crying out and saying,
"You are the Christ, the Son of God!"

Luke 4:41

Demons are alive and well, and with their voice, they attempt to torment, oppress, and bring people under their influence. The ministry of Jesus and His disciples included casting out demons. Seven came out of Mary Magdalene (see Mark 16:9). Another deliverance came about in a man who had possessed demons for a long time: *"27He wore no clothes, nor did he live in a house but in the tombs.... 30Jesus asked him, saying, 'What is your name?' And he said, 'Legion,' because many demons had entered him"* (Luke 8:27, 30). On occasion, Jesus allowed demons to speak, but in other instances, He rebuked them and didn't allow them a voice (see Luke 4:41).

We may not always recognize demons speaking to us, but it's clear from Scripture that they do. One day, this rang especially true for me while driving in my car. My then four-year-old daughter had discerned that demons were speaking to me and causing me obvious distress. She laid her tiny hand on me and said, "You bad devil, you leave my mommy alone!" As children of God filled with His Spirit, we do well not to allow the demons to speak or to have a voice in our heart and mind.

Although having passed that baton of authority to us, God's Spirit is still in the business of setting people free from demonic oppression. Jesus said, *"I cast out demons and perform cures today and tomorrow"* (Luke 13:32, NLT). In Luke 9:1, Jesus *"called His twelve disciples together and gave them power and authority over all demons."* Jesus also said, *"And these signs will follow those who believe: In My name they will cast out demons"* (Mark 16:17).

Over the years, I've had numerous spiritual face-to-face encounters with demons, both in my own life and in the lives of people around me. Demonic voices can be sly and subtle, but the closer you stay in step with the Spirit, the sooner you'll recognize them. Then, using the authority that Jesus has given you, you can command them to be silent.

Combat Discipline

I discipline my body and bring it into subjection.

1 Corinthians 9:27

A major player in the life of a soldier is physical fitness. We're all familiar with the bodily discipline of the armed forces that begins in boot camp; however, it doesn't end there. For continued endurance, staying strong is necessary; otherwise, the troops will find it difficult to endure the hardships that lie ahead. On and off the battlefield, self-control in every area is indispensable. Our fitness regime includes our spirit, our soul—or the mind, will, and emotions—and our body.

"Physical exercise has some value, but spiritual exercise is valuable in every way because it promises life both for the present and for the future" (1 Timothy 4:8, GNT). Although beneficial, the results of physical exercise are temporary because our body is temporary. Our spirit man, on the other hand, is eternal, and the way we train it today carries over into the life that lies ahead.

Former Navy SEAL, Chris Kyle, said in reference to SEAL training, although it "is extremely demanding physically and mentally.... Being a SEAL is more about mental toughness than physical prowess."[1] I find the brawny marine's statement amazing because it mimics biblical principles of the battlefield of the mind. Kyle understood where the fight lies—in the mind.

With our earthly body as the temple of the Holy Spirit, staying healthy is of paramount importance. However, this isn't the end of our workout session. Deployed on earth, I consider our tour of duty similar to 'hell week' as we engage in fierce firefights. For believers in Christ, heaven is the end of our tour of duty, where we experience the *fullness* of rest from our enemy.

As a soldier in relationship with Jesus, take hold of the promise found in 1 Timothy 4:8. Set your mind to strive for the reward of eternal life gained through disciplined spiritual exercises, such as prayer and Bible reading.

Better than Omega 3s

The memory of the righteous is blessed.

Proverbs 10:7

One morning, my family and were headed to church when I realized I forgot my car keys. I went back inside and found them lying next to a Bible, which was open on the kitchen counter. When I picked up the keys, the words of our opening scripture jumped off the page. I laughed. Although I forgot where I'd set my keys, God said my memory is blessed!

The apostle Paul tells us, as born-again children of God, *"we have the mind of Christ"* (1 Corinthians 2:16). Friends, this is better than Omega 3s, which are known to be beneficial for promoting brain health. I find that the Holy Spirit helps me remember the daily things of this earthly life. I can't count the times He's reminded me where I've misplaced things.

Once I "lost" my swimsuit for almost a year. Shopping isn't my thing, let alone shopping for swimwear! But while planning for a beach vacation, I needed my swimsuit. I prayed to Jesus about my situation, and in my mind, I saw my suit in a brown leather backpack, deep within the trunk of my car. Immediately I went to the car, and there it was!

On a more unusual note, when Levi passed away, without my knowledge, my sisters graciously did my laundry. When I couldn't find a certain pair of jeans, I asked God for help. While sitting in my kitchen, in my spirit I saw my bedroom closet, and in the closet was a stack of clothes with my jeans in the center of it. I found that the pile was full of my husband's clothes, but my jeans were in the center, just as I saw in my mind.

We've all searched for wallets, cell phones, tools, jewelry, and lots of other things, including Bibles! Remember that Jesus is a friend indeed, and a friend in time of need. Next time you misplace something, take time to ask Him, "Lord, where is that …?" Then, start receiving His promise of Proverbs 10:7, and know that your memory is blessed!

Fickle Faith

In this you greatly rejoice, though now for a little while, if need be, you have been grieved by various trials, that the genuineness of your faith, being much more precious than gold that perishes, though it is tested by fire, may be found to praise, honor, and glory at the revelation of Jesus Christ.

1 Peter 1:6–7

One day I said to God, "I don't know how You put up with me; my faith seems so fickle."

The word *fickle* means "to change frequently, especially with regard to one's loyalties, interests, or affections."[1] When we have faith, we believe or trust in something. Even after walking with the Lord for over three decades, and especially after Levi's death, one day my faith seemed up and another day down. Fickle faith is like a chameleon—always changing and adapting to its surroundings. True faith however, stands fast on the promises of Jesus Christ, the unchanging One who *"is the same yesterday, today, and forever"* (Hebrews 13:8).

Consider Peter, who walked closely with Jesus day after day; he even walked on water! As bold as I believe Peter to have been, when he saw the boisterous wind and waves, fear overtook him, and he began to sink. Jesus saved him, but asked, *"O you of little faith, why did you doubt?"* (Matthew 14:31). Later, in his fickle faith, when confronted about knowing Jesus, Peter cursed and declared to bystanders, *"I do not know the Man!"* (Matthew 26:74).

Peter said in our opening passage that our faith is more precious than gold—earth's most valuable metal. In the natural, fire purifies gold by bringing its dross to the surface. Peter wrote in verse 7 that spiritually, our faith is also tested by fire. The heat of circumstances will reveal pollutants or contaminants in our faith, which can result in wavering, small, or even dead faith. Or, maybe in your case, glowing faith!

We may think our faith is strong, and it may be. But, a firestorm of some nature is always ready to heat up our circumstances and put that faith to the test: *"Beloved, do not think it strange concerning the fiery trial which is to try you, as though some strange thing happened to you"* (1 Peter 4:12).

Just as Peter grew in faith, you can also come to an unwavering faith in Jesus Christ. But, know that it may take holding Jesus' hand through a fiery trial to bring your faith forth as gold.

A Molded Image

Then God said, "Let Us make man in Our image, according to Our likeness."

Genesis 1:26

Strongholds are fortified places that can have either a positive or a negative connotation. When negative, they're images or beliefs in our mind that are contrary to the Word of God. Oftentimes, they're very resistant to being overthrown.

My husband creates art through sculpting clay. Layer upon layer, he meticulously forms the clay until an image emerges. When completed, he takes that image to a foundry where a mold is made and molten metal is then poured into it. The result is a bronze statue.

This process of transforming clay into an image and then into bronze is similar to the formation of negative strongholds in our mind. Like an artist, the devil uses a similar process to sculpt an image within our soul. Taking a lump of lies, with calculated precision, he sculpts an image into us that's contrary to our identity in Christ.

Depending on the magnitude of my husband's projects, the amount of time required for transforming the clay to bronze varies. It can take a week, a month, or a year for the lump of clay to become a clearly visible image. In the same manner, it can take the devil a moment, a week, a month, or even years to mold us into someone other than our true character in Christ. Without the Master Sculptor's guidance, we embrace Satan's lies, which equip him with the tools necessary to sculpt into us a false identity.

Spiritually speaking, God also gave us tools with which we can demolish strongholds or false images sculpted within our souls. Don't allow the enemy of your soul to mold or shape you according to his lies. Instead, with the help of the Holy Spirit, believe the truth of God and what He says about you, as He daily transforms you into His own beautiful image.

Fire and Hammer

"Is not My word like a fire?" says the LORD,
"and like a hammer that breaks the rock in pieces?"

Jeremiah 23:29

There are two common methods to destroy bronze sculptures. One is to heat the bronze metal to 3500 degrees until it becomes molten metal. The second is demolition by a jackhammer. Pondering this process brought revelation from today's scripture as to how an unfounded belief or stronghold in the mind can be demolished.

God's Word is like a fire and a hammer that consume and destroy. As we fellowship with the Spirit of fire, the flame of His Word consumes the lies of the enemy in our wrong thinking. When He unveils truth to us, it's like a hammer breaking those lies or rocks into pieces. Amazingly, the word *rock* in Hebrew depicts a fortress or stronghold.[1] How fitting!

To varying degrees, Christ followers have in the past, or presently, harbor fortified thoughts or strongholds in their mind that are in opposition to God's thoughts. One of my former strongholds or negative thinking was that God loved men more than women. As I met with God in prayer through His Word, more and more He began to reveal His love for me. With deepened security in my relationship with Him, I began to give Him those reinforced thoughts, and He showed me how, through the Spirit and obedience to His Word, that negative thinking would be demolished.

Hold the lies that you're believing over the flame of God's Word until it incinerates those strongholds, or likewise, allow the hammer of His Word to smash them into pieces. For example, if you doubt God's love for you, meditate on John 15:9, *"As the Father loved Me, I also have loved you."* Truth as a fire and a hammer will demolish the lies you've believed. Through God's Word, you'll see the enemy's lies melt like wax and his strongholds fall to the ground in pieces!

On- and Off-Road Communion

As He sat at the table with them,
He took bread, blessed and broke it, and gave it to them.

Luke 24:30

Full of intrigue, the road to Emmaus revealed two men—possibly buddies—walking and talking, discussing current events. For these men, the topic of the day was the crucifixion of Jesus that had taken place three days earlier. Along the road, Jesus drew near to them, but their eyes were restrained so they didn't recognize Him. Undercover, Jesus walked and talked with them. Arriving at their destination, the men invited Him to stay with them. Later, sitting at the table together, Jesus *"30 took bread, blessed it and broke it, and gave it to them. 31 Then their eyes were opened and they knew Him; and He vanished from their sight"* (Luke 24:30–31).

While reading Luke 24:31, my eyes were opened much like the disciples'. They'd been prevented from seeing Him for who He was, and it wasn't until after Jesus broke bread with them that their eyes were opened and they knew Him. The moment we break bread with Him in communion is the moment we'll either come to know Him for who He truly is, or know Him more.

Heading back to Jerusalem, the two men now had even more to discuss! When they found the eleven disciples and those who were with them, they told them that Jesus *"was known to them in the breaking of bread"* (Luke 24:35).

Communion is not a time of obligation, but a precious, priceless time to intimately get to know Jesus. As revelation in the knowledge of Him emerges, the outward flow is relationship, healing, provision, and the like. Taking communion as He commanded, whether that's in a church setting or at home in our living room, He'll open our eyes as well, and we'll know Him more and more.

Eternal life is to know Him. Since this is our quest, let's gather with Him at His communion table, *"because he who feeds on [Him] will live"* (John 6:57, brackets added). As you partake of communion today, do so with the intent of getting to know Jesus better and allowing Him to open your eyes with revelation knowledge of who He is to you.

Left Hook

A righteous man may fall seven times and rise again.

Proverbs 24:16

For thirty years, my daily life has consisted of Bible reading and prayer. I consider myself a mature Christian but continue to ripen on the Vine. However, possessing a soul, I'm not immune to a "left hook," which in boxing is the most devastating blow because of how the jab connects with the jaw, nearly always producing a knockout.

At some point, we've all felt contact from our opponent, the devil, in the form of a left hook. His blow can catch even a righteous man off-guard. A jab comes because it's our contender's nature.

In a boxing match there are as many as three judges present. In a spiritual boxing match, God is our ringside referee, Jesus is our cut man, or one who attends to the fighter's wounds, and the Holy Spirit is our "trainer" or teacher.

In May 2015, the dirty fighter challenged me in the ring, blindsiding me with torment. Thankfully, with my ringside help, the round was short lived. The opposition was dealt a knockout blow! During my midnight bout, it seemed Satan had me on the ropes, but Jesus gave me step-by-step instructions to power punch my rival. First, I was to pray in tongues. Then, after a few rounds of singing the name of Jesus, along with the Holy Spirit's comfort, I fell fast asleep. When I woke, my spirit, soul, and body revealed no evidence of a fight, but I heard the Lord say, *"That was a left hook from hell."*

In the boxing world, fighters such as Evander Holyfield are known for their killer left hooks. Jesus, also known for His killer left hook, willingly got in the ring with Satan, and by going to the cross took the ultimate left hook from hell, which was due you and me. Because of His victory, the Referee holds up our hand as the victor. As born-again prizefighters, our reward is the devil's contact with a left hook from heaven!

Because the Father, Son, and Holy Spirit are present with you in the ring in your fight, your contender doesn't stand a chance. Go ahead, put up your "dukes" for the knock out!

777

The LORD has appeared of old to me, saying:
Yes, I have loved you with an everlasting love;
therefore with lovingkindness I have drawn you.

Jeremiah 31:3

Two days before Christmas, a divine assignment was before me. In a local store, a young man accompanied by two untidy young children leaned in front of me looking behind the counter, saying, "I'm not cutting in." I responded, "All is well." The words on his T-Shirt, which read "$#%& Jesus," caught my attention.

Lovingly, I said, "Young man, I couldn't help but notice your T-Shirt. Jesus loves you." He spewed only words of venom. Then, as I began to tell him of Jesus' kindness toward me in Levi's death, for a *mere* moment he softened and kindly replied, "I'm sorry about your son." Then he continued with his toxic speech.

As I shared the Good News of the cross, he responded, "I used to be a pastor." Immediately, I noticed two sixes tattooed on his right hand. Just when I thought, *Could it be?* he pointed to the 666, and said, "Lady, I'm going to hell!"

I asked, "Are you taking these two with you?" as I motioned to the children. He was speechless. I continued, "You may've been a pastor in title, but you most likely haven't met the real Lord Jesus Christ; or, if you have, you've been wounded in a way that's caused you to turn your heart from Him."

His response took me off-guard: "No one's ever been as kind to me when I wear this T-shirt as you." I replied, "My hope is that when you meet me you meet the real Lord Jesus."

Thanking God for the opportunity, I heard *"I can trust you,"* meaning, He can trust me to follow His lead with people. In prayer, instead of referring to the man as 666, considering the number seven God's number of completion, I named him 777, believing that one day he'll come to the complete saving knowledge of Jesus.

The Spirit of God within me was in hot pursuit of this man; in reality, He was relentless. Are there 777s in your life whom God wants to passionately pursue, overtaking them with His love and kindness that leads to repentance? (See Romans 2:4.) Be alert, for you never know where they may appear!

Devil-Threshing Instrument

You will be a new threshing instrument with many sharp teeth.
You will tear your enemies apart, making chaff of mountains.

Isaiah 41:15 (NLT)

Just because I meet with God in my secret place to pray, it doesn't mean the devil idly sits by and leaves me alone. This morning, attempting to sabotage my prayer time, he bombarded me with thoughts that accused God of not being good. To resist his attack, I decided to take communion. I held a cracker in my hand and began to pray and thank Jesus, remembering His sacrifice and all He's done for me.

I put the cracker in my mouth, and the moment I bit it and began to chew, the Holy Spirit quickened our opening passage to me. Symbolically, as my sharp teeth crushed the cracker, God showed me that my mouth would be "a new sharp threshing instrument having teeth" that will "thresh the mountains (or the liar's accusing thoughts) and beat them small, making the hills or the devil's lies as chaff."

In this moment, God made my mouth a threshing mechanism against the accusing thoughts, which instantly became chaff. Synonyms for the word *thresh* are: *beat, wallop, whack, clobber,* or *pummel.* You and I are to clobber the devil with the Word of God that's in our mouth.

General Foods is famous for the advertising slogan, "Wheaties, the Breakfast of Champions." This may be true for their cereal; however, in the spirit, the true breakfast of champions is the Lord's Supper! We overcame Satan by the blood of the Lamb and by the word of our testimony (see Revelation 12:11).

Our mouths are a mighty force. Proverbs 18:21 reads, *"Death and life are in the power of the tongue."* I encourage you to be the devil-threshing instrument God has designed you to be, crushing all demonic foes by speaking His Word, which is truth and life.

Dream Husband

For your Maker is your husband.

Isaiah 54:5

"Livin' the dream" is a phrase that can be used either respectfully or sarcastically. Expressed with optimism, it means we're doing what we've long desired: working a dream job, taking a dream vacation, or having a dream baby. I'm livin' the dream in my marriage, as I have a dream husband.

I, as a babe in Christ, and with Mark's renewed commitment to God, we entered into marriage. Our past, apart from Christ, left us with festering soul wounds, which made the beginning of our marriage somewhat challenging. This is usually true for every marriage, as a fallible man and woman do not equal infallibility. Despite this equation, there's a sum, which comes from Ecclesiastes 7:8, *"The end of a thing is better than its beginning."*

Whether we're married or single, God is ultimately our dream husband, as He's perfect in every way. However, in an earthly marriage, God divinely designed men in His image, fitting them with His awesome attributes, such as protector, provider, and leader. My husband reflects all these characteristics and more.

Once in Bible college, the class was asked, "Who besides Christ do you consider the most loving person in your life?" Without hesitation, I thought, *my husband.* Despite our trials, he's loved me unconditionally and continues to love me through thick and thin. When we were dating, he asked, "Will you grow old with me?" Together, we're aging gracefully.

If you are "livin' the dream" in your marriage, keep in God's graces! If you're in the midst of the furnace, don't give up. Proverbs 3:5–6 promises, *"Trust in the LORD with all your heart, and lean not on your own understanding; in all your ways acknowledge Him, and He shall direct your paths."*

If separation in any form has invaded your marriage relationship, look to the God of reconciliation. If divorce has encroached, turn to Jesus—*"the resurrection and the life"* (John 11:25). If you're a single man or woman in waiting, continue to deepen your relationship with Jesus, and when you do marry, you can bring that overflow of love and blessing with you.

Seasonal Fruit

His delight is in the law of the LORD,
and in His law he meditates day and night.
He shall be like a tree planted by the rivers of water,
that brings forth its fruit in its season.

Psalm 1:2–3

Coming from a large family of fourteen, fruit trees and a sprawling vegetable garden blanketed our property. As a child, my brothers and sisters and I spent time planting and working in the garden. We also played "Hide and Seek" in the grapevines that surrounded our home. After a lifetime of experience with fruits and vegetables, I feel as though I'm somewhat of an expert on produce.

It was customary for us growing up to eat whatever we wanted from the garden, or at least that's how I remember it. We quickly learned when to eat from the garden and when not to. Produce out of season is never tasty because it's hard or bitter. Nor did we eat foods that were overripe or rotten to the taste. The perfect time to eat from the garden was when the fruit and vegetables were in season.

I find it similar with our spiritual life. God's plans and purposes for our lives never arrive out of season but at the peak of His desired maturity. Nor does God speak a word to us out of season. Nevertheless, how often do we run ahead of God when His plans and timing are still green? Or, maybe we're overripe, not having moved in obedience when He's asked us to. We must always look expectantly to the Master Gardener, as He alone gives us our food in due season (see Psalm 145:15).

If you've made Jesus Christ the Lord of your life, He's also the Lord of your garden. Take time to savor the words of God, and meditate in them day and night. *"Be patient...see how the farmer waits for the precious fruit of the earth..."* (James 5:7). Don't rush God's plans for your life. As long as you stay planted by the rivers of the living water of the Holy Spirit, God will bring forth the spiritual fruit He desires for you in due season.

Heavenly Exposure

Have no fellowship with the unfruitful works of darkness,
but rather expose them.

Ephesians 5:11

After thirty years, this passage really came alive to me during a walk with some of my unsaved acquaintances. On one of our hikes, one woman spoke of her friend whose three-year-old granddaughter had died of cancer. I responded, "I'm so sorry for them. I know the heartache of a mother losing a child. My son passed away."

As we approached the end of the trail, this woman, with kindness and all sincerity, said, "I have a friend who's a medium and talks to the dead. She can tell you everything your son would say to you, and she's extremely accurate." In my heart, I thought, *Lord, You set me in the right place!* I responded in compassion, saying, "I'm a believer in the Lord Jesus Christ, and anything I need to know or hear about my son, Jesus tells me. I have direct communication with Him."

She said, "Oh my, you're really connected!" If given the opportunity, I would've added, "...furthermore, my son's not dead. He believes in Jesus, and though he died physically, he lives spiritually" (see John 11:25). But, two of her three dogs became vicious among themselves, to the point that one drew blood, so our conversation ended before I could speak. Even so, unfruitful works of darkness had been exposed.

Previously, I had interpreted Ephesians 5:11 to mean that we shouldn't associate with unfruitful works of darkness by living out of our carnal, fleshly nature. As true as this is, today's revelation is equally important and eye opening.

Those of us who call Jesus "Lord" are said to be as *"bold as a lion"* (Proverbs 28:1). In my situation, and at the Spirit's leading, because I spoke truth to the spirits in operation, I wasn't having fellowship with them or their unfruitful works but rather exposing them. As the righteousness of God in Christ Jesus, don't hesitate to speak up boldly so demonic forces can hear you. In doing so, their evil works will be exposed.

What's in Your Pouch?

Then he took his staff in his hand; and he chose for himself
five smooth stones from the brook, and put them in a shepherd's bag,
in a pouch which he had, and his sling was in his hand.

1 Samuel 17:40

Something came alive in my heart as I read the words *shepherd's bag*. I envisioned David toting a pouch resembling our modern-day satchel while he was in the fields with the sheep. Satchels typically have long straps, close with a flap, and are worn over the shoulder. Besides stones, I can only guess what David carried in his pouch!

I wondered what we, as modern-day shepherds, carry in our pouch while shepherding the flock of God (see 1 Peter 5:2). I concluded that, like David, we symbolically carry that which aids and protects the sheep as well as ourselves.

A shepherd can be defined as a member of the clergy who provides spiritual care and guidance for a congregation. I believe every disciple of Christ has a role of shepherding to some degree. However, Jesus, as the Good Shepherd, to aid His sheep, filled His bag with the five-fold ministry: apostles, prophets, evangelists, pastors, and teachers who are to equip and edify the body of Christ (see Ephesians 4:11).

The first and most important stone in our pouch is the Living Stone, Jesus Christ (see 1 Peter 2:4). We also carry the Word of God, or the Living Bread, as Jesus is the Bread of Life (see John 6:35). His words feed, lead, guide, and protect us and the sheep to which He has entrusted to us.

Symbolized in Scripture as water, oil, and wine, the Holy Spirit should be in our pouch at all times. Living water is to flow from our bellies, washing and refreshing ourselves then the sheep; oil represents the anointing for consecration of service and healing; and wine represents the effervescent life of the Spirit bubbling up within us. As overseers, prayer is how we fill our shepherd's bag.

Stealing a popular tag line from a credit card company, I ask you, "What's in your pouch?" Are you equipped to spiritually help yourself and those God has put in your path? There are some things we should never leave home without.

Old School but Still in Style

You shall not all do as we are doing here today—
every man doing whatever is right in his own eyes.

Deuteronomy 12:8

The topic of sexually purity is not only "old school" but hot—even among professing Christians. Now under grace and not the Law, many believe the lie that because Christ forgave us of everything, we can engage in anything.

Since God never changes, neither do His standards of forbidden sexual practices. God told Moses in Leviticus chapter 20 to tell His people not to act like the Egyptians, who represent worldliness or those who don't follow Christ. They were to not imitate the Egyptians' way of life. Specifically, He told them to never have sexual intercourse with their mother, sister, half-sister, granddaughter, aunt, daughter-in-law, brother's wife, or neighbor's wife. If a man lay with a male as he lay with a woman, both of them were committing an abomination. The only physical relationship that God honors is between a married man and woman.

Sexual practice with an animal was and is a terrible perversion to the Lord. God said that all of these detestable activities were practiced by the people of the land, and the land has become defiled. He warned His people not to engage in any of these acts (see Leviticus 18). Today, nothing has change as far as God is concerned: His commands are still in full effect.

Paul also addressed the subject in the New Testament church when he spoke to the Corinthians. Although Paul never married, God granted him wisdom to write to us about living in line with His holy standards (see 1 Corinthians 5:9–11, NLT).

Although God has strict rules on sexual purity, Jesus has good news for us—He forgives! Additionally, God makes a way of escape when temptations arise. Although not popular today, *repent* is a biblical term, meaning "change of the mind, or the seat of moral reflection, to reconsider or think differently."[1] Take time to read both the Old and New Testaments for God's viewpoint on this subject. Whether you believe the topic is old school or hot, most likely you'll find yourself "thinking differently."

This Ain't No Masquerade Party

For My eyes are on all their ways; they are not hidden from My face.

Jeremiah 16:17

Although the Masquerade Ball originated in the fifteenth century, they're still alive and well in many cultures of the world today, including within the body of Christ.

For these galas, people don elaborate costumes, and attendees wear a mask to hide their true identity. *Masquerade* is defined as "a false show or pretense or the wearing of disguise";[1] in other words, pretending to be someone you're not.

In regards to our spiritual walk, oftentimes, many of us peer through masks that hide wounds, shame, or guilt. No matter what mask we wear, Jesus knows who's behind it.

Hiding in any form is as old as the Garden of Eden, where Adam and Eve hid themselves from God because of fear (see Genesis 3:8). Perhaps you too have tried to hide from God at one time or another. "'*Can anyone hide himself in secret places, so I shall not see him?' says the* LORD" (Jeremiah 23:24).

When I was in anguish and grief with my son's death, the pain was so great that a disguise of any kind was impossible. I was hurting deeply. When people met me, they met grief face to face. Honestly, it shocked some to the point that they preferred I wore a mask. Called to walk in our new creation, the body of Christ often deprives each other of the opportunity to express genuine hurts experienced in life's circumstances. Because of this, masks are prevalent, while many walk around wounded. Had I masked my grief and "pretended" I wasn't a grieving mother, I doubt that I'd be alive today.

In 1 Samuel 10:22, men were seeking Saul. Unsuccessful, they asked the Lord, "Where's Saul?" God replied, "*There he is, hidden among the equipment.*" God didn't allow Saul to stay hidden.

If you're hiding behind a mask, before the stroke of midnight, or better yet, immediately, leave the ball and your mask behind. Until you remove your disguise, your wounds will remain hidden and unhealed. You can't hide from God, so come out from behind that mask, and allow Him to heal you.

Whose Battle?

The battle is the LORD'S.

1 Samuel 17:47

A battle raged in my mind two years after Levi departed for heaven. At this point, the Lord exposed Satan's *attempt* to take me out. Since we've all encountered the enemy on the battlefield of our mind, I hope you'll receive the following excerpt from a conversation between God and me as an encouragement for any battle you may be going through.

"Sharon, hell is at full volume trying to deceive you through loud lying lips—lies against you, against Me, and against My character in your eyes. Satan is speaking death to your heart and mind about My love for you. As a liar, a murderer, and the father of abortions, he's trying to abort the call I have on your life."

"Father, although You've delegated authority to me, I'm brokenhearted and crushed in spirit. I feel helpless, lacking any will or strength to fight. I don't even want to live, let alone fight."

"The battle is not yours, Sharon, but Mine. My Spirit draws the two-edged sword, which defeats the enemy in your heart. Turn to Me as soldiers turn to their commanding officer. A true leader will lead the troops along the surest route to safety. This is what I plan to do with you. You're wounded and brokenhearted. I alone am your shield and can protect you from the devourer."

I've learned that it's not about you and me doing anything but surrendering to Jesus to live through us. The Spirit carried me because I had no fight. Although I'm well now that Jesus has healed my broken heart, I'm still not the one doing, *"For in Him we live and move and a have our being"* (Acts 17:28).

If you're in a battle, turn to your compassionate Commanding Officer, Jesus Christ. He'll either give you specific instructions and the Spirit's wherewithal to accomplish His orders, or if you're wounded, He'll pick you up and carry you over His shoulder to safety.

GPS

*For the ways of man are before the eyes of the L*ORD*,*
and He ponders all his paths.

Proverbs 5:21

Before smart phones, I was seeking the Lord for the perfect Christmas gift for my students. At the time, I thought, *Who wouldn't like a GPS for Christmas?* In our natural world, GPS, of course, means "Global Positioning System." However, spiritually, GPS could stand for "God's Positioning System."

The incredible gift is that God positioned us in Him, in Christ. This is a gift we'll be unwrapping throughout all of eternity. It takes money to purchase and update a natural GPS, but Jesus has already purchased God's Positioning System for us and has fully loaded it with all the maps we'll ever need to live out our life's course from earth to heaven.

A GPS is only as good as its maps, and God always has the best maps available for our trip. Outdated maps can wreak havoc as we try to reach our destination. It's imperative to take time out of our day to sit with the One who's charted our course so we don't get lost, or even worse, reach a spiritual dead end called everlasting death. God's route will lead to everlasting life.

It makes no difference how long ago we purchased our GPS; we can still get the most up-to-date information for our unit by contacting the manufacturer. God is never out of date! We can contact Him at any time for whatever current information we may need.

We need to know that God won't always lead us on the shortest route but the surest route. Since there's nothing new under the sun (see Ecclesiastes 1:9), Jesus also followed God's Positioning System precisely. As the Son of Man on the earth, He never veered to the right or to the left, nor did He opt to bypass or look for the shortest route to the cross.

Our spiritual GPS provides guidance by the unfailing Holy Spirit. He'll never lead us down the wrong path. Our job is to trust and obey, stay tuned to Him only, and don't allow the devil to re-route us. If you haven't been using your GPS, it's time to start. Happy traveling!

Have Mercy on Us!

And behold, two blind men sitting beside the road, when they heard that Jesus was passing by, cried out, saying, "Have mercy on us, O Lord, Son of David!"

Matthew 20:30

The large crowd, which surrounded the blind men, told them to be quiet as they called out to Jesus, but the men only shouted louder, *"Have mercy on us, O Lord, Son of David!"*

When Jesus heard them He called after them and asked, *"'32What do you want Me to do for you?' 33They said to Him, 'Lord, that our eyes may be opened'"* (Matthew 20:32–33).

Does your calling out to Jesus arrest His attention with a response to the point that people—or the enemy—say, "Shush!"? We don't know if the multitude that followed Jesus was boisterous or quiet or if they considered the men disorderly or unclean and indigent. No matter, Jesus, attentive to their cry, heard their relentless plea.

There's an element of humility in this story as the disadvantaged men voiced their need. Many people in this situation might have gone along with the crowd and have been silenced. What do we do in a group when we have a need and the Spirit of God is moving? Do we cry out like these men, or are we like the others, yelling, "Be quiet!"? Many times, because of appearing needy or prideful, we don't speak up. I've done it! But these men wouldn't stay silent, and their tenacity paid off. *"Jesus had compassion and touched their eyes. And immediately their eyes received sight, and they followed Him"* (Matthew 20:34). Imagine this! Now imagine Jesus coming to your aid.

The year 2008 brought a noticeable decline in Mark's commission art business. While reading this passage, I cried out to the Lord, saying, "Lord have mercy on us!" Jesus responded, *"What do you want Me to do for you?"* I said, "Lord, grant us favor for work." Later in the day, we received some leads for my husband's art.

These types of testimonies are recorded in Scripture for your taking. I encourage you to cry out like the blind men! What Jesus did for them, He'll do for you. He'll provide what you ask of Him, according to His will.

NOVEMBER 19

Complete Satisfaction

In Your presence is fullness of joy;
at Your right hand are pleasures forevermore.

Psalm 16:11

While in a time of praise and worship, discouragement mounted in my heart as the holidays were nearing their fullness. With Thanksgiving only a few days away, it was now my third with my son residing in heaven. I didn't *feel* thankful, even though I had much to be thankful for.

Then the Lord blessed me with a vision, which included Jesus and my son. They stood in heaven face to face, with their feet about twelve inches apart. The two of them were holding hands, with arms extended to near maximum length. As they spun around and around, they smiled and laughed, having the time of their lives. I sensed perfect communion between the two of them. Full of joy, Levi suddenly threw his head into Jesus' chest in the midst of spinning and twirling, as if to say, "Stop! I need a rest from all this joy and exhilaration."

In the vision, by God's divine design, my son's face was directly toward me. Although not aware of my presence, Levi had what I would call the fullest smile possible. Pure contentment radiated from his being, which said, *"I'm in need of absolutely nothing."*

You and I are not yet face to face with Jesus like the heavenly saints are. However, as believers filled with His Spirit, you and I are face to face with Him in a way that we can experience a *portion* of the joy of His presence, which the heavenly saints experience to the full.

For you, me, and my son, God is El Shaddai—God Almighty, the All-Sufficient One—in whom we derive complete satisfaction. Are you satisfied or dissatisfied today? God says He satisfies the longing soul (see Psalm 107:9). He also tells us that His people shall be satisfied with His goodness (see Jeremiah 31:14). Complete satisfaction is yours today through Jesus, the giver of true joy.

Pillars of Clouds and Fire

You go before them in a pillar of cloud by day and in a pillar of fire by night.

Numbers 14:14

As the Israelites journeyed in the wilderness, God led them with a pillar of cloud and a pillar of fire. Symbolic of the Spirit's presence, these remained with the people (see Exodus 13:22). Today, for those who put their trust in Jesus, the Holy Spirit indwells us, continues to lead us day and night, and never departs from us.

Because of employment constraints, my husband and I were living apart for a time. His once-thriving international art business and my teaching ministry had disappeared. During this time, a position opened for my husband, and along with it, the chance for me to travel with him. We packed our truck, winterized our Colorado home, and by faith headed west to Washington. On our arrival, God led us to a seaside apartment. Suddenly, after one month, the provision that the job promised didn't deliver. It appeared to have dried up, similar to that of Elijah's provision at the Brook Cherith (see 1 Kings 17:7). This made it difficult to financially sustain two households.

It was apparent that the situation was out of Mark's hands. God's plan all along was to move us across the bay and into a home with an unbelieving stranger. Not making sense of these prayer results, I asked the Lord for confirmation. When I awoke the following morning, God reminded me of how He led the Israelites with the pillar of cloud and the pillar of fire. I sensed Him saying, *"I'm moving you across the bay. Are you coming?"*

As difficult as the majority of these days were, I can say now that I greatly appreciate what God accomplished in me during this time. He was asking for a deeper trust, and by His grace, I was able to yield.

If you've dug your heels in today, resisting His unknown leading, I encourage you to trust Him. He is trustworthy. You may not know where you're going, but you can trust the One who's taking you.

Go Where?

But Simon Peter answered Him, "Lord, to whom shall we go?
You have the words of eternal life."

John 6:68

One morning, feeling disheartened in grief and in my relationship with God, I read John 6:61, where Jesus asked some of His disciples, *"⁶¹Does this offend you?'.... ⁶⁶From that time, many of His disciples went back and walked with Him no more"* (John 6:61, 66). Like these disciples, I've also been tempted to walk away at times. But, by God's grace, I've never acted on that temptation.

After sharing these thoughts with some acquaintances, their facial expressions surprised me. I asked them, "Who, at one time, hasn't questioned his or her walk with Christ, especially after the death of a child?" I know I'm not the only one, although perhaps the only honest one!

I asked God to make a way for me to explain myself. God responded, *"All of the thoughts you have are not yours. Satan continually attempts to interject thoughts into the human mind. My Holy Spirit exposes his lies with the illumination of the truth of My Word. The thought of you wanting to quit loving Me wasn't your thought but Satan's. He brings a thought in the first person, baiting you to believe it's yours. It's a lie that you don't love Me or that you want to quit loving Me. You love Me because I first loved you."*

God revealed more truth to me from Jeremiah 32:40, saying, *"I will make an everlasting covenant with them: I will never stop doing good for them. I will put a desire in their hearts to worship me, and they will never leave me"* (NLT).

Following Levi's passing, my life was difficult. At times, I did feel like walking away. However, God made a covenant with me—and with you—that we'd never leave Him! Satan attempted to plant a lie, but the Spirit of truth never let that seed take root. If you're like the disciples, or like me, and are tempted to walk away, do the opposite and run to Him. No one else has the words of eternal life.

Rose of Sharon

Thus says the LORD, who created you…and He who formed you,…"Fear not, for I have redeemed you; I have called you by your name; you are Mine."

Isaiah 43:1

Names to me are important and thought provoking. God considers His own name significant, as well as the names of all mankind. Knowing us before the foundation of the world, when God speaks our name, He's declaring the meaning of His intention for creating us. God, via the angel Gabriel, instructed Mary to name her baby, Jesus. Every time we say, "Jesus," we declare, "Jehovah is salvation."

I was once introduced to a man named Ernesto, whom I encountered again six months later. I remembered his face but not his name. Not meaning to, I put my hands on my temples as if telepathic, and said, "I see an E. Your name begins with an E…your name is Ernesto!" He was flabbergasted, as was I! I said, "The reason I remembered your name is because God loves you, and He calls you by name."

It wasn't until I began researching the meaning of my own name (Sharon Rose) that I began to accept and appreciate it. On the map, Sharon is a coastal plain located in Israel between Joppa and Mount Carmel; a place well known in ancient times for fertility and beauty.

One morning in prayer, God spoke to me about my name, saying, *"Your name means 'fertile.' In Israel, the plains of Sharon are the most fruitful in all the land, with lush green grass and abundant fields of grain. Looking over the plains of Sharon, people can see its vibrant beauty and fertility. When people see you, they see your vibrant fertility and beauty in Me. You are My rose of Sharon, My lily of the valley, My lily among the thorns. In Me you bloom, even in the desert. You are the aroma of Jesus Christ, so blossom, and let them smell the fragrance of My love for you, and for them."*

Have you ever seriously considered the meaning of your name? What is God declaring every time He calls you by name? Even if you've never liked your name, receive it as if it's from God Himself, and begin to speak it proudly as a form of prophecy over your life.

Combat Fasting

The people of Moab with the people of Ammon, and others with them besides the Ammonites, came to battle against Jehoshaphat. And Jehoshaphat feared, and set himself to seek the LORD, and proclaimed a fast.

2 Chronicles 20:1, 3

Some battles necessitate a different course of action than others. Having led a lifestyle of fasting since 1986, I can attest to its benefits. The Bible speaks of its blessings; however, I often see the body of Christ frown on fasting, regarding it only as a work to obtain something or a futile attempt to crucify the flesh.

God gave me a revelation about fasting through my dog's veterinarian. My dog already had his immunizations, however it was recommended that he get a booster shot. Instantly, a thought came to me that fasting is like a booster shot! Jesus *"has blessed us with every spiritual blessing in the heavenly places in Christ"* (Ephesians 1:3). What better way to accelerate and appropriate our blessings from the spirit realm into the natural realm than through a booster of a fasting prayer?

Like Jehoshaphat, we have an enemy. And, although Satan is defeated, he's still on active duty, attempting to oppose our victory. Jehoshaphat, a warrior in battle, *"proclaimed a fast"* (2 Chronicles 20:3). Everyone gathered to seek help from the Lord, and God answered through the prophet, Jahaziel, saying, *"15Listen, all you.... Thus says the LORD to you: 'Do not be afraid nor dismayed because of this great multitude, for the battle is not yours, but God's. 16Tomorrow go down against them.... 17...Position yourselves, stand still and see the salvation of the LORD....'...Do not fear or be dismayed; tomorrow go out against them, for the LORD is with you"* (2 Chronicles 20:15–17). I like that quick, telling response!

King David, also a warrior, said, *"I humbled myself with fasting"* (Psalm 35:13). From time to time, it's beneficial for every enlisted saint to engage in fasting—not only to humble our soul, mind, will, and emotions to the will of God, but also to cleanse our physical body, resulting in renewed strength for the battle. If you haven't considered fasting for a while—or maybe never—allow the Lord to lead you in this powerful spiritual discipline.

Healing Is for Real

*Then Jesus went about all the cities and villages,
...and healing every sickness and every disease among the people.*

Matthew 9:35

B y healing every sickness and every disease among the people, Jesus was fulfilling Isaiah's prophecy written in Isaiah 53 and recorded in Matthew 8:17: *"He Himself took our infirmities and bore our sicknesses."*

I believe that healing isn't only for real but for today! Jehovah Rapha is the "Lord who heals." Sickness and disease are not God's handiwork but resulted from the law of sin and death. Thankfully, *"the law of the Spirit of life in Christ Jesus has made [us] free from the law of sin and death"* (Romans 8:2, brackets added).

God said, *"I will take sickness away from the midst of you"* (Exodus 23:25). God also *"anointed Jesus of Nazareth with the Holy Spirit and with power, who went about doing good and healing all who were oppressed by the devil, for God was with Him"* (Acts 10:38). As we read in the following scriptures, oppression in any form comes from the devil and not God: The people brought a mute and demon-pos-sessed man to Jesus. When He cast the demon out, the mute spoke (see Matthew 9:32–33). Jesus, speaking of a woman whom He healed, said that Satan had bound her for eighteen years (see Luke 13:16). And, Matthew 8:16 tells us, *"He cast out the spirits with a word, and healed all who were sick."*

The miracles Jesus performed while walking the earth were a glorious foretaste of the healing atonement He provided on the cross. I don't know why some receive His healing on this side of heaven and others don't. But we can't negate the truth of God's Word: By His stripes we are healed—spirit, soul, and body.

In regards to my broken heart, Jesus said, *"Your faith didn't heal you; I healed you."* What a joy to know it wasn't anything I did but everything that Jesus did! I'm living proof that healing is for real and for today. No matter your need, Jesus is true to His Hebrew name, Jehovah Rapha, the Lord who heals. Through His death on the cross, you are healed. Receive your healing now in Jesus' name.

Table of Grace for Twelve and More

Now the sons of Jacob were twelve.

Genesis 35:22

As the sons of Jacob were twelve, so are the sons and daughters of my dad, Merrill. My frugal father always said, "Things are cheaper by the dozen."

Revering God, my parents prayed on their children's behalf. Thankfully, because my parents are now in heaven, they're not thinking about the difficulties the dozen inflicted on them. They only see the fruit that is yet to come from their prayers.

To the best of their ability, my parents selflessly raised us as kingdom kids for kingdom purposes. My dad worked single-handedly supporting us twelve. At the same time, my mother, doing all the domestic chores, attempted to train twelve—spiritually and emotionally—and bravely went behind the wheel with each new driver. Only until I matured and had a family of my own, did I appreciate my parents' gift of sacrifice. I believe my parents are now standing before Jesus with His stamp of approval as good and faithful servants.

I also believe that the prayers of my parents were in agreement with Jesus' prayer: *"And this is eternal life, that they may know You, the only true God, and Jesus Christ whom you have sent"* (John 17:3). I'd like to see the prayers of Jesus and of my parents come to fruition on behalf of my siblings, as I assume my siblings, JoAnn, Michael, Kathy, Neal, Janet, Jim, Tom, Mary, Margaret, Robert, and Julie would. As our parents called us to the dinner table three times a day, their prayers beckoned us to His table of grace to receive eternal life, which is an intimate relationship with Jesus today that will last forever.

To a large degree, families don't eat together at the dinner table today as our family did, and although you may not be one of twelve, you're certainly part of God's family when you believe in the Lord Jesus. Because of this, Jesus says you're welcome to *"eat and drink at My table in My kingdom"* (Luke 22:30). If you're not yet part of God's family, ask Jesus to invite you in, where there'll always be a place for you at the table.

Resurrection Choices

For the hour is coming in which all who are in the graves will hear His voice and come forth—those who have done good, to the resurrection of life, and those who have done evil, to the resurrection of condemnation.

John 5:28–29

The topic of hell is hotter than the topic of heaven (no pun intended), but since Jesus addressed both, we'd do well to listen. If you've not yet been born again, this topic is for you. And, if you have been born again, this topic is also for you, as we believers need to be vocal with others in sharing the Good News of Jesus.

Jesus, equating condemnation with eternal damnation, said to the Pharisees, *"…How can you escape the condemnation of hell?"* (Matthew 23:33) Jesus is clear that hell exists.

Jesus said, *"…for if you do not believe that I am He, you will die in your sins"* (John 8:24). If you don't believe that Jesus is the One whom the Father has sent, you'll die in your sins. This may sound frightening, but at the same time, we know that Jesus took our sins upon Himself at the cross; therefore, we don't have to die in our sins.

Since eternal life is in the blood of Jesus and not good works, I believe the "good" that Jesus is referring to in our opening passage is to believe in His name for our eternal salvation. When we do so, we receive *"the resurrection of life"* and will forever live with God. On the other hand, the evil that people do is simply choosing not to believe this truth, resulting in *"the resurrection of condemnation"* or being forever separated from God.

God leaves you with the decision to accept or reject His message. However, He loves you enough that while you're still a sinner, He sent Jesus to die for you, forgive you, and reconcile you back to His Father. To believe or not believe are your resurrection choices.

Romans 10:9 tells us that if we confess with our mouth and believe in our heart, saying, "Lord Jesus, I believe that You are the Christ, the Son of God," we'll be saved and have everlasting life. Jesus is here with you now. If you've never done this, now's the time. *"Now is the day of salvation"* (2 Corinthians 6:2). Your eternal destiny awaits your choice.

The Grave at a Full Age

You shall come to the grave at a full age,
as a sheaf of grain ripens in its season.

Job 5:26

The grave contains a plethora of unanswered questions, especially when it holds the young. Shortly after Levi's death, I spoke with a woman who owned a funeral home. Her consoling words to me were, "There's no rhyme or reason to death when it comes to age. We've made preparations for one-day-olds to one-hundred-year-olds and beyond, and everything in between."

David said, *"You have made my days as handbreaths, and my age is as nothing before You; certainly every man at his best state is but vapor"* (Psalm 39:5). Until Jesus' return, everyone will succumb to physical death and its grip. And no matter what the age—nineteen or ninety—our life is but a vapor.

Reading our opening passage, I saw an analogy of a sheaf's fullness and my son's death that I'd never considered previously. A sheaf is a mature bundle of grain stalks laid lengthwise and tied together after harvest. The word *full* denotes completeness, maturity, or old age.

In regards to grain, it's not the seed's coat that blooms, but the seed within. The seed's coat falls away and dies as the fruit emerges. Our physical body, the coat for our spirit man, also falls away in death. Although laid lengthwise in the grave, the spirit of the dead and their fruit remain to be resurrected to eternity.

Although my son went to the grave physically at nineteen, I believe that like a sheaf of grain, spiritually his life was mature, full, ripe, and in season. In death, his body now lay lengthwise, but his spirit and fruit continue with God.

You've heard the saying, "You can't judge a book by its cover." Spiritually, we can't judge a body by its cover either, as God alone knows the plans behind the curtains of eternity and the age required for a full harvest. I challenge you to think outside the box of this earthly life and into the unseen eternal world of the Spirit of the Living God, even though, during your life, His ways will never be completely understood.

Hold On

The end of a thing is better than its beginning.

Ecclesiastes 7:8

Jesus brought this prophetic word to me during a church service: *"Some of you want a divorce. Hold onto Me because in Me the end of your marriage is better than the beginning. I am the Beginning and the End"* (see Revelation 1:8). What an encouragement to hang in there and hold on!

In a conversation with Jesus regarding divorce, the Pharisees said, *""4Moses permitted a man to write a certificate of divorce, and to dismiss her.' 5...Jesus answered and said to them, 'Because of the hardness of your heart he wrote you this precept'"* (Mark 10:4–5). Unchecked resentment in marriage carries the potential to harden a spouse's heart.

For some, marriage is a battle, and for everyone it can be been rough at times. If you're honest, at least once, the temptation to throw in the towel has crossed your mind; if not, then maybe murder! Life certainly offers ample opportunities to consider divorce, but ideally, as covenant people, it's for better or for worse. As a reflection of Christ and His bride, the Church, a Christian marriage isn't about us individually, but rather God, our spouse, and our children. Therefore, I encourage you, *"if it is possible, as much as depends on you, live peaceably"* (Romans 12:18), with each other.

Jesus said, *"6But from the beginning of the creation, God 'made them male and female. 8...and the two shall become one flesh'; so then they are no longer two, but one flesh. 9Therefore what God has joined together, let not man separate"* (Mark 10:6, 8–9). Even though God's ultimate plan is that no man separate what He has joined, with Jesus, there's forgiveness in divorce.

If Jesus isn't a part of your marriage, invite Him in. If He's involved, He'll be faithful to guard you from the evil one. As disciples of Christ not everything is easy, but with God, all things are possible, including everlasting marriage. Hold onto Jesus and His promise that *"the end of a thing is better than its beginning!"*

Blood Stained

He was clothed with a robe dipped in blood,
and His name is called The Word of God.

Revelation 19:13

While taking communion, I heard the Lord say, *"Because of My body and because of My blood, you are blood stained."* Blood-stained clothes are not something I would desire to wear. However, when it comes to the precious blood of Jesus, I'm grateful my garments are saturated.

A seemingly oxymoronic, heavenly conversation reads:

"13Then one of the elders answered, saying to me [John], 'Who are these arrayed in white robes, and where did they come from?' 14And I said to him, 'Sir, you know.' So he said to me, 'These are the ones who come out of the great tribulation, and washed their robes and made them white in the blood of the Lamb.'" (Revelation 7:13–14, brackets added).

How is clothing made white with blood? As odd as it sounds, this is exactly how God does spiritual laundry. At the transfiguration of Jesus, reference is made to an earthly launderer. *"His clothes became shining, exceedingly white, like snow, such as no launderer on earth can whiten them"* (Mark 9:3). That's some kind of white! Tide detergent cannot compete!

Because of our sin nature, a trip to God's cleaners is necessary, as the blood of Jesus is the *only* refiner's soap for that nature. Revelation 1:5 tells us, He *"loved us and washed us from our sins in His own blood."* This makes our spiritual clothing white or clean. I used to enjoy going to the Laundromat because I could get all of my laundry done in one shot. That's how God's laundry process works. *"With His own blood [Jesus] entered the Most Holy Place once for all, having obtained eternal redemption"* (Hebrews 9:12, brackets added).

Is it time for you to go to the Laundromat? Don't put it off any longer! Jesus is waiting for you. And in one shot, as you confess with your mouth and believe in your heart that God raised Jesus from the dead, your clothes, or spirit, will shine and be exceedingly white like snow with His blood.

Waiting during Combat

Wait on the LORD; be of good courage, and He shall strengthen your heart; wait, I say, on the LORD!

Psalm 27:14

For military recruits of all ranks—both natural and spiritual—waiting is a mandatory process. Staying put is not always an easy test. However, when used effectively, a hiatus can be beneficial. For both types of soldiers, downtime used wisely ensures the next assignment's success.

Because highly functional weapons are important to both forces, while waiting, I'd see to it that mine were clean and fully loaded so I could *"be ready in season and out of season"* (2 Timothy 4:2). For encouragement, I'd stay connected to God, family, and friends. Anyone who *"isolates himself seeks his own desire"* (Proverbs 18:1). As for morale, I would take time getting to know fellow soldiers and not withdraw from the troops or the body of Christ (see Hebrews 10:25).

Delays happen in God's army. We're either waiting on God, or He on us, or we might be waiting on others. The disciples waited in Jerusalem for the promise of the Holy Spirit (see Acts 1:4), and Simeon waited for the consolation of Israel (see Luke 2:25). David's men had to wait at Jericho until their beards grew back (see 1 Chronicles 19:5), and Christ followers are waiting for the return of the Lord.

Weary in my waiting, one day Jesus said to me, *"I, too, am waiting!"* Surprised, I hadn't previously thought of Jesus as One who waits! However, He's yet to reap His harvest at the end of the age (see Revelation 14:15–16). Once again, He warmed my heart, understanding my humanness.

Second Peter 3:9 says, *"The Lord is not slack concerning His promise* [to you]*"* (brackets added). His very character is faithfulness. He's your God of appointment, not disappointment. Whatever it is you're waiting for, know that if it's in the Lord, it's worth the wait.

Walking Out of the Tomb—Part 1

Jesus...came to the tomb. It was a cave, and a stone lay against it.

John 11:38

Reading John 11:38–44 during a time of prayer and fasting, Jesus spoke to me saying, *"Like Lazarus, you're dead in a cave—a grave—with a stone of unbelief rolled over your heart; unbelief that's telling you that I'm not good because Levi came home."* His words lovingly pierced my heart. He began flooding me with revelation as if He was in the flesh talking with me as He did with Martha over 2000 years ago.

Arriving at the tomb, Jesus commanded, *"Take away the stone"* (John 11:39). I clearly sensed Him saying, *"It's not your responsibility to take away the stone. I'll do this for you, as the stone's too heavy for you."* This is amazing grace!

Martha responded, *"Lord, by this time there is a stench, for he has been dead four days"* (John 11:39). God said to me, *"The unbelief is a stench, and it's been four years since Levi died."* I felt like the man in the Bible who said, *"Lord, I believe; help my unbelief!"* (Mark 9:24). Jesus spoke to Martha four days after Lazarus' death, and Jesus was speaking to me, exactly four years after Levi's death.

Jesus asked Martha, *"Did I not say to you that if you would believe you would see the glory of God?"* (John 11:40). The morning of Levi's death, God said, *"I know the thoughts that I think toward you...thoughts of peace and not of evil, to give you a future and a hope."* Later that afternoon, hearing the news, I questioned how a child going to heaven warrants plans of peace and hope. God reminded me as He did Martha, *"If you'd believe that I have a future and a hope for you, you'd see the glory of God."*

If a stone of unbelief covers your heart and has buried you in a grave where God's glory is covered, don't despair. Jesus has a specific and perfect plan to pull you from that grave. Tomorrow, I'll share the plan He had for me.

Walking Out of the Tomb—Part 2

Now Jesus loved Martha and her sister and Lazarus.

John 11:5

Before Levi's accident, we prayed for his safety; after his death, we prayed for his physical resurrection. Not receiving the answers we expected, my faith in God's goodness was shipwrecked; after all, Jesus compared my faith with Lazarus'—a dead man.

As Jesus cried with a loud voice to Lazarus, Jesus spoke to me from John 11:43, saying, *"Sharon, come forth! Your responsibility is to come when I call, as Lazarus arose when I called him."* His words were life giving. *Only God* could raise me; He was my *only* hope. At God's call, Lazarus came from the grave, bound with grave clothes and his face wrapped in a cloth (see John 11:44). Likewise, I came out of my grave with a cloth of unbelief over my face, temporarily blinding me from seeing God's true love for me.

Jesus spoke to the bystanders, saying, *"Loose him, and let him go"* (John 11:44). Symbolically, here, the bystanders were my brothers and sisters in Christ. The morning of this revelation, I went to church when God instructed me to allow the "bystanders" to pray for me. It would be through their prayer of agreement that the grave clothes of unbelief would be loosed, so I could go free. It happened just as Jesus said.

John 11:38 reads, *"Jesus, again groaning in Himself, came to the tomb."* I've heard it said that Jesus groaned at the people's unbelief. I don't believe that Jesus groaned at me because of my unbelief. Instead, I felt only love, compassion, and mercy, which is what we should all encounter when our grave clothes are removed.

Jesus is able to move the heavy stones from your heart and raise you up from even the darkest tomb. If you're in a grave today, allow Jesus to call you out, take your grave clothes off, and set you free once and for all. His way of doing this will look different for everyone, but as you follow His lead, He'll usher you into freedom.

Covenant Maker

I will make an everlasting covenant with them:
I will never stop doing good for them.
I will put a desire in their hearts to worship me, and they will never leave me.
I will find joy doing good for them and will faithfully and wholeheartedly
replant them in this land. …I will do all the good I have promised them.

Jeremiah 32:40–42 (NLT)

With Levi's departure to heaven, every part of my life was difficult. Even my long-time friendship with God, which had always *seemed* so rock solid, was tested.

Although brokenhearted and crushed in spirit, I wasn't forsaken. In this time of grief I sat in my prayer chair, and my soul said, "God I don't think I want to walk with You anymore; it's just too hard." Perhaps anguish has at one time touched the depths of your being as it did mine.

God's unfailing mercy, compassion, and friendship are truly a mystery. While sharing my thoughts with Him, His Spirit led me to our opening passage. God filled my heart to overflowing with His loving kindness, which also permeated my body and soul. He not only cut a covenant with Jesus, saying that He'd never leave us, but the covenant included us never leaving Him. We don't often hear that part.

As I sat with the Lord, He helped me to understand that no matter how excruciating the circumstances, He and I are in relationship for the long haul. Because Jesus promised, *"I am with you always, even to the end of the age"* (Matthew 28:20), we can pledge the same promise to Him.

Jesus didn't promise that life would be a bed of roses. In fact, He told us, *"In the world you will have tribulation"* (John 16:33). But, then He goes on to say, *"but be of good cheer, I have overcome the world."* Unless Jesus returns in this moment, there'll be more tears ahead. We shouldn't dwell on this but just acknowledge it as fact. Likewise, we shouldn't ignore the difficulties around us by being like the ostrich with its head in the sand.

If you're overcome with circumstances beyond what you think you can bear, take hold of Jesus and the surety of His everlasting covenant. Walk with the One who has overcome the world and promises to never leave you.

Praise during Combat

*Now when they began to sing and to praise,
the Lord set ambushes against the people.*

2 Chronicles 20:22

A remarkable similarity between earthly and spiritual battalions is praise. A military cadence is a song sung by troops while running or marching. Many have a call-and-response structure where one soldier initiates a line, and the remaining soldiers complete it, building camaraderie. There are other benefits to this type of song, which include keeping the soldiers moving in step as a unit or in formation. The mental and physical advantages make for a healthier, more cohesive unit.[1]

In 2 Chronicles 20:21, King Jehoshaphat appointed people to sing and praise the Lord as they went out before their enemy army. While they sang, the Lord intervened by setting up ambushes and destroying all of their enemies. The result was dead bodies everywhere; no one escaped. Is this the victory you anticipate when you praise the Lord in your battles? It should be!

No musical instruments are required to praise our way to victory. We only need to open our mouths and sing. As we praise God, whether we do it individually or as a unit, the body of Christ becomes a unified force to administer a lethal blow to the enemy. In battle, praise is not a natural carnal weapon, but a spiritual one, as praise flows from our spirit and not our flesh. Therefore, as we sing like larks, not only do we receive the benefits of praise, but God does as well. And, the enemy receives his due, which is humiliation.

King Jehoshaphat wasn't the only one who praised his way to victory in the battle. The strapping king and warrior, David, also understood the effects of praising God in battle and in his personal life. In Psalm 18:3, he said, *"I will call upon the Lord, who is worthy to be praised; so shall I be saved from my enemies."*

If you're in battle circumstances, do as David or Jehoshaphat's army did: Sing your way to victory! As you praise the Lord, expect Him to set up ambushes that will ensure the devil's defeat.

Divine Trash Truck

"… the Dung Gate"

Nehemiah 2:13 (NLT)

Of Jerusalem's gates, the Dung Gate mentioned in the book of Nehemiah 2:13 was used for the disposal of rubbish.

One morning in prayer, I heard the trash truck in the driveway, picking up our garbage. A prayer arose from my confused and angry, but also grieving heart: "Father, by Your Spirit, help me take out the trash in my heart this morning—rubbish in the form of lies, wrong thoughts, and attitudes that might cause my soul to stink."

Some might frown on the thought that we can stink as believers. If, in our spirit, we are the fragrance of Christ, isn't it possible at times that our soul can have a stench from the works of the flesh (see Galatians 5:19–21)?

As a Christ follower, I'm not pleased whenever I catch myself making choices that stink. After all, I'm named from Song of Solomon 2:1–2, the rose of Sharon and the lily of the valley—amazingly fragrant flowers!

Once, when my children were very young, we were shopping, and my cart was filled to capacity. I came to the exit door when a security worker asked me for my receipt. I had no idea where I put it! Frustrated, I murmured, "You're a thorn in my back side." That wasn't a fragrant, Christ-like attitude.

Despite our flesh, if we're open to God's voice, the Holy Spirit will reveal our trash and jog our memory as to what is true and sweet smelling about us, which is the Holy Spirit in us, not our carnal nature. Jesus took our trash upon Himself at the cross (see 1 Peter 2:24), and He loves us enough to tell us when our soul doesn't smell like roses. When we forget that truth, the Holy Spirit is gracious to remind us that it's time to take out the trash.

Has the trash truck come to your house? Thankfully, not every day is trash pickup. I hope this is the case for your soul. However, if you need daily service, His mercies are new every morning (see Lamentations 3:23).

Are You Born Again?

"Do not marvel that I said to you, 'You must be born again.'"

John 3:7

Before responding to Christ's invitation of salvation in my own life, the term *born again* was peculiar. Leading up to my miraculous re-birth, three of my friends professed to know God and to be born again. Observing their actions, by all comparison, I looked great! Why did I need their God? Deceived with self-righteousness, I thought I wasn't living nearly as badly as they were. My justification was that I didn't claim to know Him; I only knew *of* Him!

In a conversation with Nicodemus, a ruler of the Jews, Jesus said, *" '³Most assuredly, I say to you, unless one is born again, he cannot see the kingdom of God.' ⁴Nicodemus said to Him, 'How can a man be born when he is old? Can he enter a second time into his mother's womb and be born'"* (John 3:3–4)? Have you ever asked these same questions? I did!

⁵*"Jesus answered, [Nicodemus] 'Most assuredly, I say to you, unless one is born of water and the Spirit, he cannot enter the kingdom of God. ⁶That which is born of the flesh is flesh, and that which is born of the Spirit is spirit'"* (John 3:5–6, brackets added). To enter into God's kingdom, we all must experience two births. The first is a natural birth, through the flesh of our mother's womb. The second is a spiritual birth, through the Holy Spirit.

Unless we emerge from the flesh of the physical womb, we'll never *enter into*, or *see* with our natural eyes, the world into which we are born. And if we're not born again by the Spirit of God, we won't *see* with our spiritual eyes, hear with our spiritual ears, or *enter into* the things of the Spirit.

If you're not sure where you stand with Jesus, He's lovingly waiting for you to respond to His invitation: *"Whoever calls on the name of* [Jesus] *shall be saved"* (Romans 10:13, brackets added). *Whoever* includes you! Don't wait a moment longer; take Him up on it!

The Street Called Straight

So the Lord said to him, "Arise and go to the street called Straight,
and inquire at the house of Judas for one called Saul of Tarsus,
for behold, he is praying."

Acts 9:11

Shopping with an old friend, we meandered into a clothing boutique, where we spoke briefly with a young saleswoman then left the store.

Six months later, during a time of prayer and fasting, I awoke straight out of sleep at 3:00 a.m. In my mind, I saw the face of the young saleswoman. God spoke to me, *"I want you to tell this young woman these sequences of events. Tell her that she's on My heart. Let her know I love her and that I have sent you."* I responded, "Lord, I don't know her name." He said, *"Her name is Paige. I'd like you to go to her shop on the day you have the Bible college Christmas party. Give her a Christmas card, and bake her some cookies."*

Doing what the Lord asked of me, when I arrived at the store, I told a man who was working there, "I'm looking for a woman named Paige." He responded, "She's not in today; she's not feeling well. I'm her fiancé. Can I help you?" I shared per God's instruction. His surprise was evident, and he recommended I try back in a couple of days. I left the cookies and prayed a blessing over him.

Although I didn't connect with Paige until after the New Year, my faith soared! At our meeting, she shared her compelling story. The very day I came to the store was the day she prayed to God that if He was real, to please send help, as she was pregnant and experiencing medical complications.

I felt as though I was living out of the book of Acts! Ananias didn't have access to a written New Testament, but He had a relationship led by the Holy Spirit. Today we have the written Word from which God speaks, but He also speaks to us as He did Ananias—by His Spirit.

Perhaps the Spirit is directing you to your street called Straight. If so, obey His voice. You'll be amazed at the mighty opportunities He has waiting for you.

A Woman's Choice

*Charm is deceitful and beauty is passing, but a woman
who fears the LORD, she shall be praised.*

Proverbs 31:30

Attending a meeting, I spent time with a group of precious women who were not professing Christians. As I observed their actions, clearly I saw a reflection of how I lived before I was born again. This environment also revealed to me how far Christ has removed me from my past and continues to transform me into His image.

For you gentlemen reading this, don't turn the page just yet! As father, husband, brother, and friend, your role is vital. By encouraging the women in your life to live wisely, you're helping them as well as yourselves, as they find security in their divinely designed role of being a woman.

The Bible describes two types of women, one more palatable than the other; nevertheless, both need to be addressed:

"A foolish woman is clamorous; she is simple, and knows nothing." (Proverbs 9:13)

"A gracious woman retains honor..." (Proverbs 11:16)

"The wise woman builds her house, but the foolish pulls it down with her hands." (Proverbs 14:1)

Ladies, God loves you either way. However, I can attest to having lived both foolishly and wisely, and with the Holy Spirit's help, choosing the wiser is far better; for us and everyone around us!

Ladies, there's no reason to raise a feminist fist; God is on your side. He can do more for you than you'll ever achieve independently of Him. In God's eyes, you're already equal in value to your male counterpart, yet beautifully unique, with magnificent contrasting roles.

Jesus loves women! The cross and the Gospels are proof of this. When a woman is encouraged to respect the Lord and choose wisely, she'll be complimented not only by her children, but her husband (see Proverbs 31:28). So, women, walk wisely according to the scriptures; and men, make it easy for the women in your life to make the right choices.

Obedience—Paths of Rest

*Ask for the old paths, where the good way is, and walk in it;
then you will find rest for your souls.*

Jeremiah 6:16

Wherever the scenery lends itself, hiking, biking, and walking are activities I enjoy. I've found when engaging in such recreation, signs speak along the trail and proclaim a variety of instructions, including warnings.

While hiking with a new acquaintance who professed Jesus as a young girl, I realized that spiritually, she'd lost her way after many years. Our conversation reminded me of a universal warning sign that described her current position. The signpost, found on footpaths, reads, "Stay on path." Despite its intent to protect, the sign often goes either unnoticed or ignored.

It's best to never deviate from a path's warning signs. When we do occasionally veer off our spiritual walkway, as everyone does from time to time, the sooner we sense the Holy Spirit's loving course correction, the better, as repercussions begin immediately but subtly. We could wander aimlessly for days or years before realizing we're off-course, then wonder, *How did I end up here?*

It's important to remember that, as citizens of heaven and as temporary travelers passing through this life, *some* our past choices have positioned us where we find ourselves today, and *some of* our current choices will position us on the path that lies ahead.

On another occasion, a friend and her family encountered a five-foot rattlesnake while hiking. I asked, "Was the snake lying on the trail?" She responded, "No, we went off the path."

Once walking a path that towered over the ocean, I saw a sign posted: "Stay on path, as cliffs below are unstable." Tempted to view the beauty, but remembering my friends, with God's grace I heeded the sign.

If you've strayed from your spiritual path, God knows exactly where you are. He has a "map app." Just ask, and He'll re-route you or help you stay put! But don't wait; the sooner you get back on your path the better.

DECEMBER 10

Papa's Heart—Man's Pen

The LORD said to me, "Take a large scroll, and write on it with a man's pen."

Isaiah 8:1

As the writers of the Bible took a man's pen in hand and wrote by the inspiration of the Holy Spirit, we too, take pen in hand as God continues to speak intimately to us through His Spirit. Had I not taken a pen in hand during my prayer times, this book may not have come about. I believe the following words of love and encouragement are for you, and for me, from Papa's heart through my pen:

"I have loved you with an everlasting love. When you call to Me, I respond. You make My heat skip a beat when I know you're contemplating getting together with Me. Where I am there is liberty. You're free to choose: to love and to give; and the best part is that you're free to choose to spend time with Me.

"Remember all of My paths for you are mercy and truth. I'm holding you as closely, if not more closely, than a mother holds her child. I have a resolute grip on you. There's no one thing or person who can snatch you from My hand. You are mine! I fight fiercely for you! I defend you from enemies even when it sometimes doesn't appear that way.

"Have a wonderful day in the peaceful presence of My beloved Son, Jesus Christ, and My Holy Spirit, who's ever present with you."

Many are familiar with God referring to King David as a man after His own heart. But how often do we consider that God is a God after our heart? I never believed God needed anything from me, but I've come to realize that He longs for, and thoroughly enjoys, my love and attention.

Now that our daughter has her own family, our hearts skip a beat when our children want to spend time with us. God's the same with us: *"The LORD delights in you"* (Isaiah 62:4). Believe and receive these words, and believe Papa's heart of love for yourself.

Revealing Light

Nor do they light a lamp and put it under a basket,
but on a lampstand, and it gives light to all who are in the house.

Matthew 5:15

Today I'm putting the light of the Holy Spirit's revelation on the lamp stand of this page. Don't be fooled or misled by false gods who claim to illuminate or who claim to be *the* light. Jesus boldly declared, *"I am light of the world. He who follows Me shall not walk in darkness, but have the light of life"* (John 8:12).

Spiritual revelation comes *only* when the Holy Spirit makes something that has previously been concealed known to us. One of my favorite accounts of this is in Acts 9, where Saul, like a terrorist, breathed threats and murder against the Lord's disciples. I think we can agree that Saul was in the dark.

Traveling on the road to Damascus, Saul encountered the Light of revelation Himself, Jesus Christ. Suddenly, a light shone around Saul from heaven, causing him to fall to the ground. Although he heard a voice, he saw no one (see Acts 9:3–4). Saul was trembling and astonished. Imagine yourself in Saul's shoes! Audible or inaudible, communication from *the* Light brings revelation. And, with revelation, comes instruction, as Jesus revealed to Saul the error of his ways.

Immediately following, through a man named Ananias, Jesus revealed what He wanted Saul to do from that point on: *"15Go, for he is a chosen vessel of Mine to bear My name before Gentiles, kings, and the children of Israel. 16For I will show him how many things he must suffer for My name's sake"* (Acts 9:15–16).

Jesus chooses how and when He'll reveal Himself to us. He may appear physically, in a vision, or perhaps through His Word, the Holy Bible. When He does, it may terrify us, or we may be in awe. But, whatever its effect, we'll know that we've encountered Jesus Christ Himself, for the Light of His revelation will transform us spirit, soul, and body.

Have you had a "road to Damascus" experience yet? If not, get ready!

The Red Velvet Box

*Oh, that men would give thanks to the LORD for His goodness,
and for His wonderful works to the children of men!*

Psalm 107:8

A yard ornament in the form of a "For Sale" sign adorned our front lawn. Normally, homeowners would be thrilled to show their home when selling it, but with our son's recent departure to heaven, that wasn't at the forefront of my mind.

One day, a realtor and client made their scheduled appearance. As they were leaving, I was walking up the driveway when the client leaned out of the car window and said, "I found a red velvet box full of money by your well head. I placed the box on your kitchen counter." Upon closer inspection, the velvet box, which was full of holes, appeared as if the dogs got a hold of it. Inside, to my amazement, was $250.

I considered the mystery of the circumstances, as each home in our community came with several acres of land. Did someone put the box on the porch, and the dogs dragged it away? More disconcerting, did our dogs take the prized box from a neighbor's porch? High winds were a regular occurrence in our area, so perhaps the box blew onto our property. Lost in thought, I heard the words, *"Sharon, there are more fifties on the property."*

Anticipation filled my heart. In this inch-by-inch treasure hunt, I scoured our five-acre parcel and found discolored fifty-dollar bills strewn about. God only knows how long they were out there. In total, I discovered $550! I wondered if even more money had blown away in the wind. After asking the neighbors about the box, to this day, we can only conclude that the mystery is the goodness of God revealing His wonderful works to His children.

God may not instruct you to search for money on your property; however, the kindness He showed me is the same kindness He wants to show you in the form of a personalized red velvet box. Our God is full of good surprises, and I pray He'd surprise you in a mighty way as He did me!

Pride Can't Hide

Let not the foot of pride come against me.

Psalm 36:11

In marriage, a concession to *"give yourselves to fasting and prayer"* is found in 1 Corinthians 7:5–6. Each time God has led my husband and me to these things, the results have been life changing.

During one fast, I had been thinking negatively about my husband, so I cried to God for help. God instructed me to call Sue—my eighty-year-old Christian friend. After a couple of rings and hearing her voice, I said, "Sue, I'm in a battle." She said, "Do whatever the Lord asks you to do, and leave the results with Him."

Before that call, I sensed that God wanted me to share Isaiah 58:6 with my husband: *"Is this not the fast that I have chosen…to let the oppressed go free, and that you break every yoke?"* But after twenty-five years of marriage, I hesitated, fearing exposure and revealing insecurity. Instantly, I sensed a tangible evil presence in the room; it was lurking, hindering, and silent.

God spoke, saying, *"A demonic spirit of pride is in the room with you, trying to keep you from doing what I'm asking of you. This spirit doesn't want to be exposed or come to the light or into the truth that it's a spirit of fear of abandonment, attempting to lead you to believe that you're the one afraid of being abandoned."*

Immediately, I ran to my husband and blurted out, "This is the fast God has chosen! I'm afraid that you'll abandon me!" He prayed a tender, reassuring, healing prayer over me.

God made it clear that it's not a person but a demonic spirit of pride that influences the heart. If there's something hidden, hounding you, turn to God for His plan of exposure, *"For there is nothing hidden which will not be revealed, nor has anything been kept secret but that it should come to light"* (Mark 4:22).

Betrayed

The Lord Jesus on the same night in which He was betrayed took bread.

1 Corinthians 11:23

Betrayal is a part of the human experience. Even Jesus encountered it. We all know about His betrayer. In life, we cross paths with people who resemble Judas, and regrettably, we ourselves are also disloyal at times.

I once met with grief through a new acquaintance. This person contacted me and requested a syllabus for a class I was teaching. Thinking I was helping, I gladly emailed the file. I wasn't prepared for the hurtful response I received the following morning. The attack wasn't directed at my writing but at me personally. I felt as though I had been kissed by Judas.

Crushed, I took the issue to the Lord. He revealed that I'd missed a clue. This clue came two days prior in my prayer time, which stemmed from 2 Corinthians 12:7—*"a thorn in the flesh was given to me, a messenger of Satan to buffet me."*

Unmasking truths, God showed me that the acquaintance was Satan's courier and thorn. However, reminded that criticism typically holds an ounce of truth, a vision came to me, in which I saw a "No trespassing" sign staked in the ground. The Holy Spirit revealed the sign's meaning, which was that I had unlawfully encroached on the private property of the heart of my acquaintance. In the thick of grief with the death of my son, I had done that unknowingly through a conversation we'd had.

The second nugget came from our opening scripture. The night of His betrayal, Jesus took the bread. Had grief not been companion to this conversation, it would've been different. Through this experience, God lovingly showed me that the perfect time to take communion is in the midst of betrayal.

I tried to remedy the situation by mailing a card of apology, but it was returned, stamped, "address undeliverable." As you take the Lord's Supper, remember His death and all that He did for you. Doing so will make it easier to forgive others. *"Even as Christ forgave you, so you also must do"* (Colossians 3:13). An open seat awaits you at His communion table, even—perhaps, especially—in the midst of betrayal.

God Is Not Spock

God created man in His own image.

Genesis 1:27

Happily, I'm created in the image of God and not of Vulcan Spock from *Star Trek,* where Vulcans strive to live by logic with no interference of emotions. Even humans, however, attempt to suppress emotions through various methods, including will power, medication, meditation, intimidation, drugs, or alcohol.

Society has taught men that showing emotion is contrary to masculinity and spirituality, when Scripture says otherwise. Referred to in masculine imagery, God is capable of anger, hate, and laughter. Jesus, masculine in human flesh, wept, and He made a whip and wrecked havoc in the temple.

Was the cross without feeling? God, as the Holy Spirit, can be grieved. The image of King David dancing before the Lord certainly doesn't resemble an emotionless Spock. And, should a man's response to his wife's affection in the bedroom be emotionless?

Ecclesiastes 3:5 reminds us that there's *"a time to embrace, and a time to refrain from embracing."* Therefore, concerning emotions, there's a time to embrace them and a time to refrain from embracing them, but not a time for disregarding them all together.

I once said that when women cry, people call their display "emotion," yet when men get angry, it's simply called "anger." This is society's way of disassociating men with emotion.

The ministry of Operation Restored Warrior has touched me after viewing a snapshot of their healing ministry in the movie *Holy Ghost Reborn* and through attending alumni gatherings with my husband. These veteran warriors help restore wounded warriors—spirit, soul, and body. It's refreshing to see how these warrior men engage emotion at their core. They're not mortified when moved to tears with the deep love and affection of their God, Father, Savior, Friend, Brother, and Warrior, Jesus Christ.

When it comes to emotions, do you mirror the image of Jesus or that of Spock? It's okay to be emotional when it comes to your relationship with the Lord—even you, men! For God has created us that way.

The Traffic Light

Obey My voice.

Jeremiah 11:7

At alarming rates, it seems that motorists are disobedient to traffic laws. Unfortunately, I've seen as many as six motorists at a time intentionally run a red light. Once, while stopped at a red light at a major intersection, a driver suddenly pulled around me from behind at a high rate of speed, nearly clipping the rear end of my car and spewing gravel at my windshield. Proceeding full throttle through the intersection, he ran the red light.

While sitting at another red light, a thought came to me correlating our earthly and spiritual lives in regards to the traffic signal and its functions. The different colors of red, green, and yellow provide specific instruction to motorists, promoting safety, order, and timed access to the right of way.

Even in the natural, we need to obey traffic laws. When we obey laws of the land that are not contrary to God's laws, we're obeying God (see Titus 3:1). But, God has also set up lifesaving spiritual traffic signals for His children: red—"stop" or "do not proceed"; green—"go, but check your surroundings before you proceed, as you may encounter danger or rebellious motorists running red lights"; and yellow—"proceed with caution, or *if* necessary, stop."

When motorists don't obey traffic signals, there can be grave consequences, such as injuries, court appearances, fines, jail time, loss of their drivers' licenses, and even fatalities.

There are also consequences for spiritual motorists. We can't afford to run God's red lights and be what I call a "red runner." We also shouldn't stay put when God says, "Go! Your light is green." And, we can't just sit cautiously at His yellow lights—maybe for years!

Don't be like Pharaoh, who said, *"Who is the Lord, that I should obey His voice?"* (Exodus 5:2). Jesus told us in John 8:12, *"I am the light of the world."* Red, green, or yellow, obey the Light!

The Saints

O King of the saints!

Revelation 15:3

I n the 1960s, a TV series aired Simon Templar, a British fictional character, as a Robin Hood-like criminal known as The Saint, perhaps because of his initials, S.T. With humor and off-putting remarks, he would leave a calling card at his "crimes"—a stick figure of a man with a halo. Today, the halo continues as a symbol for a saint.[1]

Originally, some religious organizations considered martyrs, who had put their faith in Christ, to be saints. Over time, after a lengthy process of investigation, religious institutions began to canonize people as saints, even if they weren't martyred. A panel of theologians approved people based on their virtue in their earthly and *assumed* heavenly lives. The final ballot then lay with the highest church officials.[2] Although its intent is to honor, the practice of canonization is not in line with Scripture.

Throughout the Bible, sainthood comes not from men, but from God. Our saintliness as Christ followers doesn't stem from our good works, working miracles, or our prayers for others. Before Christ's work on the cross, the prophet Isaiah stated, *"For all of us have become like one who is unclean, and all our righteous deeds are like a filthy garment"* (Isaiah 64:6, NASB). Now, only because of the righteousness of Jesus Christ and His atoning work, does anyone possess saintly qualities. We can't do *one good thing* or in any way *add* to the atoning work of Christ to gain His favor.

In Romans 15:25, Paul said, *"I am going to Jerusalem to minister to the saints."* These people were alive. Paul again addressed the church, saying, *"those who are sanctified in Christ Jesus, called to be saints"* (1 Corinthians. 1:2). And, in Romans 12:13, we're encouraged to distribute to the needs of the saints. Saints who have passed on have no needs; they're in the presence and fullness of God.

I'll close with Paul's words in Galatians 4:16, *"Have I therefore become your enemy because I tell you the truth?"* I hope not! Begin to see yourself as a saint, because in God's eyes, all who put their faith in Jesus Christ are saints, including you.

Fire that Doesn't Scorch

They saw these men on whose bodies the fire had no power;
the hair of their head was not singed nor were their garments affected,
and the smell of fire was not on them.

Daniel 3:27

For two consecutive summers, Colorado Springs had devastating fires. Many homes were destroyed, countless acres consumed, and sadly, lives were lost.

The location of the city in which we lived was under a mandatory evacuation. Suffocating air in the form of thick smoke mingled with ash filled the atmosphere. Like an avalanche, the fire roared down the mountain behind my house. In the midst of dangerous flames only one hundred yards from my home, I had a chuckle with God. I said, "Lord, I've packed only Levi's belongings, and he's up in heaven with You!"

Although I didn't have to pass through the fire of losing my home to flames, I did walk through the fire of Levi's passing. I'm not making light of the devastating loss people incurred during the wildfires. However, for me, the potential loss of my home couldn't compare to the loss of my son.

We have Christian friends whose homes did burn to the ground. They testified that despite their loss, God turned things around for good. They have nicer homes than before, and they feel their families are closer now than before the fire. Although Levi's absence is forever with me, I can also testify that God has worked things for my good. The most significant is a deeper revelation and relationship with God Himself.

These endings sound to me like the Hebrews boys in the fiery furnace. King Nebuchadnezzar, looking into the furnace, said, *"Look!...I see four men loose, walking in the midst of the fire; and they are not hurt, and the form of the fourth is like the Son of God"* (Daniel 3:25).

Even under the death penalty, the Hebrew boys didn't bow to circumstances but declared, *"our God whom we serve is able to deliver us"* (Daniel 3:17). If you're in fiery circumstances, declare God's faithfulness in your furnace of affliction. Like these boys, Jesus will be in your midst to deliver you, and you too, will come out without even a hint of smelling like smoke (see Daniel 3:27).

Jesus—Deeper Still

You are my hiding place.

Psalm 32:7

In 1943, in German Nazi-occupied Netherlands, the ten Boom family risked their lives hiding Jews in their home. Despite their brave efforts, betrayal came to the family, which resulted in imprisonment in concentration camps. The movie *The Hiding Place* depicts their true story.[1]

In 1976, this movie was my first glimpse of the Holocaust. It moved me to tears, anger, and confusion with merciless humanity. I watched and listened to Corrie, a survivor of the ten Boom family, whom I wrote about earlier. I sat speechless as she spoke lovingly of God, despite having survived unspeakable horrors. Then in her eighties and wrinkled with age, she glowed with a heavenly beauty. Looking directly into the camera, with a gentle voice and a thick Dutch accent, she said, "No pit is so deep that He is not deeper still."[2] Her statement about Jesus never left my unregenerate heart.

At the time, without Christ and intrigued with ten Boom, I admired her brutal honesty. She didn't deny her experience with anger and bitterness or the battle that raged within her to forgive the cruel camp guard, who beat her sister Betsy, ultimately causing her death while in the camp.

Thirty-eight years later, I watched the movie again but had no recollection of ten Boom's second statement, in which she admitted to having questions after experiencing the Holocaust: "Some questions remain, but they are not to be feared. Our heavenly Father holds all things in His hand, even our questions." Today, I can still see her face, looking into my eyes saying, "No pit is so deep that He is not deeper still. With Jesus, even in our darkest moments, the best remains and the very best is yet to be."[3]

I've found her statement to be accurate in every way. In the pit following Levi's death, Jesus is deeper still. If you're in a pit today or have questions about God's faithfulness, no matter how deep your trouble, take your feelings and questions to the Lord. You too will discover that Jesus is deeper still.

Love Nugget

But he who looks into the perfect law of liberty and continues in it, and is not a forgetful hearer but a doer of the work, this one will be blessed in what he does.

James 1:25

In 1999, my husband was off to Las Vegas. Although there are righteous people living there, "Sin City" as it's called, wasn't a place I wanted my husband to visit, for any "good" reason. Because of my insecurities and knowing how I felt, he purchased a gold nugget necklace for me and wrote the following love note to accompany it:

God gives all His children nuggets—Nuggets of Knowledge, Nuggets of Truth, Nuggets of Wisdom. God gave me all the above. My wife, my little gold nugget, I love you!!!

Being at war with fearful thoughts, unfortunately my husband's act of kindness didn't calm my heart. After all, "What happens in Vegas stays in Vegas." God spoke to me during this time, saying, *"Sharon, love thinks no evil"* (see 1 Corinthians 13:5). I complained to God, *"How's it possible for me not to think evil with my husband surrounded by such darkness?"* God responded no further.

In my husband's absence, God helped me to look into the perfect law of liberty— His Word. By doing so, I didn't forget what I was reading or hearing, but I began to do the work by taking my thoughts captive and thinking about what was true and honorable about my husband.

When Mark returned, temptation lurked in my heart to act contrary to love, but the power of God kept me looking to the Holy Spirit to restrain my tongue. Then, during our conversation, Mark asked, "Don't you need some clothes?" He handed me $750. (It was not the result of gambling!) At that moment, the Lord said, *"Only a doer of the word is blessed; not one who merely hears and does nothing!"*

I received two gold nuggets: one, a token of my husband's love; and the second, the blessing of a deeper relationship with God through trust and obedience. You may hear the Words of God often, but until you act on them, you won't receive His nuggets of blessing. Wait no longer; become a doer of the Word today.

"Shell Shocked"

*You will keep him in perfect peace, whose mind is
stayed on You, because he trusts in You.*

Isaiah 26:3

*F*ire fight is a term used on the battlefield to depict an exchange of bullets
between two sides. As a platoon of believers, in the battlefield of our mind,
shootouts frequently emerge between the enemy's lies and the Spirit's voice of truth.

Considering this analogy of warfare, "shell-shocked" soldiers came to mind. This
was a term coined during World War I to describe the reaction of some servicemen
to the trauma of battle. It was a response to the intensity of the bombardment
and fighting that produced a helplessness manifested as panic, fear, flight, or the
inability to reason, sleep, walk, or talk.[1] While the terms *Combat Stress Reaction*,
or *Post-Traumatic Stress Disorder* (PTSD) have replaced this expression, it's often
identified as the signature injury of war.

In the Lord's army, we can also experience combat fatigue, tension, or the feeling of
being "shell shocked" from the barrage of enemy lies and their traumatic effects.
Initially, anxiety, fear, loss of sleep, or the inability to reason or even persevere can
occur. In these cases, the resting of our mind and body is essential for recovery to
take place.

When taken captive, a prisoner of war no longer has a voice. When we take lying
thoughts captive in our minds, like POWs, we refuse these lying spirits permission
to speak. Some of us haven't experienced the natural battlefield, but I know we've
encountered the battlefield in our mind, which may have caused distressing shell
shock. *"But thanks be to God, who gives us the victory through our Lord Jesus
Christ"* (1 Corinthians 15:57).

A key role in the battlefield of our mind is to maintain focus and clarity with the
words of the apostle Paul, "It is not I, but the grace of God which was with me that
labored" (see 1 Corinthians 15:10). As you allow grace to work, it will enable you to
keep your mind stayed on Jesus, who'll always faithfully keep you in perfect peace
in the midst of any enemy firefight.

Hook in My Heart

The Babylonians catch people with hooks, as though they were fish.
They drag them off in nets and shout for joy over their catch!

Habakkuk 1:15 (GNT)

In prayer, I said, "Lord, Satan put out the bait that's all too familiar to me, and I took it! Now I have a hook in my heart. Please cut the barb off of the hook, so I can be free." Each one of us from time to time takes the bait of Satan—hook, line, and sinker! I took the familiar bait of envy, believing that God has favorites.

By design, the fishhook is made to enter smoothly into its prey. But once hooked, the barb is the part of the hook that prevents the fish from getting away. In its attempt to become free, the fish can become critically injured or die. Sometimes, however, the fish do get away.

Satan also designs fishing lures that are enticingly smooth. Once we take his bait, we're like fish fighting for our lives to be free of the barb that holds us. Sometimes the truth hurts as much as the barb. According to James 1:14, knowingly or unknowingly, we're tempted when we're drawn away by our own desire and enticed.

Since childhood, having longed for the affection and attention of my parents among my eleven siblings, envy hooked my heart, and the competition to be loved and noticed by them was fierce. Satan uses this fleshy desire as a lure in my life, baiting me with the lie that God also has favorites. With the Holy Spirit's help, I'm getting off the hook sooner, and often, avoiding it altogether.

James 4:7 instructs us, "…*submit to God. Resist the devil and he will flee from you.*" And, Romans 13:14 says to, "*put on the Lord Jesus Christ, and make no provision for the flesh, to fulfill its lusts.*"

I'm sure you love God and desire to submit to Him. And, you want to live free of all hooks. But, occasionally you might get snagged. Don't take the bait! If you do get hooked, Jesus is there to release you. If you've recently taken the enemy's bait, turn to the Lord to get you off the hook.

The Blessed Life

One's life does not consist in the abundance of the things he possesses.

Luke 12:15

There's no doubt we're blessed in Christ. In fact, the word *bless* is mentioned over 400 times in the Bible. Many Christians may not see themselves as blessed because they believe that the "blessed life" is merely bliss and prosperity; a life exempt of trials, tribulation, or sorrow. And for those who do experience difficulty, it's because of their choices. It's true that our choices can lead to pain and problems. However, the disciples came face to face with hardship even after making the right choices and embracing the atoning work of Jesus.

The apostle Paul wrote, "*8We are hard-pressed on every side, yet not crushed; we are perplexed, but not in despair; 9persecuted, but not forsaken; struck down, but not destroyed*" (2 Corinthians 4:8–9). Romans 8:35–36 continue with struggles, but verse 37 encourages us, "*Yet in all these things we are more than conquerors through Him who loved us.*"

Luke 1 gives an account of Zacharias and Elizabeth, who were righteous before God, walking in all of God's commandments and ordinances. Luke 1:6 describes them as "*blameless.*" Verses 13–17 tell us that Elizabeth was about to give birth to John the Baptist, who would eventually pave the way for Jesus. There was no greater prophet than their own son (see Luke 7:28)! Blessing and favor certainly surrounded them.

Even so, the couple later experienced unspeakable anguish and grief with John's beheading (see Matthew 14:10). Today, some parents face the horrors of their children being beheaded by ISIS. I consider myself blessed, but I also faced anguish and grief with Levi's death.

In meditating on the "blessed life," I became more aware of the true blessing, which is Jesus, walking us through the dangers and sorrows of this life. He helps us to the other side, whether that's on earth or in heaven. The "blessed life" isn't about what we possess but rather in our friendship with Jesus.

Your life may not be filled with roses, but you're still blessed. Jesus will always be with you, walking you through any difficulty. Take His outstretched hand and experience your own blessed life.

Hopes and Dreams

Now hope does not disappoint.

Romans 5:5

When wrestling with a crucial decision of direction, the Holy Spirit gave me a dream. In it, I was determined to find a certain pair of blue jeans. After ransacking every closet in my home, I went into my son's room where I saw a clothesline stretched across the room with clothes hanging on hangers. Determined, I rapidly flipped through every garment.

Unexpectedly, out of the left corner of my eye, I noticed an empty mouse trap. Thinking nothing of it, and moving my eyes back toward the clothesline, a mutated animal suddenly appeared, heading to the trap. It had the head of a field mouse with the elongated body of a weasel. It didn't startle me or cause fear; it was just odd enough to catch my attention and distract me from continuing to look for the jeans. Then I woke up.

The Holy Spirit revealed that the jeans represented the direction I diligently sought to find. The weasel-like mouse was the devil distracting me from finding that direction. The Lord said to me, *"The devil is distracting you with disappointment in your current circumstances, which is a trap."* God then prompted my heart with Romans 5:5—*"Now hope does not disappoint."* That rang my bell, as I knew disappointment had gripped my heart.

Still in my bed, in my mind, I saw myself walking to a dictionary and opening to the word *disappoint;* that was my cue to get out of bed. The definition was: "to defeat of expectation…; to hinder from the possession or enjoyment of that which was intended, desired, hoped or expected."[1]

The term *M.O.* or *Modus Operandi* means "the way someone does something, or the way of committing a crime."[2] Satan's M.O. is to block or stop the things we're hoping for or expecting from God.

The Father, Son, and Holy Spirit are always cheering you on when it comes to obtaining the things you're believing for. Keep on believing, and don't allow Satan to distract you. You can be sure that the God of hope won't disappoint.

Are You Trusting in a Savior or Santa?

For there is born to you this day in the
city of David a Savior, who is Christ the Lord.

Luke 2:11

The following is a news post that I read online: "'Tis the season for giving and good cheer, but it looks like for one shopping mall, Santa and his not-so-friendly little helper may have missed that memo. [A young autistic girl] stood in line for 30 minutes with her pit bull service dog, Pup-Cake when she was shooed away because of Santa's fear of pit bulls."[1]

This story is terribly sad to me, not because Santa refused the girl, but because she was led to trust in a make-believe character. Because Satan is the father of lies, I never wanted a lie from my lips to be one that my child heard in regards to Santa Claus.

St. Nicholas, or Santa Claus, truly lived at one time. Born in the third century, "his wealthy parents, who raised him to be a devout Christian, died in an epidemic while Nicholas was still young." Adhering to the words of Jesus, he sold what he owned and gave the money to the poor.[2]

Although beginning with good intentions, the St. Nicholas of yesterday is nothing like the *god* of Santa Claus today. Countless fairytale Christmas poems, songs, and now movies, portray him as alive, faithful, and one to whom you can share your heart. Supposedly, he knows when you've been naughty or nice and gives gifts conditionally, via sleigh and chimney.

Today, I'd like to encourage you to cling to the real reason for the season, which is Jesus Christ. He's not imaginary but alive and well. Sitting on His throne, He invites all to come to His lap as little children. Poles apart from Santa, Jesus, through His Spirit, goes about doing good, whether you're naughty or nice (see Acts 10:38). He gives gifts unconditionally, and every good and perfect gift is from Him (see James 1:17). And, unlike Santa, Jesus isn't afraid of anything, including pit bulls!

10,000 Reasons

Bless the Lord, O my soul.

Psalm 103:1

The lyrics of Matt Redman's song, "10,000 Reasons," resonated in my heart today:

"You're rich in love and You're slow to anger
Your name is great and Your heart is kind
For all Your goodness I will keep on singing
Ten thousand reasons for my heart to find
…Bless the Lord oh my soul…"[1]

Because of Jesus, there are 10,000 reasons and more for us to bless God. Even in the death of my son, by His grace, thoughts of gratitude filled my heart. I thanked God that I didn't see Levi die. More importantly, because my family and I believe that *"God has given us eternal life, and this life is in His Son"* (1 John 5:11), we're grateful that we'll live with Levi forever. This book, including today's entry, is a record of those many blessings.

Through the ministry Operation Restored Warrior, a man named Robert came across Mark's artwork, and through this, our healing journey was communicated. He and his brother, Joe, along with ORW, gave us a gift of $10,000! My soul then had 10,000 more reasons to bless the Lord!

The latter part of Redman's lyrics are: *"And on that day/When my strength is failing/ The end draws near/And my time has come/Still my soul will/Sing Your praise unending/Ten thousand years/And then forevermore."*

Every blessing from God, no matter its size, is noteworthy and praiseworthy. However, our greatest blessing is found in 1 John 5:20—*"And we know that the Son of God has come and has given us an understanding, that we may know Him who is true; and we are in Him who is true, in His Son Jesus Christ. This is the true God and eternal life."*

Today, I encourage you to praise God for all of His 10,000s of blessings. And, even when your end draws near, continue to praise Him for 10,000 years and forevermore!

Table 12—Part 1

I thought it good to declare the signs and wonders that the
Most High God has worked for me.

Daniel 4:2

Mark and I had attended an alumni dinner with Operation Restored Warrior. With arranged dinner seating, little did we know how divinely positioned we would be. My husband meandered through the crowd while I went to Table 12 to reserve seats. As fellow tablemates approached, we introduced ourselves on a first-name basis. I asked one couple, "Do you live here?" They said, "No, we live in Eagle, Colorado." I replied, "Where in Eagle?" After they responded, I said, "I don't know why I asked where you live in Eagle. I don't know a thing about Eagle other than my son died there."

The man whose name was Dan asked, "Was your son's name Levi?" Surprised, I responded, "Yes, his memorial is on I-70 East at the 149-mile marker." Dan continued, "...Levi Patrick?" My heightened response was, "Yes." He said, "I was at the scene of your son's accident. I leased that property and was working in the field when I saw a big cloud of dust. I walked toward the cloud, and when the dust settled, I realized what had happened. My first thought was that he was so young, and I wondered if he knew Christ."

We all stood stunned. In my heart I asked, *God, what's happening?* It had been five years since Levi passed, and until that divine moment, Dan and I knew nothing about each other.

My husband arrived at the table, and we shared the miracle story again. As the evening came to a close, we exchanged contact information with Dan and his wife, along with tears and hugs. Then Dan shared another tender moment that only God could orchestrate, saying, "I staked some rebar in the field where Levi lay to rest. I took the palm branch from church on Palm Sunday, weaved it into a cross, and placed it on the rebar. Each day I went into that field, having heard Levi's name on the news, and I talked to him."

As we'll see in the continuation of this devotional tomorrow, there's no limit to God's faithfulness and unfailing love. You can trust Him with your darkest moments.

Table 12—Part 2

And the power of the Lord was present to heal them.

Luke 5:17

In yesterday's devotional, God sent a man—not just any man, but a Christian man—knowing that one day our paths would cross. Since Dan wasn't an Operation Restored Warrior alumnus, but a guest, I continued to ask God what all this meant. God replied, "Dan needs healing." What better way to heal than through meeting Levi's parents, who could put his heart to rest regarding Levi's faith in Christ.

One of my deepest wounds in Levi's death was wondering where God was through it all. I thought I'd dealt with the anger I felt toward Him with Levi's passing, and by His grace, to a degree, I had. However, God orchestrated the circumstances at Table 12 because I also needed healing. After meeting Dan, *every ounce* of anger I had toward God concerning Levi's death was gone.

Through this meeting, God assured me, *"I was God in Dan; I was Christ, the hope of glory, in Levi; and My Holy Spirit hovered over the entire situation."* This brought complete healing to my heart, enabling me for the first time to continue living with what God had called me to do.

After parting ways, I realized I failed to get a photo of Dan to share with our daughter. I prayed for an opportunity. The following morning, Mark and I stood at Levi's highway memorial site, when Dan drove by in his truck. Recognizing us, he honked, and we waved. The occasion didn't lend itself for a photograph, as a fence and service roads separated us. We later headed back for our last alumni meeting. At our arrival, Dan pulled up next to us in the parking lot—another divine setup. I got the photograph after all.

Like Daniel, *"I thought it good to declare the signs and wonders that the Most High God has worked for me"* (Daniel 4:2). God is Most High above all gods, and when we give our lives to Him, He works in ways beyond just us. Put your faith in Him, and see what signs and wonders He'll do—not just for you, but for those around you as well.

Angel Escorts

For He shall give His angels charge over you, to keep you in all your ways.

Psalm 91:11

Psalm 91 is a passage widely read and prayed in regards to protection. We pray this promise, believing that no harm will come to us. Today, this passage has an entirely new meaning for me.

I wrote earlier about Levi going to be with Jesus on March 27 and how my husband and I talked with him on the phone that morning. We showered him with prayers and "I love you's," and assured him that his favorite meal would be awaiting him. After that call, we prayed again, since we can never pray too much for our kids. We prayed that God would send legions upon legions of angels to protect Levi as he traveled. Three hours after that prayer, Levi was in heaven.

Months after Levi's passing, while thinking about prayers prayed, and those prayers appearing unanswered, God surprised me, saying, *"I answered the prayers you prayed for Levi."* In my heart, I responded, *"Excuse me?"* He reminded me of our request for legions of angels. God said, *"I did send legions upon legions of angels to Levi, only they escorted him home."* God did keep His Word! He did give His angels charge over my son, and He did keep him in all his ways, even unto death.

Have you prayed for something in which the answer didn't come about as you expected? I'm certain you have, possibly in many areas. The Lord says, *"8For My thoughts are not your thoughts, nor are your ways My way…. 9For as the heavens are higher than the earth, so are My ways higher than your ways, and My thoughts than your thoughts"* (Isaiah 55:8–9).

God has a way with words! My family continues to pray Psalm 91 and trust in His protection. However, we now know, that His protection can manifest with an eternal perspective that we cannot comprehend. I encourage you to pray Psalm 91, which is God's heart of protection for you. Pray for Him to send angels all around!

Home Plate

I press toward the goal for the prize of the upward call of God in Christ Jesus.

Philippians 3:14

Words can't express how much I miss Levi. At the completion of this book in 2017, he has been a heavenly resident for seven years. Yet, God continues to meet me in very real and personal ways, comforting me with yet another glimpse of Levi in a vision, playing baseball.

With the bases loaded, Levi was up to bat. After hitting an inside-the-park home run, Levi ran with all his might as the crowd looked on with anticipation. Arriving at home plate, the umpire relayed Levi's outcome to eager stadium spectators. Raising both arms together to shoulder level, and with a sweeping motion to his sides, he shouted, "Safe!"

In a spiritual sense, Levi played the game of baseball on earth, and kept his eye on the ball, or Jesus. With the Holy Spirit as his manager, Levi ran both hard and smart. By sharing the truth of Jesus with his teammates, symbolically, Levi loaded the bases with players who will also finish the game as he did, arriving at home plate—heaven—where God the Umpire gives the final call of "Safe!"

In this revelation, Jesus impressed my heart with this thought: I'm still in the game of life, or spiritual baseball, and there are many more plays yet to be played. Therefore, like Levi, by the Spirit of Grace, I'm called to play the game well and trust that the heavenly Umpire knows my appointed arrival to home plate and will signal me "safe."

I don't know about you, but at times I want to throw my bat or quit, getting out of the game all together. However, as a team player, we all have a vital role to play, and that is to help each other make it to home plate. I encourage you along with myself to, *"14...press on toward the goal* [home plate] *to win the* [heavenly] *prize of the upward call of God in Christ Jesus"* (Philippians 3:14, AMP, brackets added).

Fellow teammates, the upward call is the call of "Safe!" given when we cross home plate. Batter up!

One Way

*Jesus said to him, "I am the way, the truth, and the life.
No one comes to the Father except through Me."*

John 14:6

We couldn't end on a better note than by declaring the true meaning of the name of Jesus, "Jehovah is Salvation." *"Salvation is found in no one else, for there is no other name under heaven given to mankind by which we must be saved"* (Acts 4:12, NIV).

When dealing with eternal life and death, it's said that Jesus is narrow minded in His thinking, or His beliefs are intolerant and limited in range and lack the willingness or ability to appreciate alternative views. It's true that Jesus has only one view: *"¹³Enter by the narrow gate; for wide is the gate and broad is the way that leads to destruction, and there are many who go in by it. ¹⁴Because narrow is the gate and difficult is the way which leads to life, and there are few who find it"* (Matthew 7:13–14). The way of Jesus, although narrow, is life giving.

Jesus also said, *"⁷I am the door of the sheep. ⁸All who ever came before Me are thieves and robbers.... ⁹...if anyone enters by Me, he will be saved, and will go in and out and find pasture"* (spiritual security) (John 10:7–9). God's requirement is for His flock to enter through Jesus, the Good Shepherd, the Door of the sheep. The good news is that *"whoever calls on the name of the LORD shall be saved"* and enter the sheepfold (Acts 2:21). When we call, He answers.

If you've already encountered Jesus and accepted His salvation, wonderful! But, if you're still a lost sheep, wandering, remember that Jesus knows your whereabouts. You can recognize Him as the Shepherd holding a sign that reads: *"I am the way, the truth, and the life."*

When Jesus reveals Himself to you and offers His hand, you need only to respond by saying yes. Confess with your mouth the Lord Jesus and believe in your heart that God raised Him from the dead, and as He promised, you *will* be saved (see Romans 10:9). The time is now. I pray you won't wait another moment to receive the greatest gift ever given.

The grace of the Lord Jesus Christ, and the love of God, and the communion of the Holy Spirit be with you all. Amen.

2 Corinthians 13:14

Levi Patrick
1991–2010

This devotional is dedicated in celebration of Levi's life. His nineteen years were short, yet filled with passion for Christ and to see the lost saved. There isn't a day that goes by that I don't think of him. Thank you, Levi, for being such an amazing son and for loving Jesus with everything you had. I love you.

2007

Sasha and Levi

Forever the Best of Friends
Israel Family Vacation

2017

Nate, Sasha, and Emery Samuel
(Our Son-in-law, daughter, granddaughter, and baby on the way!)

Devotional—June 17th
Devotional—June 27th

2009

Levi and Alan

Lewis Palmer Football Awards Night
Alan—Mentor and Friend
Devotional—June 14th

2009
Austin and Levi

Homecoming Party
Austin—Best Friend from Childhood
Devotional—May 17th

2016

Mark, Miracle Man–Dan, and Sharon

Devotionals—December 27-28th

Notes

January 7

1. *Vine's Complete Expository Dictionary of Old and New Testament Words*, rev. ed. (Nashville, TN: Thomas Nelson, Inc., 1992), p. 264, s.v. "gird."
2. Ibid.

January 16

1. Julie Ann Allen, *You Only Think God Is Silent* (Bloomington, IN: Westbow Press, 2005).

January 20

1. James Strong, *Strong's Exhaustive Concordance of the Bible* (Nashville, TN: Thomas Nelson, Inc., 1990), Greek Dictionary p. 78, s.v. "chronos." (See also p. 39, s.v. "kairos.")

January 22

1. Dave Roberson, *The Walk of the Spirit—The Walk of Power: The Vital Role of Praying in Tongues* (Tulsa, OK: Dave Roberson Ministries, 1999).

February 2

1. *New Oxford American Dictionary*, ver. 2.2.1 (New York, NY: Oxford University Press, 2005), s.v. "complain."

February 4

1. *Vine's Complete Expository Dictionary of Old and New Testament Words*, rev. ed. (Nashville, TN: Thomas Nelson, Inc., 1992), p. 593, s.v. "spirit."

February 10

1. James Strong, *Strong's Exhaustive Concordance of the Bible* (Nashville, TN: Thomas Nelson, Inc., 1990), Hebrew Dictionary p. 76, s.v. "nagid."

February 11

1. *New International Bible Dictionary* (Grand Rapids, MI: Zondervan Publishing House, 1987), p. 113, s.v. "Baal."
2. *New Oxford American Dictionary*, ver. 2.2.1 (New York, NY: Oxford University Press, 2005), s.v. "kiss."

February 22

1. Stephanie Johnson, *Abandoned,* directed by John Laing (Auckland, NZ: Movie Maker, 2015), TV movie (TV One).

March 7

1. *New Oxford American Dictionary,* ver. 2.2.1 (New York, NY: Oxford University Press, 2005), s.v. "bow."

March 8

1. James Strong, *Strong's Exhaustive Concordance of the Bible* (Nashville, TN: Thomas Nelson, Inc., 1990), Greek Dictionary p. 70, s.v. "tamelon."

March 11

1. Simon Thomas, "The origins of S.O.S. and Mayday," Oxford Dictionaries, July 1, 2014, http://blog.oxforddictionaries.com/2014/07/sos-mayday/.

March 13

1. James Strong, *Strong's Exhaustive Concordance of the Bible* (Nashville, TN: Thomas Nelson, Inc., 1990), Greek Dictionary p. 16, s.v. "astheneia."
2. *Vine's Complete Expository Dictionary of Old and New Testament Words,* rev. ed. (Nashville, TN: Thomas Nelson, Inc., 1992), p. 324, s.v. "infirmity."

March 14

1. William Goldman, *Princess Bride,* directed by Rob Reiner (Beverly Hills, CA: Act III Communications, 1987), film.

March 18

1. Dr. M. R. DeHann, "The Life Is in the Blood," The Chemistry of the Blood, Sermon 4, http://jesus-is-savior.com/BTP/Dr_MR_DeHaan/Chemistry/04.htm.

March 26

1. James Strong, *Strong's Exhaustive Concordance of the Bible* (Nashville, TN: Thomas Nelson, Inc., 1990), Greek Dictionary p. 42, s.v. "koinonia."

April 1

1. James Strong, *Strong's Exhaustive Concordance of the Bible* (Nashville, TN: Thomas Nelson, Inc., 1990), Greek Dictionary p. 54, s.v. "paradeisos."

April 3

1. Dr. David Hilber, "Vision Ready Is Mission Ready," *Exchange and Commissary News* (May 2011), www.ebmpubs.com/ECN_pdfs/ecn0511_TacticalEyewear.pdf.

April 5

1. *New Oxford American Dictionary,* ver. 2.2.1 (New York, NY: Oxford University Press, 2005), s.v. "comfort."

2. James Strong, *Strong's Exhaustive Concordance of the Bible* (Nashville, TN: Thomas Nelson, Inc., 1990), Greek Dictionary p. 54, s.v. "parakaleo."

April 20

1. *New Oxford American Dictionary,* ver. 2.2.1 (New York, NY: Oxford University Press, 2005), s.v. "insanity."

2. James Strong, *Strong's Exhaustive Concordance of the Bible* (Nashville, TN: Thomas Nelson, Inc., 1990), Hebrew Dictionary p. 33, s.v. "halal."

April 21

1. LMFAO, "I'm Sexy and I Know It," *Sorry for Party Rocking,* Interscope, 2011, https://www.azlyrics.com/lyrics/lmfao/sexyandiknowit.html.

April 22

1. James Strong, *Strong's Exhaustive Concordance of the Bible* (Nashville, TN: Thomas Nelson, Inc., 1990), Greek Dictionary p. 29, s.v. "entole."

2. *Vine's Complete Expository Dictionary of Old and New Testament Words,* rev. ed. (Nashville, TN: Thomas Nelson, Inc., 1992), p. 639, s.v. "tradition."

May 1

1. James Strong, *Strong's Exhaustive Concordance of the Bible* (Nashville, TN: Thomas Nelson, Inc., 1990), Hebrew Dictionary p. 126, s.v. "tiqvah."

2. Ibid., s.v. "qqvah."

May 10

1. *Vine's Complete Expository Dictionary of Old and New Testament Words,* rev. ed. (Nashville, TN: Thomas Nelson, Inc., 1992), p. 662, s.v. "vision."

2. *American Dictionary of the English Language: Noah Webster 1828,* online ed. (Springfield, MA: G & C Merriam Co., 2013), s.v. "vision," http://webstersdictionary1828.com/Dictionary/vision.

May 11

1. *Vine's Complete Expository Dictionary of Old and New Testament Words,* rev. ed. (Nashville, TN: Thomas Nelson, Inc., 1992), p. 639, s.v. "trance."

May 25

1. James Strong, *Strong's Exhaustive Concordance of the Bible* (Nashville, TN: Thomas Nelson, Inc., 1990), Greek Dictionary p. 45, s.v. "lutron." (See also p. 14, s.v. "apolutrosis.")

May 28

1. Melody, *Love Is in the Earth: A Kaleidoscope of Crystals—The Reference Book Describing the Metaphysical Properties of the Mineral Kingdom* (Wheat Ridge, CO: Earth Love Pub House, 1995).

June 8

1. James Strong, *Strong's Exhaustive Concordance of the Bible* (Nashville, TN: Thomas Nelson, Inc., 1990), Greek Dictionary p. 57, s.v. "peripipto."
2. Ibid., p. 56, s.v. "periasmos."
3. *New Oxford American Dictionary,* ver. 2.2.1 (New York, NY: Oxford University Press, 2005), s.v. "cakewalk."

June 10

1. "#49: Private Investigator Terminology: Common Words Used by Private Investigators," P. I. Advice, published January 4, 2013, www.privateinvestigatoradvicehq.com/49-private-investigator-terminology-common-words-used-by-private-investigators.

June 17

1. Smokey Robinson and Ronald White, "My Girl," *The Temptations Sing Smokey,* Gordy (Motown), 1964, www.genius.com.

June 20

1. Bobby McFerrin, "Don't Worry Be Happy," *Don't Worry, Be Happy,* EMI, 1988, www.bobbymcferrin.com/don't-worry-be-bobby/.

June 22

1. "Nail it," IdioMeanings, http://www.idiomeanings.com/nail-it/.

June 23

1. Gary Martin, "Loose lips sink ships," Phrasefinder, https://www.phrases.org.uk/meanings/237250.html.

June 26

1. John Lennon and Paul McCartney, "Help!" *Help!* Parlophone Records, 1965, www.genius.com.

2. David Sheff and John Lennon, *All We Are Saying: The Last Major Interview with John Lennon and Yoko Ono* (New York, NY: St. Martin's Griffin, 2000).

June 29

1. Louisa M. R. Stead, "'Tis So Sweet to Trust in Jesus," public domain, 1882, http://library.timelesstruths.org/music/Tis_So_Sweet_to_Trust_in_Jesus/.

July 1

1. James Strong, *Strong's Exhaustive Concordance of the Bible* (Nashville, TN: Thomas Nelson, Inc., 1990), Hebrew Dictionary p. 51, s.v. "yatsar."

July 5

1. *New International Bible Dictionary* (Grand Rapids, MI: Zondervan Publishing House, 1987), p.140, s.v. "Bethesda."

July 14

1. James Strong, *Strong's Exhaustive Concordance of the Bible* (Nashville, TN: Thomas Nelson, Inc., 1990), Greek Dictionary p. 52, s.v. "optomai." (See also p. 37, s.v. "ide.")

July 17

1. "Heart Disease and Atherosclerosis," WebMD, www.webmd.com/heart-disease/atherosclerosis-faq.

July 20

1. Robert Schenkkan and Andrew Knight, *Hacksaw Ridge,* directed by Mel Gibson (Cross Creek Pictures, Pandemonium Films, Permut Presentations, and Vendian Entertainment, 2016), film.

July 29

1. Mari J. Frank, *Safeguard Your Identity* (Laguna Niguel, CA: Porpoise Press, 2005).

August 3

1. James Strong, *Strong's Exhaustive Concordance of the Bible* (Nashville, TN: Thomas Nelson, Inc., 1990), Greek Dictionary p. 62, s.v. "ptuo."

August 4

1. Kelly McPherson, *Sniper: Deadliest Missions,* directed by Emre Sahin (Los Angeles, CA: Karga Seven Pictures, 2010), TV movie (A&E Television Networks).

August 8

1. Helen Reddy and Ray Burton, "I Am Woman," *I Don't Know How to Love Him,* Capitol Records, 1971, www.lyricsdepot.com/helen-reddy/i-am-woman.
2. James Brown, "It's a Man's Man's Man's World," *It's a Man's Man's Man's World,* King, 1966, www.azlyrics.com/lyrics/jamesbrown/itsamansmansmansworld.
3. Adam Clarke, *Clarke's Commentary on the Bible,* vol. 6 (Nashville, TN: Abingdon Cokesbury Press).

August 10

1. Alexander Pope, "An Essay on Criticism" (Oxford University: W. Lewis, 1711), line 527.

August 12

1. "Corrie ten Boom, 'How to Forgive,'" YouTube video, 7:14, posted by "PastorsStudy," May 9, 2011, www.youtube.com/watch?v=3cfp51vLZb4-.
2. Ibid.

August 16

1. *Vine's Complete Expository Dictionary of Old and New Testament Words,* rev. ed. (Nashville, TN: Thomas Nelson, Inc., 1992), p. 533, s.v. "reward."

August 17

1. "Arthur Fletcher, Former Head of United Negro College Fund," National Public Radio, July 17, 2005, http://www.npr.org/templates/story/story.php?storyId=4757704.

September 7

1. *Alaska, the Last Frontier,* executive producers: Daniel Soiseth, Grant Kahler, Cameo Wallace, and Philip Day (Los Angeles, CA: Discovery Studios, 2011), TV series (Discovery Channel).

September 8

1. James Strong, *Strong's Exhaustive Concordance of the Bible* (Nashville, TN: Thomas Nelson, Inc., 1990), Greek Dictionary p. 68, s.v. "sumpascho."

September 14

1. Edwin Schupman, "Code Talking," National Museum of the American Indian, www.nmai.si.edu/education/codetalkers/html/chapter4.html.

September 16

1. Frances Goodrich, Albert Hackett, and Frank Capra, *It's a Wonderful Life*, directed by Frank Capra (Los Angeles, CA: Liberty Films, 1946), film.

September 18

1. Christian Expressions by Dayspring, Dayspring Cards, Siloam Springs, Arkansas.

September 26

1. Corrie ten Boom, and John and Elizabeth Sherrill, *The Hiding Place:The Triumphant True Story of Corrie Ten Boom* (New York, NY: Bantam Books, 1974), p. viii.

October 4

1. "What is an IED??" *San Jose Mercury News*, December 13, 2006, http://www. mercurynews.com/2006/12/13/what-is-an-ied/.

October 6

1. James Strong, *Strong's Exhaustive Concordance of the Bible* (Nashville, TN: Thomas Nelson, Inc., 1990), Hebrew Dictionary p. 46, s.v. "yabesh."

October 7

1. *Vine's Complete Expository Dictionary of Old and New Testament Words*, rev. ed. (Nashville, TN: Thomas Nelson, Inc., 1992), p. 492, s.v. "prophecy."

October 8

1. *Vine's Complete Expository Dictionary of Old and New Testament Words*, rev. ed. (Nashville, TN: Thomas Nelson, Inc., 1992), p. 593, s.v. "spirit."

October 13

1. *Vine's Complete Expository Dictionary of Old and New Testament Words*, rev. ed. (Nashville, TN: Thomas Nelson, Inc., 1992), p. 557, s.v. "seed."

October 19

1. James Strong, *Strong's Exhaustive Concordance of the Bible* (Nashville, TN: Thomas Nelson, Inc., 1990), Greek Dictionary p. 16, s.v. "harpazo."

October 21

1. "The Name and Attributes of God," My Redeemer Lives Christian Ministry, http://www.myredeemerlives.com/namesofgod/el-shaddai.html.

October 29

1. John Lennon and Paul McCartney, "All You Need Is Love," *Magical Mystery Tour,* Parlophone Records, 1967, https://www.beatlesbible.com/songs/all-you-need-is-love/.

November 1

1. Chris Kyle, Scott McEwen, and Jim DeFelice, *American Sniper* (New York, NY: William Morrow and Company, 2012), pp. 24, 37.

November 3

1. *New Oxford American Dictionary,* ver. 2.2.1 (New York, NY: Oxford University Press, 2005), s.v. "fickle."

November 5

1. James Strong, *Strong's Exhaustive Concordance of the Bible* (Nashville, TN: Thomas Nelson, Inc., 1990), Hebrew Dictionary p. 83, s.v. "cela."

November 14

1. *Vine's Complete Expository Dictionary of Old and New Testament Words,* rev. ed. (Nashville, TN: Thomas Nelson, Inc., 1992), p. 525, s.v. "repent, repentance."

November 15

1. *New Oxford American Dictionary,* ver. 2.2.1 (New York, NY: Oxford University Press, 2005), s.v. "masquerade."

December 4

1. "Military Cadence," Wikipedia, last modified September 23, 2017, https://en.wikipedia.org/wiki/Military_cadence.

December 17

1. "Simon Templar," Wikipedia, last modified August 19, 2017, https://en.wikipedia.org/wiki/Simon_Templar.
2. "The Process of Beatification & Canonization," Eternal Word Television Network, www.ewtn.com/johnpaul2/cause/process.asp.

December 19

1. Allan Sloane, Lawrence Holben, Corrie ten Boom, and John and Elizabeth Sherrill, *The Hiding Place,* directed by James F. Collier (Minneapolis, MN: World Wide Pictures, 1975).

2. Ibid.

3. Ibid.

December 21

1. Adam Hochschild, *To End All Wars: A Story of Loyalty and Rebellion, 1914–1918,* reprint ed. (New York, NY: Mariner Books, 2012), pp. xv, 242, 348.

December 24

1. *American Dictionary of the English Language: Noah Webster 1828,* online ed. (Springfield, MA: G & C Merriam Co., 2013), s.v. "disappoint," http://webstersdictionary1828.com/Dictionary/disappoint.

2. *The American Heritage New Dictionary of Cultural Literacy,* 3rd ed. (Boston, MA: Houghton Mifflin Company, 2005), s.v. "modus operandi," http://www.dictionary.com/browse/modus-operandi.

December 25

1. "Santa, Elf Fired after Refusing to Pose with Little Girl and Her Service Dog," From the Trenches World Report, December 2, 2014, http://fromthetrenchesworldreport.com/santa-elf-fired-after-refusing-to-with-little-girl-and-her-service-dog/113495.

2. "Who Is St. Nicholas?" St. Nicholas Center, www.stnicholascenter.org/pages/who-is-st-nicholas.

December 26

1. Matt Redman, "10,000 Reasons," *10,000 Reasons,* Chordant Distribution Group, 2011, www.Myktis.com/songs/10000-reasons.